China's Human Rights Lawyers

In this extensive account of human rights lawyers in China, Eva Pils shows how these practitioners are important as legal advocates for victims of injustice and how bureaucratic systems of control operate to subdue and marginalise them. The book also discusses how human rights lawyers and the social forces they work for and with challenge the system. In conditions where organised political opposition is prohibited, rights lawyers have begun to articulate and coordinate demands for legal and political change.

Drawing on hundreds of anonymised conversations, the book analyses in detail human rights lawyers' legal advocacy in the face of severe institutional limitations and their experiences of repression at the hands of the police and state security apparatus, along with the intellectual, political and moral resources lawyers draw upon to survive and resist. Key concerns include the interaction between the lawyers and their bureaucratic, professional and social environments and the forms and long term political impact of resistance. In addressing these issues, Pils offers a rare evaluative perspective on China's legal and political system, and proposes new ways to assess domestic advocacy's relationship with international human rights and rule of law promotion.

This book will be of great interest and use to students and scholars of law, Chinese studies, socio-legal studies, political studies, international relations, and sociology. It is also of direct value to people working in the fields of human rights advocacy, law, politics, international relations, and journalism.

Eva Pils is a Reader in Transnational Law at King's College London, Dickson Poon School of Law.

Routledge Research in Human Rights Law

Available titles in this series include:

The Right to Development in International Law
The Case of Pakistan
Khurshid Iqbal

Global Health and Human Rights
Legal and Philosophical Perspectives
John Harrington and Maria Stuttaford

The Right to Religious Freedom in International Law
Between group rights and individual rights
Anat Scolnicov

Emerging Areas of Human Rights in the 21st Century
The role of the Universal Declaration of Human Rights
Marco Odello and Sofia Cavandoli

The Human Right to Water and its Application in the Occupied Palestinian Territories
Amanda Cahill

International Human Rights Law and Domestic Violence
The effectiveness of international human rights law
Ronagh McQuigg

Human Rights in the Asia-Pacific Region
Towards Institution Building
Hitoshi Nasu and Ben Saul

Human Rights Monitoring Mechanisms of the Council of Europe
Gauthier de Beco

The Positive Obligations of the State under the European Convention of Human Rights
Dimitris Xenos

Vindicating Socio-Economic Rights
International Standards and Comparative Experiences
Paul O'Connell

The EU as a 'Global Player' in Human Rights?
Jan Wetzel

Regulating Corporate Human Rights Violations
Humanizing Business
Surya Deva

The UN Committee on Economic, Social and Cultural Rights
The Law, Process and Practice
Marco Odello and Francesco Seatzu

State Security Regimes and the Right to Freedom of Religion and Belief
Changes in Europe Since 2001
Karen Murphy

The European Court of Human Rights in the Post-Cold War Era
Universality in Transition
James A. Sweeney

The United Nations Human Rights Council
A Critique and Early Assessment
Rosa Freedman

Children and International Human Rights Law
The Right of the Child to be Heard
Aisling Parkes

Litigating Transnational Human Rights Obligations
Alternative Judgements
Mark Gibney and Wouter Vandenhole

Reproductive Freedom, Torture and International Human Rights
Challenging the Masculinisation of Torture
Ronli Noa Sifris

Applying an International Human Rights Framework to State Budget Allocations
Rights and Resources
Rory O'Connell, Aoife Nolan, Colin Harvey, Mira Dutschke and Eoin Rooney

Forthcoming titles in this series include:

Jurisdiction, Immunity and Transnational Human Rights Litigation
Xiaodong Yang

Children's Lives in an Era of Children's Rights
The Progress of the Convention on the Rights of the Child in Africa
Afua Twum-Danso Imoh and Nicola Ansell

Human Rights Law in Europe
The Influence, Overlaps and Contradictions of the EU and the ECHR
Kanstantsin Dzehtsiarou, Tobias Lock, Theodore Konstadinides and Noreen O'Meara

Nomadic Peoples and Human Rights
Jérémie Gilbert

Business and Human Rights in South East Asia
A Global Imperative for States and Corporations
Mahdev Mohan and Cynthia Morel

China's Human Rights Lawyers
Advocacy and Resistance
Eva Pils

Extraterritoriality and International Human Rights Law
The Spatial Reach of African Human Rights Treaties
Takele Soboka Bulto

Human Rights Law and Personal Identity
Jill Marshall

In Pursuit of Human Rights
NGOs, Pedagogy and Praxis in Grassroots Africa
Joanne Coysh

Indigenous Peoples, Title to Territory and Resources
The Transformative Role of Free Prior & Informed Consent
Cathal M. Doyle

The Law and Practice of the European Social Committee
Francesco Seatzu and Amaya Ubeda de Torres

Reconciling Cultural Diversity and International Human Rights Obligations
The Compatibility Approach in the Practice of International
Human Rights Institutions
Michael K. Addo

The Right to Equality in European Human Rights Law
The Quest for Substance in the Jurisprudence of the European Courts
Charilaos Nikolaidis

Social and Economic Rights in Theory and Practice
A Critical Assessment
Helena Alviar Garcia, Karl Klare and Lucy A. Williams

China's Human Rights Lawyers

Advocacy and Resistance

Eva Pils

Routledge
Taylor & Francis Group

LONDON AND NEW YORK

First published 2015
by Routledge
2 Park Square, Milton Park, Abingdon, Oxon OX14 4RN

and by Routledge
711 Third Avenue, New York, NY 10017

Routledge is an imprint of the Taylor & Francis Group, an informa business

© 2015 Eva Pils

British Library Cataloguing in Publication Data
A catalogue record for this book is available from the British Library

Library of Congress Cataloging-in-Publication Data
Pils, Eva, author.
   China's human rights lawyers and contemporary Chinese law / Eva Pils.
      pages cm—(Routledge research in human rights law)
   Includes bibliographical references and index.
   ISBN 978-0-415-87084-9 (hardback)—ISBN 978-0-203-79606-1 (ebk)
   1. Civil rights lawyers—China.   2. Human rights workers—China.
   I. Title.
   KNQ1601.C48P55 2014
   342.5108'5—dc23   2014001439

ISBN: 978-0-415-87084-9 (hbk)
ISBN: 978-0-203-79606-1 (ebk)

Typeset in Baskerville
by Keystroke, Station Road, Codsall, Wolverhampton

MIX
Paper from
responsible sources
FSC
www.fsc.org   FSC® C013604   Printed and bound by CPI Group (UK) Ltd, Croydon, CR0 4YY

Contents

Acknowledgements   xi
List of abbreviations   xiii

1   Perspectives on human rights advocacy in China   1

External perspectives on human rights advocacy in China 1
The human rights movement in China: an internal perspective 5
Chinese human rights lawyers as a contentious issue 6
Constraints on research and the use of sources for this book 10
The structure of this book 15

2   Quests for justice and legal advocacy in Chinese history   20

The imperial era: tradition and counter-tradition 21
The promises of liberalism and the spectres of totalitarianism 30
Limited legal reconstruction in the Reform and Opening era 39
The rise of weiquan *(rights defence) 47*
The enduring significance of historical conceptions of justice 51

3   The place of rights advocacy in 'the system'   58

Rights' place in the system: overview 58
Encountering common grievances 66
The institutions to address injustices 85
Marginalisation and identification 93

4   Courtroom advocacy   104

Rules and practices limiting courtroom advocacy 105
Limited achievements in courtroom advocacy 121
The dispersal of rights advocacy into the wider community 133

5   Bureaucratic control of the legal profession   146

The signs of control 146
The control complex of justice bureaux, lawyers' associations and the Party 147
Lessons of the struggle of X Law Firm 170
Dimensions and limitations of bureaucratic control 176

6   Relationship with the security apparatus   189

Police surveillance, 'chats', tracking and following and casual violence 191
Limited uses of the formal criminal process 202
Enforced disappearance and torture 211
'Persuasive' and 'caring' Party–State terror 221
The 'dual state' logic of Party–State control 224

7   Resistance and wider legal and political advocacy   232

The logic of resistance to Party–State control 233
Advocacy of and through openness and democratic expression rights 237
Advocacy and resistance through association 248
Novel forms of civic activism: the New Citizen Movement and its repression 255
The goal of inclusive transformation 266

8   Stability, reform and rights advocacy   274

Implications for stability discourse and rights lawyer categorisations 275
*Implications for legal reform, 'constructive' rule of law discourse and agency in
change 279*
Implications for human rights advocacy 283

Index   287

Acknowledgements

I am indebted to many people for their support. First and foremost, I want to thank all of my interlocutors, human rights lawyers and others working with them. They have most generously shared experiences and insights, and many times been kind and optimistic when they seemed to have every reason to be angry and despairing. I am sorry I cannot acknowledge them by name, as their contributions have all been anonymised.

Second, I am very grateful to those who have helped me with writing this book, some by reading drafts and many more by discussing the issues the book is about. Among these are most importantly Stephen Guest and Mike McConville, who have been available as fellow scholars to talk to throughout the writing process, and have with surpassing kindness and patience read and commented multiple times on every chapter. I cannot thank them enough. They were also among the friends who helped me deal with the inevitable psychological and practical set-backs while writing this book, including the forced disappearances of some rights lawyers, including interlocutors for this book, in the first half of 2011. Those who have read and commented on chapters and early drafts included Oscar Chase, Joy Chia, Cindy Estlund, Barry Friedmann, Ben Liebman, Tom Kellogg, Josh Rosenzweig and Frank Upham. I would also like to thank four anonymous reviewers of my book proposal for their great comments and suggestions and Jiang Jue and Zhang Yihong for their excellent research assistance in the late stages of this book. All errors are, of course, mine.

For sharing insights in discussions about human rights and human rights advocacy in China and elsewhere I would like to thank: in Hong Kong, Amy Barrow, Nicholas Bequelin, Jean-Philippe Béja, Chris Buckley, Jean-Pierre Cabestan, Chan Ka-Wai, Chine Chan, Cheung Yiu-Leung, Joy Chia, Surabhi Chopra, Geoff Crothall, Fu Hualing, Han Dongfang, Jiang Jue, Jin Huaiyu, Swati Jhaveri, Nina Jorgensen, Robin Munro, Stephen Pan, Dinusha Panditaratne, Patrick Poon, Roseann Rife, Flora Sapio, Aaro Samuli Seppänen, Christoph Steinhardt, Teng Biao, Sebastian Veg, Maya Wang, Alainna Wrigley, Wu Fengshi, Xu Yan, Verna Yu, Yu Xingzhong, Zeng Jinyan and Zhang Yihong. Elsewhere, Chen Yu-Jie, Joan and Jerry Cohen, Sophie Cornford, Jeremy Daum, Jacques DeLisle, Ed Donovan, Cindy Estlund, Corinna-Barbara Francis, Terry Halliday, Sharon Hom, Joey Lee, Li Xiaorong, Joan Liu, Sida Liu, Elizabeth Lynch, Nicola

Macbean, Otto Malmgren, Carl Minzner, Andy Nathan, Eileen and Paul Mooney, Tom Kellogg, Sophie Richardson, Christina Sadeler, Marina Svensson, Tim Millar, Frank Upham, Liz Wickeri, diplomats from some twelve diplomatic representations in Beijing, and of course, all my anonymous interlocutors again.

Lastly, I am greatly indebted to two research institutions: the Faculty of Law at the Chinese University of Hong Kong, where I was previously employed, and, the US–Asia Law Institute at New York University School of Law, where I have been a visitor many times. I will always be especially grateful to Jerry Cohen at New York University for the inspiration his work continues to be.

List of abbreviations

ABA	American Bar Association [美国律师协会]
ACLA	All China Lawyers' Association [中华全国律师协会]
BLA	Beijing Lawyers' Association [北京市律师协会]
CCP	Chinese Communist Party [中国共产党]
CECC	Congressional–Executive Commission on China [美国国会及行政部门中国问题委员会]
CHRD	Chinese Human Rights Defenders [人权捍卫者]
CL	People's Republic of China Criminal Law [中华人民共和国刑事诉讼法]
CPL	People's Republic of China Criminal Procedure Law [中华人民共和国刑事诉讼法]
HRW	Human Rights Watch [人权观察]
ICCPR	International Covenant on Civil and Political Rights [公民及政治权利国际公约]
ICSECR	International Covenant on Social, Economic and Cultural Rights [经济, 社会和文化权利国际公约]
INGO	international non-governmental organisation [国际非政府组织]
LGBT	Lesbian, gay, bisexual and transgender [女同性恋者, 男同性恋者, 双性恋者和跨性别者]
MOJ	People's Republic of China Ministry of Justice [中华人民共和国司法部]
NGO	non-governmental organisation [非政府组织]
NPC	National People's Congress [全国人民代表大会]

NPCSC   Standing Committee of the National People's Congress
         [全国人民代表大会常务委员会]
OPS   One Party System
         [一党制]
PRC   People's Republic of China
         [中华人民共和国]
RTL   Re-education Through Labour
         [劳动教养]
SPC   People's Republic of China Supreme People's Court
         [中华人民共和国最高人民法院]
UDHR   Universal Declaration of Human Rights
         [世界人权宣言]
UN   United Nations
         [联合国]
UPR   Universal Periodic Review
         [普遍定期审议]
USA   United States of America
         [美国]

1 Perspectives on human rights advocacy in China

The lawyers at the centre of this book represent a small number – probably fewer than one in a thousand licensed lawyers in China; and of these 200 or so (in absolute numbers),[1] a significant number have already been barred from practicing. Their professional advocacy is ridden with failures. Their political influence would be nil but for the people they represent and work with. They themselves are at constant risk of being detained, harassed and abused.

Yet they play pivotal roles, both in China's legal practice and in political resistance against its current Party–State system. Their advocacy shows that although the Party–State is organised on Leninist principles, this system cannot be understood without attention to the rights it purports to protect (and sometimes does protect). Chinese rights lawyers' work also challenges the view that 'human rights' stands only for inefficacious international institutions, culturally detached advocacy, or a simply obsolete idea; it shows that the values underpinning rights and law are of abiding appeal in China today. An account of their efforts therefore not only affects the evaluation of China's legal and political system, but also allows us to assess domestic advocacy's challenges to transnational civil society and international human rights diplomacy from new critical angles.

External perspectives on human rights advocacy in China

The principle that public power must not violate rights justifies the immense coercive power of the State;[2] and therefore all rights advocacy challenges government

---

1 As of December 2013, a rights lawyer thought there were some 200 lawyers considering themselves to be 'human rights lawyers' in the People's Republic of China (PRC) (#19 2013-7), and some 130 PRC lawyers had elected to join a *weixin* (social media) chat group calling itself '人权律师团 [human rights lawyer group]' requiring a formal pledge to the goals of the group (observation). Similar groups with overlapping membership exist on different social media.
2 The very point of the idea of rights, as understood here, is to restrain government power by requiring justification of its coercive uses. E.g. Dworkin: Ronald Dworkin, *Taking Rights Seriously* (Duckworth: London, 1977) Chapters 2 and 3; *Law's Empire*, Harvard University Press, Cambridge, MA: 1986.

power at some level. The right not to be tortured is a good example; it supports criticism of governments that torture people. Although different theories of human rights diverge in many ways, including on the question of what rights are most central and deserve to be called 'human rights', they lead to similar conclusions when the violation of certain basic rights is concerned. The argument about torture, for example, is that it undermines human capabilities and human agency,[3] that in many instances it unjustifiably inflicts (physical) pain;[4] and that it violates the 'right to be regarded as a human being whose dignity fundamentally matters'.[5]

Lawyers' human rights advocacy is most centrally associated with the uses of procedures and channels provided by domestic systems and the international community to decide whether power exercise in specific cases was justified. It is this sense of advocacy that matters most to Chinese human rights lawyers' work discussed in this book, whereas claims for State provision of welfare is less central to it. (Transnational NGOs' work, focusing on the equally important task of monitoring and exposing abuses, is important for example through monitoring what happens to domestic rights defenders and on occasion by providing material support.) Viewed from an international perspective, domestic rights advocacy can localise challenges to specific government authorities. Again, torture is a good example. Some 35 years ago any rights-based criticism of torture in China came largely from outside the country;[6] but today, as the State has publicly recognised the right not to be tortured and carried out legal reforms creating institutionalised complaint channels, it comes also from legal professionals who are in a sense part of the system they fight, and who complain, for example, about torture that occurs in police detention centres, prison cells and – sometimes – even courtrooms.

In repressive systems, human rights advocacy invariably edges toward political resistance, since the political morality that supports the idea of human rights holds political obligation – a duty to obey the laws of the political community – to depend on respect for such rights, which the repressive system denies. The idea of a right to resistance to tyrannical government derives from this argument.[7]

---

3 Alan Gewirth, *Human Rights*, University of Chicago Press, Chicago: 1982; James Griffin, *On Human Rights*, Oxford: Oxford University Press, 2008.
4 2010; John Tasioulas, 'Human rights' entry in *Routledge Companion to the Philosophy of Law*, Routledge, London, 2012.
5 Dworkin, *ibid*.
6 Roberta Cohen discusses what she characterises as a 'bland and cautious' first foreign government statement on human rights in China, issued by the Carter administration of the US in 1978, as well as international NGOs such as Freedom House and Amnesty International, in 'People's Republic of China: the human rights exception', *Occasional Papers/Reprint Series in Contemporary Asian Studies* no. 3 – 1988 1, University of Maryland School of Law, Baltimore, 1988; http://digitalcommons.law.umaryland.edu/cgi/viewcontent.cgi?article=1085&context=mscas, accessed 1 January 2014.
7 One might, for instance, cite Locke on the people's 'right to resume their original liberty' when the legislature forfeits the power the people had put into their hands. John Locke, *Second Treatise on Government*, Chap. XIX Sec. 222, 1689, text available at http://constitution.org/jl/2ndtr19.htm; or Ronald Dworkin, *Justice for Hedgehogs*, Harvard University Press, Cambridge, MA: 2010, at p. 321.

It is reflected in the 1789 Declaration of the Rights of Man and the Citizen,[8] as well as in the 1948 Universal Declaration of Human Rights,[9] for example. A total violation of all obligations to protect human rights – entailing the breakdown of corrective mechanisms such as court adjudication – can justify not only domestic resistance but even, at least as an abstract possibility, foreign intervention.[10]

It is therefore of relevance not only to historians that international and transnational organisations and governments have consistently described China's human rights record as bad, on its own and in international comparison. Substantive criticism was advanced in the 2009 and 2013 Universal Periodic Review (UPR) processes, for example,[11] the 'inconsistent, eclectic [and] incomplete' nature of this process notwithstanding.[12] UN Special Rapporteurs such as Manfred Nowak in 2006 have also been sharply critical[13] and individual States such as the United States of America and Sweden publish their own annual reports on countries including China;[14] detailing many instances and aspects of (reported) human rights violations on the part of the Chinese State.

There is, of course, controversy about how appropriate criticism of the Chinese government for its human rights record is, or even about whether it is appropriate at all, given that China is a non-western country, a developing country and emerging economy, and a country whose government explicitly rejects political liberalism. This controversy can in my view never get away from the more basic question of whether human rights are important in China; but then, in addition to concerns about criticising the Chinese government,

8 Declaration of the Rights of Man and the Citizen, approved by the National Assembly of France, 26 August 1789, at http://avalon.law.yale.edu/18th_century/rightsof.asp, accessed on 21 December 2013: 'The aim of all political association is the preservation of the natural and imprescriptible rights of man. These rights are liberty, property, security, and resistance to oppression.'

9 The Universal Declaration of Human Rights, Preamble: 'Whereas it is essential, if man is not to be compelled to have recourse, as a last resort, to rebellion against tyranny and oppression, that human rights should be protected by the rule of law', at http://www.un.org/en/documents/udhr/, accessed 21 December 2013.

10 Some theories make the ability of human rights arguments to set aside the principle of non-intervention in sovereign states a guiding criterion for deciding *what* human rights we have. John Rawls, *The Law of Peoples*, Harvard University Press, Cambridge, MA: 1999; discussing Rawls' idea for China: Stephen Angle, 'Decent democratic centralism', 33 *Political Theory* 518 (2005).

11 Relevant documentation concerning China's last review on 22 October 2013 is available from UPR info, 'Review 2013'/China, at http://www.upr-info.org/Review-2013-1696.html, accessed 2 January 2014.

12 Rhona K.M. Smith, 'More of the same or something different? Preliminary observations on the contribution of the Universal Periodic Review with reference to the Chinese experience', 10 *Chinese Journal of International Law* 3 (2011), 565–586.

13 'United Nations Special Rapporteur highlights abuses in China', UN Press Release, 2 December 2005, at http://www.unhchr.ch/huricane/huricane.nsf/view01/677C1943FAA14D67C12570C B0034966D?opendocument, accessed on 21 December 2013; Manfred Nowak, 'Fact-finding on conditions on torture and ill-treatment and conditions of detention', 1 *Journal of Human Rights Practice* (2009) 101–119.

14 See e.g. for the U.S. State Department Country Report 'China' (2010) http://www.state.gov/documents/organization/160451.pdf.

there has also always been a more global and profound kind of scepticism about the idea of (human) rights. From Bentham's early positivism to Marx, Marxist, Marxian and various 'postmodern' views of law, critics have regarded rights either as derivative creations of law, which, in turn, is sourced in political power; or as potentially deceptive expressions of power relations that law and rights serve to support, rather than challenge or change. Some scholars in these traditions have argued that human rights are late expressions of imperialism and that 'global neocapitalism and human-rights-for-export are part of the same project', for example.[15]

Lastly, not only scholars who reject the idea of rights, but also some scholars who are sympathetic to it have described it as part of a secular faith. Thus Koskenniemi, who has argued that international law is in crisis, has also expressed the hope that faith in international law understood as a set of liberal principles with an 'emancipatory promise' could be regained.[16] If this analysis is correct, we may regard human rights advocates as at best members of a community of faith constituted by the 'global human rights movement',[17] some sort of global religion that has followers and priests; and we must perhaps ask ourselves if rights' and rights advocacy's importance is limited to those who share the faith[18] and such faith may be lost.

These attitudes of scepticism should be noted and considered; but I would suggest that no critical engagement is possible if we do not at least consider what human rights advocacy looks like from the inside. To do this, it is necessary to engage those who choose to engage in rights advocacy in the rather hostile conditions of the Chinese system directly on the tenets of their convictions; and this is best done without assuming their attitudes or actions to be based in incommunicable articles of faith.

15 Costas Douzinas, for example, argues that 'despite differences in content, colonialism and the human rights movement form a continuum, episodes in the same drama . . . bringing civilization to the barbarians . . . There is little difference between imposing reason and good governance and proselytizing for Christianity and human rights. They are both part of the cultural package of the West, aggressive and redemptive at the same time.' Costas Douzinas, 'Seven theses on human rights (3)', at http://criticallegalthinking.com/2013/05/23/seven-theses-on-human-rights-3-neoliberal-capitalism-voluntary-imperialism/, accessed 30 December 2013.

16 Martti Koskenniemi, 'What should international lawyers learn from Karl Marx?', in Susan Marks (ed.), *International Law on the Left: Re-examining Marxist Legacies*, Cambridge University Press, Cambridge, 2011, chapter 1.

17 Henry J. Steiner, Philip Alston and Ryan Goodman, *International Human Rights in Context: Law, Politics, Morals*, 3rd ed., 2007, for a discussion of the history of the global human rights movement. For a critical discussion, see Samuel Moyn, *The Last Utopia: Human Rights in History*, Belknap Press, Cambridge, MA: 2010.

18 So far as the Chinese Party–State engages with these debates at the international level, it is part of the international institutional framework supposed to protect human rights but has also used arguments echoing the sceptical and relativistic arguments advanced from outside China and sometimes to associate human rights with outside threats to its sovereignty or even hostile attacks, and with the inside threat of subversion. For a discussion of this last aspect, see Dong Yunhu and Chang Jian (董云虎, 常健, editors), 中国人权建设 60 年 [*60 Years of Establishing Human Rights in China*], Nanchang, Jiangxi People's Press: 2009, especially Chapter 8, pp. 304 f.

The human rights movement in China: an internal perspective

Considered through the eyes of the domestic lawyers who try to address them from within, human rights problems in China look quite different from what the external perspective would suggest. Drawing on practices of legal advocacy in concrete cases, discussing how case-based advocacy expands and relates to wider legal and political advocacy, the present account depicts an, in many aspects, dysfunctional system, but not one whose basic elements someone outside China cannot recognise; and this non-liberal system with an, at times, explicit anti-rights rhetoric is not 'the other' system with which the world has no connection but, rather, a possible system ours could become more like. As this study seeks to understand lawyers' role in the Chinese human rights movement,[19] it seeks to capture and interpret their experiences and views, their hopes and difficulties, starting from how they themselves presented these, under the protection of anonymity and unadulterated by the public persona they have been given in media and other more personalised reports.

In the domestic Chinese rights movement or *weiquan* movement, the ideas of human rights (*renquan*) and natural (human) rights (*tianfu renquan*), civil rights (*gongmin quanli*), basic rights (*jiben quanli*), constitutional rights (*xianfa quanli*), legal rights (*hefa quanli / quanyi*) and rights *tout court* (*quanli*) are used fairly eclectically.[20] In addition to these terms there is the ubiquitous term 'rights defence', *weiquan*, which could be read as a contraction of the words *weihu* and *quanli*.[21] The differences between the various terms denoting rights appear to matter less than the common ideas underlying them. Echoes of the Mencian 'Mandate of Heaven' (*tianming*)[22] and uses of traditional terms for wrongs and injustice are evidence of the vernacularisation of rights language;[23] and citizen action often emphasises the democratic and revolutionary potential of rights. Accordingly, at least so far as domestic perspectives are described and interpreted here, I will use 'human rights' in an open sense; and I will give preference to the terms 'rights', 'rights defenders' and 'rights lawyers,' reflecting the open Chinese usage.

---

19 In his study of the historical origins of the idea of human rights (in the west), Tierny observes that, setting aside the question of whether people in historical eras without words for human rights had such rights, it is still important to ask in which kind of *Zeitgeist* environment individuals could think of and articulate this particular idea, and how the idea is to be understood in the particular context in which it is articulated. Tierny, *The Idea of Natural Rights: Studies on Natural Rights, Natural Law and Church Law 1150–1625*, Wm. B. Eerdmans Publishing Company, 1997, chapter 1. This question can clearly be asked with regard to China, too.

20 In Chinese characters, 人权, 天赋人权, 公民权利, 基本权利, 宪法权利, 合法权利/权益, 权利.

21 In Chinese characters, 维权 (维护权利).

22 In Chinese characters, 天命.

23 Eva Pils, 'Taking *yuan* (冤) seriously: why the Chinese government should stop suppressing citizen protest against injustice', forthcoming in *Temple International and Comparative Law Journal*. On vernacularisation, Sally Engle Merry, *Human Rights and Gender Violence: Translating International Law into Local Justice*, Chicago University Press, Chicago: 2005.

Chinese human rights lawyers as a contentious issue

Reflecting a widely held opinion about Chinese human rights lawyers, perhaps especially among the circles of those involved in collaborative rule of law reform projects, but clearly also beyond, an academic commentator wrote in 2011 that:

> [T]he horrendous and inexcusable plight of the handful of Chinese lawyers whose abuse has been reported is largely irrelevant to, and tells us little about, the everyday work of most Chinese lawyers and their interactions with the justice system.[24]

Human rights lawyers have received attention not only from academia but also from the news media, human rights NGOs and the diplomatic community ever since the term *weiquan* started being widely used, initially as an idea promoted by the government, and especially when, around 2005, the persecution of rights lawyers started in earnest. It is perhaps not surprising that the renown rights lawyers thus obtained might not have had much appeal for those who were interested in a detached and serious study of the wider Chinese legal system and its rule of law reform as such. At the same time media attention has also drawn praise and admiration for human rights lawyers, praise whose effects have been complex and not always beneficial.

Picking up on the positive coverage of the idea of rights defence in Party–State-controlled domestic discussions in the 1990s,[25] the first scholarly discussions considered them largely as lawyers participating in 'public interest law' activities, i.e. in a constructive role supporting what was also thought to be the political leadership's ultimate goal of a more independent judiciary and better rights protection.[26] From this perspective, it must have seemed natural, at least initially, to categorise *weiquan* lawyers depending on the extent to which they could be regarded as 'constructive' in this way. Academic literature has provided categorisations, or taxonomies. In a classic piece, Cullen and Fu, who adopt their taxonomy as a 'descriptive-analytical tool,' argue that the three types of lawyer they describe ('moderate', 'critical' and 'radical') are different mainly with regard to the kinds of case they adopt. They say that these typologies are recognised within the *weiquan* community, within society and within government, emphasise the types of case rights lawyers work on:

> Moderate *weiquan* lawyers prefer to work through legal rather than political means. They limit their advocacy to legal issues and justify their legalistic

---

24 John Wagner Givens, 'The silent majority: China's other lawyers', *Huffington Post*, 29 July 2011, at http://www.huffingtonpost.com/john-wagner-givens/the-silent-majority-china_b_912135.html, accessed 2 January 2014.

25 Discussed in Chapter 2.

26 E.g. Benjamin Liebman, *Legal Aid and Public Interest Law in China*, 34 *Texas International Law Journal* (1999) 211.

approach on the ground of professionalism. They persuade their clients, in one way or another, to limit their action to what is permissible in law and to channel their grievances and demands through the court system. For example, moderate lawyers have prohibited their clients from sit-ins, rallies or demonstrations. While moderate lawyers may be identified with a cause, the cause is often more immediately related to individual cases.[27]

By contrast, what the authors term 'critical' *weiquan* lawyers:

> [B]uild on good (personal/financial) foundations, and stress results over grandstanding. These lawyers are highly critical of the OPS [One Party System] and the legal system, but recognize the lack of viable alternatives over the near-to-medium-term future. They sharply criticize the system, but at the same time are cautious about the language used and the manner through which the criticism is expressed. They stress commitment to the 'system' but demand that the system try and live up to its rhetoric ... One key feature distinguishing critical from moderate lawyering is the sensitivity of the cases. Critical weiquan lawyers take cases with political ramifications. They prefer cases that are politically sensitive, but not politically prohibitive.
>
> [. . .] At the top of the weiquan pyramid are the limited number of radical lawyers who distinguish themselves by representing the most sensitive cases and identifying completely with political dissidents and their political causes ... In general, lawyers can become radical either with respect to the causes they identify with or with respect to the methods they use. A lawyer is radicalized when he or she represents and identifies with the 'enemies' of the state. This will often lead to harsh criticism of the political and legal system. Given China's concern with political stability, a lawyer would also be labelled radical when he or she goes beyond legal representation by organizing and leading clients in extra-legal political confrontations.[28]

Peerenboom describes radical *weiquan* lawyers more explicitly by what he regards as their methods and goals:

> Radical lawyers take on highly sensitive political cases involving dissidents and Falun Gong. Their methods are more extreme, including organizing mass demonstrations and social movements, or even advocating violence. Their goals may include overthrow of the Party–state ... they tend to alienate the general public and their fellow lawyers, and provide a pretext

---

27 Fu and Cullen, '*Weiquan* (rights protection) lawyering in an authoritarian State: building a culture of public-interest lawyering', *China Journal*, 59 (2008), 111–127 at p. 116. See also Richard Cullen and Fu Hualing, 'Climbing the *weiquan* ladder: a radicalising process for rights-protection lawyers', 205, *China Quarterly*, 40–59, at http://journals.cambridge.org/action/displayFulltext? type=1&fid=8243497&jid=CQY&volumeId=205&issueId=-1&aid=8243495, accessed 21 December 2013 ('*weiquan* lawyering').
28 Fu and Cullen, '*Weiquan* lawyering', *supra*.

for the government to delegitimize and suppress the *weiquan* movement, as many less radical lawyers have pointed out.[29]

These categorisations and taxonomies are clearly important to understanding contemporary discussion of *weiquan* as a social practice. But an initial examination of radical lawyers suggests that such terminology reflects and may reinforce perceptions of lawyers as, variously, sensationalised side issues 'irrelevant to the work of most Chinese lawyers', 'as irritants worsening the situation of 'moderate' lawyers', or as larger-than-life heroes and martyrs; and the academic merits of the above taxonomies categorising and sub-categorising in these ways notwithstanding, can draw attention from who these lawyers are, what they do, and how they interact with the wider legal and political system in China as individuals, beyond coverage in media reports, international rights advocacy and comments.[30] The vocabulary of the radical can also be taken to commend the moderate and critical, and lawyers who bear these labels for their willingness to stay within the law and – in Peerenboom's case – for not advocating violence.[31]

On the side of the (here negatively understood) 'radical', for example, one author describes Chen Guangcheng, a blind lay rights defender who, a few months after moving to the US, accused his initial sponsor of giving in to Chinese government pressure to abandon him,[32] as 'rebellious' and 'aggressive,' as well as an 'uncompromising rebel,' and someone 'causing . . . trouble':

> Chen's conviction drove him to tactics which even most activist lawyers eschew, especially in combination: 1) his case touched on a nationally sensitive issue (the one-child policy) 2) he included over a thousand plaintiffs and attempted to open the door for over a hundred thousand more 3) he lacked the government connections that help protect other activist lawyers 4) he

---

29 Randall Peerenboom, 'Searching for political liberalism in all the wrong places: the legal profession in China as the leading edge of political reform?', (8 September 2008), *La Trobe Law School Legal Studies* Research Paper No. 2008/7, at http://ssrn.com/abstract=1265080, or http://dx.doi.org/10.2139/ssrn.1265080. In other publications, Peerenboom has characterised 'radical' lawyers in similar terms but without claiming that they advocate violence.

30 It may also be hard to identify specimens fitting the 'radical' category defined on these terms (especially Peerenboom's definition): Jonathan Benney, *Defending Rights in Contemporary China*, Abingdon, Routledge: 2012.

31 In the present context, the notion of the moderate rights defence lawyer is generally invoked to invite sympathy. Xu Zhiyong, detained in July 2013 on spurious charges, had made a very prominent contribution in the New Citizen Movement discussed in Chapter 7. Shortly after his criminal detention on suspicion of 'gathering a crowd in a public place to disrupt order', a smuggled video was published in which Xu calls on others to join the New Citizen Movement from his detention centre. Within a short time, for example, the BBC, the *Economist*, *Guardian*, *New York Times*, *Reuters* and the *Washington Post* (on one of the blogs it runs), etc., had described Xu as 'moderate'.

32 Having suffered illegal house-arrest and imprisonment, Chen escaped and moved to the United States with his family in March 2012. He accepted the offer of a one-year-fellowship at NYU Law School's U.S.-Asia Law Institute, but later criticised NYU for giving in to 'pressure' from the Chinese government to discontinue his tenure as visiting scholar, without substantiating these accusations and attracting commentary in the media and other circles.

liaised with foreign media 5) public protest was involved ... Most lawyers would probably have *avoided serious reprisals by giving up* after losing in the lower court and having an appeal ignored. They likely would have chosen less *aggressive* tactics, for example, by bringing a much smaller group of plaintiffs (even one of China's lawyers most experienced at suing the state has never filed a case with over 700 plaintiffs). It is difficult to assess whether less aggressive tactics would ultimately have been more successful, but it is likely that they would have *kept Chen out of trouble*. (emphases added)[33]

This assessment suggests that giving up might have been 'more successful' but without elucidating how or in what way. It appears to argue that the risk of reprisals is by itself evidence of 'aggressive' tactics and that the likelihood of serious reprisals would be a compelling reason for anyone not wishing to be 'aggressive' to give up.[34] It leaves several questions open, not least the question of how we should understand the characterisation as 'aggressive', and appears to relegate rights lawyers who refuse to give up to a category of individuals whose few members appear unhinged, unable to 'keep out of trouble' and generally suspect, because they make choices that others would reject.

On the other side of this polarised discussion of human rights lawyers, the vocabulary of 'heroes', 'crusaders' and so on,[35] also raises concerns and leaves questions unanswered. If heroes are people who act in the service of others, accepting risks to themselves and without anticipating external gain for themselves,[36] some of the individuals who were interlocutors for this project are undoubtedly heroes. But, at least in popular literature and in the media, the word 'hero' is used in many different ways, and hero narratives sometimes

---

33 John Wagner Givens, 'Chen Guangcheng: still raising heck', *Huffington Post, 3* July 2013, at http://www.huffingtonpost.com/john-wagner-givens/chen-guangcheng-nyu_b_3541948.html.

34 The author might have added that Chen and his supporters in China attempted to draw attention to this lawsuit by other means, for example, by organising free legal education classes delivered pro bono by lawyer friends, seeking to get the police to investigate defamatory slogans against Chen Guangcheng appearing in his village, and by providing legal consultation to people more widely. Anonymous, '谁是陈光诚 [Who is Chen Guangcheng?]', independent documentary film, 2011, available at http://vimeo.com/34059688, accessed 4 January 2014.

35 E.g. David Kilgour, 'Canada can help imprisoned Chinese hero Gao Zhisheng', *The Métropolitain*, 25 March 2010, at http://themetropolitain.ca/articles/view/793; John Taylor, 'Lawyer Zhou – China's new hero', 28 September 2004, at http://www.abc.net.au/foreign/content/2004/s1205375.htm; Florian Godovits, 'Manfred Novak discusses two of China's heroes', 28 July 2009, at http://www.theepochtimes.com/n2/world/manfred-nowak-united-nations-gao-zhisheng-hu-jia-china-20247.html and http://www.epochtimes.de/manfred-nowak-massive-repressionswelle-an-uiguren-470416.html; Alexa Olesen, 'Blind lawyer a legal crusader in China', *Washington Post*, 20 July 2006, at http://www.washingtonpost.com/wp-dyn/content/article/2006/07/20/AR2006072000315.html.

36 Zimbardo's definition of heroism: 'First, it's performed in service to others in need – whether that's a person, group, or community – or in defense of certain ideals. Second, it's engaged in voluntarily, even in military contexts, as heroism remains an act that goes beyond something required by military duty. Third, a heroic act is one performed with recognition of possible risks and costs, be they to one's physical health or personal reputation, in which the actor is willing to accept anticipated sacrifice. Finally, it is performed without external gain anticipated at the time of the act.' http://greatergood.berkeley.edu/article/item/what_makes_a_hero.

indicate a judgement made by others (as in the expression 'someone's hero'), which would make heroes similar to celebrities or 'heroes' of any random cause (regardless of their moral views or moral courage). Understood in this latter, wider sense of a mediated third-person assessment, the idea of the hero can draw justified scepticism, especially when it is not clear whom or what a particular hero is to be associated with. The, at times, adulating tone of some representations of rights lawyers might equally invite puzzlement, as for instance when it is said of Lawyer Gao Zhisheng that he is 'often called' or 'has won the sobriquet "China's conscience"',[37] however well meant and expressive of deep and well-deserved respect this way of describing him likely is. Some of the distinctions, awards and general attention given to rights lawyers, moreover, appear closely associated with political figures and with their views and projects, which the lawyer in question may not understand well, perhaps not even be close to, or have any opportunity to form an opinion about.[38] Gao Zhisheng, then, is a hero in Zimbardo's sense, but being the hero of the various groups who make him into one may not help the effort of doing justice to who he is, or indeed to his public persona.

Engaging with the views and debates briefly outlined above, the present study seeks to show that rights lawyers do matter to the legal profession and China's legal system as a whole, as can be understood from a systematic study of the institutional conditions they work in, their professional work with clients, inter-action with the wider legal profession and wider legal system, encounters with Party–State repression, and political ideals, aspirations and advocacy. It has used conversations held under the protection of anonymity in the hope of getting views and comments unadulterated by the public personae rights lawyers have acquired. It seeks an empirical response (with the limitations I set out below), in an effort to address puzzles to which categorisations not embedded in actual empirical data can give rise, in order to offer a more finely grained account of the people involved, their actual working lives, motivations and aspirations.

Constraints on research and the use of sources for this book

The fieldwork for this account is based on conversations conducted with 97 individuals based in different Mainland Chinese cities (mostly Beijing) and

---

37 Cp. David Kilgour, 'Conscience of China: Gao Zhisheng', 8 May 2010, *Epoch Times*, http://www.theepochtimes.com/n2/opinion/gao-zhisheng-conscience-of-china-34982.html; Elissa Cooper, '"China's conscience" missing in action', *Christianity Today*, 23 February 2009, at http://www.christianitytoday.com/ct/2009/october/34.38.html.

38 For example, a commission named after a US Congressman 'adopted' lawyer Gao Zhisheng as one of the first two prisoners selected for the new Defending Freedoms Project of the Tom Lantos Human Rights Commission in January 2013, at a time when Gao had spent about four years first in strict extra-legal detention and then in prison, almost totally cut off from general information. Congressman Wolf wrote, 'I have chosen to advocate for you . . . Your faith is an inspiration as is your pursuit of justice even at great risk to your personal safety and well-being . . . You have my promise that I will be your friend and will not be silent in the face of your suffering.' Gao would probably welcome this attention; but might be ill equipped to gauge the implications of his 'adoption' by Wolf from a prison cell in Xinjiang. 'Wolf supports Chinese prisoner through "Defending Freedoms" Project', 24 January 2013, at http://wolf.house.gov/press-releases/wolf-supports-chinese-prisoner-through-defending-freedoms-project/, accessed 2 January 2014.

working on cases in places all over China. Most of the conversations used directly in quotations here were conducted between April 2010 and January 2013, most were one on one, and the majority were audio-recorded.[39] In some cases, comments used in this book were made at closed door seminars and on similar occasions. Some 73 of the interlocutors sought out for formal conversations have a professional law background, in most cases a licence to practise law held at some point (as mentioned, a number of rights lawyers have had their licences taken away or suspended). Other interlocutors include human rights defenders without a professional law background, petitioners, citizen journalists and videographers.

The rights lawyers' statements are the centrepiece of this account. From these conversations, the reality of rights lawyers' professional roles and lives in the Chinese legal system can be gleaned. In many instances, the statements gathered from lawyers about particular cases or causes could be corroborated to some extent by news reports or by conversing with different actors who had participated in the same case, by participation in private or semi-open online chats (e.g. via Skype), or by access to documents and reports made available, for the most part, online.

Inevitably, this project was affected by limitations resulting from the nature of the topic and the legal and political system. A major limitation was the lack of access to trial hearings. Even assuming that it would have been possible to get access to ordinary court hearings – this is difficult at least for foreigners[40] – it would have been clearly impossible to obtain access in cases in which one of the already 'sensitive' lawyers at the centre of this study was acting, given also that the cases they appeared in were themselves 'sensitive;' and thus my observation of this aspect of the legal process was limited to outside court buildings. Occasionally I met clients together with lawyers, and I had some separate conversations with lawyer's clients (not in detention).

With three or four exceptions, the lawyers spoken to could be described as *weiquan* or 'human rights' lawyers. The initially small circle of lawyers working on human rights widened and acquaintances and their contacts deepened as this study progressed, and as the Party–State repression of lawyers got worse. In 2009 Teng Biao, himself a human rights lawyer and scholar, estimated that there might

---

39 Consent to recording and use for this project was obtained in all cases. Some particularly constrained conversations were held with the interlocutor's consent only to take notes. In some cases, notes were taken directly after the conversation and consent to use was confirmed subsequently, due to special circumstances. The individuals have been randomly numbered for the purpose of anonymisation; and only I have accessed the recordings of conversations. References to public statements by rights lawyers in media interviews, essays, blog postings, documentary films and so on are provided with full citations.

40 Some years earlier, I had some opportunities outside the context of this project to attend trial hearings in ordinary cases with no rights lawyer involvement; but it should be noted that the character of the hearing was likely affected by the fact it was being observed. Similarly, while I have interacted with Chinese officials from many different authorities within the broader legal system, including Public Security Bureau officers, judges, procurators, and Ministry of Justice officials, this was not in the context of the present project.

be 'a few dozen of us';[41] whereas in 2012, he estimated their number to have grown to over 100 but remain below 200.

The individuals who contributed were selected on the basis of personal acquaintance or through personal introductions. They 'qualified' for being interviewed by virtue of their experience with human rights defence, in most cases current, in one or two cases years back. They were approached by phone, over the internet, via intermediaries (usually rights lawyers), or in person. Many of the individuals approached know each other as colleagues or occasional collaborators, and in some cases as friends. I have known some of them since 2004 and I approached many interlocutors by obtaining their contact details from people I already knew, including in some cases from individuals and organisations outside Mainland China. While in some cases only one conversation was held and recorded for the purposes of this book, there was a core group of one or two dozen interlocutors central to China's human rights movement, with whom I met at least a dozen times, and with whom I jointly attended meals, seminars, conferences, retreats and so on, augmenting the amount of time spent in informal conversation or as an observer–participant of rights lawyer events. On such occasions, I made the acquaintance of another few dozen rights lawyers who were not formally sought out for recorded conversations, but whose experiences and comments also came to shape my understanding of this topic.

Generally, contact requests were successful. Only in one case did I not receive any reply to my enquiry if a conversation was possible with an individual I had met a few years earlier, and gave up after a few attempts. In another case, a lawyer whom I had previously met explained in a text message that they had returned to their hometown due to 'the bad air in Beijing'. In numerous instances, meetings became impossible or had to be called off when the lawyers were hour-arrested or forcibly disappeared, and it was not possible to re-establish contact or even if contact could be made to arrange meetings in all cases after the rights lawyers were released from forced disappearances.

The circumstances in which the conversations were arranged and conducted varied. Generally, arrangements were made through the internet or over the phone, and meetings took place in coffee shops, restaurants, offices, parks or in the private residence of the interlocutor. Sometimes, appointments were made days in advance and through voice-Skype to minimise the risk of the authorities becoming aware of the appointment. In one case, a lawyer suggested that I should go to a place where he could often be found whenever I was in town, rather than making an appointment that might trigger instructions not to meet me. In one case, I arranged a first meeting with my interlocutor through Skype communication with his friend, another interlocutor and was not sure whom exactly I was meeting as I had mentioned several names of interest to me. In the case of Gao Zhisheng, it would have seemed impossible to arrange to meet him,

---

41 Teng Biao, 'The law on trial in China', *Washington Post*, 25 July 2009, at http://www.washingtonpost.com/wp-dyn/content/article/2009/07/24/AR2009072402940.html.

and we just went to his residence when we heard he had been returned there after a long-term forced disappearance.

Interlocutors generally thought that it was possible, if not likely, that they were being monitored in some way (and I thought so too during some of the conversations). For instance, it seemed possible to most interlocutors that at least their electronic communications (phone conversations, phone text messages, email, internet chat services and social media) were monitored and in a few cases, they explained why they had positive knowledge that this was so.[42] Several interlocutors reported about their phones 'playing up' at certain times;[43] they attributed this to interference from the authorities.

During face-to-face meetings many thought that it was possible to listen in on conversations led for the purpose of this study via electronic devices, such as mobile phones:

> See, our conversation right now might be listened in on. But we don't need to take any counter-measure, such as taking the battery out of our phones, because we actually don't care, do we?[44]

Some interlocutors believed that there was additional surveillance through microphones and surveillance cameras installed, for instance, in coffee shops,[45] in public parks[46] and in private homes.[47] In one case, the person under surveillance had himself been instructed to audiotape conversations with visitors, and to hand over the audio-recordings to the police afterwards.[48]

Many interlocutors were, in fact, under surveillance at certain times, covert or ostentatious, and on numerous occasions, the interlocutor pointed out plain-clothes persons sitting or walking nearby or following us. Face-to-face meetings also included sitting in a flat with a human rights defender couple as the police was knocking on the door demanding admission (without any warrant, and unsuccessfully on that day); visiting interlocutors in their monitored homes and work environments and, on occasion, meeting interlocutors under house arrest; and meeting family and friends of primary interlocutors at times when they themselves were detained or 'being travelled' or when they were voluntarily avoiding their own homes to spare their families harassment.

On occasion, measures to escape electronic surveillance were taken, indicating that the interlocutor did mind being monitored. Forms of avoidance included

---

42 E.g. #2's story in 2009. See also Chapter 6.
43 E.g. 'Yesterday I gave an interview to [foreign newspaper] about [another lawyer]. Since last night, my phone has been playing up especially badly ... I think that just confirms our judgement; they're really worried and cagey about the case of [the other lawyer].' Skype conversation #9 2010 (on file).
44 #52 11 1:16.
45 Conversation #22 2011-3.
46 Conversation #5, #27 2010-1.
47 This concerns the case of a friend of the author belonging to *weiquan* circles, who was not formally interviewed in the course of this project.
48 Conversation #8 2010-1.

meeting somewhere without taking electronic equipment along, taking batteries out of mobile phones or placing them in containers blocking off signals,[49] using special mobile phones with newly bought SIM card numbers among a few friends or family members at certain times,[50] simply whispering.[51] Sometimes ommunication was arranged through middlemen and could take place in person only, with all electronic communication being avoided.

Only on a few occasions did interlocutors express fear or show signs of fear, for example constantly checking for plainclothes officers or listening or video-recording devices. But there was a pervasive consciousness of risk. As of December 2013, of the 97 interlocutors, four of the lawyers and three other rights advocates had served or were serving prison sentences[52] and two more interlocutors had been placed under criminal investigation detention. Two interlocutors, had served a Re-education Through Labour sentence. Some 17 lawyers and 10 other rights advocates had been in police detention other than criminal investigation detention for periods of at least a day; in some cases their detention took the form of a forced disappearance of up to two months and in one case over a year. Some 27 of the lawyers and nine other advocates were confirmed to have been beaten by plainclothes police, uniformed police or other officers of the *sifa jiguan* (judicial authorities)[53] at some point; some of these persons had been tortured by various physical and psychological methods. The majority of interlocutors who had been beaten had been beaten more than once; and for some lawyers, scuffles and beatings – casual violence at the hands of the authorities – appeared to have become a common experience.

While the sense that all conversations were possibly recorded by the police or internal security services did not reduce their value as such, the point of anonymisation as a standard technique of sociological research became at times rather elusive. Not only might their stories and cases identify the better known interlocutors despite efforts to conceal their identity, but also, in a political environment so far deviating from the 'normal' of western liberal democracies in which these techniques were devised, did interlocutors think it unlikely that they might 'disclose' anything that was not already known to the authorities in the course of a conversation.

Most of the individuals sought out for conversation have some sort of 'public' or online persona: they have blogs and/or microblogs, and some of them have given media interviews and public lectures, or published essays on human rights issues. Materials of this nature, as well as large quantities of other written and audio-visual sources of every description (including in some cases online chats in writing), have also been used to gain a better understanding of the issue at hand. As a result, several persons lead a 'double life' in this study: they are quoted by

---

49 Conversation #8 2010-1, #9 2010-3, # 22.
50 #9 2011-2.
51 # 7 2011-1.
52 As a consequence, they lost their licences in accordance with the Law on Lawyers.
53 In Chinese characters, 司法机关.

name with reference to publicly available sources, and in anonymised form with reference to personal conversations. The possibility of inferring from a public to an anonymised persona has been reduced as far as possible using standard social science techniques; but, of course, such inferences cannot be entirely precluded.

The structure of this book

Chapter 2, discussing the history of legal advocacy and quests for justice in China, argues that the human rights movement, of which lawyers are part, has been the result of a confluence of two different factors, popular demands for redress for injustices, and political–legal reforms creating broadly liberal institutions, including that of the lawyer. Both of these have a history extending back in time well beyond the founding of the PRC, whereas official accounts of the current system and its history at best draw on a sanitised, adulterated version of the Chinese moral tradition.

Discussing the central features of the current legal and political system relevant to lawyers' rights advocacy, as well as the grievances and rights violations at the centre of human rights cases, Chapter 3 characterises the PRC's system as affected by inherent tensions. Rights lawyers and other rights advocates hold the Party–State to the promises it has made to its citizens to protect rights, for example through the PRC Constitution and further laws and regulations, whereas the Party–State tends to view rights advocacy as 'destabilising' and hence illegitimate. As rights lawyers protest the system, they identify with their clients, and are increasingly marginalised along with their clients.

Chapter 4, discussing how lawyers conduct advocacy in court and similar settings, examines how the system-inherent conflict outlined in Chapter 3 affects legal, especially judicial practices. Drawing on lawyers' accounts of their advocacy experiences, it argues that rights lawyers have in the past decade created new and more effective patterns of advocacy to overcome the obstacles known from studies of ordinary litigation practices. Yet because it effectively disturbs the routine of judicial practices, and because it depends on publicity for (however limited) success, forceful legal advocacy is often pushed outside State-provided and State-controlled fora, with further reaching consequences; and it is as a result of their successes that rights lawyers have come under increasing pressure from the justice bureaucracies and security apparatus.

Chapters 5 and 6, discussing bureaucratic control of the entire legal profession by the justice bureaucracies and control of rights lawyers by the security apparatus, argue that adapting to the inbuilt contradiction between the institutions of rights and law, on the one hand, and the command principle that is its basic form of power exercise, on the other, the Party–State has kept the institutional reform machine going, nourishing hopes of slow but sure progress toward rule of law. At the same time it has aspired to achieve total managerial control over the legal process, and sharpened its denunciations of 'western' rule of law. Repression reaches (pervasively) far into the recesses of 'ordinary' lawyers' professional advocacy; it constitutes a compelling reason to reject facile narratives of incremental liberalisation. Legislative reforms in the general direction of increased liberalisation are not pointless but they do nothing to impede a worsening of repression, because it is possible for the Party–State's system to accommodate opposed trends – to accommodate, in Fraenkel's language, a concurrent rise of the state of norms and the state of measures, a change that cannot translate into 'rule of law' construction.[54] Control systems have been perfected; they have become less crude but not any less repressive in their effects.

The invasive nature of repression techniques used against rights lawyers, the most invidious of which are discussed in Chapter 6, are indicative of a logic of total denial of liberty that is reminiscent of 20th-century totalitarian systems. But if taken seriously, freedom also encompasses the freedom of individuals inside the system to stop the descent into the ever tightening control of the post-totalitarian State. Drawing on this argument, Chapter 7, examining the wider political consequences of rights lawyers' advocacy, observes that confronted with extra-legal measures, a rising number of lawyers' advocacy has become more systemic, organised and overtly political and less concerned with the futile wish to 'stay within the law' in recent years. Important relationships of mutual support between rights lawyers, people seeking redress for grievances, people intellectually attracted to the values rights lawyers stand for, and the democratic opposition (these constitute overlapping groups) are being formed. Since in becoming more connected and politically activist, lawyers make the choice to popularise their causes by addressing the flaws of the political system head on, at the cost of attracting the label of subversiveness and further persecution, these new developments are likely to deepen the crisis of the legal system in the longer term. Chapter 8 discusses the implications of these findings for wider discourse about stability, legal reform and human rights advocacy.

Bibliography

International law instruments

Universal Declaration of Human Rights, passed by the United Nations General Assembly on 10 December 1948, at http://www.un.org/en/documents/udhr/.

---

54 Ernst Fraenkel in his book *The Dual State (Der Doppelstaat)* tried to capture the character of the German political system, as it had developed from about the 17th century until then. He uses the distinction between what he calls the 'normative' and the 'prerogative state' (state of measures, state of norms) to capture the fact that a formalistically conceived rule according to laws can be entrenched, even as rule of law is undermined by the dual state in both of its aspects, including the fundamentally arbitrary power mechanisms characterizing the classical, 20th-century totalitarian system. The idea of the dual state has been applied to non-totalitarian systems such as that of the Federal Republic of Germany, especially by the political left. Ernst Fraenkel, *The Dual State. A Contribution to the Theory of Dictatorship*, translated by E.A. Shils, Oxford University Press, New York: 1941.

Books and articles

Angle, Stephen, 'Decent democratic centralism', 33 *Political Theory* 518 (2005).

BBC, 'Activist speaks from Chinese jail', 8 August 2013, at http://www.bbc.co.uk/news/world-asia-china-23624034, accessed 5 January 2014.

Benney, Jonathan, *Defending Rights in Contemporary China*, Routledge, London and New York, 2012.

Branigan, Tania, 'China's human rights situation is getting worse, says US official,' *Guardian*, 2 August 2013, at http://www.theguardian.com/world/2013/aug/02/china-human-rights-worse-us, accessed 5 January 2014.

Buckley, Chris, 'A leading Chinese human rights advocate is detained in Beijing', *New York Times*, 17 July 2013, at http://www.nytimes.com/2013/07/18/world/asia/china-detains-a-leading-human-rights-advocate.html?_r=0, accessed 5 January 2014.

Chin, Josh, 'Prominent Chinese activist releases jail video', *Washington Post* ChinaRealTime blog, 8 August 2013, at http://blogs.wsj.com/chinarealtime/2013/08/08/prominent-chinese-activist-releases-jail-video/, accessed 5 January 2014.

Cohen, Roberta, 'People's Republic of China: the human rights exception', *Occasional Papers/Reprint Series in Contemporary Asian Studies* 3 (1988) 1, University of Maryland School of Law, Baltimore, 1988, at http://digitalcommons.law.umaryland.edu/cgi/viewcontent.cgi?article=1085&context=mscas, accessed 1 January 2014.

Cooper, Elissa, '"China's conscience" missing in action,' *Christianity Today*, 23 February 2009, at http://www.christianitytoday.com/ct/2009/october/34.38.html, accessed 5 January 2014.

Cullen, Richard and Fu, Hualing, 'Climbing the *weiquan* ladder: a radicalising process for rights-protection lawyers', 205, *China Quarterly*, 40–59, at http://journals.cambridge.org/action/displayFulltext?type=1&fid=8243497&jid=CQY&volumeId=205&issueId=-1&aid=8243495, accessed 21 December 2013.

Dong, Yunhu and Chang, Jian (董云虎，常健, editors), *60 Years of Establishing Human Rights in China* (中国人权建设 60 年), Jiangxi People's Press, Nanchang, 2009.

Douzinas, Costas, 'Seven theses on human rights (3)', at http://criticallegalthinking.com/2013/05/23/seven-theses-on-human-rights-3-neoliberal-capitalism-voluntary-imperialism/, accessed 30 December 2013.

Dworkin, Ronald, *Justice for Hedgehogs*, Harvard University Press, Cambridge, MA, 2010.

Dworkin, Ronald, *Law's Empire*, Harvard University Press: Cambridge, MA, 1986.

Dworkin, Ronald, *Taking Rights Seriously*, Duckworth, London, 1977.

Fraenkel, Ernst, *The Dual State. A Contribution to the Theory of Dictatorship*, translated by E.A. Shils, Oxford University Press, New York, 1941.

Freedom House, 'China continues to target "Citizen Movement" with arrest of Xu Zhiyong', at http://www.freedomhouse.org/article/china-continues-target-new-citizens-movement-arrest-xu-zhiyong, accessed 5 January 2014.

Fu, Hualing and Cullen, Richard, 'Weiquan (rights protection) lawyering in an authoritarian state: building a culture of public-interest lawyering' *China Journal*, 59 (January 2008), 111–127 at p. 116.

Gewirth, Alan, *Human Rights*, University of Chicago Press, Chicago, 1982.

Givens, John Wagner, 'Chen Guangcheng: still raising heck', *Huffington Post*, 3 July 2013, at http://www.huffingtonpost.com/john-wagner-givens/chen-guangcheng-nyu_b_3541948.html, accessed 5 January 2014.

Givens, John Wagner, 'The silent majority: China's other lawyers', *Huffington Post*, 29 July 2011, at http://www.huffingtonpost.com/john-wagner-givens/the-silent-majority-china_b_912135.html, accessed 2 January 2014.

Godovits, Florian, 'Manfred Novak discusses two of China's heroes', 28 July 2009, at http://www.theepochtimes.com/n2/world/manfred-nowak-united-nations-gao-zhisheng-hu-jia-china-20247.html, accessed 5 January 2014.

Griffin, James, *On Human Rights*, Oxford University Press, Oxford, 2008.

Kilgour, David, 'Conscience of China: Gao Zhisheng', *The Epoch Times*, 8 May 2010, at http://www.theepochtimes.com/n2/opinion/gao-zhisheng-conscience-of-china-34982.html, accessed 5 January 2014.

Kilgour, David, 'Canada can help imprisoned Chinese hero Gao Zhisheng', *The Métropolitain*, 25 March 2010, at http://themetropolitain.ca/articles/view/793, accessed 5 January 2014.

Koskenniemi, Martti, 'What should international lawyers learn from Karl Marx?,' in Susan Arks (ed.), *International Law on the Left: re-examining Marxist legacies*, Cambridge University Press, Cambridge, 2011, Chapter 1.

Liebman, Benjamin, 'Legal aid and public interest law in China', 34 *Texas International Law Journal* (1999) 211.

Locke, John, *Second Treatise on Government*, Chap. XIX Sec.222, 1689, text available at http://constitution.org/jl/2ndtr19.htm.

Merry, Sally Engle, *Human Rights and Gender Violence: translating international law into local justice*, Chicago University Press, Chicago, 2005.

Moyn, Samuel, *The Last Utopia: Human Rights in History*, Belknap Press, Cambridge, MA, 2010.

Nowak, Manfred, 'Fact-finding on conditions on torture and ill-treatment and conditions of detention', 1 *Journal of Human Rights Practice* (2009) 101–119.

Olesen, Alexa, 'Blind Lawyer a legal crusader in China', *Washington Post*, 20 July 2006, at http://www.washingtonpost.com/wp-dyn/content/article/2006/07/20/AR2006072000315.html, accessed 5 January 2014.

Peerenboom, Randall, 'Searching for political liberalism in all the wrong places: the legal profession in China as the leading edge of political reform?,' *La Trobe Law School Legal Studies* Research Paper No. 2008/7, at http://ssrn.com/abstract=1265080 or http://dx.doi.org/10.2139/ssrn.1265080.

Pils, Eva, 'Taking *yuan* (冤) seriously: why the Chinese government should stop suppressing citizen protest against injustice', 25 *Temple International and Comparative Law Journal* (2011) 285–327.

Rawls, John, *The Law of Peoples*, Harvard University Press, Cambridge, MA, 1999.

Smith, Rhona K.M., 'More of the same or something different? Preliminary observations on the contribution of the Universal Periodic Review with reference to the Chinese experience', 10 *Chinese Journal of International Law* 3 (2011), 565–586.

Steiner, Henry J., Alston, Philip and Goodman, Ryan, *International Human Rights in Context: Law, Politics, Morals*, 3rd ed., Oxford University Press, Oxford and New York, 2008.

Tasioulas, John, 'Human rights' entry, in *Routledge Companion to the Philosophy of Law*, Routledge, London, 2012.

Taylor, John, 'Lawyer Zhou – China's new hero', 28 September 2004 at http://www.abc.net.au/foreign/content/2004/s1205375.htm, accessed 5 January 2014.

Teng, Biao, 'The *law* on trial in China', *Washington Post*, 25 July 2009, at http://www.washingtonpost.com/wp-dyn/content/article/2009/07/24/AR2009072402940.html, accessed 5 January 2014.

Tierny, Brian, *The Idea of Natural Rights: Studies on Natural Rights, Natural Law and Church Law 1150–1625*, Wm. B. Eerdmans Publishing Company, Cambridge, 1997, Chapter 1.

UN Press Release, 'United Nations Special Rapporteur highlights abuses in China', 2 December 2005, at http://www.unhchr.ch/huricane/huricane.nsf/view01/677C19 43FAA14D67C12570CB0034966D?opendocument, accessed 21 December 2013.

U.S. State Department Country Report 'China' (2010), at http://www.state.gov/documents/organization/160451.pdf.

'Wolf supports Chinese prisoner through "Defending Freedoms" Project', 24 January 2013, at http://wolf.house.gov/press-releases/wolf-supports-chinese-prisoner-through-defending-freedoms-project/ accessed 2 January 2014.

Wong, Gillian, 'Chinese rights activist: citizens should seek rights', 8 August 2013, at http://bigstory.ap.org/article/jailed-china-activist-citizens-should-seek-rights, accessed 5 January 2014.

Yu, Verna 'Activists call for release of Xu Zhiyong and end to crackdown', *South China Morning Post*, 30 July 2013, at http://www.scmp.com/news/china/article/1292947/legal-scholar-teng-biao-and-hong-kong-rights-groups-call-release-moderate, accessed 5 January 2014.

Zimbardo, Philip, 'What makes a hero?', 18 January 2011, at http://greatergood.berkeley.edu/article/item/what_makes_a_hero, accessed 5 January 2014.

Websites, blog and microblog entries

'Declaration of the Rights of Man and the Citizen, approved by the National Assembly of France', 26 August 1789, at http://avalon.law.yale.edu/18th_century/rightsof.asp, accessed 21 December 2013.

[United Nations] Universal Periodic Review, 'Review 2013'/China, at http://www.upr-info.org/Review-2013-1696.html, accessed 2 January 2014.

Documentary and multimedia sources

Anonymous, 谁是陈光诚 [Who is Chen Guangcheng?], independent documentary film, 2011, available at http://vimeo.com/34059688.

2 Quests for justice and legal advocacy in Chinese history

The government and other actors use historical attitudes toward individual quests for justice in contemporary debates about rights and justice in China; and understanding how they do this is important. The current official 'harmony' discourse largely seeks to draw arguments against such quests and legal advocacy from the Chinese tradition, and Marxist–Leninist and Maoist conceptions of political morality seek to portray rights as incompatible with the true goal of history. Against these views, I argue toward a reading of history that shows how concern with the situation of the vulnerable individual and individuated demands for justice have been articulated all along in China's tradition in this Chapter. Evidence for individuated concern can be found, for example, in the Confucian moral tradition, in popular uses of the concept of *yuan*,[1] 'injustice', as a conception of injustice, and in historical forms of professional *songshi*[2] advocacy on behalf of litigants before the imperial magistrate. The traumatic experiences of the PRC's persecution of lawyers and destruction of legal institutions under Mao Zedong certainly did not promote the cause of liberal, rights-centred justice; but they have strengthened current rights lawyers' belief in the need for a rule of law-based system.

There is an important caveat to the argument outlined in the following: mainstream political doctrine in imperial China largely kept preventing individual complaints from being appreciated as anything other than appeals to the personal moral rectitude of officials in power, whose intervention on behalf of the complainant was sought through institutionalised channels. Until scholars and officials were confronted with liberal political theories, government in China therefore did not consider creating political or legal institutions that systematically recognised and protected a fully fledged idea of individual rights; and after a brief flourishing in the post-imperial order, that idea continued to be vilified in the early decades of the PRC. It is for this reason only that human rights and legal advocacy are associated with western political theories in China – not, I argue, because there is anything un-Chinese in the related ideas of protecting individual rights and delivering justice through independent adjudication. There are good reasons for

1 In Chinese characters, 冤.
2 In Chinese characters, 讼师.

thinking of those ideas as lying dormant, waiting to be revived in the political and legal practices of imperial China by the beginnings of Chinese liberalism in the 19th century.

To make this argument is important, because the struggle for liberal ideas is also a struggle for a liberal evaluation of history; it is directly relevant to the evaluation of the role of law and rights in our time. Today liberal, rights-centred conceptions of justice compete not only with traditional, wrongs-centred (*yuan*-centred) ones, but also with those of the orthodox Party–State canon, which has changed greatly over time but generally focused on aspects of human or social need and welfare. The past has a presence not only because in the actuality of individual quests for justice people use traditional concepts such as that of *yuan*.

Past injustices of the PRC such as those of the Anti-rightist Movement and the Cultural Revolution matter also because they were never adequately addressed and continue to present a spectre that rights advocates want to prevent from recurring. Yet in order to do so, they must fight the PRC legal and political system's post-totalitarian features.

The imperial era: tradition and counter-tradition

The government and social elite's view of legal advocacy in imperial China was largely that they were socially harmful; and the person widely considered to have been China's first legal advocate, Deng Xi, is often adduced as an example.

Deng Xi lived in the state of Zheng in the 6th century BC. He was a scholar belonging to the School of Names or School of Dialectitians, who advised people in legal disputes, wrote a penal code on bamboo, a cheap and widely available material, and devised methods by which ordinary people might make written submissions to the ruler by open or private letter. The ruler considered these activities so dangerous that he had Deng Xi executed and his corpse publicly displayed for the moral edification of the people.[3] Deng Xi's example reverberated through the centuries, according to many historians of Chinese law; it reflects an official attitude of distrust and hostility toward the figure of the legal advocate.

In Deng Xi's story, the condemnation of legal advocacy is based on the argument that he turned falsehood into truth and the impermissible into the permissible and vice versa.[4] Beyond criticism of legal sophistry and beyond

---

3 In one case, Deng Xi is reported to have advised both sides. 'The Wei river was extremely high. A person from the house of a rich man of Zheng drowned. Someone found the body. The rich man asked to buy it back. The man demanded very much money. The rich man told Deng Xi about it. Deng Xi said, "Calm down about it. There's certainly no one else he can sell it to." The one who found the body was troubled by this and told Deng Xi about it. Deng Xi replied to him too by saying, "Calm down about it. There's certainly nowhere else they can buy it."' (18.4/453). As Fraser points out, the assessment given in both instances was correct; yet it was taken to be an example of lawyerly deviousness. Cited from Chris Fraser, 'Deng Xi's exploits (supplement to entry on School of Names)', at http://plato.stanford.edu/entries/school-names/exploits.html, accessed 23 October 2013.

4 'He turned wrong into right and right into wrong. There was no standard of right and wrong, and what was admissible and inadmissible changed daily. Those he desired to win would thereby win;

asserting that his advice was capricious, lacking constancy and principle, the story also reflects a deeper distrust toward law in general, which has come to be regarded as a central feature of Confucian political philosophy.[5] The Analects of Confucius considered the use of edicts (*zheng*)[6] and punishments (*xing*)[7] inferior to government by virtue (*de*)[8] and rites or socially accepted standards of appropriateness (*li*):[9]

> Lead the people with governmental measures and regulate them by law and punishment, and they will avoid wrongdoing but will have no sense of honour and shame. Lead them with virtue and regulate them by propriety, and they will have a sense of shame and, moreover, set themselves right.[10]

The bamboo penal code seemed dangerous to the ruler, just because it was easily transmittable: it could be copied and passed on to anyone.[11] It could become a publicly available set of rules; these rules, once publicly known, could be argued about. Imperial governments appeared averse to being tied to public rules; and even the punitive rules they created were left open by catch-all provisions. A provision of the Great Qing Code of 1646, in effect until 1912, for example, threatened 40 blows of the lighter bamboo to anyone who did 'what ought not to be done',[12] without further definition. Rules of this kind are so morally perfectionist that they invite disregard in social practice, especially if they are not made more operable through an institutionalised practice of public legal interpretation and argument. But the power to punish they symbolise is fearfully wide and undivided.

those he desired to be found guilty would thereby be found guilty. (18.4/454).' Cited from Chris Fraser, 'Deng Xi's exploits (supplement to entry on School of Names)', at http://plato.stanford.edu/entries/school-names/exploits.html. This passage is also discussed at Li Qian (栗茜), '中国古代的讼师制度 [The system for legal advocates in ancient China]', 12 September 2009 at http://bjgy.chinacourt.org/article/detail/2012/09/id/887408.shtml, accessed October 23 2013. Ulrich Theobald, entry on 'Master Deng Xi' at *China Knowledge* website, http://www.chinaknowledge.de/Literature/Diverse/dengxizi.html, accessed 23 October 2013.

5 Bodde, Derk and Morris, Clarence, *Law in Imperial China* (Cambridge, MA: 1967): 'The *li* (. . .) constitute both the concrete institutions and the accepted modes of behaviour in a civilised state' (*ibid.*, p. 19). Bodde and Morris note that by the time of the Tang dynasty, the breach between Confucianism and Legalism had been 'effectively closed.' *Ibid.*, p. 20.
6 In Chinese character, 政.
7 In Chinese character, 刑.
8 In Chinese character, 德.
9 In Chinese character, 礼.
10 Confucius, *Analects*, II.3. 子曰: 道之以政, 齐之以刑, 民免而无耻。道之以德, 齐之以礼, 有耻而格. Available at http://www.guoxue.com/gxrm/gxrm-24.htm, accessed 23 October 2013. The expression here translated as 'law and punishment' is represented by the single character *xing* (刑) whose central meaning is legal punishment (as in *xingfa*, penal or criminal law). Translation by Liu Shu-Hsien, in *Understanding Confucian Philosophy: Classical and Sung-Ming*, Praeger Publisher, Westport, MA: 1998, at p. 20.
11 The government until then had operated a system of ad hoc royal edicts transmitted through bronze vessels, to which most people were unlikely to have easy access. Ulrich Theobald, entry on 'Master Deng Xi' at http://www.chinaknowledge.de/Literature/Diverse/dengxizi.html.
12 Section 386 of the Great Qing Code [大清律例] reads: (不应为): 凡不应得为而为之者笞四十 事理重者杖八十律无罪名所犯事有轻重各量情而坐之. An excerpt of the Great Qing code is available at http://www.dushu.com/showbook/101196/1042017.html, accessed 23 October 2013.

Even though there is no evidence that Deng Xi challenged the ruler's edicts directly; that he tried to do more than hold the ruler to standards extrapolated from the edicts themselves, any interpretation that is not a mere repetition of what has already been said can lead to dissension about which interpretation is best. In the official view, dissension, especially if given public expression, was undesirable and indicative of political problems. To support this view, governments could draw on the Confucian Analects, for example:

> 'Confucius said, "(. . .) When the Way prevails in the Empire, the Commoners do not express critical views".'[13]

Even though Confucian philosophy concedes that there is value in pointing it out to the ruler when he is wrong, the above comment suggests that in direct contrast to liberal accounts such as those by Mill and Kant, it sees no value in free argument as such. This entails a practical difficulty with addressing complaints or remonstrations to the government: this must be done at one's own risk. Unless he succeeds in persuading the authorities of the correctness of his remonstration, the critic may be rebuked, even punished, with perfect apparent justification. But, if there is no acknowledged value in criticism ultimately found to be wrong, will any but the most virtuous and self-critical of rulers acknowledge the value of being criticised by his subjects? The *Analects of Confucius* do not suggest, at least not clearly, that the State (the ruler) should institute procedures protecting people who remonstrate wrongly, or procedures for deciding cases remaining controversial. By contrast, political theories in the liberal analytical moral tradition defend both the objectivity of normative judgements, and free speech and controversial (adversarial) legal argument.

The moral tradition as captured in fables and other narratives is awake to these problems. Commenting on the authoritarian conception of the relationship between truth and power such views support, for example, a contemporary human rights lawyer remarked:

> We have a proverb, 'pointing to a deer and calling it a horse.'[14] An important minister around the time of the Second Qin Emperor needed to get rid of some people. Well, how to do that? He got a deer and said, 'that's a horse

---

13 Confucius, *Analects*, 13.15. (*zi yue: tian xia you dao, ze shu ren bu yi*) 子曰：天下有道，则庶人不议 See D.C. Lau, *Confucius, The Analects.* Translated with an Introduction by D.C. Lau, Penguin Books, London: 1979. From this perspective, there would be a moral duty to tell the ruler when he was wrong. But it would not seem so important that people could themselves say objectively wrong things with impunity, especially politically or morally wrong things; so there is no theoretical foundation for a right to freedom of expression. Joseph Chan reaches a somewhat similar conclusion in Joseph Chan, 'A Confucian perspective on human rights for contemporary China', in Joanne R. Bauer and Daniel A. Bell (eds.), *The East Asian Challenge for Human Rights* (Cambridge University Press, Cambridge: 1999). Given the Confucian emphasis on education, tolerance and forbearance, as well as on 'doing the right thing for the right reason', this view might still accommodate honest mistakes or disagreements based in genuine conviction on both sides. The Confucian attitude to public dissension emerging from these passages is, at any rate, one of cautious rejection.
14 In Chinese characters, 指鹿为马.

there.' Only a few people, considering themselves clever, insisted, 'but that's a deer!' All those who had said so were got rid of.[15]

The suppression of advocacy in official conceptions of a good legal system thus appears to have philosophical roots in attitudes with a long tradition, as expressed in this story. The discomfortingly tight logic of this view has been criticised as one of the aspects of *renzhi*,[16] 'rule by men', and contrasted unfavourably with *fazhi*,[17] the 'rule of law' yet to be achieved in contemporary China.

Perceiving the fundamental nature of the concern about public dissension, scholars have long pointed to a difference between the Chinese tradition and not only liberalism but also the philosophical debates of classical western antiquity, they have pointed to the importance of public argument in Greece, for example.[18] The contrast is well captured in a comparison between Socrates, celebrated for his fearless expression of his views and discussed critically for his acceptance of the verdict against him as one of 'law', and Deng Xi, relegated to outright contempt and comparative oblivion. Liberal scholar He Weifang attributes the 'failure' of Chinese classical society to produce 'a legitimate and professionalized class of lawyers'[19] to the fact that while in classical European antiquity, public discussion and controversial argument prefigured contemporary liberal litigation practice in public court hearings, no such practice existed in the Chinese tradition.[20] Expressing a similar view, scholars Ye Qing and Gu Yuejin write:

> Legal defence [*bianhu*][21] by itself means demanding that the ruler protect individual rights and interests, it means democracy, it means that in deciding whether a person's conduct amounts to crime and should be punished the ruler listen to that person's explanation and account, that this person be allowed to defend themselves and engage in argument. At this level, it is obvious that the ruler would not easily acknowledge legal defence. Legal scholarship in China's ancient times was not enamoured of this profession which had sprung up of its own. For one thing they feared that this kind of profession might lead to all sorts of speech in extra-legal areas and lead the ordinary people not to obey, to be insurgent in their minds, and not to distinguish [correctly] between right and wrong. For another, they feared that its emergence might shake the 'uniformity of the law' which was the basis of

---

15 #21 2010-2. The person at the centre of this story is in fact a minister of the Second Qin Emperor, who succeeded the First Qin Emperor.

16 In Chinese characters, 人治.

17 In Chinese characters, 法治.

18 He Weifang, 'The nascence and growing pains of a professionalised legal class', *Columbia Journal of Asian Law* 19 (2005) 238.

19 He Weifang, *ibid.*

20 '贺卫方教授演讲实录——中国律师的时代使命[Transcript of Professor He Weifang's speech – the mission of the Chinese lawyer], available at http://forum.acla.org.cn/showflat.php?Board=22&Number=450759, accessed 2005; link broken; text now available at http://bbs.esnai.com/thread-1636077-1-1.html.

21 In Chinese characters, 辩护.

the ruler (*junwang*),[22] that it might lead people to controversies within the [framework of the] law and to 'legal knowledge' that would allow people to challenge the edicts of the ruler.[23]

And, discussing the difference between the concept of *songshi*, litigation master, and the concept of the lawyer on western liberal terms, scholar Qiu Zhihong observes that right until the end of the last, Qing Dynasty, local officials never abandoned their sense of threat from, and righteous condemnation of, these legal professionals, who advised people on how to argue before the imperial magistrate. Even in the late Qing Dynasty, officials felt justified in 'punishing' such advocates for their activities:

> In the Illustrated Annals of Wushen, in the first year of the Xuantong era [i.e. 1909], there was one illustrated essay titled 'A new method for getting the common people not to bring lawsuits' and in the essay the method was specifically described as follows: 'whenever it comes to hearing complaints, request to know who helped the complainant write the complaint, and then summon this person and make them kneel before the magistrate [*Yamen*] as a punishment [*ti'an fagui*].[24] This will result in a gradual decline in litigation cases.'[25]

Official accounts of the imperial tradition have generally emphasised the traditional value of 'harmony' (*hexie*)[26] as a Party–State concept. Sometimes, they have also done so to justify equally hostile attitudes toward litigation and legal advocacy in the present. The vocabulary of 'harmony', 'conciliation' and 'peace', in Chinese, *he*,[27] is part of the moral philosophy canon as well as of everyday vocabulary, e.g. in the phrase, 'holding harmony dear' (*yi he wei gui*).[28] Since 2006, the political leadership has made use of this vocabulary to support its efforts to maintain 'social stability' and downplay social disparity. The expression 'socialist harmonious society'[29] suggests that differences of wealth, status and power are

---

22 In Chinese characters, 君王.
23 Ye Qing 叶青, Gu Yuejin 顾跃进, 律师制度研究 [*A study of the system for lawyers*] (Shanghai Academy of Social Sciences Press: 2005), pp. 26 f.
24 In Chinese characters, 提案罚跪.
25 Qiu Zhihong (邱志红), '从"讼师"到"律师"：从翻译看近代中国社会对律师的认知 [From "litigation masters" to "lawyers": analysing the understanding of lawyers in modern Chinese society from translations]', in 近代史研究, 3 *Studies of Modern History* (2011) posted 16 September 2011, at http://jds.cass.cn/Item/21623_5.aspx, accessed 25 October 2013, with citation to 时事报馆编：《戊申全年画报》第 34 册, 1909 年, 第 17 页.
26 In Chinese characters, 和谐. *The Contemporary Chinese Dictionary* at 2121 (entry on *hexie* (和谐)).
27 In Chinese character, 和.
28 In Chinese characters, 以和为贵.
29 中共中央关于构建社会主义和谐社会若干重大问题的决议 [Resolution on the Construction of a Socialist Harmonious Society] (promulgated by the Chinese Communist Party Central Committee, passed Oct. 11, 2006) Sixth Plenary Session, 8–11 October 2006, *reprinted in CPC Central Committee on Building a Socialist Harmonious Society and a Number of Major Issues* (中共中央关于构建社会主义和谐社会若干重大问题的决议), *Xinhua News Agency* (18 October 2006), http://news.xinhuanet.com/politics/2006-10/18/content_5218639.htm, accessed 24 October 2013.

acceptable as long as suitable efforts are made to cater to welfare needs[30] and that disharmony – political opposition, protest, resistance – in society is unacceptable.[31] (Sometimes, as observed later, today's rulers also exhibit the same kind of attitude through Marxist–Leninist anti-rights rhetoric.) Seeking to distance themselves from what they perceive to be a largely authoritarian Chinese tradition, rights lawyers, in turn, quite frequently express their hopes of getting away from the Chinese past, and moving forward, as it were, toward modernity and (liberal) universal values (*pushi jiazhi*).[32]

Yet just as the severe curtailing of a right to criticise,[33] so too has the critical appraisal of legal advocates and the role of law in governance historically been controversial. Alternative readings of their role in history have always been possible. Different ways of reading history, ways that oppose official orthodoxy, can serve to challenge the 'harmony'-centred account of the imperial tradition preferred by the present government. For one thing, even on Confucianism's own terms, contemporary official uses of 'harmony' can ring false. The Confucian Analects say, 'A noble person will achieve conciliation based on principle but not blind union. A small person will blindly seek to unite, but cannot achieve principled conciliation.'[34] Since harmony has value, it is important, but conciliation must be principled, not blind – it must not disregard or compromise other moral values such as for example that of justice.[35] Yet, indifferent to such important recognitions of other moral values in the Confucian tradition, contemporary propaganda has largely remained blind to uses of 'harmony' to justify the repression of quests for justice; it has failed to distinguish 'union' (*tong*)[36] and 'harmony' (*he*).

For another, official doctrines' apparent, principled disregard for freedom of speech notwithstanding, argument and open criticism of the powers that be could nevertheless be valued in practice. The fact that Deng Xi engaged with the codes in a critical way did, after all, attract notice. His role could be seen in a different, more favourable light, despite the apparent vilification of his character and achievements. He dared to challenge officially held views; to do so publicly, and to counter accusations by presenting cases in a different light. The instructions for

---

30 Leila Choukroune and Antoine Garapon, 'The norms of Chinese harmony: disciplinary rules as social stabiliser', 3 *China Perspectives* 36 (2007) 36–38, available at http://chinaperspectives.revues.org/document2013.html, accessed 24 October 2013.

31 It is also similar to the idea of 'scientific development perspective', (科学发展观) discussed in Chapter 3. For a discussion of the Scientific Development Perspective by President Hu Jiantao, see 科学发展观重要论述摘编 [Scientific Development Perspective Archive], http://theory.people.com.cn/GB/68294/137720, accessed 24 October 2013.

32 In Chinese characters, 普世价值.

33 Joshua D. Rosenzweig, 'China's battle over the right to criticise', *Far Eastern Economic Review* (2009), available at http://chinadigitaltimes.net/2009/05/joshua-rosenzweig-chinas-battle-over-the-right-to-criticize/, accessed 24 October 2013.

34 In Chinese characters, 君子和而不同, 小人同而不和. Confucius, Analects XIII 23 at 207 (Cai Xiqin ed., Lai Bo and Xia Yuhe trans., *Sinoligua* 1994); see Confucius, *The Analects* 13 (Raymond Dawson ed., 1993).

35 Cp. Stephen C. Angle, 'Human rights and harmony', 30 *Human Rights Quarterly* 76 (2008) 78–80.

36 In Chinese character, 同.

writing open letters (*xianshu*)[37] with whose invention tradition credits him[38] were
a logical extension of this approach to the laws; and they were 'dangerous' only
by the same logic.[39] Chinese history is, in fact, replete with loyal officials pointing
out obvious problems of maladministration and injustice, and (willingly) suffering
the consequences; one example of such an official is Qu Yuan,[40] whose heroic
death is celebrated to this day. If the mainstream tradition views Qu Yuan with
approval also because he complied with traditional conceptions of honour by
doing away with himself, having challenged his ruler, such traditional approval is
perhaps not so different from admiration for Socrates' equanimous compliance
with the order to do the same. And beyond that of approval of scholar–officials
engaging in criticism, China also has a popular tradition of submitting grievances,
grievances that can be brought by entirely ordinary people. This tradition draws
on the powerful concept of *yuan*, 'wrong' or injustice, to be discussed in a moment.

From the perspective of the lawyer who told it, there also seem to be two
different points to the above story of the deer: on the one hand, a self-deprecatory
one – those who, 'considering themselves clever', protest that it *is*, in fact, a deer,
are superficially pointing out a fact of trivial obviousness and paying with their
lives for doing so. But then, they are also resisting an unscrupulous and irrational
ruler, whose ruthlessness and cruelty – and opposition to the moral teachings of
Confucianism – is legend in Chinese history. Stories like these are the repositories
of a popular counter-tradition that offers radically different evaluations of advocacy and resistance to authority. Thus Qiu Zhihong, acknowledging the popular
counter-tradition that supported and sometimes celebrated especially talented
songshi also mentions popular literature's role in this.[41]

Lastly, it has long been recognised that the Confucian rejection of written laws
and codified punishments did not prevent imperial governments from using
them;[42] and by using law the authorities also subjected themselves to its rules.
A pithy record of the end of Deng Xi himself, indeed, states: 'They killed him, *but
they used his bamboo penal code*' (emphasis added).[43]

This indicates acceptance, however grudging, of the utility of having written
rules allowing the standardisation of government practices by means of such

---

37 In Chinese characters, 县书.
38 Reportedly the government prohibited not only open letters but also private submissions of
    petitions. Ulrich Theobald, *ibid.* This did not prevent a flourishing practice of petitioning from
    emerging.
39 Li Qian (栗茜), '中国古代的讼师制度 [The system for legal advocates in ancient China]',
    12 September 2009, at http://bjgy.chinacourt.org/article/detail/2012/09/id/887408.shtml.
    Li Qian notes that the publication and circulation of legal codifications continued prohibited
    throughout imperial China; and even the compilation of legal cases was forbidden in some places
    and at some times.
40 In Chinese characters, 屈原.
41 Qiu, *ibid.*, mentions that debates at the time differentiated between 'litigation masters' (讼师) and
    'litigation tricksters' (讼棍) to distinguish between good and bad individuals in this role.
42 Bodde and Morris, *ibid.*, note that the legalist and Confucian traditions had been merged.
43 Li Qian (栗茜), '中国古代的讼师制度 [The system for legal advocates in ancient China]',
    12 September 2009, at http://bjgy.chinacourt.org/article/detail/2012/09/id/887408.shtml;
    Fraser, *ibid.*, notes that it was more likely Zi Chan's successor Si Chuan who ordered Deng's
    execution.

rules. Government practice from at least the second Han Dynasty onward merged the grand traditions of Confucianism and legalism in practice, despite not fully owning up to its legalist influences.[44] Imperial legal codes were in use from then on, even though their circulation was limited, and those who, like Deng Xi, engaged in helping people involved in litigation before the magistrate as litigation masters were in fact tolerated, even though they continued to be denounced. Their role might be hushed up as something of an embarrassment to the system, and scholars of legal history have straightforwardly characterised their profession as an 'underground' one;[45] but for all that they could be indispensable. Popular tradition revered many imperial magistrates who combined traits of the judge and the investigator–detective,[46] as well as famous legal advocates. Legal practice made use not only of an unacknowledged legal advocate's profession but also of manuals and collections of edicts, etc.; and the value of codification was recognised in legal practice. Tacitly, the importance of advocacy was acknowledged even when it was dogmatically frowned upon and officially denounced.[47]

Not only were legal advocates at some level recognised as important part of the legal system as practised, individual quests for justice through petitioning to government offices were equally of recognised importance, and had a place accorded to them in the system. Given the moral earnestness (for lack of a better word) pervading the Confucian tradition this is hardly surprising. Confucian philosophers might express preference for harmony but that could not amount to a licence to disregard moral principle; on the contrary, as noted, 'A noble person will achieve conciliation based on principle but not blind union.'[48] The idea of 'harmony' could not possibly justify the repression of all substantively legitimate protest as 'disharmonious' or 'destabilising' in any moral tradition.

Reflecting the central importance of personal moral rectitude in Confucian philosophy, the contemporary language of protest, its forms and images, also draws on the Chinese tradition: not only that of Confucian ideas as they were taught to members of the elites and those who hoped to join them, but also

---

44 Bodde and Morris, *ibid.*; Klaus Muehlhahn, *Criminal Justice in China: A History*, Harvard University Press, Cambridge, MA: 2009, Chapter 1, especially at pp. 23 ff.

45 Du Jin distinguishes persons employed as legal advisers (师爷) or secretaries (书吏) and litigation masters, (讼师). Du Jin, 'Lawyers in the Ming and Song dynasties', public research seminar, the Chinese University of Hong Kong Faculty of Law, 25 April 2013.

46 Judge Bao 包拯 (999–1062) is the best known exemplar; cp. Wilt L. Idema *Judge Bao and the Rule of Law*, World Scientific Publishing, Singapore: 2010. Judge Di (Dee) is another example. Cp. Website devoted to Robert van Gulik's work on Judge Di at http://www.ude.de/gulik/, accessed 7 November 2013.

47 Fu Guoyong's 2012 book represents a recent attempt to do justice to China's indigenous tradition of legal advocacy. Fu Guoyong, 追寻律师的传统 [*In quest of a lawyer tradition*], Beijing United Publishing Company, Beijing: 2012.

48 In Chinese characters, 君子和而不同, 小人同而不和. Confucius, Analects XIII 23 at 207 (Cai Xiqin ed., Lai Bo and Xia Yuhe trans., *Sinoligua* 1994); see Confucius, *The Analects* 13 (Raymond Dawson ed., 1993).

on more popular traditions. It does so especially through a traditional conception of wrongs and injustice. *Yuan*, 'a wrong',[49] is a traditional concept that is part of the modern, ordinary quest for justice in China. As a traditional moral concept, *yuan* can be understood as analogous to the concept of rights in modern political settings, because it constitutes an alternative way of capturing the ruler's political responsibilities towards the ruled. Even though the traditional submission of grievances, *shen yuan* or petitioning (*xinfang*)[50] is different from asserting rights through the court system, in modern China, people with grievances often engage in both practices concurrently and petitions can also be directed to courts, so that the systems, in fact, overlap.[51]

While capturing concern for how injustice affects the individual person and can become personal tragedy, *yuan* as a concept is still different from rights in several ways. First, *yuan* invokes a traditional conception of natural justice and order that can also be found in popular Chinese literature;[52] it is an idea that lives on in stories more than in the State philosophy of Confucianism (or what was taken for it). For example, in Guan Hanqing's popular 13th-century drama, *The Injustice to Dou'E* (*Dou'E Yuan*),[53] a falsely accused woman predicts unnatural phenomena to occur as a reaction to her execution, and her *yuan hun*, her 'wronged spirit', later ensures that these prophesies come true.[54]

Yuan is, second, also connected to an idea of moral obligation starkly different from the idea of justice of the liberal tradition. Wrongs conceived as *yuan* do not merely generate a right to redress; rather, seeking redress also becomes a duty the wronged person has to fulfil. This makes sense if one considers justice mainly in the light of a personal virtue – one that requires personal effort[55] – and if one takes seriously the idea that injustice is not merely personal grievance but also a disruption of universal laws that – in the absence of a private/public divide – one may have a personal duty to uphold. The duty to seek justice can be owed to a person who died a wrongful death, for instance. It vests not only with the person

---

49 The online dictionary *Chinese Dictionary* (汉语词典) translates *yuan* (冤) as 'bad luck, enmity, injustice, or wrong.' *Definition of* yuan, *Dictionary*, http://tw.18dao.net/%E6%BC%A2%E8%AA%9E%E8%A9%9E%E5%85%B8/%E5%86%A4, accessed 3 November 2013.

50 In Chinese characters, 信访. Minzner, Carl F., 'Xinfang: an alternative to formal Chinese legal institutions', 42 *Stanford International Law Journal* 103 (2006), at: http://ir.lawnet.fordham.edu/faculty_scholarship/3, at 109–20 (providing a detailed definition, historical background, and modern description of the Xinfang system).

51 Du Bin (杜斌), '上访者：中国以法治国下幸存的活化石 [*Petitioners: Living Fossil Under Chinese Rule by Law*]', Hong Kong: 2007. The title page depicts a petitioner in traditional petitioning garb (hat and cloak), prominently displaying the character 冤.

52 For example, this concept is reflected in works such as Pu Songling (蒲松龄), 聊斋志异 [Strange Tales from a Chinese Studio], available in translation by John Minford, Kindle Books: 2006.

53 In Chinese characters, 窦娥冤.

54 Guan, Hanqing (关汉卿). '感天动地窦娥冤 [*The Injustice to Dou'E that touched Heaven and moved Earth*]', Yuan Dynasty (1271–1368), http://www.tianyabook.com/lnz/doueyuan.htm.

55 See *id*. This would correspond to the traditional concept of *yi* (义), which translates as 'duty', 'righteousness' and 'justice.' Feng Yu-lan characterises 'doing the right thing for the right reason' as an aspect of the idea of 义. Fung (Feng) Yu-lan, ed. by Derk Bodde, *A Short History of Chinese Philosophy*, Macmillan, New York: 1948, at p. 42.

who suffered injustice or his surviving relatives; it can also be inherited by the descendants of the person who was originally involved in a quest for justice, as they assume a filial duty to seek justice for their parent.[56]

Third, *yuan* supports certain assumptions of political subordination built into a political system with concentrated, paternalistically exercised power. The image of the wronged person, the *yuanmin*,[57] is a 'kneeling' image, as one scholar put it in conversation.[58] It is an image corresponding to the expression 'father and mother official', *fumuguan*,[59] supposed to indicate the caring and loving attitude that is the ideal of the imperial-era Confucian official.

It is the intimacy, trust, supplication and submissiveness implicit in the image of the kneeling petitioner turned toward an individual official or official building, that illustrates perfectly why a professional legal advocate is *not* meant to be part of this traditional picture: the presence of the lawyer might strengthen the individual seeking justice but it would lessen the appeal that rests in the supplicant's weakness. But the importance of the concept of *yuan* in the moral tradition of China, the wealth of popular tales it has created testifies to the Chinese moral tradition's creation of its own political practices informed by respect and concern for the individual person's grievance; its own recognition of the principle that justice must be done.

In sum, there is an important historical practice of legal advocacy as well as an indigenous tradition of bringing grievances and protesting injustice in China. Both have in some ways corresponded to the authoritarian conceptions of political order that have dominated this tradition: legal advocates were used but given little official recognition, and traditional patterns of quests for justice were submissive appeals to power whose recognition was supposed to be strengthened, not challenged, by making such appeals. But it has been argued here that the conception of justice underlying *yuan* supports that of rights, because it is based in concern for the wronged individual seeking justice. In the actuality of protest and quests for justice in China today, it certainly contributes to fuelling, as well as challenging, the idea of human rights, and it represents an important cultural resource for challenging official accounts of the Chinese moral tradition that seek to cleanse it from 'disharmonious' ideas.

The promises of liberalism and the spectres of totalitarianism

Even though there are, as outlined below, significant continuities connecting today's system for lawyers to earlier periods, the PRC's founding myth is that 1949 marks the beginning of a 'New China', of a total break with the past, a past that

---

56 Eva Pils, 'Taking *yuan* (冤) seriously: why the Chinese government should stop suppressing citizen protests against injustice', 25 *Temple International and Comparative Law Journal* (2011) 285–327.
57 In Chinese characters, 冤民.
58 Author conversation (2010, not audio-recorded).
59 In Chinese characters, 父母官.

has only in more recent years become useful as a resource from which to draw arguments against 'western' rights advocacy and universal values. The contemporary human rights movement, by contrast, has on numerous occasions claimed connections with the past, especially the late imperial and post-imperial (Republican) reform eras; and claiming these connections can serve directly to question the legitimacy of the current political system. The rejection of the current system is all the stronger because of the un-redressed injustices of the Mao Zedong era, about many of which official accounts have for obvious reasons stayed silent.

The imperial tradition had been inimical to the idea of the independent legal advocate of the European enlightenment, but after the defeat of the Qing Dynasty in the Opium Wars and in the war with Japan, the imperial government saw a need to introduce reforms, and legal codes were drafted that would have introduced the basic elements of a legal system modelled on western systems. These efforts foundered when the Qing Dynasty broke down in 1911; but even as failed efforts, they had further reaching influence. Many of the basic concepts Chinese law operates with today, including that of rights, *quanli*,[60] and that of lawyers, go back to late Qing reform discussions and translations from the Japanese and European languages. The word used for lawyers, 'master of the laws', in modern language, *lüshi*,[61] appearing in the draft Civil and Criminal Procedure Code produced by Qing reformers in 1906,[62] replaced the old expression 'litigation master', *songshi*[63] or – sometimes – 'litigation trickster', *songgun*.[64] It marked a different conception of legal workers and placed lawyers for the first time in the State-designed framework for the legal process. In 1912, after the demise of the Qing, the so-called Beiyang government then led by Yuan Shikai, a former Qing general, enacted the first law formally establishing a legal profession in China in 1912.[65] In the ensuing three decades, the Republic of China continued working with this pre-republican model while drawing up further codifications resulting in the November 1941 Law on Lawyers.[66] The legal profession,

---

60 In Chinese characters, 权利. Stephen C. Angle's account of the history of translations of texts on international law, and the way 'rights' came to be translated in the 19th century by using the character for 'power', *quan* and then routinely combining it with the character for 'profit', *li*, emphasises that these terms became charged with 'normative' and 'positive' (attractive, good) meaning, quite distinct from an early pejorative use of *quan-li*, for instance by Xunzi (3rd century BC) Angle, *Human Rights in Chinese Thought: A Cross-Cultural Inquiry*, Cambridge University Press, Cambridge: 2002, at pp. 108 and 109, respectively.

61 In Chinese characters, 律师.

62 Liu Guiming, '律师百年与律师精神 [100 years of history of the legal profession and the spirit of the legal profession]', prepared for the 2012 Annual Meeting of 律师文摘 *[Lüshi wenzhai]* 3 March 2013, available at http://blog.legaldaily.com.cn/blog/html/81/2441181-32856.html, accessed 26 October 2013.

63 In Chinese characters, 讼师.

64 In Chinese characters, 讼棍.

65 Liu Guiming, *ibid.*

66 Liu Guiming, *ibid.* discussing the Republic of China's Law on Lawyers, (律师法) of 1 November 1941.

modelled on a civilian codified legal system, expanded rapidly in these decades.[67]

The concepts of rights, law and citizenship, were central to the new legal order created by late Qing and early Republican reformers. Uses of the concept of citizen, as Professor Merle Goldman has pointed out, go back to the scholar–reformers in the declining years of the Chinese empire, in particular Liang Qichao and Kang Youwei.[68] Goldman quotes Kang Youwei's comment that: 'Since all the people have the right to participate in assemblies and they all have the responsibility to be concerned about their country, they are all called citizen.' This was a statement reflecting the liberal principles embraced in the reform era.[69] The 1906 Draft Code and 1908 Draft Constitution recognised basic rights, including that of freedom of speech and of criminal defence, and the laws of the Republican era were based in liberal legal principles.

But even as Republican legal reform was underway, the Civil War between Kuomintang and Chinese Communist Party threatened the liberal order being created. According to the founding tenets of Marxism, law, legal rights and lawyers are part of a set of values corresponding to capitalist–bourgeois society; they are described as 'values' only in the sense that they reflect the material conditions created by capitalism and are necessarily related to the distribution of power in capitalist society; and they are, according to Marxism, bound to wither away along with the material conditions established by capitalism, which will be replaced by socialism or communism as a higher stage of social development. The model of the Soviet Union, followed in the first decade of the PRC, and the idea of 'socialist legality' permitted uses of the law, but only within narrowly defined limits; Soviet legal doctrine did not – could not – recognise the moral force of rights as part of any legal system. In line with its ideological commitments, the Communist Part repealed the laws of the Republican era wholesale.

The reality of developments in 'liberated' areas under Communist Party dominion, and of the PRC's first decade attests to the fact that even after the Communist takeover the idea of legal advocacy along liberal lines remained attractive. The Communist Party abolished all the Republican era laws, and its early decision to combat 'black lawyers (*hei lüshi*) and litigation masters (*songshi*)'

---

67 Alison O'Connor, 'China's lawyers and their training: enduring influences and disconnects', in Stanley B. Lubman, *The Evolution of Law Reform in China: an Uncertain Path*, Edward Elgar Publishing, Cheltenham: 2012, pp. 545–567 at p. 553 f.
68 Merle Goldman, *From Comrade to Citizen: The Struggle for Political Rights in China*, Harvard University Press, Cambridge, MA, and London: 2005, at p. 11; Cp. 公民者, 担荷一国之责任, 共其利害, 谋其公益, 任其国税之事, 以共维持其国者也 Ma Xiaoquan (马小泉), Citizen autonomy: a continuing topic mentioned for a century – an analysis of Kang Youwei's gongmin zhizhi bian (1902) [公民自治:一个百年未尽的话题—读康有为《公民自治篇》(1902 年)], Academic Research (学术研究), 2003 (10), available at, http://d.wanfangdata.com.cn/Periodical_xsyj 200310023.aspx, accessed 25 October 2013.
69 Chen Tong argues that lawyers' newspaper advertisements, making use of the concepts of legal rights and human rights (法权 and 人权) reflected the public's acceptance of these concepts. Chen, Tong (陈同), '上海本土律师的出现 [The Emergence of Local Lawyers in Shanghai]', in Fu Guoyong (傅国涌 ed.), 追寻律师的传统 [*In Quest of A Lawyer Tradition*], Beijing United Publishing Company, Beijing: 2012, at pp. 16 f.

showed that lawyers and legal advocacy, remnants of the post-imperial reforms, were politically suspect.[70] But the new government also created rules allowing for legal representation and criminal defence, by 'public defenders' (as opposed to 'lawyers').[71] The legal system built in the 1950s, modelled on that of the Soviet Union, explicitly recognised the need for lawyers. By 1954, 'legal advisor centres' allowing for the provision of legal services outside the narrow area of representation in litigation had been established on a trial basis;[72] and by 1957 a draft 'Law on Lawyers' had been produced. This reversion to the term *lüshi* was an important indication of continuity. After all, early members of the Party had themselves experienced persecution and in some cases obtained legal assistance from sympathetic outsiders to the Party,[73] such as the lawyer and first PRC Justice Minister Shi Liang, who had received legal education in the Republican era law schools.[74]

But after these first few years, the Communist Party under Mao Zedong performed a dramatic turn against legal advocacy and, later, the very idea of law, in two decades of intensifying persecution of lawyers and other legal professionals, beginning with the Anti-Rightist Movement and culminating in the conflagration of the Cultural Revolution. Having established, 'according to incomplete statistics', a total of 870 legal advice centres and some 18,000 lawyers by June 1957,[75] the legal profession was virtually extinguished in the Anti-rightist movement which attacked factions within the Party considered to be leaning to the right. The exercise of the legal profession was deemed to be a sign of 'loss of [ideologically correct] standpoint' and an effort to help criminals. The lawyers' system was characterised as a 'capitalist thing;' therefore, it must be 'annihilated.'[76] The Cultural

---

70 关于取缔黑律师及讼棍事件的通报[Notice on the Revocation of Black Lawyers and Litigation Masters], promulgated by the PRC Ministry of Justice on October 17, 1950, available at http://www.cnki.com.cn/Article/CJFDTotal-HXZB195101112.htm, http://wuxizazhi.cnki.net/Search/HXZB195101112.html, accessed 3 November 2013.

71 In the 'liberated' areas ('bases') controlled by the Chinese Communist Party, lawyers were not denied a place in the legal system, but their position was qualified in some locations – for instance, in the Shaanxi Base it was stipulated that 'workers [sic] have a right to legal representation.' Liu Guiming, *ibid*.

72 Liu Guiming, *ibid*.

73 Wu Lilan and Lin Qi (吴立岚、林淇), '法庭上的吴开生 [Wu Kaisheng in Court]', in Fu Guoyong, 追寻律师的传统 [*In quest of a lawyer tradition*], Beijing United Publishing Company, Beijing: 2012, pp. 147–179, discusses the memoirs of Wu Kaisheng, a lawyer who joined the Kuomintang yet provided forceful legal defence to one of the early Communist party members, Chen Geng (陈赓).

74 Shi Liang (史良) defended, among others, Communist Party members Deng Zhongxia, Ren Baige and Fang Zhida (邓中夏、任白戈、方知达). She was herself detained for political reasons at one point, saved only through intervention by Soong Ch'ing-ling. According to the scholar Liu Guiming, Shi's background and experiences led her to support clear safeguards for criminal defence lawyers in the very early regulatory framework introduced during her tenure as Justice Minister, which ended in 1954, the year when the first PRC Constitution stipulated a right to criminal defence. Liu Guiming, *ibid*. Ms Shi is also understood to have supervised the persecution of legal professionals as 'rightists' in the 1950s.

75 Liu Guiming, *ibid*. Liu adds that the provision of legal services could be safeguarded in all cities with a population of over 3 m by June 1957.

76 Liu Guiming, *ibid*.

Revolution, 1966- 1976, led not only to the labelling of any remaining lawyers as belonging to the 'Stinking Ninth Category',[77] of intellectuals.

The basic attitude of rejection of (liberal) legal institutions and legal values that can be found in Marxism, complemented by 'Mao Zedong Thought's' account differentiating between contradictions amongst the people and contradictions between the people and its enemies,[78] was used to justify these actions. To quote from a well-known editorial of the *People's Daily* in 1969:

> Army, police, courts, and other branches of the state machinery are instruments for class oppression. To the enemy class, they are the instruments of suppression. Being a violent force, they are not at all benevolent. They have the single aim to deprive the reactionaries of the right of speech, which is to be granted only to the people. Dictatorship will be practiced with respect to the class enemies, whereas democracy will be practiced among the people ... Covered by the curtain that 'all men are equal before the law', the class enemies not only are not objects of dictatorship, but they receive the law's protection. They will enjoy the democratic rights in the same way as the masses of the people, since there will be 'impartiality' toward all'.

In its total rejection of impartiality and equality as legal values, this analysis represents a stringent and novel conception of class-based justice, a conception justice in which individuals play no part, only the classes to which they are declared to belong – a conception that cannot be found in the traditional Chinese moral canon. But the rejection of legal advocacy that follows it is not so novel; it echoes the concern of the traditional, imperial system with fruitless argument and morally illicit efforts to help the guilty avoid punishment. From this perspective, the PRC government appears to lapse back into the attitude of the traditional, autocratic government that views legal advocacy as posing unjustified challenge to political power:

> According to the stipulations of the 'Organizational Law of the People's Court', criminals may hire lawyers to defend them. The primary purpose of the appearance of the lawyer in court to defend the criminal has as its starting point 'making it advantageous for the defendant'. The lawyer, therefore, will try to find favorable evidence from the facts of the case, the criminal's motivation, cause-and-effect relationships, and principles of the law that will reduce the guilt and responsibility of the criminal. The prosecutor will make the prosecution on behalf of the state. In court,

---

77 Discussed in Yuan Qi, Zou Guoliang and Wen Chaoli (袁起, 邹国良, 文朝利), 60 年语录 (1949–2009): 60 年共和国的沧桑巨变 [*Quotations from 60 years (1949–2009): 60 years of vicissitudes in the Republic*], China Development Press, Beijing: 2009; Boye Lafayette De Mente, *Chinese Etiquette & Ethics in Business*, McGraw-Hill, Whitby: 1994, at p. 91.

78 Mao Zedong (毛泽东), 1957, 'On the correct handling of contradictions among the people', (translation) in Selden, Mark, *The People's Republic of China: A Documentary History of Revolutionary Change*, New York Monthly Review Press, 1979.

therefore, one will insist on his evidence for prosecuting against the case while the other will try to defend the case on the basis of his principles. The argument is usually endless and the counterrevolutionaries are perfectly capable of taking advantage of their right to defense, their right to appeal, and the legal restrictions on the instruments of dictatorship to pursue their 'legal' struggle.[79]

By the end of the Cultural Revolution, 'the legal profession had to be rebuilt very nearly from scratch.'[80] Universities had for the large part suspended teaching, courts, procuracies and the police were widely considered to be dysfunctional, and the Ministry of Justice had been dissolved altogether.

For the few legal professionals who survived this period and returned to working as lawyers; persecution by the Communist Party was a traumatic lesson on why rule of law and liberal legal values were important. Lawyer Zhang Sizhi[81] comments on the impression his own persecution as a 'rightist' left:

> They spent over a year 'fixing' me. That was no laughing matter. The entire court was mobilised. They publicly announced that I was the main target of this campaign, and the word at the time was that any cadre above the rank of Party section head (党员科长) must cease work and focus on criticising Zhang So-and-So. Quite interesting, that. The struggle [sessions] were very acerbic, very intense.

Having worked as a judge until 1956, before being reassigned to work as a lawyer, Zhang was 'investigated' on suspicion of being a counterrevolutionary before eventually being labelled as a rightist. Describing the experience of being 'struggled' prior to the eventual 'condemnation' as rightist, Zhang comments:

Interviewer:	So you must have felt really lonely at the time? Was there anyone helping you?
Zhang Sizhi:	No one.
Interviewer:	Was there anybody who said you had been falsely accused (*yuanwang*)?
Zhang Shizhi:	No one.
Interviewer:	You had to fight all by yourself.

79 People's Daily (人民日报), 'Completely smash the feudal capitalist and revisionist legal system', 2 *Chinese Law & Government* 4 (1969–1970); in English translation from http://mesharpe.metapress.com/link.asp?id=rpw84w8w70644l15, accessed 26 October 2013.
80 Alison O'Connor, *supra*, at p. 556.
81 Lawyer Zhang Sizhi was recruited for a Communist Party support group while he was receiving legal education under the Republican era system. Despite having served as judge for about nine years, he 'remembers almost no cases' he handled while serving as a judge recruited in 1948. Zhang Sizhi and Xiao Hong (张思之，晓虹), '张思之：律师应站在公权力的对立面 [Zhang Sizhi: the lawyer should stand opposed to public power]', in 腾讯-深度对话第71期 (Tengxun In-depth Dialogue no. 71), 16 June 2010, at http://www.politicalchina.org/printnews.asp?newsid=179588, accessed 26 October 2013.

Zhang Sizhi: All by myself. So now, when I handle some [criminal] defence cases I am not all that worried. It has to do with the training I received at the time; so I've got to thank them, really. It was really intense. They 'fixed'/'struggled' me from 1956 all through 1957 and eventually passed a verdict saying that having conducted an investigation, [it had been decided that] Zhang Shizhi was not a counter-revolutionary. I said, 'You can't do this. You knew all along that I was not a counter-revolutionary. You've got to be clearer.' Because in fact, during the [earlier] campaign, they had used all sorts of methods such as sending fabricated messages in the name of a spying organization to entrap me, and so on; they did all these sorts of thing. I said, 'Why didn't you include that letter in your investigation?'[82]

Describing how, recognised as a person opposed to the Anti-Soviet campaign,[83] he knew there was no chance of escaping a 'rightist' verdict:

I understood only too well. At the time some people tried to persuade me to engage in 'self-criticism'. They said, 'Think about it, Sizhi, don't you want to make a "self-criticism" and be done with it?' But I said, 'I'm going to be [labelled rightist] whether or not I engage in self-criticism. Sorry, no, I am not going to do another self-criticism.' And sure enough, I was categorized as a rightist.[84]

The Party–State power Zhang describes confronting here shares, despite its ostentatious distancing from the imperial past, the power to determine authoritatively what a politically 'correct' view is; and it condemns Zhang, then a lawyer, on account of his professional identity as someone whose public role is to support dissension from, resistance to the authorities in the context of the legal process. In that sense, it is similar to imperial governments.

What gives special relevance to the persecution of lawyers in the Mao Zedong era is that the current government has not distanced itself completely from that era and that, indeed, the past years have seen various official efforts to reclaim Mao's legacy, as discussed in greater detail later. If the struggle for liberal ideas in China is also a struggle for a liberal re-evaluation of history, no historical events are more central to this contemporary struggle than the Anti-Rightist

---

82 Zhang Sizhi and Xiao Hong, *ibid*.
83 '肃反' as well, see here http://baike.baidu.com/view/5121309.htm.
84 Zhang Sizhi and Xiao Hong, *ibid*. 'As a result, from 1956 [when I had been expelled from the position as judge] to 1957 I only got to handle one and a half cases [as a lawyer]. This is how it happened.' Zhang was sent to 'rehabilitation through labour'; as usual at the time, his term of internment as a farm labourer was not fixed. He was released and allowed to work for some time as a middle school teacher after 15 years, before eventually being ordered to resume work as a lawyer. Zhang Sizhi and Xiao Hong, *ibid*.

Campaign and the Cultural Revolution. Regardless of how personal their connection with these times is – only a very few lawyers today were lawyers then – they matter because today's government never completely distanced itself from these movements.

Against this background, it is understandable that rights lawyers see in all of Chinese history the period of Republican China as the most hopeful era. The experiences of the Republican, the warlord the late Qing era's struggle for liberal principles have stayed relevant and influence the present generation of human rights lawyers; especially if the connection is of a personal nature – as in the case of a rights advocate who said she 'inherited' this vocation from her grandfather:

> Grandpa was persecuted during the Cultural Revolution and died in 1966. He had loved the army [as he had attended the Whampoa Military Academy] and loved common people and he tried to help the common people; that's why, after Liberation, he was to some extent protected. While he hadn't been a lawyer by name he did legal work for common people; he had many books in his home (. . .) The government at the time still had some use for these people; at the time they lacked people with certain skills including legal skills.
>
> But when they were no longer useful, they 'struggled' them. They persecuted him as a dosser (*diao er lang dang*).[85] They killed so many people!
>
> Dad also chose to study law (. . .) Before Liberation he worked on some death row cases; students would come and seek him out. This was before military tribunals. (. . .) [After Liberation] he worked for the government and he didn't want to talk about this – he kept going on sick leave. [During the Cultural Revolution] I don't remember clearly [what happened then] because I was rather small and he would not talk to us about things. But my brothers were older and they would be told some things; they knew he had been persecuted. Even though he was [held] close by there was no way of visiting him [at the time] because the police would follow. (. . .) He had a very bitter experience; he thought that before Liberation things had still made some sense. [But still] he wanted me to do law. So, initially we still had some hope. He thought I was the most suitable to do law work. That's why I studied law.[86]

Contemporary human rights lawyers in their thirties and forties make clear references to the Republican and even late Qing era; they repudiate the experiences of the Anti-Rightist Campaign and the Cultural Revolution. Lines connecting Late Qing and contemporary liberalism are consciously redrawn and re-emphasised when, for example, liberals consciously choose the centenary of the Qing Constitution (never in force) to launch 'Charter 08' or to celebrate one hundred years of history of the Chinese legal profession; or when they use

---

85 In Chinese characters, 吊儿郎当.
86 From #52011-1; also: #5 2010-1. Order of sentences has been changed for the sake of chronological coherence.

concepts and even calligraphies originating in the early 20th century.[87] Complicated, traumatic or shameful experiences, in turn, are important to those seeking for angles from which to understand and criticise the current government:

> I am an idealist. This is partly due to my 'bad' family background. During the political campaigns in the early years of the People's Republic, my father had been labelled a landlord. As a result of this, other children treated me with bias.[88]

In recent years, rights lawyers have also expressed anxiety that the Cultural Revolution might return:

> The more violent-leaning they [the government] become the less they can understand the value of rights defence ... there is an inner logic between the emergence of repression of rights lawyers, of the voices of reason, and the emergence of violence; a connection of inner necessity ... and in future there could be more large scale violence.
>
> [...] The authorities are not merely refusing to reflect but also obstructing reflection [*fansi*].[89] If a major disaster has happened in society and there is no reflection, it may come again.[90]

An understanding of these eras' historic injustices can also heighten their sense of personal responsibility. A young lawyer in his early thirties remarked in conversation:

> It is often said that the feudal times and the Cultural Revolution have left us with these ideas [of authoritarianism]. But Lawyer A (a much older lawyer) once said to me, 'You keep saying that the Mao Era was bad. But you mustn't just say that it was just Mao himself who was bad. You must also think about what the cadres at the time did.'
>
> His meaning was, I think, that we cannot just think about the past as past, we must also think about each individual person's responsibility in the present. So now when it comes to [the repression of] Falun Gong and rights defence, we can also not keep silent all the time. Each individual person has responsibility.[91]

87 Li Xiaorong and Zhang Zuhua (李晓荣, 张祖桦, editors), '零八宪章 [Charter 08]', Kaifang Press, Hong Kong: 2009, translated by Perry Link, Charter 08, *New York Review of Books*, 15 January 2009, at http://www.nybooks.com/articles/archives/2009/jan/15/chinas-charter-08/, accessed 4 January 2014.
88 #25 2011-1.
89 In Chinese characters, 反思.
90 #9 2010-2.
91 #7 2011-2.

In sum, the first half of the 20th century contains especially important reference points for rights lawyers. For them, the late imperial and post-imperial reform era matters, largely because it is the era when liberal ideas are first given an institutional manifestation; the Republican era can be seen as one of experimentation and unfulfilled promise. The period from 1957–1979 matters for different reasons, because it saw such devastating persecution under the current ruling Party; it is an era that has left Chinese society with haunting spectres. As the ruling Party is unable entirely to repudiate what it did then, and given its continued commitment to a Leninist political Party–State structure, today's government remains burdened with the crimes of this era,[92] but also supported by its genuine achievements. Its efforts to construct the Chinese tradition as one of repressive 'harmony', suppress the memory of Republican China, and control the historical record of the Mao Zedong era, have helped to forestall challenges to its purported authority so far, but they have also limited its ability to reform.

Limited legal reconstruction in the Reform and Opening era

The reform era under Deng Xiaoping revived liberally oriented reforms, but only within narrowly defined limits. Drawing in some areas on draft laws that had been kept locked away for 20 years and longer, the leadership revived and re-established the legal institutions of the judiciary, the procuracy, and the police, as well as the Ministry of Justice (which had been completely shut down). It passed new laws and regulations; opened law schools (by now, several hundred); and 'propagated legal knowledge' (*pufa*).[93] In drawing on the models created in the PRC's first decade, the leadership accepted some of those models' institutional premises, including for instance the separation of functions implied by allocating adjudicative, legislative and executive powers to separate institutions, and the acceptance of in principle adversarial trials allowing for legal defence.

The idea of 'ruling the country in accordance with law' (*yi fa zhi guo*),[94] seemed to indicate a promise on behalf of the authorities that the government would be bound by the new laws it created, too: under these new rules, contracts would have to be fulfilled and property protected; the violation of another's property or personal rights could trigger claims to damages, even against the government, which could be sued in 'administrative litigation', formalised in 1989.[95] No one must be falsely accused and no one mistreated

---

92 Liu Xiaobo (刘晓波), 'The Cultural Revolution has never ended', (文革从来没有结束), at http://blog.boxun.com/hero/2006/liuxb/17_1.shtml, accessed 27 October 2013.

93 In Chinese characters, 普法.

94 In Chinese characters 依法治国 Jiang Zemin heightened the popularity of this phrase by using it in a law lecture to senior party officials in 1996 with reference to Deng Xiaoping's reform policies. See Yang Deshan (杨德山), '依法治国, 以德治国 [Ruling the Country in Accordance With Law, Ruling the Country in Accordance with Virtue]', 6 September 2002, at http://news.xinhuanet.com/newscenter/2002-09/06/content_552721.htm, accessed 26 October 2013.

95 PRC Administrative Procedure Law, [中华人民共和国行政诉讼法], adopted and promulgated on 4 April 1989 and effective as of 1 October 1990.

in detention; officials breaking the law faced not only Party discipline but also criminal punishment and other legal action.

From a Party–State perspective, however, the idea of 'ruling the country in accordance with law' was much more limited. Although the Marxist–Maoist belief that law was an 'instrument of oppression of the antagonistic classes' came to be criticised if not (as some argue) abandoned,[96] the Deng era replaced it with a barely less narrow idea of law: the idea that law was essentially *made* by (or, that it had a social source consisting in) the ruling power. While contemporary positivists argue that judges must needs make law at certain times, however, under the rules and principles articulated in the PRC Constitution and its 2000 Legislation Law the power that made rules also had not only the authority to interpret them but also to ensure compliance with them;[97] and the Party's power to make rules that must (also) be respected was never abandoned.[98] Evidently, the Party–State meant to stay in full control of the laws it was making and the legal process it created for implementation of these laws. From this perspective, 'ruling the country in accordance with law' was at best meant to legitimise continued one-Party rule. Human rights, that epitome of a bourgeois–liberal, universalist conception of law connecting it to inherent moral requirements, may have appeared far fetched and rather irrelevant to the leadership at the time, given its Marxist background and increasingly welfare-utilitarian outlook reflected in phrases such as 'governing for the good of the people' (*zhi zheng wei min*).[99]

Reflecting the limited goals of 'ruling the country in accordance with law', the 1982 Constitution purported to be committed to contradictory principles; liberal scholars' shorthand way of expressing this criticism was to say that the Constitution's Chapter 1 (about State organisation) and Chapter 2 (about rights) were fundamentally irreconcilable.[100] China's legislative structure and other political decision-making structures follow the logic of rulers, however small,

96   Carlos Lo, 'Socialist legal theory in Deng Xiao-ping's China', 11 *Columbia Journal of Asian Law* (1997) 469. As discussed below, the Maoist theory of contradictions is being revived.

97   PRC Constitution, Articles 62 and 67 clarify this for the NPC and its Standing Committee, for example. The Constitution of People's Republic of China [中华人民共和国宪法], adopted on 4 December 1982, last revised in 2004; Wang Zhenmin (王振民), 中国违宪审查制度 [*Constitutional review in China*], Chinese University of Politics and Law Press, Beijing: 2004, at p. 372.

98   Perry Keller analyses this problem in 'Sources of order in the Chinese legal system', 42 *American Journal of Comparative Law* 4 (1994) 711–759, at pp. 754–759. For a discussion post-2000 Legislation Law, see Randall Peerenboom, *China's Long March Toward Rule of Law*, Cambridge University Press, Cambridge: 2002, Chapter 6 ('The legislative system: battling chaos').

99   In Chinese characters, 执政为民. Hu Jintao in 2003. See, e.g., Xinhua News, '胡锦涛在学习贯彻"三个代表"重要思想理论研讨会作重要讲话：真心学三个代表 立党为公执政为民是标志 [Hu Jintao gives an important speech during the study meeting for the earnest study of the guiding thoughts of the "Three Represents:" sincerely studying the Three Represents, establishing the party in the common interest, and governing for the good of the people should be [our] aims]', 1 July 2003, at http://news.xinhuanet.com/news center/2003-07/01/content_948197.htm, accessed 27 October 2013.

100 E.g. Teng Biao, 'Rights defence, microblogs, and the surrounding gaze: the Rights Defence Movement online and offline', in *Locating Civil Society: Communities Defending Basic Liberties*, Special Issue of *China Perspectives*, 2012 / no.3.

effectively making their own rules, following the principles of 'democratic central-ism'[101] and the democratic 'mass line',[102] allowing for directives and incidental intervention from above. Rule according to proponents of democratic centralism is rule by theoretically undivided power; it is theoretically incompatible with the protection of fundamental rights such as the Constitution's Chapter 2 enumer-ates, because it rules out 'bottom-up' challenges to political (including legislative) decisions once they have been made. A tension between the idea of legal rights securing the position of the individual vis-à-vis the State and that of 'democratic–centralist' rule making, therefore runs through the entire current legal and political system. It is compounded by the fact that the true holder of power, the Party, has no clearly defined and consequently no clearly limited role in the constitutional framework and is widely understood to be exempt from 'rule in accordance with law, as discussed further in Chapter 3'.[103]

However, while there was no clear indication that the Deng era's 'reform and opening' was intended to mean genuine respect for human rights, let alone wider political opening; there was a certain degree of relaxation of control, and there were efforts to rehabilitate some of the victims of political injustice.

Party–State conceptions of legal and political order were explicitly, expressly juxtaposed with popular conceptions of order and popular demands. From the start, therefore, popular voices of dissent played a different role in the reform and opening era. Two events at the very beginning of the reform era illustrate the different visions for a post-Mao Zedong order – the first Democracy Wall Movement of 1978–1979, a popular action making use of 'big character posters' to express criticism of and demands toward the government, on the one hand; and the trial of the 'Gang of Four', the small group that had exerted political control, on the other.

Begun as an initially tolerated campaign of criticism against Mao Zedong in support of the new leadership's efforts to destroy Maoist remnants represented by the 'Gang of Four', the Democracy Wall movement quickly became a forum for expressions of criticism against the current government, culminating in Wei Jingsheng's proposal that a 'fifth modernisation', the protection of human rights, was indispensable to the success of genuine modernisation.[104] A rights lawyer in his sixties, who was serving as a soldier at the time, recalls his first encounter with a Big Character Poster wall in Shanghai:

---

101 Democratic Centralism (民主集中制): 'The minority obeys the majority; party members have complete freedom to discuss and criticize before any issue is decided; after it is decided, everyone must implement the decision of the organization no matter what their view; the subordinate must implement the resolutions and directives of the superior, they may present their views to the superior, but they must still implement these resolutions and directives before they are changed by the superior.' Cited from Stephen C. Angle, 'Decent democratic centralism', 33 *Political Theory* (2005) 4.

102 Xu Chongde (徐崇德), (中华人民共和国宪法史) [*A Constitutional History of the People's Republic of China*], Fujian People's Press, Fuzhou: 2003, at p. 309.

103 Chapter 3 addresses the views of He Weifang, Zhang Qianfang and Jiang Shigong, among others.

104 Jonathan Spence, *The Search for Modern China*, Norton, New York: 1990.

The first time I was given an idea of human rights was in 1979, when we were aboard a ship carrying out repairs in Shanghai . . . It happened to be the period in which the 'Democracy Wall' movement occurred. So I was right there when it happened, and I got weekly leave, which I used to go to People's Square to read the big wall posters.[105] Among the ones that left a rather deep impression upon me was one [you could see] almost as you got to the Square, that read, 'We Commemorate Sun Yat-Sen.'

And then I also saw another one, one complaining about Mao, that was written particularly badly, with many characters written wrongly, but it was somebody speaking from his heart . . . complaining against Mao Zedong with all these wrongly written characters. You could tell that there must be some people who really loathed Mao Zedong!

I also saw a long essay, written very beautifully, that discussed human rights. At the time, I recall, it was discussing five different human rights, the 'right to life', the 'right to property', the 'right to pursue happiness', and – I have forgotten which other rights. But it drew my attention when I saw it at that time. It left a deep impression.[106]

It is of note that this commentator, who was to become a lawyer almost as soon as it became possible to take this professional path, had never heard of human rights in 1979 – but it is no less important that there were people there, presumably of an older generation and an educated background allowing them to 'write beautifully', who could connect back to the liberal tradition and revive ideas to become central to much of social protest in the decades to come. Of course, doing so was risky, since for the first decade of reform and opening, human rights remained an officially largely repudiated concept; and many participants in the Democracy Wall movement were persecuted.[107]

The Democracy Wall movement was an early indication of the forces that could be unleashed once popular protest was allowed to occur at all. The trial of the Gang of Four, by the same token, provided an early indication of the limited extent to which law was to figure in the handling of political and other conflicts, at a time when little other empirical evidence was available. It indicated that the Party–State emphasised criminal punishment and other punitive systems, and that it would use the legal process following the form of the trial organised on liberal and adversarial terms but continue to impose severe limits on procedural rights and, in particular, the rights of the defence. It also indicated the Party–State's inclination to use the criminal legal process for 'educational' and

---

105 See, for a discussion of big character posters, Hua Sheng, 'Big character posters in China: a historical survey', 4 *Journal of Chinese Law* (1990) 234.
106 #21 2010-1. The lawyer went on to talk about how in the eighties, after leaving the army and enrolling to study, he was attracted to 'capitalist' liberal texts and how friends gave him 'secret' texts written by Liu Binyan and others.
107 Author conversation with an 'ordinary' participant in the movement, left unable to find work and subsisting in penury after release from prison, in the summer of 2010.

propaganda purposes.[108] As Cohen showed for the earliest decades of the PRC, the public trial represented a 'constitutional model' but not the normalcy of secrecy in criminal trials then; and as Clarke and Feinerman wrote as late as in 1995, even a public trial – along the lines of Cohen's 'constitutional model' 'is any trial with an audience, regardless of how that audience is selected'.[109]

Jiang Qing's trial (as the most significant of the Gang of Four trials) was a trial 'with an audience' and with participation from criminal defence lawyers, but without effective procedural safeguards for even basic rights of the defendant. Criminal defence lawyer Zhang Sizhi recalls with 'regret' not having treated Jiang Qing better. In the one meeting he was allowed with her, he recalls being told that two jailors had repeatedly thrown her to the ground for six hours on end during the 'isolated interrogation' for the 'investigation' of her crimes:[110]

> Those words were spoken from her own mouth and no mistake. Later when I read the materials [I saw that] she had also said that to other people, which shows that this matter wasn't necessarily fabricated. But when we now look at all the official things [records] – oh, how very civilised we were to her that evening [when she was detained and questioned]. [Those records] don't say that she was repeatedly thrown to the floor for six hours on end. But I tell you, what I thought at the time was, 'Those throws were too light, only six hours, too short! What's six hours? And how many people did you harm?' At the time that was how I thought, so I remember this matter with great precision. But having thought about it in a more detached manner after it was over, I am now really unable to judge what actually happened then.[111]

Rendered more poignant by the fact that the defendants had shown no commitment whatsoever to protecting the accused while in power, this trial was a

---

108 Discussed in Jiang Jue, 'The practice of "criminal reconciliation" (*xingshi hejie*) in the PRC criminal justice system', PhD dissertation at the Chinese University of Hong Kong (2012) on file with author.

109 Mao Zedong, 'On the correct handling of contradictions among the people' (1957), posted at http://www.etext.org, from Mao Tse-Tung, *Four Essays on Philosophy* (Peking, 1968). According to this theory, 'the contradictions between ourselves and the enemy and the contradictions among the people must be resolved by different methods. To put it briefly, the former are a matter of drawing a clear distinction between ourselves and the enemy, and the latter a matter of drawing a clear distinction between right and wrong.' *Ibid.* In Clarke and Feinerman's analysis, 'The traditional identification of law and compulsion with dictatorship and enemy classes . . . has made it difficult to accept the notion that courts and law are the proper institutions for handling [non-antagonistic] contradictions. Therefore a wide variety of institutions labelled "administrative" have come into being . . . the much used phrases "punished according to law" mean not "punished according to proper legal procedures" but "given a formal punishment under the Criminal Law".' Clarke and Feinerman, 'Antagonistic contradictions: criminal law and human rights in China', 141 *China Quarterly* (1995), at http://docs.law.gwu.edu/facweb/dclarke/pubs/Clarke%20and%20Feinerman,%20Antagonistic%20Contradictions.pdf, at p. 136.

110 Zhang Sizhi and Xiao Hong, *ibid.*

111 Zhang Sizhi and Xiao Hong, *ibid.*

show trial in which the Party–State could be relatively confident of controlling the process:[112] all publicly available records, as indicated in Lawyer Zhang's comment, could be screened to eliminate any trace of Party–State wrongdoing in the Gang of Four's prosecution; and as other political trials, so, too was this one used to lay down a claim to legitimacy and draw a clear dividing line between the defendants and the Party–State establishment remaining after it had publicly enacted a purge of opposed factions.

Despite its status as a political trial,[113] the trial of the Gang of Four had nevertheless exemplary value explaining more general traits of the legal process reconstructed in the reform and opening era. From the 'educational' (propaganda) perspective adopted in this sort of legal process, there is no need for protections of the individual caught up in it; the 'political' trial is not in principle different from ordinary trials that are also used to serve 'educational' goals. If adopted stringently, it undermines the liberal assumptions made in what Cohen called the 'constitutional' legal process.[114]

Certain features of the criminal process and other legal processes in the reform era have followed logically from this basic premise: it is sensible *not* to use the trial as a process to determine the guilt or innocence of the suspect/defendant, since as Clarke and Feinerman observe, there is no interest in showing that the authorities could be in the wrong; since this is so, it may on occasion be opportune to replace the adjudicative process with one where a negotiated outcome is reached (with or without a public audience) under the direction of the authorities, and where who is right is at best a minor consideration; and there is no barrier to the use of 'law enforcement' as part of political campaigns projecting the power of the Party–State to impose punishment. Substantively punishment can be understood to be merited by virtue of an 'authoritative' decision that it is appropriate, and conflict is to be resolved in such as manner as to ensure peace, not justice.

Because there are authoritative decisions, however, and because the rights and interests of the individual participating in the legal process are not important, that process may be reopened whenever it is deemed opportune, and it may be opportune to do so for instance in the event that it is discovered that the authorities have made a mistake. The disciplining and punishing of officials guilty of errors, as well as the correction of errors itself, serve the reaffirmation of political authority, of conveying an appropriate educational message, as

---

112 Video recordings (short clips) are available online.
113 Otto Kirchheimer, *Political Justice: The Use of Legal Procedure for Political Ends*, Princeton University Press, Princeton: 1961.
114 In her work, Jiang Jue discusses in particular the perspective of a legal scholar who has entirely rejected the understanding of the criminal legal process suggested by the 'constitutional' perspective and, instead of analysing it using the well-known categories of investigation stage, trial stage, and so on, introduces new categories. Jiang Jue, *supra* Chapter VI and Li Changsheng (李昌盛), '刑事庭审的中国模式: 教化型庭审 [The Chinese Pattern of Criminal Trial: *Bildung* Trial]', 1 法律科学(西北政法大学学报 [*The Science of Law*], 1 *Journal of the Northwest University of Political Science and Law* (2011) 131.

Rosenzweig has argued;[115] nevertheless, concern with correctness is an important concession with this sort of system makes toward the value of justice, and it is also what shows this sort of system to bear a family resemblance to the liberal 'constitutional' trial.

These features of the legal system as just described relate to the non-liberal influences relevant in the past; and they continue to matter to how institutions are designed and to substantive arguments in legal practice today. For example, until the mid-1990s, the written laws and regulations did not recognise a presumption of innocence. The laws stipulated blanket crimes such as 'hooliganism',[116] and allowed the use of analogy in the criminal justice process.[117] The latter aspects made the system created in the 1980s appear similar to late Qing law; a provision of the Great Qing Code of 1646, in effect until 1912, had threatened 40 blows of the lighter bamboo to anyone who did 'what ought not to be done',[118] without further definition. There are extensive procedural possibilities for obtaining retrials; and court litigation is but one of two major avenues used by citizens to obtain redress for injustice; the other, the petitioning system, has often been compared to petitioning in the imperial tradition, and characteristically is the system that draws most obviously on the language of *yuan*.

In the area of economic liberties and individual entitlements to welfare, the 1980s saw a tentative and gradual abandonment of Marxist–Leninist and Maoist practices such as the planned economy and collective organisation of production, and their replacement with a welfarist, utilitarian perspective. Marxism and utilitarianism have convenient similarities, however; while their political (popular) attraction appears to lie in a concern with everyone's welfare, both Marxism and utilitarianism are unable fully to account for the moral importance of individual rights. As discussed in greater detail in Chapter 3, rights have remained neglected in the reform and opening era, supposed to be subordinate to general welfare considerations decided on in an authoritarian manner by the Party–State. This is less apparent in the Party–State's rather obviously self-serving suppression of freedoms such as that of speech in the name of 'social stability' – after all, one of the most enduring defences of freedom of speech and thought is in essence utilitarian[119] – and it is plausible that it is in the area of political and civil liberties

---

115 Joshua D. Rosenzweig, 'China's battle over the right to criticise', *supra*.
116 Jerome A. Cohen and Margaret K. Lewis, 'The enduring importance of police repression: Laojiao, the rule of law and Taiwan's alternative evolution', in Jean-Philippe Béja (ed.), *The Impact of China's 1989 Tian'anmen Massacre*, Routledge, London: 2011; *Challenge to China: How Taiwan Abolished Its Version of Re-Education Through Labor*, Berkshire Publishing, Great Barrington: 2013.
117 Article 79 of the 1979 PRC Criminal Law (中华人民共和国刑法 [Criminal Law of the People's Republic of China], adopted on 1 July 1979, promulgated on 6 July 1979, and effective as of 1 January 1980, at http://www.novexcn.com/criminal_law.html): 'Crimes that are not expressly defined in the Specific Provisions of this Law may be determined and punished in according to whichever article in the Specific Provisions of this Law that covers the most closely analogous crime, but the judgment shall be submitted to the Supreme People's Court for approval.' This law is no longer effective. Cp. Jerome A. Cohen, *The Criminal Process in the People's Republic of China, 1949–1963: An Introduction*, Harvard University Press, Cambridge, MA: 1968, at pp. 336 ff.
118 Section 386 of the Great Qing Code, *supra*.
119 John Stuart Mill, *On Liberty*, Longman, Roberts & Green, London: 1869.

that the reform era system has stayed most committed to its Marxist–Maoist and Leninist origins. A statist form of utilitarianism is perhaps most clearly apparent in the manner in which the Party–State brushes aside individual rights in its intense efforts to promote economic growth for instance through urban construction, which is supposed to be in the public interest, understood on welfare–utilitarian, aggregate grounds. It is also apparent in the way in which the Party–State under the new system accepted the surge in corruption that has characterised the current era.

The authoritarian and educational outlook of the reform era system made campaign-style administration of justice an eligible method of *pufa*, dissemination of legal knowledge, while at the same time rendering the system blind to the rights violations they led to. A rights lawyer who grew up in the 1970s and 1980s recalls the case of a young unmarried couple charged with crime when the girl became pregnant, as among the early experiences that left an impression:

> My uncle was the criminal defence lawyer for the boy. His parents would come to our home and say, he of all ought not to be punished harshly – such a good boy! Everybody agreed how unfortunate it was that this had happened in the middle of a strike-hard campaign. But there was nothing one could do. They were both sentenced to death.[120]

The larger political development of the 1980s indicates that despite its successes and beneficial overall effects for welfare, governance in the reform era could not cope with the groundswell of protest against many aspects of the system. At a deeper level, the system continued to display commitments to irreconcilable principles.

Popular protest rose during the 1980s. It included notably corruption and, in a rather abstract and philosophical sense, also intellectualist complaints about the lack of human rights protection. Jonathan Spence and others have commented that while those demanding democracy and human rights were clearly in earnest, they did not necessarily have a very good understanding of these concepts.[121] But even as at a level of political theory many issues may have appeared hazy the popular groundswell of protest prepared the ground for a vernacularisation of the idea of human rights that was to take place only after 4th June 1989 and that was one of the unintended consequences of 'Opening and Reform':

> The 1980s student democracy movement shouted slogans opposing corruption and calling for human rights, democracy and press freedom, but it was unable to connect these abstract slogans with people's actual lives and interests . . . But [today] rights defenders use individual cases – forced relocation and land seizures, population planning, injustice, personal liberty, labour rights, food safety – to create this relationship: they are not only

120 #23 2010-2.
121 Spence, *supra*.

able to defend the interests of ordinary people, but can actually promote democracy and rule of law at the same time.[122]

The discussion in this section has argued that the frequently observed and commented upon fundamental tension between the Leninist and liberal political conceptions in the current PRC Constitution mark two radically opposed kinds of attitude toward law and rights, especially toward popular criticism of government. Even though the Party has adopted quite different political principles during its 65 years in political control, it has not abandoned the totalitarian/post-totalitarian attitude of total rejection of political opposition to itself; and the PRC Constitution and embracing of liberal principles in the Deng Xiaoping reform era was therefore bound to lead to conflict.

If the current human rights movement has chances of succeeding, however, it is not because liberalism as a set of ideas will vanquish other ideas; that, indeed, is entirely unlikely. Rather, drawing on this and the argument of earlier sections, it seems that in contemporary China, two strands of quests for justice come together and their forces unite: the rights movement with its roots in liberal political philosophy, and the indigenous tradition, the vernacular forms of popular protest represented by traditional conceptions of injustice such as *yuan*.

Professor Yu Jianrong of the Chinese Academy of Social Sciences whose early work focused on China's petitioning system, wrote in 2007:

> On the streets of Beijing you can see thousands of petitioners. They have changed the name of the Supreme People's Court 'Office For Receiving Petitioners' into 'Office For Receiving the Wronged'. They say that they belong to a particular nationality, one that exists in addition to the People's Republic fifty-six other nationalities: namely, the Tribe of the Wronged (*yuanmin* 冤民).[123]

It is because both *yuan* and rights are 'back' with a vengeance that a popular human rights movement emerges in the later years of the current reform era.

The rise of *weiquan* (rights defence)

This chapter has so far argued that liberalism, rising from the 19th-century's reception of western political ideas, had become an important political force in China by the beginning of the PRC, with support also from some Party members, and that the ideas of rights and democracy it encompasses were not eradicated

---

122 Teng Biao, 'What is rights defence?', in Stacy Mosher and Patrick Poon (eds.), *A Sword and a Shield: China's Human Rights Lawyers*, China Human Rights Lawyers Concern Group, Hong Kong: 2009.

123 Yu Jianrong (于建嵘), '中国的骚乱事件与管治危机 [China's unrest incidents and governance crisis]', transcript of a presentation at University of California Berkeley lecture, 30 October 2007, available at http://www.clb.org.hk/chi/node/140745, accessed 27 October 2013.

even in the disastrous period of the Cultural Revolution; rather, they 'survived' as ideas and values cherished by those who had suffered and survived persecution. With the beginning of legal reconstruction, these ideas were again brought into play by those entrusted with new positions in the legal system and in the rapidly expanding field of legal education.

After the June Fourth massacre and ensuing persecution of democracy activists, looked on by most current rights lawyers as a series of important but already distant events,[124] the promise of law, in particular that of rights protection, may if anything have become more important – as the democracy movement appeared to have failed for the moment, the then adolescent generation of people born in the late 1960s and 1970s were especially likely to put their hope in the possibility that the Party–State might of its own accord put reforms into place that would protect citizens against its own power. These hopes were encouraged by signs that the Party–State was willing to accept the value of human rights, even though its first (1991) *White Book on Human Rights* presented a defensive interpretation of the concept, and arguably began a process of conceptual dilution that continues until today, and even though after it signed the ICCPR in 1998, China failed to ratify this treaty.

The judicial leadership, especially under SPC President Xiao Yang, co-author of a book entitled *Toward an Age of Rights*, encouraged judicial professionalism;[125] and law schools taught law making very explicit comparative references to western systems, so much so that some of those who had studied law at the time said they had learned far more about the US Constitution in their constitutional law course than about that of the PRC. Of central importance to such courses was the question of how best to enforce constitutional rights and thus, cases such as the US case *Marbury vs. Madison* played a prominent role. In a constitutional law course I audited in Beijing in 2003, at the height of the period of human rights optimism, much discussion was devoted to the question of how to institutionalise a system of constitutional review of State acts including laws and regulations; and articles and books about the topic of *xianzheng*,[126] constitutionalism or 'constitutional governance', proliferated.

Widely reported and discussed cases indicted support from the legal authorities and from the largely controlled print media. In 2001 in the *Qi Yuling* case, the Supreme People's Court appeared to abandon its stance that the judiciary was not

---

124 Discussed in Eva Pils, 'The practice of law as conscientious resistance', in Jean-Philippe Béja (ed.), *The Impact of China's 1989 Tian'anmen Massacre*, Routledge, London: 2010.

125 According to Yu Xingzhong, judicial professionalism discourse in the PRC did not simply reiterate liberal western discourse; rather it became a field for contentious exchanges between scholars and judges falling into three distinct camps of 'official policy defenders' wary of too much professional independence of judges, 'eager experimenters' intent on widening the autonomous space of the judiciary and 'dispute resolvers anchored in traditional Chinese culture', represented by the majority of basic level court judges, who rejected judicial professionalism. Yu Xingzhong, 'Judicial professionalism in China: from discourse to practice', in William P. Alford, Kenneth Winston and William C. Kirby (eds.), *Prospects for Professionalism in China: Essays on Civic Vocations*, Routledge, London: 2009.

126 In Chinese characters, 宪政.

allowed to apply the Constitution directly in deciding cases; it opined that the plaintiff Qi Yuling's constitutional right to education had been violated by the defendant, another private party. The decision was celebrated by then SPC Vice President Huang Songyou as 'China's *Marbury vs. Madison* in an essay published online. In 2003 in the 'Sun Zhigang Incident', using a legal mechanism introduced in 2000, three young academics successfully challenged the constitutionality of a regulation that served as the legal basis for one of China's many administrative detention systems, by writing an open 'suggestion letter' to the National People's Congress Standing Committee. While they did not obtain an annulment of the regulation in question by the National People's Congress, the regulation's creator, the State Council, revoked it. Characteristically, national newspapers reported on the incident reproducing a comment purportedly made by Sun's father, to the effect that if only it helped to promote legal construction, his son would not have died in vain.[127]

It was in this climate of reform optimism that *weiquan*,[128] or 'rights defence', emerged in the 1990s, initially as an officially propagated idea, which the Party–State sought to promote through the distribution of rights defence manuals and wall posters. In line with its positivistic assumption that rights were essentially granted by the State, and relying on its tight control of all legal institutions (discussed in greater detail in Chapter 3), the authorities seemed to assume that the defence of rights in the courts and through other essentially State-controlled systems could be controlled and that, like also the petitioning system, its controlled uses would serve as a sort of safety valve for popular discontent with the government.

But, from the perspective of liberal lawyers and scholars including some persons in authority, such as SPC Vice President Huang Songyou, rights defence was not – could not – be constrained in this way. Scholar and lawyer Teng Biao, one of the co-authors of the Sun Zhigang letter, describes the main methods of rights defence in the following way:

> Mainly it is the intervention of lawyers or rights defenders in a specific case ... The goal is to use the legal process to demonstrate the power of the law and protect the rights of the party concerned, to call on the government to abide by the law, to expose the unlawful actions of officials, to use the court of public opinion to monitor law enforcement departments when necessary, or to defend civil rights through legal arguments in court. This also includes launching public interest lawsuits, signing open letters regarding a case, commenting publicly on a particular legal policy, and all other legally-permissible means of monitoring the government and promoting the development of rule of law.[129]

---

127 Xinhua News, '本网记者现场直击孙志刚案庭审 [Live broadcast on the criminal trial in the Sun Zhigang case]', 20 June 2003, at http://news.xinhuanet.com/newmedia/2003-06/10/content_911471.htm, accessed 28 October 2013.
128 In Chinese characters, 维权.
129 Teng Biao, 'What is rights defence?', *supra*.

Perhaps the most important aspect of the emergence of *weiquan* was that, as indicated by Teng Biao in the passage cited earlier, the use of individual cases to promote liberal political ideas served to popularise and vernacularise[130] the idea of human rights far beyond professional or academic circles. Petitioners used the expression 'human rights' with increasing confidence and fluency, especially after the expression 'The state respects and protects human rights', together with a stronger provision safeguarding private property rights had been included in a 2004 constitutional amendment. Frustrated with the judicial system and the system for bringing petitions – 'Letters and Visits' – they began denouncing these systems as root causes of the violation of their human rights:

> At the time when they reinstituted the lawyers system the ordinary people generally still thought that lawyers were people just helping the bad people . . . But gradually they changed their mind; this had to do with the rise of rights consciousness among the people.[131]

Less than 25 years after the total denunciation of the term during the Cultural Revolution and less than 15 years after the persecutions triggered by the June Fourth massacre, human rights were back as part of a vocabulary used actively and widely to challenge State authorities.

In the actuality of popular protest and petitioning practice, 'rights defence', *wei quan*, and petitioning or 'bringing grievances', *shen yuan*,[132] are frequently combined. *Yuan* has almost no place in the official language of contemporary law. This makes it a concept that is part of the popular counterculture of ordinary people, petitioners seeking justice. In its focus on individual grievances, *yuan* could be called a proto-liberal idea: it is one of the concepts that draw attention to the individual's position in the legal and political system and insist on the individual's moral importance in that system: the person who has been wronged ought to be attended to, their wrong ought to be righted. Functionally, it may be argued, *yuan* is therefore similar to rights.

If the image of the *yuanmin* is a 'kneeling' image,[133] the petitioner kneeling in front of a government or court building, prostrating herself toward the building as a symbol of Party–State authority, replicates the age-old image of the supplicant commoner submissively seeking official protection. By contrast, the citizen who asserts her rights is standing, confronting the authorities on ideally equal terms – demanding justice, not begging for it. Lawyers speaking up in open court, citizens standing with their backs turned toward the court building, holding up protest signs and chanting protest slogans, are not seeking the attention of the authorities in a submissive manner; rather they are – at least also – speaking to the public and

---

130 Sally Engle-Merry, *Human Rights and Gender Violence: Translating International Law into Local Justice*, University of Chicago Press, Chicago: 2006.
131 #24 2010-1.
132 In Chinese characters, 伸冤.
133 Author conversation (2010).

their message is potentially a political one even if it focuses on a particular case.[134] The more assertive attitude of *weiquan* assumes a clearly public and potentially confrontational relationship between citizens and the government; it invites public attention and scrutiny. Lawyers do not wear petitioner garments; also by their clothes they will generally locate themselves at the modern, liberal end of the spectrum; but they work with people who are less clearly committed to liberal values. They well understand the emotional power of this concept and the political ideas it evokes; and they use it, sometimes, to draw analogies between the current government and that of imperial dynasties.

The combination of using the Party–State's own promises of rule by law, actively seeking popular support through connections with clients that were established naturally by 'rights defence (*weiquan*) lawyers', and drawing on liberal political ideas represented a challenge to the existing order:[135]

> The ruling Party. . . . always thought that lawyers must be serving them . . .
> Now of course they have a sort of resentment, to varying degrees, toward
> lawyers; lawyers are not a community they welcome, and their tolerance is
> waning . . . Their understanding of rights and rules, of political power being
> constrained by these, is just not very clear. Did you see what Wu Si wrote in a
> recent issue of *Yanhuang Chunqiu*?[136] He said, 'The leadership doesn't read
> books, they only read documents.' Too true: what we who have studied
> law and politics consider to be commonly understood, they [don't
> know about].[137]

The enduring significance of historical conceptions of justice

In this chapter I have outlined the ideas and political developments that created a setting in which, toward the end of the last century, a professional engagement with and defence of rights by professional lawyers could develop as a widely noted and politically significant social practice. I have also sought to locate the beginnings of the Chinese human rights movement, of which human rights lawyers have become an indispensable part, in the emergence of Chinese liberalism as an intellectual tradition dating back to the last century with a greatly ruptured and fragmented history. Even though they represent different

---

134 The example of two lawyers holding up a sign that reads 'Lawyers Demand Access to Case Files' is discussed in Chapter 4.

135 For a discussion contrasting the leadership's instrumentalism with rights-centred attitudes, see Jacques De Lisle, 'Traps, gaps and law in China's transition', in *Is China Trapped in Transition? Implications for Future Reforms*, Oxford Foundation for Law, Justice and Society, 2007, at p. 7.

136 Along similar lines, Wu Si criticises an official close to Mao Zedong, Chen Yonggui (陈永贵) for only reading documents, not books: Wu Si (吴思), 陈永贵沉浮中南海：改造中国的试验 [*Chen Yonggui's ups and downs in Zhongnanhai: an experiment with changing China*], Huacheng Press, Guangzhou: 1993.

137 #24 2010-1.

interpretations of justice and good governance, the political ideas associated with theories (philosophies) that continue influential in Chinese society should not be thought of as compartmentalised or controlled by any one section of the political community, but rather as ideas contested and challenged within Chinese society.

This is as true of the pre-Republican moral tradition, which produced the concept of *yuan*, injustice, as it is of the modern era, which produced the concept of rights: the government, it has been shown, has been unable to control either of these ideas, and both have been successfully used to challenge the government. The emergence of the legal profession since the early 20th century has been part of a struggle for the liberal idea of rights, which despite its failures has kept alive ideas started by late Qing Dynasty reformers, and which has inspired the contemporary human rights movement. The emergence of the *weiquan* movement, however, can only be understood if both liberal and traditional conceptions of (in)justice are taken into account and their significance for contemporary social movements recognised. Since rights lawyers operate at the interface between legal advocacy and the human rights movement, their emergence should be understood against this background, as a development that would not have been possible without legal professionalism and without the periodic rises of popular discontent and protest that have characterised the reform and opening era.

Only by clarifying the contemporary movement's relationship with the past can we understand its position vis-à-vis the current political system, and its promise of political change. Much of the account given in ensuing chapters draws on events, cases and rights lawyers' experiences during the decade since the 2003 'Sun Zhigang Incident', a decade when this challenge was more clearly perceived and met with increasingly severe repression.

Bibliography

Historical laws

Great Qing Code [大清律例] (1646), in use during the Qing Dynasty (1644–1912).
Republic of China's Law on Lawyers [中华民国律师法], enacted and promulgated on 1 November 1941 by the Republican Government.

Constitution and NPC laws

PRC Administrative Procedure Law [中华人民共和国行政诉讼法], passed on 4 April 1989, promulgated on 4 April 1989 and effective as of 1 October 1990.
PRC Constitution [中华人民共和国宪法], passed on 4 December 1982, promulgated and effective as of 4 December 1982, last revised on 14 March 2004.
1979 PRC Criminal Law [中华人民共和国刑法], passed on 1 July 1979, promulgated on 6 July 1979, and effective as of 1 January 1980, at http://www.novexcn.com/criminal_law.html, no longer effective.

Rules and regulations

Ministry of Justice Notice on the Revocation of Black Lawyers and Litigation Masters [关于取缔黑律师及讼棍事件的通报], promulgated on 17 October 1950 at http://www.cnki.com.cn/Article/CJFDTotal-HXZB195101112.htm, http://wuxizazhi.cnki.net/Search/HXZB195101112.html.

Other official documents

Chinese Communist Party Central Committee Resolution on the Construction of a Socialist Harmonious Society [中共中央关于构建社会主义和谐社会若干重大问题的决议], passed on 11 October 2006, reprinted in CPC Central Committee on Building a Socialist Harmonious Society and a Number of Major Issues [中共中央关于构建社会主义和谐社会若干重大问题的决议], Xinhua News Agency (Chinese Communist Party Central Committee 18 October 2006), at http://news.xinhuanet.com/politics/2006-10/18/content_5218639.htm.

Books and articles

Angle, Stephen C., 'Human rights and harmony', 30 *Human Rights Quarterly* 76 (2008) 78–80.

Angle, Stephen C., 'Decent democratic centralism', 33 *Political Theory* 4 (2005).

Angle, Stephen C., *Human Rights in Chinese Thought: A Cross-Cultural Inquiry*, Cambridge University Press, Cambridge: 2002.

Béja, Jean-Philippe, 'Is jail the only place where one can "live in truth"?', in Jean-Philippe Béja, Fu Hualing and Eva Pils (eds.), *Liu Xiaobo, Charter 08 and the Challenges of Political Reform in China*, Hong Kong University Press, Hong Kong: 2012.

Bodde, Derk and Morris, Clarence, *Law in Imperial China*, Harvard University Press, Cambridge, MA: 1967.

Cai, Xiqin, Lai, Bo and Xia, Yuhe, *Confucius. The Analects*, Sinolingua, Beijing: 1994.

Chan, Joseph, 'A Confucian perspective on human rights for contemporary China', in Joanne R. Bauer and Daniel A. Bell (eds.), *The East Asian Challenge for Human Rights*, Cambridge University Press, Cambridge: 1999.

Chen, Tong (陈同), '上海本土律师的出现 [The emergence of local lawyers in Shanghai]', in Fu Guoyong (傅国涌 ed.), 追寻律师的传统 [*In Quest of A Lawyer Tradition*], Beijing United Publishing Company, Beijing: 2012.

Choukroune, Leila and Garapon, Antoine, 'The norms of Chinese harmony: disciplinary rules as social stabiliser', 3 *China Perspectives* (2007) 36–38, at http://chinaperspectives.revues.org/document2013.html.

Clarke, Donald C. and Feinerman, James V., 'Antagonistic contradictions: criminal law and human rights in China', 141 *China Quarterly* (1995), at http://docs.law.gwu.edu/facweb/dclarke/pubs/Clarke%20and%20Feinerman,%20Antagonistic%20Contradictions.pdf 136.

Cohen, Jerome A., *The Criminal Process in the People's Republic of China, 1949–1963: An Introduction*, Harvard University Press, Cambridge, MA: 1968.

Cohen, Jerome A. and Lewis, Margaret K., *Challenge to China: How Taiwan Abolished Its Version of Re-Education Through Labor*, Berkshire Publishing, Great Barrington: 2013.

Cohen, Jerome A. and Lewis, Margaret K., 'The enduring importance of police repression: Laojiao, the rule of law and Taiwan's alternative evolution', in Jean-Philippe Béja (ed.), *The Impact of China's 1989 Tian'anmen Massacre*, Routledge, London: 2011.

Confucius/Kong Zi (孔子), 论语 [*Analects*], compiled in the 4th century BC; translation by Cai Xiqin, Lai Bo and Xia Yuhe, *Confucius. The Analects*, Sinolingua, Beijing: 1994.

De Lisle, Jacques, 'Traps, gaps and law in China's transition', in *Is China Trapped in Transition? Implications for Future Reforms*, Oxford Foundation for Law, Justice and Society, 2007.

De Mente, Boye Lafayette, *Chinese Etiquette & Ethics in Business*, McGraw-Hill, Whitby: 1994.

Du, Bin (杜斌), 上访者：中国以法治国下幸存的活化石 [*Petitioners: Living Fossil Under Chinese Rule by Law*], Ming Pao Publications, Hong Kong: 2007.

Fraser, Chris, 'Deng Xi's exploits (supplement to entry on School of Names)', at http://plato.stanford.edu/entries/school-names/exploits.html.

Fu, Guoyong (傅国涌), 追寻律师的传统 [*In quest of a lawyer tradition*], Beijing United Publishing Company, Beijing: 2012.

Fung (Feng), 'Yu-lan', in Derk Bodde (ed.), *A Short History of Chinese Philosophy*, Macmillan, New York: 1948.

Goldman, Merle, *From Comrade to Citizen: The Struggle for Political Rights in China*, Harvard University Press, Cambridge, MA and London: 2005.

Guan, Hanqing (关汉卿), '感天动地窦娥冤 [*The Injustice to Dou'E that touched Heaven and moved Earth*]', Yuan Dynasty (1271–1368), at http://www.tianyabook.com/lnz/doueyuan.htm.

He, Weifang, 'The nascence and growing pains of a professionalised legal class', *Columbia Journal of Asian Law* 19 (2005) 238.

Idema, Wilt L., *Judge Bao and the Rule of Law*, World Scientific Publishing, Singapore: 2010.

Jiang, Jue, 'The practice of "criminal reconciliation" (*xingshi hejie*) in the PRC criminal justice system', PhD dissertation at the Chinese University of Hong Kong (2012).

Keller, Perry, 'Sources of order in the Chinese legal system', *American* 42 *Journal of Comparative Law*, 4 (1994) 711–759.

Kirchheimer, Otto, *Political Justice: The Use of Legal Procedure for Political Ends*, Princeton University Press, Princeton, 1961.

Koenig, Stefan, *Vom Dienst am Recht – Rechtsanwälte als Strafverteidiger im Nationalsozialismus* [*On service to the law – lawyers as criminal defenders under National Socialism*], Walter de Gruyter & Co., Berlin: 1987.

Lau, D.C., *Confucius, The Analects*, Penguin Books, London: 1979.

Li, Changsheng (李昌盛), '刑事庭审的中国模式: 教化型庭审 [The Chinese Pattern of Criminal Trial: *Bildung* Trial]', 1 法律科学 (西北政法大学学报 [*The Science of Law*], 1 *Journal of the Northwest University of Political Science and Law* (2011) 131.

Li, Qian (栗茜), '中国古代的讼师制度 [The system for legal advocates in ancient China]', 12 September 2009, at http://bjgy.chinacourt.org/article/detail/2012/09/id/887408.shtml.

Li, Xiaorong and Zhang, Zuhua (李晓荣, 张祖桦), '零八宪章 [Charter 08]', Kaifang Press, Hong Kong; 2009, translated by Perry Link, Charter 08', *New York Review of Books*, 15 January 2009, at http://www.nybooks.com/articles/archives/2009/jan/15/chinas-charter-08/, accessed 4 January 2014.

Liebman, Benjamin L., 'Assessing China's legal reforms', in Stanley B. Lubman, *The Evolution of Law Reform in China: An Uncertain Path*, Edward Elgar Publishing, Cheltenham: 2012.

Liu, Guiming (刘桂明), '律师百年与律师精神 [100 years of history of the legal profession and the spirit of the legal profession]', 3 March 2013, at http://blog.legaldaily.com.cn/blog/html/81/2441181-32856.html.

Liu, Shu-Hsien, *Understanding Confucian Philosophy: Classical and Sung-Ming*, Praeger Publishers, Westport, MA: 1998.

Liu, Xiaobo (刘晓波), 'The Cultural Revolution has never ended [文革从来没有结束]', 13 May 2006, at http://blog.boxun.com/hero/2006/liuxb/17_1.shtml.

Lo, Carlos, 'Socialist legal theory in Deng Xiao-ping's China', 11 *Columbia Journal of Asian Law* (1997) 469.

Lubman, Stanley B., 'Introduction' to *The Evolution of Law Reform in China: An Uncertain Path*, Edward Elgar Publishing, Cheltenham: 2012.

Ma, Xiaoquan (马小泉), 'Citizen autonomy: a continuing topic mentioned for a century – an analysis of Kang Youwei's gongmin zizhi bian (1902) [公民自治:一个百年未尽的话题—读康有为《公民自治篇》(1902年)]', *Academic Research* (学术研究), 10 (200310), at http://d.wanfangdata.com.cn/Periodical_xsyj200310023.aspx.

Mao, Zedong, 'On the correct handling of contradictions among the people' (1957), at http://www.etext.org, from Mao Tse-Tung, *Four Essays on Philosophy*, Foreign Languages Press, Peking: 1968.

Merry, Sally Engle, *Human Rights and Gender Violence: Translating International Law into Local Justice*, University of Chicago Press, Chicago, 2006.

Mill, John Stuart, *On Liberty*, Longman, Roberts & Green, London: 1869.

Minzner, Carl F., 'Xinfang: an alternative to formal Chinese legal institutions', 42 *Stanford International Law Journal* 103 (2006), at http://ir.lawnet.fordham.edu/faculty_scholarship/3.

Muehlhahn, Klaus, *Criminal Justice in China: A History*, Harvard University Press, Cambridge, MA: 2009.

O'Connor, Alison, 'China's lawyers and their training: enduring influences and disconnects', in Stanley B. Lubman, *The Evolution of Law Reform in China: an Uncertain Path*, Edward Elgar Publishing, Cheltenham: 2012.

Randall Peerenboom, *China's Long March Toward Rule of Law*, Cambridge University Press, Cambridge: 2002.

People's Daily (人民日报), 'Completely smash the feudal capitalist and revisionist legal system', 2 *Chinese Law & Government* 4 (1969–1970), at http://mesharpe.metapress.com/link.asp?id=rpw84w8w70644l15.

Pils, Eva, 'Taking *yuan* (冤) seriously: why the Chinese government should stop suppressing citizen protests against injustice', 25 *Temple International and Comparative Law Journal* (2011) 285–327.

Pils, Eva, 'The practice of law as conscientious resistance', in Jean-Philippe Béja (ed.), *The Impact of China's 1989 Tian'anmen Massacre*, Routledge, London: 2010.

Pu Songling (薄松龄), 聊斋志异 [*Strange Tales from a Chinese Studio*], available in translation by John Minford, Kindle Books: 2006.

Qiu, Zhihong (邱志红), '从"讼师"到"律师":从翻译看近代中国社会对律师的认知 [From "litigation masters" to "lawyers": analysing the understanding of lawyers in modern Chinese society from translations]', 近代史研究 (*Studies of Modern History*) 3 (2011), at http://jds.cass.cn/Item/21623_5.aspx.

Rosenzweig, Joshua D., 'China's battle over the right to criticise', *Far Eastern Economic Review* (2009), at http://chinadigitaltimes.net/2009/05/joshua-rosenzweig-chinas-battle-over-the-right-to-criticize/.

Sheng, Hua, 'Big character posters in China: a historical survey', 4 *Journal of Chinese Law* (1990) 234.

Spence, Jonathan, *The Search for Modern China*, Norton, New York: 1990.

Teng, Biao, 'Rights defence, microblogs, and the surrounding gaze: the Rights Defence Movement online and offline', in *Locating Civil Society: Communities Defending Basic Liberties*, Special Issue of *China Perspectives* 2012/3.

Teng, Biao, 'What is rights defence', in Stacy Mosher and Patrick Poon (eds.), *A Sword and a Shield: China's Human Rights Lawyers*, China Human Rights Lawyers Concern Group, Hong Kong: 2009.

Wang, Zhenmin (王振民), 中国违宪审查制度 [*Constitutional review in China*], Chinese University of Politics and Law Press, Beijing: 2004.

Wu, Lilan and Lin, Qi (吴立岚、林淇). '法庭上的吴开生 [Wu Kaisheng in Court]', in Fu Guoyong (傅国涌 ed.), 追寻律师的传统 [*In quest of a lawyer tradition*], Beijing United Publishing Company, Beijing: 2012.

Wu, Si (吴思), 陈永贵沉浮中南海：改造中国的试验 [*Chen Yonggui's ups and downs in Zhongnanhai: an experiment with changing China*], Huacheng Press, Guangzhou: 1993.

Xu, Chongde (徐崇德), 中华人民共和国宪法史 [*A Constitutional History of the People's Republic of China*], Fujian People's Press, Fuzhou: 2003.

Yang, Deshan (杨德山), '依法治国，以德治国 [Ruling the country in accordance with law, ruling the country in accordance with virtue]', 6 September 2002, at http://news.xinhuanet.com/newscenter/2002-09/06/content_552721.htm.

Ye, Qing (叶青), Gu, Yuejin (顾跃进), 律师制度研究 [*A study of the system for lawyers*], Shanghai Academy of Social Sciences Press, Shanghai: 2005.

Yu, Jianrong (于建嵘), '中国的骚乱事件与管治危机 [China's unrest incidents and governance crisis]', transcript of a presentation at University of California Berkeley lecture, 30 October 2007, at http://www.clb.org.hk/chi/node/140745.

Yu, Xingzhong, 'Judicial professionalism in China: from discourse to practice', in William P. Alford, Kenneth Winston and William C. Kirby (eds.), *Prospects for Professionalism in China: Essays on Civic Vocations*, Routledge, London: 2009.

Yuan, Qi, Zou, Guoliang and Wen, Chaoli (袁起，邹国良，文朝利), 60 年语录 (1949–2009): 60 年共和国的沧桑巨变 [*Quotations from 60 years (1949–2009): 60 years of vicissitudes in the Republic*], China Development Press, Beijing: 2009.

Zhang, Sizhi and Xiao, Hong (张思之、晓虹), '张思之: 律师应站在公权力的对立面 [Zhang Sizhi: the lawyer should stand opposed to public power]', in 腾讯-深度对话第71期 (Tengxun In-depth Dialogue no. 71), 16 June 2010, at http://www.politicalchina.org/printnews.asp?newsid=179588.

Websites, blog and microblog entries

Confucius, *Analects*, excerpt at http://www.guoxue.com/gxrm/gxrm-24.htm.

Definition of *yuan*, Dictionary, at http://tw.18dao.net/%E6%BC%A2%E8%AA%9E%E8%A9%9E%E5%85%B8/%E5%86%A4.

Great Qing Code [大清律例] excerpt, at http://www.dushu.com/showbook/101196/1042017.html.

Scientific Development Perspective Archive [科学发展观重要论述摘编], at http://theory.people.com.cn/GB/68294/137720.

Theobald, Ulrich, entry on 'Master Deng Xi' at *China Knowledge* website, http://www.chinaknowledge.de/Literature/Diverse/dengxizi.html.

Website devoted to Robert van Gulik's work on Judge Di, at http://www.ude.de/gulik/.

Xinhua News, '胡锦涛在学习贯彻"三个代表"重要思想理论研讨会作重要讲话：真心学三个代表 立党为公执政为民是标志 [Hu Jintao gives an important speech during the study meeting for the earnest study of the guiding thoughts of the "Three Represents": sincerely studying the Three Represents, establishing the party in the common interest, and governing for the good of the people should be [our] aims]', 1 July 2003, at http://news.xinhuanet.com/newscenter/2003-07/01/content_948197.htm.

Xinhua News, '本网记者现场直击孙志刚案庭审 [Live broadcast on the criminal trial in the Sun Zhigang case]', 20 June 2003, at http://news.xinhuanet.com/newmedia/2003-06/10/content_911471.htm.

Presentations and recorded speeches

Du, Jin, 'Lawyers in the Ming and Song dynasties', presentation at a public research seminar, the Chinese University of Hong Kong, 25 April 2013.

He Weifang, '贺卫方教授演讲实录 —— 中国律师的时代使命 [Transcript of Professor He Weifang's speech – the mission of the Chinese lawyer]', 6 September 2002, at http://bbs.esnai.com/thread-1636077-1-1.html, http://news.xinhuanet.com/newscenter/2002-09/06/content_552721.htm.

3 The place of rights advocacy in 'the system'

[I]n all systems whose origin lies in Leninism, there is a need to suppress enemies incessantly in order to keep up mobilisation within [the Party]. Since they no longer have a political theory, they now must rely on material interests to maintain unity. But with the passage of time, that, too, weakens. Then one [official] starts questioning, 'Why are you a division head and I am only a section head?' So they have to find new enemies, Falun Gong, Tibetans, Uighurs, rights defenders, underground religions, and so on, to persuade [their own people] that 'if we don't stand together, we can't control them.'[1]

A number of factors determine the place of rights and rights advocacy in China. These include the design of the legal system as part of a wider 'system' (*tizhi*),[2] the status of rights in the legal system and vis-à-vis the Party, the nature of major grievances and rights violations the system produces, and mechanisms and practices that limit lawyers' ability to use rights to challenge and improve the system effectively from within. Because of these factors, rights lawyers' ethical obligations, in many other systems defined by the justified expectations of clients, on the one hand, and those of the wider public (or the State) and legal profession, on the other, are here almost exclusively felt toward their clients, whom they regard as victimised by the system, and with whom they come to identify the more they themselves are marginalised.

Rights' place in the system: overview

Many common grievances affect a number of different rights including the right of access to justice;[3] which can require rights defenders to decide on where

---

1 # 25 2013-1(3).
2 In Chinese characters, 体制.
3 On the broader topic of access to justice in China, Jayshree Bajoria, 'Access to justice in China', 16 April 2008, at http://www.cfr.org/china/access-justice-china/p15745; Fu Hualing. 'Access to justice in China: potentials, limits, and alternatives', draft (September 2009), at http://papers.ssrn.com/sol3/papers.cfm?abstract_id=1474073. International law does not explicitly protect an abstract right to access to justice but this right is implicit in substantive and procedural rights

they should concentrate their efforts; and the chances of succeeding in rights defence cases vary also depending on what and whose rights are involved, as well as on how (if at all) the authorities try to justify rights violations. In this context, it is first necessary to consider the place of rights in the wider legal–political system.

Scholarly debates about rights in 'the system'

As noted earlier, the 1982 Constitution's Chapters 1 and 2 (about State organisation and rights, respectively) manifest an inherent tension, which directly affects the place of rights in 'the system.'[4] The principles of 'democratic centralism' and 'People's democratic dictatorship', on the one hand, constitute rule by theoretically undivided power, since the interests of the Party and of the people are, at least in orthodox Party perspective, always identical.[5] On the other, the rights listed in Chapter 2 of the Constitution presuppose a principle of clear limitation of public power by rights, which would at least require judicial institutions with a mandate to enforce rights against the institutions exercising public power.

Taken at face value, the Constitution in its Chapter 2 does guarantee a number of fundamental rights, including the right to equality before the law, the right to vote, freedom of speech, freedom of assembly and association, freedom of religion, freedom and security of the person, freedom from insult, freedom from violation of the home and the privacy of correspondence. This also includes certain socioeconomic rights. The Constitution's Article 5 states that 'All state organs, the armed forces, all political parties and public organisations and all enterprises and institutions must abide by the Constitution and the law. All acts in violation of the Constitution and the law must be investigated. No individuals or organisations are above the Constitution or the law.' An amendment in 2004 added the phrase 'the State respects and preserves human rights' to Article 33. The Constitution also lists duties of citizens including the right and duty to work (Article 42) and the duties to safeguard China's unity, honour and defend the motherland, and to safeguard the Constitution (Articles 52–55). It also stipulates in its Article 51 that the exercise of constitutional rights may not 'infringe upon the interests of the State, of society or of the collective, or upon the lawful freedoms and rights of other citizens.' While this language indicates some difference from liberal democratic constitutions, the Constitution's rights catalogue is open to liberal–restrictive interpretation, and broadly similar to that of liberal democracies.

At the international level, China is State party to a number of important human rights treaties, including notably the International Covenant on Social,

(see for example Article 2 ICCPR, Article 8 UDHR). Relevant domestic constitutional provisions include Articles 33, 37 and 41 of the PRC Constitution.

4 See discussion in Chapter 2.

5 Wu Tiaohe (吴调和), '党是人民利益的代表 [The Party is the Representative of the People's Interests]', *Shi Dai Chao Magazine* (时代潮), 2006/3, at http://www.people.com.cn/GB/paper83/16850/1480483.html, accessed 22 December 2013. On democratic centralism (民主集中制), see also Chapter 2.

Economic and Cultural Rights (ICSECR) and the Convention against Torture, and it has signed (albeit not yet ratified) the International Covenant on Civil and Political Rights (ICCPR).[6] An ever growing body of legislation hierarchically ranking beneath constitutional guarantees created in the reform and opening era concretises certain constitutional rights in the NPC (statutory) laws such as the Criminal and Administrative Procedure Laws and the Property Rights Law.

Groups of centrally important protected rights include, first, social and economic rights.[7] Second, there are liberty and security of the person: the Constitution protects in Article 37 the personal liberty and bodily integrity of Chinese citizens, as do the ICCPR and ICESCR. A number of further statutory and other provisions outlaw or criminalise certain uses of violence by the State against its citizens. Third, the Constitution (Articles 35 and 36) and laws protect the rights to freedom of speech, assembly and association and of religion; and Article 41 articulates a right to submit complaints and suggestions to the State authorities.[8] Article 33 of the Constitution safeguards the principle of equality before the law, and Article 48 explicitly stipulates equal rights for women. Although partly modelled on Soviet-style (Leninist) constitutions, the provisions of the PRC Constitution evoke the general idea of what Hart described as 'the distinctive structure of a municipal legal system' on which his descriptive analysis of the concept of law was based[9] – a legal system in which legislative, adjudicative and administrative functions are separated out into different institutions (the People's congresses, the People's courts and the People's government) and in which authoritative propositions of law can be identified in accordance with formal criteria. According to the PRC Constitution, the NPC is the highest legal authority; in addition to legislation, it has the function of appointing high officials of the other branches of government, of ensuring the enforcement of the Constitution and of interpreting NPC legislation (Articles 62 and 67 on NPC Standing Committee (NPCSC)). Article 126 of the Constitution stipulates that the courts adjudicate cases independently.

Since the beginning of the reform era, liberal scholars who are part of institutionalised academia (sometimes referred to as the 'liberal faction' or *ziyoupai*)[10] have argued for mechanisms that could strengthen the institutional protection of rights, such as judicial independence and rights restrictions only by NPC legislation. In making these arguments, scholars such as Jiang Ping, Xia Yong, He Weifang, Cai Dingjian and Zhang Qianfan, have exerted great influence on

---

6 See Bayefsky, 'The United Nations Human Rights treaties – China', as of 20 September 2011, at http://www.bayefsky.com/bycategory.php/state/36. For a discussion of the relationship between domestic law and international law, see Bjoern Ahl, 'Chinese law and international treaties', 39 *Hong Kong Law Journal* (2009), at http://www.cesl.edu.cn/eng/upload/201106214048086.pdf.

7 The phrase *shengcun quan* (生存权), often used in these contexts, in its narrower meaning captures the right to livelihood or subsistence.

8 Cp. Mindy Kristen Longanecker, 'No room for dissent: China's laws against disturbing social order undermine its commitment to free speech and hamper the rule of law', 18 *Pacific Rim Law & Policy Review* 2 (2009).

9 H.L.A. Hart, *The Concept of Law*, 2nd ed., Oxford University Press, Oxford: 1994, e.g. at p. 17.

10 In Chinese characters, 自由派.

those who have received legal training. Even though the majority of scholars might be cautious to identify with particularly outspoken liberals,[11] such as He Weifang, Xiao Han and Zhang Xuezhong, it is reasonable to expect that the majority of law graduates have imbibed basic beliefs in the role of law and constitutional rights in curbing public power; and the Party–State discourse of *yi fa zhi guo*[12] has in some ways supported the liberal legal discourse.[13]

Rights and the Party

A challenge liberal scholars face, however, is how to account for the role of the Party. Discussions of the Party in published textbooks are generally limited to an abstract level. For example, a collection of lectures by Zhang Qianfan, a liberal constitutional scholar, discusses 'political parties' in one chapter, the first four sections of which are devoted to the function of political parties in western liberal multiparty systems. The fifth section discusses the Party structure in China, addressing the existence of so-called 'democratic parties' (or 'satellites') in addition to the Party, explaining the function of Party Central's 2002 *Regulations on Selection and Appointment of Party and Government Cadres*,[14] the implications of dualist government and Party committees at village governance level, and calling for a 'rule-of-law transformation of the governance model':

> The traditional model of governance has been one of 'power concentration': in the whole of the State, control by the ruling Party's organisations permeates all corners of society. At the centre, the ruling party controls subordinate Party organisations through a top-down system of governance and, by extension, government at all local levels. Internal to the Party, power is concentrated in one highest-level organisation [*jituan*],[15] and at times even in the person of a particular leader ... [T]he long-standing practice of this governance model and the democratic and rule-of-law ideals manifested in the Constitution are in some tension.[16]

Zhang Qianfan has also observed that not only does the Party control State agencies, but also it is not part of the constitutional framework, as it is only mentioned in the Constitution's Preamble. The Party and its 'satellites' are not registered as legal entities in China, 'thus leaving no ground for estimating their legal status and capacities.'[17] Regarding the difficult but centrally important question of whether

---

11 Aaro Samuli Seppänen, *Useful Paradoxes: Ideological Conflicts in the Chinese Rule of Law Discourse*, PhD dissertation, Harvard, September 2012; draft on file with author; at pp. 162 ff.
12 In Chinese characters, 依法治国.
13 Discussed in Chapter 2.
14 Zhang Qianfan (张千帆), 宪法学讲义 [Constitutional Law Lectures], Peking, 2011, at p. 407.
15 In Chinese characters, 集团.
16 Zhang Qianfan, *ibid.*, at p. 409 (存在着一定的紧张关系).
17 Zhang Qianfan's *The Constitution of China. A Contextual Analysis*, also discusses the role of the Party as the originator of rules called 'latent', *ibid.*, at pp. 97 ff., an expression drawing on the scholar Wu Si's work.

or how the Party as an organisation is subject to the law's coercive rules and principles, scholars have suggested that as an 'organisation' in the sense of Article 5 of the PRC Constitution, it is, like its members as individual persons, subject to the Constitution and laws.[18] But the Party's potential legal liability for rights violations remains an abstract possibility, and arguments addressing more specific problems for which the Party might be accountable can attract censorship and criticism as 'subversive', as in the case of constitutional scholars He Weifang, who suggested that a Party breakup into opposed forces could be beneficial,[19] and Zhang Xuezhong, who lost his academic position over the publication of an electronic book, *The New Common Sense – The Nature and Effects of One-Party Dictatorship*.[20]

From a liberal perspective, the strategy of the Sun Zhigang Incident seems appropriate:[21] the strategy of assuming that the system the text of the PRC Constitution envisages (or seems to promise)[22] will at some point be implemented. For this to happen, however, the State must be treated as if it were not a Party–State – as though public power were only that which was legitimately held by the authorities of the State, as set out in the Constitution, but not the greater power that is in fact wielded by the Party.[23] While liberal scholars are therefore critical of the existing political–legal structure – and in doing so they may rely on calls for a separation of the Party and the State in the 1980s[24] – they might sometimes also, on an admittedly uncharitable reading, be taken to lend support to a charade that helps the Party to obscure its role. Although this may not be intended, the strategy of 'taking the play for real' risks perpetuating the belief, potentially useful to the authorities, that China is in the process of reforms aiming to realise the liberal constitutional model. It may support the view that advances toward the rule of law can be ensured only if change is allowed as a process of corrective, incremental reforms and if nobody rocks the boat too badly, a position which some liberal constitutional and political scholars outside China, such as for instance

---

18 Seppänen, *supra*, at p. 180 attributes this view to Xin Chunying.
19 He Weifang, *In the Name of Justice: Striving for the Rule of Law in China*, Brookings Institute Press, Washington, DC: 2013, Chinese People's Liberation Army National Defence University (中国人民解放军国防大学), '较量无声 [Silent Contest]', 2013, available at http://www.youtube.com/watch?v=M_8lSjcoSW8 (accessed 31 December 2013), a propaganda film, suggests He Weifang is connected to western enemy forces.
20 Electronic copy on file with author. Andrew Jacobs, 'Chinese professor who advocated free speech is fired', *New York Times*, 10 December 2013, at http://www.nytimes.com/2013/12/11/world/asia/chinese-professor-who-advocated-free-speech-is-fired.html?_r=0.
21 Sun Zhigang's death in a custody and repatriation centre led to the State Council's revocation of a regulation on 'Custody and Repatriation' regulation criticised as unconstitutional (discussed in Chapter 2).
22 Albert Chen uses the insightful characterisation of the PRC Constitution as a 'semantic' one: Albert H.Y. Chen, 'Constitutions and values in three Chinese societies', working paper, 17 September 2009, at http://ssrn.com/abstract=1474731 p. 10.
23 Zhang Qianfan, *ibid.*, questions explicitly how an organisation consisting of 6% of the population can represent the people as a whole (at p. 409).
24 Kenneth G. Lieberthal and David M. Lampton characterise the relationship between the Party and the State as one between 'principal and agent', in *Bureaucracy, Politics and Decision-making in Post-Mao China* (1992), Part One; available at http://publishing.cdlib.org/ucpressebooks/view?docId=ft0k40035t;brand=ucpress.

Wang Tiancheng and Mo Zhixu, reject.[25] It can also encourage adherence to a formalist conception of law and focus on the idea of legal authority – the belief that such authority originates from the words of the Constitution and from legislative enactment, as procedural criteria of validity.

Some scholars critical of the 'liberal faction' have proposed a different way of understanding China's constitution, namely, in the words of Jiang Shigong, as an 'unwritten' one, which in addition to the PRC Constitution as text accounts for 'constitutional customs' and other propositions that allow such scholars to describe the role of the Party as paramount.[26] It is no accident that Jiang Shigong has been the main translator of Carl Schmitt's work into Chinese, and that Zhu Suli, author of some essays defending Party leadership on pragmatist grounds, is the most important translator of Richard Posner.[27] Drawing on authoritarian or (morally more attractive) utilitarian theories, their accounts focus more on the reality of political–legal practices; they better capture the system's own utilitarian and authoritarian (or paternalistic or totalitarian) arguments seeking to justify some of its systematic rights violations. The challenge these accounts face, in turn, is that they may abandon critical distance from the power structure they describe and, indeed, to varying degrees embrace and support the existing power structure. Like those of the conservative socialists their theories cannot adequately account for the idea of rights.

While conservative socialists embrace the Marxist position that law (and by implication, rights) is in contradiction with the aims of socialism, hence useful only in limited contexts and so far as subject to Party prerogatives, and damaging when it promotes capitalist values (such as private property),[28] less orthodox scholars supportive of existing power structures and policies, are less clear in their stances on rights. Officials of the Party and State maintain a similar ambivalence, with high-level directives under the new Xi Jinping leadership rejecting the 'western' idea of human rights as a universal value,[29] even as human rights remains a staple topic of international relations and as China joins the UN Human Rights Council.

---

25 Wang Tiancheng (王天成) is critical of reform incrementalism (渐进改革主义) in 大转型——中国民主化战略研究框架 [The great transition – a framework for studying strategies of democratisation in China], Hong Kong: 2012 (especially Chapters 5, 7, 8). #2 2013-11.

26 Jiang Shigong (强世功), 'Written and unwritten constitutions: a new approach to the study of constitutional government in China', [中国宪法中的不成文宪法——理解中国宪法的新视角], 36 *Modern China* 1 (2010) 12–46, at http://www.lishiyushehui.cn/modules/topic/detail.php?topic_id=282, accessed 27 October, 2013; Jiang Shigong (强世功), 图施耐特和"大众宪法", [Tushnet and the "populist constitutional law"], 11 *Dushu* (读书(2004) 122–131, at http://www.civillaw.com.cn/article/default.asp?id=55048, accessed 27 October 2013.

27 Cp. Zhu Suli (朱苏力), 波斯纳及其他——译书之后 [Posner and other matters – after translating his book], Beijing: 2004.

28 For a discussion of conservative socialists including Luo Gan, Gong Xiantian and Lin Zhe, see Seppänen, *supra* (Chapter 3).

29 ChinaFile, 'Document No. 9', at http://www.chinafile.com/document-9-chinafile-translation, accessed 30 December 2013 (with further links). See also Liu Jie, 'A biased view of China', *China Daily*, 30 January 2012, at http://www.chinadaily.com.cn/cndy/2012-01/30/content_14502312.htm; Dong Yunhu, Chang Jian (董云虎, 常健, editors), *Six Decades of Building Human Rights in China* (中国人权建设 60 年), Jiangxi People's Press, Nanchang: 2009.

Rights lawyers' perspective on 'the system'

Without (for the most part) actively participating in academic debates, practising lawyers bring an important perspective to the understanding of the constitutional structure, because they are daily confronted with practical aspects of the system. Rights lawyers are attracted to liberal positions; and they, too, use the strategy of speaking to the State as though there were no Party; but in their line of work, there is little point in pretending not to see the Party's role in the system as it actually functions, and their confrontations with the authorities compel them to engage with the 'justifications' the system offers. Like liberal scholars, they call for respect for the written norms of PRC law 'as if' these were taken seriously by the Party–State; but rights lawyers are also compelled to realise that human rights advocacy is on principle subversive of the political power concentration the system favours.

'The system' (*tizhi*)[30] as rights lawyers, academic critics and others discuss it, is that of the Party–State with its interconnected institutions.[31] It includes the formal political–legal institutions of the Party–State; but also those other political actors that are under the Party–State's control.[32] Thus, 'the system' as a concept is quite open; but talking about the system means clearly to include the Party and its various agencies. For example, in discussing the judicial process one would account for the role of the so-called legal and political committees of the Party; and in discussing detention systems one would account for 610 offices in charge of handling Falun Gong practitioners, Discipline and Inspection Commission as the entity handling investigation of Party members, and petitioning offices running 'black (unofficial) jails'. In discussing academia, it would be understood that the academic establishment, so far as it is under Party–State control, is part of the system; as are in most contexts the lawyers' organisations such as the All China Lawyers' Association, whose role is discussed in Chapter 5. 'The system' in these usages represents an antithesis to a political community whose institutions of government and the State can be meaningfully juxtaposed with those of civil society.[33] Despite many differences, the system to that extent resembles those of eastern European countries where dissidents called for the establishment of a civil society, for 'living as if' in ways similar to 'taking the play for real'.[34]

30 In Chinese characters, 体制.
31 For exemplary uses of 'the system', see e.g. Zhang Boshu (张博树), 中共党专制逻辑的 28 个命题 [28 Propositions concerning the CCP's Dictatorship]', 109 *Human Rights in China Biweekly* (中国人权双周刊 (12 July–25 July 2013), at http://city.mirrorbooks.com/news/?action-viewnews-itemid-95190, accessed 25 December 2013.
32 See, further, Susan Lawrence and Michael S. Martin, 'Understanding China's political system', *Congressional Research Service Paper*, 20 March 2013, at www.fas.org/sgp/**crs**/row/R41007.pdf.
33 Some scholars inside and outside China continue to argue that China does not have a civil society (yet). See, for example, Jean-Philippe Béja in *Civil Society against Democracy?*, Conference paper on file with the author; http://www.usc.cuhk.edu.hk/PaperCollection/Details.aspx?id=7423.
34 Entry on Adam Michnik, *A Dictionary of Political Biography*, at http://www.oxfordreference.com/view/10.1093/oi/authority.20110803100155343, accessed 25 December 2013; Chen Yongmiao (陈永苗) makes explicit references to Michnik in '大陆沦陷区的"民国党人" [The "Republicans"

This language cuts through the distinction between the Party and the State that is cultivated in legal establishment discourses. The use of expressions such as 'inside' or 'outside the system' (*tizhi nei/ tizhi wai*)[35] captures, albeit in an imprecise way, a person's or organisation's attitude toward or position vis-à-vis the system. Similarly, the expression *kao tizhi*,[36] 'relying on the system', generally indicates the use of contacts and other ways of getting things done that are favoured by the system. When lawyers or journalists, for example, 'rely on the system', this may require accepting compromises between what is professionally desirable and what is required to stay safe and supported by 'the system'.

It is in facing this system that lawyers seek to defend rights safeguarded in the laws, the Constitution and international treaties. Their progress through the institutions of the legal system, too, is shaped by the characteristics of this wider system. The fact that constitutional rights and rights safeguarded by international treaties to which the Chinese State is a party cannot be protected by judicial means[37] is therefore only part of the problem. Another part is that even if constitutional rights were enforceable through an adjudicative mechanism, the conceptual framework within which they are expected to function does not clearly envisage the Party as possible perpetrator of rights violations. For this reason, rights lawyers not only make reference to the abstract provisions of the Constitution as if these provisions could be cited in judicial contexts. They and their sympathisers take the further step of challenging the existing order as illegitimate, arguing 'as if' the ICCPR and other central human rights treaties had been fully recognised by the authorities; and complaining about individual rights violations. Thus, a joint human rights lawyer appeal combined the call for the establishment of a constitutional court with that for the release of all prisoners of conscience, naming 44 such prisoners criminally detained in the first nine months of 2013, and characterising them as 'the nation's conscience and the country's backbone'. It added the observation:

> If they do not have the basic rights of citizens, 'the people' will always be subjects, never citizens.
>
> A 'State' that does not protect its citizens' basic rights is never a People's Republic but always a dictatorship.[38]
>
> A 'Constitution' that cannot protect the citizens' basic rights is not a 'Constitution' but, rather, waste paper.[39]

---

on the Occupied Territory of the Mainland]', 8 June 2012 at http://www.peacehall.com/news/gb/pubvp/2012/06/201206082208.shtml, accessed 25 December 2013.

35 In Chinese characters, 体制内 / 体制外.
36 In Chinese characters, 靠体制.
37 See discussion below.
38 In Chinese characters, 专政.
39 'Chinese human rights lawyers: appeal to safeguard human rights and realise constitutional government', 4 December 2013, at http://www.siweiluozi.net/, accessed 10 December 2013.

Encountering common grievances

> After I joined Lawyer X's law firm [in 2004], I started meeting many petitioners. I began to understand their lives and learned about the unfair treatment they had suffered. My first reaction was shock, because before, all the information we got, at school and in society, was always glorious. How wonderful this society was, how ordinary people's lives were getting better and better all the time: we mostly heard about those things. Then when I got [to the new firm], suddenly what I heard was almost exclusively negative.[40]

A wide spectrum of wrongs forms the basis of rights lawyering in China. Common grievances include criminal process wrongs such as torture, wrongful convictions and extrajudicial incarceration;[41] forced evictions, housing demolitions and land expropriations; food and medicine poisoning; forced abortions; discrimination; internet censorship; labour rights violations; 'law enforcement' abuses; psychiatric and other medical abuses; official corruption and official dereliction of duty; and pollution of the air, soil and groundwater.

Until the rise of the Chinese internet some 10 or 15 years ago, there were few opportunities even for learning about them and censorship continues to limit our understanding of them. Only some of these social grievances, sometimes expressed through jokes and verses,[42] translate into human rights-based complaints, and some centrally important human rights concerns can hardly be called popular grievances; among these are the rights of the LGBT community and to some extent rights against gender-based discrimination, because discrimination in these areas is socially entrenched.

The young lawyer cited above reported shock and, later, a sense of empathy and obligation toward victims of rights violations. A number of lawyers reported in similar ways how a particular case, a particular client, touched them and started them on a career of rights defence, sometimes right at the beginning of their professional careers, in other cases after many years of practice. Cases and encounters that are remembered as significant to the lawyer's further career development include, for example, seeking civil compensation from the lawyer's home region for a girl crushed to death in a motor accident; seeking civil

---

40 #14 2010-1.
41 In the context of criminal justice, the death penalty is also a human rights violation according to the view taken here. But, case advocacy generally focuses on death sentences as wrongful for an independent reason such as the innocence of the defendant. The group 'China Against Death Penalty' (http://www.cadpnet.org/en/show.asp?ID=146, accessed 31 December 2013) engages both in criminal defence and wider advocacy against the death penalty as such.
42 Such as for instance the following one: 'The people have money – you embezzle it; the people have women – you rape them; the people have homes – you demolish them; the people have comments – you delete them; the people have difficulties – you make a show [of being concerned] about them; the people have wrongs – you lock them up; the people have concerns – you delay handling them; the people have doubts – you fabricate [answers]; the people have property – you move it aside; the people have sufferings – you evade dealing with them; the people have unborn children – you abort them; the people have stalls – you overturn them. The people call you bastards, but you call yourselves father-and-mother officials.' On file with author, from an online-based chat group including some 130 human rights lawyers, December 2013.

compensation for negligent injury of a young boy (in the case of Gao Zhisheng);[43] land-grab cases (these became 'trigger' cases for several lawyers); seeking civil compensation for a person beaten to death in police detention; the criminal defence of students involved in political discussions; criminal defence for a person persecuted for their religion; and the experience, while still working as a public prosecutor, of seeking to convince superiors at the People's Procuracy that the case against a defendant was flawed because he had obviously been badly tortured and had retracted his confession at trial.[44] In all of these cases, the encounter with a client focused their attention on the fate of the individual for whom they came to feel responsible, sometimes in emotionally complex ways. In the case of the tortured defendant, for example, despite the interlocutor's strenuous efforts to obtain a review of the evidence by remonstrating with his superiors, the defendant was convicted and executed; and this case appeared to weigh on his mind even more than the experiences of supervising executions, some of which were botched.

It seemed that cases in which the Party–State's agencies had deprived clients of their liberty or injured or killed them were most likely to produce such deep impressions. But it is one of the peculiarities of the Chinese system that such cases can arise in widely different legal contexts including not only the criminal process but also, for example, land and eviction disputes, disputes around online and offline expression, disputes about legal residency status and petitioning. In all these cases, the system can come down with full force on a person deemed guilty of infraction, sometimes, even of minor rules, or considered to present a threat to a Party–State goal of overwhelming importance, such as 'stability preservation'.[45] Depending on the specific context, the connections between Party, State and other actors can be crucial for understanding the nature of the injustice; an experience of total, concentrated power or *jiquan*[46] that Ai Weiwei (in conversation with Herta Mueller) once called hard to describe and compared to 'rain – you know what it's like when you stand in it.'[47] The experience of being caught up in injustice and seeking redress can make individuals feel that they are up against a power that has many means, including but not limited to those of the legal process, at its disposal to subdue and coerce them. While violence and restrictions of liberty are extremely important, there are significant other means, techniques, and powers: the ability of the system, for example, to get an employer to fire

---

43 Gao Zhisheng, *A China More Just*, Broad Press USA, New York: 2007, Chapter 3.
44 These examples draw on a number of conversations including #6 2011-1; #14 2010-1; #19 2011-1; #21 2010-1; #22 2010-1; #252013-3; #62 2012-1; #85 2013-1; #95 2013-1.
45 Rights lawyers frequently cited the common phrase, 维稳压倒一切 – 'stability preservation trumps everything.' In its earlier form '稳定压倒一切', 'stability trumps everything', it can be traced back to 4 June. On the current form, see Guangzhou Daily, 孟建柱赴乌鲁木齐指导维稳强调当前新疆工作维稳压倒一切 [Meng Jianzhu travels to Urumqi to guide stability preservation, emphasises that in current work in China, stability preservation trumps everything]', 5 September 2009, at http://gzdaily.dayoo.com/html/2009-09/05/content_692660.htm, accessed 1 January 2014.
46 In Chinese characters, 集权.
47 Ai Xiaoming (艾晓明), 艾晓明访艾未未谈网络、艺术与公民问责 [Ai Xiaoming visits Ai Weiwei, discusses the internet, art and civic responsibility], 25 November 2013, at http://canyu.org/n81956c9.aspx, accessed 26 December 2013.

a person, get a landlord to terminate a private rental contract, get an internet company to shut down a client's blog and get a school to deny admission to a targeted person's child. In all of the preceding examples, the security apparatus may be thought to be involved; but this is not always evident.

The Party–State does not seek to justify all of the rights violations that occur; indeed it has outlawed and criminalised many. But, its welfare–utilitarian and authoritarian (post-totalitarian) outlook explains the systemic nature of some of these violations, including the systematic perpetration of certain crimes such as torture by the Party–State.

Grievances stemming from social and economic rights violations

Among the cases arising from experiences of exploitation, dispossession, and material deprivation, forced evictions and land-grabs (usually taking the form of expropriations) are a notable example. They are widely understood to be one of the major causes of social discontent and unrest in China. At least 50 million rural citizens are said to have been affected by land takings (expropriation) decisions, according to Chinese government figures.[48] Rural citizens lose land held in socialist collective ownership, and are often compelled to abandon their former homes and move elsewhere, while their homes are destroyed and the land used for projects such as infrastructure or urban construction. Adding to this number are those evicted from their urban homes, standing on land already State owned.[49] The law provides for compensation as well as resettlement according to a complex system of rules; but for myriad reasons, it may fail to make adequate provision, especially in rural cases; and evictees do not get to share in the benefits derived by officials and property developers from acquiring the land they lived on. An unknown fraction of those affected by expropriations and evictions are not satisfied and are willing to protest. A land expropriation in a major coastal city (for a railway station and residential construction) affected about 8,000 households in 2009, to give an example; and initially a few hundred, but following repression, only a handful of people were willing to complain to the government.[50] To put things in perspective, the Three Gorges Dam project is thought to have caused the relocation of over 1 million people (as of 2012).[51]

48 China Daily, 'Rural land disputes lead to social unrest in China', 6 November 2010, at http://www.chinadaily.com.cn/china/2010-11/06/content_11511194.htm, accessed 26 December 2013.
49 Cp. Eva Pils, 'Contending conceptions of ownership in urbanising China', in Fu Hualing and John Gillespie (eds.), *Resolving Land Disputes in East Asia*, Cambridge University Press, Cambridge: forthcoming; Hua Xinmin (华新民), 华新民：土地私有产权从来就没有消失过, 29 June 2011, at http://news.qq.com/a/20110701/000579.htm, accessed 26 December 2013.
50 The case of Mrs L. and her community is discussed in Eva Pils, 'Waste no land: property, dignity and growth in Urbanising China', 11 *Asian-Pacific Law & Policy Journal* 2 (2010) 1–48, at http://blog.hawaii.edu/aplpj/files/2011/11/APLPJ_11.2_pils.pdf, accessed 26 December 2013.
51 Sui-lee Wee, 'Thousands being moved from China's Three Gorges – again', Reuters, 22 August 2012, at http://www.reuters.com/article/2012/08/22/us-china-threegorges-idUSBRE87L0ZW 20120822. See also: Qian Yanfeng, '"Most homes" to be demolished in 20 years', *China Daily*, 7 August 2010, at http://www.chinadaily.com.cn/china/2010-08/07/content_11113982.htm, accessed 26 December 2013.

Not all these grievances translate easily into legal claims. At the level of domestic law, while Article 13 of the Constitution and lower level legislation rule out expropriations and demolitions not serving a 'public interest need', the practices and power relations are such that a big property developer in 2010 was able to comment that 'as long as it's for urban construction it's always in the public interest';[52] and the State's authorities (including the courts) have been virtually impervious to arguments about public interest. Despite a legislative attempt to define projects *not* in the public interest in the context at least of urban demolitions in 2011, reports about the practice of evictions do not suggest any significant improvements.[53] Although the problems of eviction and land-grab grievances are recognised as factors of social instability, the system clearly also provides continued support for the welfare–utilitarian view that extreme sacrifices can be justifiably exacted from individuals the protection of whose rights would stand in the way of improving aggregate welfare, and the Party–State asserts the power to determine what is good for the people. The official slogans used to convey this message are ubiquitous at eviction sites, for example: 'Support the National Construction Project',[54] 'Thoroughly Implement the Scientific Development Perspective, Build a World City with Chinese Characteristics!' and 'Advance in Solidarity, Revive China, Love the Motherland, Build the Motherland!'[55] The right to housing safeguarded by international human rights law plays virtually no role in institutionalised domestic legal discourse on this topic, although it is occasionally invoked in popular protest.[56] The legal claims evictees are most likely to be able to enforce are those for compensation and resettlement in accordance with the law.

Similar welfare–utilitarian arguments are used to justify a number of other rules and policies with grave rights-violating consequences. These include rules and policies concerning environmental pollution, the household registration system that justifies differential public services, and the system restricting the number of allowed births (often referred to as 'One Child Policy');[57] and these various sets of rules and policies affect one another. Thus, for example, the fact that household registration determines where one is entitled to public services, such as schooling and healthcare, leads to enormous differences in the levels of

52 Yang Ming (杨明), '北京华远集团董事长任志强: 不存在非公共利益拆迁 只要是城建都是公共利益 [Ren Zhiqiang, Chairman of the Board of Beijing Yuayuan Group, comments that there is no such thing as demolition and relocation not in the public interest]', *Liaowang Dongfang Zhoukan* [瞭望东方周刊], 10 February 2012, at http://finance.ifeng.com/opinion/zjgc/20100210/1822226.shtml, accessed 26 December 2013.
53 国有土地上房屋征收与补偿条例 [Regulation on compensation for expropriation of buildings on state-owned land], promulgated by the State Council, effective from 21 January 2011 AI. 2011 regulation.
54 Banner displayed on condemned buildings at an eviction site (Beijing, July 2009), picture on file with author.
55 Billboards (Beijing Taoranting), January 2013, picture on file with author.
56 Examples are discussed in Eva Pils, 'Contending conceptions', *supra*.
57 Relaxation of this policy was announced in December 2013. China News, '全国人大常委会组成人员认为, 国务院有关部门要继续坚持计划生育的基本国策, 依法有序稳妥地实施单独两孩政策', 25 December 2013, at http://www.chinanews.com/gn/2013/12-25/5659946.shtml. As long as birth control as such remains, opportunities for abuse are likely to arise.

such services, and contributes to the problem of migrant worker children not having access to urban public schools, if they live with their parents.[58] The fact that Chinese citizens are, in principle, required to remain in the place of their household registration, where rural residents normally have a share in collective land ownership and access to social services, has contributed to the phenomenon of 'cancer villages' – if the land these rural residents have rights in is polluted, there may be no viable economic alternative to remaining on the polluted land.[59] Under the State-imposed permit system for giving birth, to give another example, the Party–State determines the number of persons allowed to be born, supposedly in accordance with assessments of how many births are likely to serve the goal of general welfare.[60] Again because the systems just mentioned are connected and overlap, so-called 'children born in excess' are routinely denied household registration, which turns them into non-persons without legal status and consequently no access to public services at all, no State ID cards and no entitlement to a passport and has given rise to a practice of demanding a 'social welfare fee' for obtaining a household registration for these excess children.[61] In all these contexts, there is ample opportunity for official rent seeking and other forms of corruption.

Because practices and systems such as land expropriations and housing demolitions, the household registration system and Party–State birth planning meet with resistance, further problems and the potential for rights violations are likely to arise in the context of their implementation and enforcement. For example, the law that requires evictees to enter into compensation agreements with the government leads to use of pressure tactics that can include threats, intimidation and beatings. In the expropriation case just mentioned, the father of a 'holdout' household was badly beaten by unknown thugs, the child was denied access to a local public school on the grounds of her mother protesting and the mother was alternately threatened and given inducements to get her to sign an agreement; as she continued complaining, she was subject to illegal detentions in black jails.[62] Evictions and land-grabs have also been connected to protest suicides, as well as cases of persons dying while resisting violence in

58 Yeqing Huang, Fei Guo and Yiming Tang, 'Hukou Satus and social exclusion of rural-urban migrants in transitional China', 3 *Journal of Asian Public Policy* 2 (2010) 172–185, at http://www.tandfonline.com/doi/pdf/10.1080/17516234.2010.501160; Li Cheng, 'Hukou in a human rights perspective' (2008 Dissertation) available at http://www.duo.uio.no/publ/jus/2008/77477/77477.pdf, accessed 26 December 2013; Eva Pils, 'Citizens? The legal and political status of peasants and peasant migrant workers in China', in Liu Xiangmin (ed.), 制度, 发展与和谐 [System, Development, and Harmony], Hong Kong: 2007, 173–243.

59 Lee Liu, 'Made in China: cancer villages', *Environment Magazine* (March/April 2010), at http://www.environmentmagazine.org/Archives/Back%20Issues/March-April%202010/made-in-china-full.html, accessed 26 December 2013.

60 Li Cheng, 'Hukou in a human rights perspective' (2008 Dissertation) available at http://www.duo.uio.no/publ/jus/2008/77477/77477.pdf, accessed 26 December 2013.

61 Xi Wang (希望, a pen name), '中国14名律师要求审计署公布社会抚养费的去向 [14 lawyers seek public disclosure on where social welfare fees have gone from the National Audit Bureau]', 2 September 2013, at http://www.rfa.org/mandarin/yataibaodao/renquanfazhi/nu-09022013155348.html.

62 Eva Pils, 'Waste no land', *supra*.

eviction or demolition, in some cases in a violent manner, resulting in injury or death of others.[63]

The authorities are more likely to acknowledge and address complaints related to material interests such as can be satisfied with money, than complaints related to immaterial values, civil and political rights, or challenges to their coercive power.[64] For example, government appears to have made efforts to raise compensation levels and improve provisions for those evicted; but the system remains intransigent toward criticism of the land tenure system as such. Rights defenders will emphasise the sense of basic safety and belonging that comes from having a home and is protected by the right to housing; but regardless of the experiences of dislocation and powerlessness they may produce, land expro-priations, demolitions and related issues are generally understood to be not about the 'if' but rather about the 'how', of such measures. There is widespread anger about the system leading to tragedies such as protest suicides, suggesting that the wrongs of forced eviction are not limited to material losses. But facing a multitude of problems evictees and their lawyers, rather than trying to stop evictions, generally focus on stopping uses of Party–State-centred violence in the process, and on obtaining better compensation and resettlement arrangements: 'Those who really don't want to leave are extremely few. The government usually finds some way of getting them to leave. These are issues of negotiation.'[65]

Complainants have better chances of success also in other contexts, if their complaints relate to discrete economic interests that can be satisfied without fundamentally upsetting or challenging the system, its power distribution and power centres. In the area of labour, for example, confrontational collective labour action is considered illegal; officially there are no State-recognised independent labour unions;[66] and labour protest may be criminalised;[67] but

---

63 Amnesty International, 'Standing their ground: thousands face violent evictions in China', released in October 2012, at http://www.amnesty.org/en/library/info/ASA17/001/2012/en, accessed 30 December 2013; Eva Pils, 'Contending conceptions', *supra*. On the problems visited on migrants: Michael Bristow, 'China closes migrant worker schools', 1 September 2011, at http://www.bbc.co.uk/news/world-asia-pacific-14743222, accessed 27 December 2013; Dan Chung and Tania Branigan, 'China's migrant families suffer under hukou', 15 March 2010, at http://www.guardian.co.uk/world/video/2010/mar/15/china-migrant-workers, accessed 27 December 2013; China Law Professor Blog (Donald C. Clarke), 'The famous Hukou editorial', 26 March 2010, at http://lawprofessors.typepad.com/china_law_prof_blog/2010/03/the-famous-hukou-editorial.html, accessed 27 December 2013.
64 The Benthamite utilitarianism of this position is also reflected in the second sentence of Lawyer Tong Lihua (佟丽华), 为了正义/ *Strive for Justice* (Beijing. 2009). 'My understanding of justice is the greatest happiness for the greatest number.' *Ibid.*, at p. 1. Tong Lihua's public interest work is accepted by the authorities.
65 #39 2012-1.
66 The 1995 Labour Law, 1999 Contract Law, 2005 Trade Union Law, 2007 Labour Dispute Mediation and Arbitration Law, 2008 Labour Contract Law and further laws and regulations regulate labour contracts and labour relations. The right to strike was excised from constitutional right guarantees in 1982. Cp. Chang Kai (常凯), '论中国的罢工权立法 [On the Legislation of Right to Strike in China]', 19 February 2011, at http://blog.sina.com.cn/s/blog_51bd78fc0100ogl9.html. See also China Labour Bulletin, 'Unity is strength: the workers' movement 2009–2011, 11 October 2011, at http://www.china-labour.org.hk/en/node/101134, accessed 27 December 2013.
67 China Labour Bulletin, *ibid.*

de facto collective action takes place, and workers mobilise and organise in increasingly complex ways.[68] In individual relationships between employers, back wages is characterised as the most common problem,[69] as worker's compensation stipulated by contract and safeguarded as a human right (cp. ISCESCR Article 7)[70] is often withheld; but labour rights advocacy cases can be won. They are largely taken on by specialised labour rights lawyers, and there are domestic and international NGOs such as *Dagongzu* Services Centre in Guangdong and China Labour Bulletin in Hong Kong, that provide specialised legal advocacy.[71] By comparison, there are no similarly visible domestic 'grassroots' organisations supporting those affected by forced evictions and land expropriations, although some law firms have developed specialisations in evictions;[72] and it is widely thought that eviction disputes are more 'sensitive' because they more directly target government agencies and touch more directly on the fundamentals of the economically so important land tenure system, which gives much power to the government.

Similar differences can be observed in discrimination cases. All aspects of social discrimination can be publicly discussed and criticised; but it is difficult to mount legal challenges to them, especially when – as, for example, with household registration-based discrimination – differential treatment is required or enabled by laws and regulations.[73] Simply put, the more pervasive and Party–State centred a form of discrimination, and the more it is supported by stability and welfare arguments, the harder it is to challenge. Thus, in the area of employment discrimination, civil society groups dedicated to rights protection against disease-based employment discrimination such as the well-known NGO Yirenping have successfully used legislation to challenge persistent discriminatory practices in the context of contagious diseases such as Hepatitis B and AIDS/HIV;[74] and the chief reason why AIDS/HIV discrimination is harder to oppose is that it is more likely to challenge the Party–State. But in the area of *hukou* discrimination, which is based on the laws and regulations of the State,

---

68 China Labour Bulletin, *ibid.*

69 China Labour Bulletin, 'Wages in China', entry, 10 June 2013, at http://www.clb.org.hk/en/node/100206, accessed 27 December 2013.

70 Today's labour contract law recognises non-written employment contracts, reflecting widespread practice. Cp. Mary Gallagher, 'Legislating harmony: labour law reform in China', draft (2008), at http://www.erb.umich.edu/Research/Initiatives/colloquiaPapers/GallagherRevisedPaperJan08.pdf, accessed 27 December 2013.

71 See for their websites, http://blog.sina.com.cn/dgzngo (广东番禺打工族服务部 *Dagongzu* Service Centre) and http://www.clb.org.hk/en/ (China Labour Bulletin), accessed 31 December 2013.

72 Most notably the Beijing Cailiang Law Firm (http://www.cai-liang.com/), accessed 30 December 2013.

73 Timothy Webster, 'Ambivalence and activism: employment discrimination in China', (2011) Vanderbilt Journal of Transnational Law at http://digitalcommons.law.yale.edu/cgi/viewcontent.cgi?article=1000&context=ylas, accessed 27 December 2013.

74 Webster, *ibid.* Also see Zhou Ruiping (周瑞平), '中国首例艾滋病就业歧视案详情披露 [Details of China's first AIDS discrimination case disclosed]', *Legal Weekend* (法治周末), 12 January 2011, at http://news.sina.com.cn/c/sd/2011-01-12/004521799440.shtml, accessed 27 December 2013.

advocacy faces greater challenges despite the pressing challenges produced by discrimination in healthcare, education and other public services. There has as of early 2014 not been a case of effective *hukou*-based employment discrimination litigation accepted and substantively adjudicated by a court;[75] and there is little social mobilisation to promote the rights and interests of rural residents and persons without *hukou*.

In sum, a wide range of different policies implemented in the name of general welfare, affecting such diverse issues as land, housing, birth planning, access to public services, legal recognition as a citizen and resident, labour rights and protection against serious harm from pollution, are taken to justify the view that individual sacrifices are necessary; and justifications are clothed in the language of general welfare, economic development and the 'scientific development perspective', a political slogan coined by Hu Jintao.[76] While a complex multitude of rights may be infringed in these various scenarios and contexts, rights defenders in many of them focus on redressing distributive injustices, in the context of which the Party–State is sometimes responsive to complaints, and on addressing Party–State-centred violence, complaints to which the authorities are generally less responsive.

The discussion above has already shown that from the perspective of these doctrinally held and propagated views, further rights-violating means of enforcing a correct understanding and ensuring compliance are – at some level – justified and systemically practised; they include 'thought education' and various forms of physical coercion. The wider issues of censorship and thought and speech crimes and of system-centred violence are discussed in the following section.

Grievances centred in restrictions of liberty

If the authorities justify restrictions of social and economic rights and indignities inflicted in their wake primarily by (albeit flawed) utilitarian arguments, 'justifications' for uses of various restrictions of thought and personal liberty can often be found in an authoritarian, paternalistic attitude toward citizens; an attitude that in some of its aspects such as 'brainwashing' is reminiscent of the totalitarian systems of the 20th century, and may be accurately called

---

75 Lin Ping (林坪), '中国首例户籍就业歧视案被法院驳回 [China's first hukou discrimination case rejected by the Court]', *Radio Free Asia*, 4 December 2013, at http://www.rfa.org/mandarin/yataibaodao/renquanfazhi/yl-12042013160724.html?searchterm:utf8:ustring=%E6%88%B7%E5%8F%A3, accessed 27 December 2013; Radio Free Asia, 中国多位学者、律师联署呼吁消除计生与户籍捆绑政策 [Several scholars and lawyers in China sign joint statement calling for abolition of restrictive birth control and hukou policies], 5 December 2013, at http://www.rfa.org/mandarin/Xinwen/huji-12062013101031.html? searchterm:utf8:ustring=%E6%88%B7%E5%8F%A3, accessed 27 December 2013.

76 Coined in 2007 this slogan is generally taken to mean a perspective on development that includes growth, but also sustainable development, social welfare, a person-centred society and a harmonious society. See Xinhua Net, '科学发展观 [Scientific Development Perspective]', Xinhua Net, at http://news.xinhuanet.com/ziliao/2005-03/16/content_2704537.htm, accessed 31 December 2013.

'post-totalitarian'.[77] In contrast with the grievances discussed above, however, the law justifies restrictions of liberty of the person and violations of the right to life and physical integrity only within narrow limits. It is recognised that restrictions of personal liberty must be couched in the form of statutory law; and many forms of violence, including physical torture and false imprisonment, are outlawed and have been criminalised.[78] State restrictions on freedom of mind are by contrast much less clearly limited.[79]

Means by which the system restricts the freedom of thought, conscience and expression include administrative censorship and the criminalisation of certain kinds of speech and religious manifestation. Crimes used to curb the right to free speech include social order crimes such as 'creating a disturbance',[80] State secrets crimes,[81] the crimes of subversion and inciting subversion,[82] the crime of

77 The traits and effects of the current system in China are in several respects different from 20th-century totalitarian systems. China does not fulfil all of the criteria drawn up, e.g. by Friedrich and Brzezinski: '(1) an official ideology which is to direct society to a final state of mankind, (2) a hierarchically organised, dictatorially led Party to which the State bureaucracy (and every institution) is subordinated; (3) a politically instructed police terror, directed against arbitrarily defined opponents [and] encompassing the entire population as well as the Party; (4) the State monopoly on information, news and (5) a concentration of all of the means of domination in the hand of the party and the State so that finally (6) the economy becomes subordinated to bureaucratic co-ordination and central control.' Cited in Klaus Mueller, 'East European studies, neo-totalitarianism and social science theory', TIPEC Working Paper 03/7, at www.trentu.ca/tipec/3muller7.pdf, accessed 27 December 2013. The State does not have an information monopoly in China, and the economy is not (entirely) State directed, for example. Neither is Chinese society 'atomised' in the sense of Hannah Arendt, (*The Origins of Totalitarianism*, Harcourt, Brace, Jovanovich, New York: 1973), since citizens can communicate and connect in myriad largely State-independent ways. However, subordination to Party directives, police terror, and a proclaimed Party ideology remain aspects of the current system. If the image of 20th-century totalitarianism is one of squares and stadia filled with people shouting on cue in communication with their leader, today's post-totalitarian one is perhaps that of the person in front of a computer screen, connected but alone; alone but under surveillance via electronic devices or in person, and subject to in some cases instant online censorship.
78 Article 238, 247 and 248 in Criminal Law, CECC translation at http://www.cecc.gov/pages/newLaws/criminalLawENG.php and Article 18, 50 and 54 in Criminal Procedure Law, CECC translation at http://www.cecc.gov/resources/legal-provisions/criminal-procedure-law-of-the-peoples-republic-of-china.
79 There are a few limited areas in which limiting the limitations of free speech is discussed. For example, the introduction of a 'public figure' exception in defamation law contexts has been under discussion for some time. Yi Xing (易兴), 论公众人物的隐私权 [On the Right to Privacy of Public Figures], (2009) available at http://www.civillaw.com.cn/article/default.asp?id=44964, accessed 27 December 2013.
80 Article 293 Criminal Law, CECC, translation at http://www.cecc.gov/pages/newLaws/criminalLawENG.php. Longanecker, *supra*.
81 Article 111 CL, CECC translation at http://www.cecc.gov/pages/newLaws/criminalLawENG.php. HRIC, 'State Secrets: China's Legal Labyrinth' (2009), at http://www.hrichina.org/sites/default/files/PDFs/State-Secrets-Report/HRIC_StateSecrets-Report.pdf, accessed 27 December 2013.
82 Art. 105 (2) CL, CECC translation at http://www.cecc.gov/pages/newLaws/criminalLawENG.php. Teng Biao, (滕彪), 'The political meaning of the crime of "subverting state power"', in Béja, Fu and Pils, *Liu Xiaobo and Challenges of Constitutional Reform in China*.

defamation[83] and of obscenity.[84] It also targets religion: the 'crime' of 'abusing an evil cult to undermine implementation of the law'.[85] Censorship beneath the level of criminalisation potentially affects all areas of professional, social and political life; but, as scholars and other observers have pointed out, has not been effective in suppressing many messages in the era of the internet and social media. While, especially since the social media have allowed citizens to spread their messages ('everybody has a microphone'),[86] censorship has triggered much criticism, satire and resistance, it is only rarely perceived as a judicially actionable grievance; and as discussed below, judicial complaints against some censorship measures have been blocked.

The legal provisions quoted and from further laws and regulations governing censorship, as well as the way they are used in practice, indicate that the Party–State in charge of all this censorship hovers between consequentialist pre-occupation with the social and political effects of expression, and paternalistic, post-totalitarian preoccupation with the eradication of ideas and convictions deemed wrong, just for the sake of ensuring 'correct political thought'. The authorities are unable to police all public (let alone private) expression and are reduced to policing what they consider socially especially harmful. Yet once individuals have been identified as targets of measures to suppress expression, these targets can be subjected to treatments aimed at obtaining statements of repentance and spiritual or political reform from them. When this happens, the post-totalitarian system's measures hark back to the (totalitarian) Mao Zedong era, as some rights lawyers have come to experience for themselves.[87]

The numerous institutions in charge of censorship and internet controls, including the Propaganda or 'Publicity' Department and the State Council Information Office,[88] are also involved in the 'stability preservation' offices whose activities are discussed in Chapter 6; and much censorship is outsourced, for example to internet companies. It is in the nature of 'stability preservation' conducted by these entities that the same content of speech can be treated differentially depending on who the speaker is, and that comments that would not

---

83 Article 243 CL, CECC, translation at http://www.cecc.gov/pages/newLaws/criminalLawENG.php. Joshua D. Rosenzweig, 'China's battle over the right to criticise', *Far Eastern Economic Review*, 5 May 2009.

84 CL Article 246 CL, CECC, translation at http://www.cecc.gov/pages/newLaws/criminal LawENG.php.

85 Article 300 CL, CECC translation at http://www.cecc.gov/pages/newLaws/criminalLawENG.php.

86 The sociologist Yu Jianrong famously used this phrase in an interview. Zhang Xiong, 'Yu Jianrong is all the rage', *Nandu Zhoukan*, 8 December 2010, http://www.nbweekly.com/magazine/cont.aspx? artiID=12431, accessed 27 December 2013; translated by Stacy Mosher in Marina Svensson and Eva Pils, *An Anthology of writings by Professor Yu Jianrong of the Chinese Academy of Social Science in English Translation* [working title].

87 Discussed in Chapter 6.

88 For discussions of the institutions in charge of media censorship, see Isabella Bennet, 'Media censorship in China', Council on Foreign Relations Website, 24 January 2013, at http://www.cfr.org/china/media-censorship-china/p11515, accessed 27 December 2013; David Bandurski, 'What happened at the Beijing News', 15 September 2011, at http://cmp.hku.hk/2011/09/15/15432/, accessed 27 December 2013.

trigger any reaction from the mouth or keyboard of one person become a reason for suppression in the case of another;[89] it is not (in the post-totalitarian era) the content of speech but its social effects that 'justify' repression, as one can see from the rule that criminal prosecutions for social media posts are triggered only if there has been a certain social reaction to a posting, and that also instructs courts to measure the social 'harmfulness' by determining, e.g. the number of downloads/clicks and in content 'subversive' posting has received.[90]

Similarly, faith-based groups are persecuted on the grounds of claimed social or political harmfulness. Members of a variety of faith-based communities, including certain house-churches (unregistered churches), groups drawing on strands of Daoism and Buddhism such as Guanyin Fa Men and Falun Gong have been affected by prosecution under Article 300 of the Criminal Law; as well as by other repression under direction of the so-called 610 Offices, established in 1999 (on 10 June 1999) to deal with investigation, monitoring and controlling Falun Gong,[91] after Falun Gong had provoked the Party–State by staging a demonstration outside the central government complex of Zhongnanhai.[92] Tibetan Buddhism and Islam in Xinjiang have also been affected by especially severe persecution, including criminal prosecutions; and ethnic and religious persecution overlap in these contexts.

The closely related freedoms of assembly and association are also limited. For lawyers, compulsory membership and the Party–State supremacy over social organisations (*shehui tuanti*),[93] as well as the general principle that no more than one civil society organisation for each topic of concern is needed, not only hinder the rise of State-recognised independent lawyers' associations.[94] Reforms in recent years added restrictions on foreign financial support; and relaxed registration requirements for service NGOS have not included advocacy NGOs – the latter have remained more severely restrained.[95] Since 2000, moreover, the

---

89 Teng Biao, *supra*. A lawyer related being called in by the police, 'Only so they could reprimand me and ask me to delete [certain] tweets!' #26 2011-12. The tweets expressed quite general, everyday complaints.

90 Human Rights in China, Liu Xiaobo's 1st and 2nd instance defence statements at http://www.hrichina.org/en/content/3206 and http://www.hrichina.org/en/content/3210, accessed 27 December 2013.

91 Sarah Cook and Leeshai Lemish, 'The 610 Office: policing in the Chinese spirit', 11 *China Brief* 17 (2011), at http://www.jamestown.org/uploads/media/cb_11_43.pdf, accessed 27 December 2013.

92 610 Offices are generally assumed by lawyers to be involved in the judicial process in any Falun Gong case and they are thought to have influence on the judicial decision in all such cases. Their function has reportedly since been expanded to cover other religious groups and to serve wider purposes of 'social management'. Voice of America (Mandarin Desk), 吉林 610 办公室阻 挠律师依法辩护 [A Jilin 610 Office obstructs lawyer's lawful criminal defence], 13 September 2010, at http://www.voanews.com/chinese/news/china/20100913-lawyer-harrased-102769329. html, accessed 27 December 2013. See also #25 T on obstruction of criminal defence lawyers to attend client's trial.

93 In Chinese characters, 社会团体.

94 Wu Fengshi and Chan Kin-man, 'Graduated control and beyond: the evolving government–NGO relations', 3 *China Perspectives* (2012) 9.

95 Wu Fengshi and Chan Kin-man, *ibid.*; Raymond Li, 'Rights groups miss out on easing of registration rules for NGOs', *South China Morning Post*, 12 March 2012, at http://www.scmp.com/

Ministry of Civil Affairs Provisional Measures for Banning Illegal Social Organisations have provided a tool to control organisations trying to exist without registration.[96] The criminal law and parallel systems of punishment can also be used specifically to target civil society associations and assemblies, 'subversive' activities carried out in groups and 'illegal assembly'.[97]

Lawyers and scholars have argued that the criminalisation of expression, association and manifestations of faith is unconstitutional. Regarding speech crimes, some have argued that specific crimes such as that of 'inciting subversion' constitute censorship in violation of the Constitution's guarantee of freedom of speech in Article 35.[98] With slightly different emphasis, others have argued that this constitutional guarantee is empty in the post-totalitarian conditions of the current system. Thus, Teng Biao says, the Party has never abandoned the principle of political power monopoly, and therefore the safeguard for freedom of speech is 'an empty clause, not to say a trap ensnaring those who rely on it'.[99] Rights lawyers' criticism has also addressed the fact that the post-totalitarian Party–State is compelled to apply its punitive rules in a highly arbitrary fashion, because it would be impossible to police everybody's expressed thoughts in the way totalitarian systems attempted to do with (at least) greater success.[100] As Yang Guobin and others have shown, so much expression can evade internet censorship today; and much content that could easily be deemed 'subversive' by the authorities can be spread online and even offline.[101]

Regarding the crime of 'abuse of evil cults to impede the implementation of the law', rights lawyers have argued that in the absence of explicit legislative (statutory) criminalisation of Falun Gong the assessment that Falun Gong was an 'evil cult' was unfounded; that criminal convictions violated freedom of religion, protected by Article 36 of the PRC Constitution, human rights instruments, etc.[102] They have also pointed to the fact that only an SPC judicial opinion serves

news/china/article/1188742/rights-groups-miss-out-easing-registration-rules-ngos, accessed 26 December 2013.
96 取缔非法民间组织暂行办法 [Provisional Measures on Banning Illegal Social Organisations] issued by Ministry of Civil Affairs, 10 April 2000, available in Chinese and English translation at http://www.chinadevelopmentbrief.cn/?p=712, accessed 26 December 2013. Karla Simon discusses these in 'The regulation of civil society organisations in China', (2011), athttp://ssrn.com/abstract=1781075. Also: Karla Simon, *Civil Society in China: The Legal Framework from Ancient Times to the 'New Reform Era'*, Oxford University Press, Oxford: 2013.
97 Article 296 CL, at http://www.cecc.gov/resources/legal-provisions/criminal-law-of-the-peoples-republic-of-china, accessed 26 December 2013.
98 Guo Guoting (郭国汀), 废除或修改煽动颠覆国家政权罪 [Abolish or revise the crime of inciting subversion], at http://blog.boxun.com/hero/200811/guoguoting/3_2.shtm, accessed 27 December 2013.
99 Teng Biao, 'The political meaning of the crime of "subverting state power"', translated from the Chinese by Pinky Choy and Eva Pils, in Jean-Philippe Béja, Fu Hualing and Eva Pils, *Charter 08 and Challenges to Constitutionalism in China*, Hong Kong University Press, Kong Kong.
100 Teng Biao, *ibid.*
101 Yang Guobin, *The Power of the Internet in China: Citizen Activism Online*, Columbia University Press, Columbia, OH: 2009.
102 Article 36, PRC Constitution.

as basis for the classification of Falun Gong as 'evil sect', and to the incoherent internal structure of Article 300:

> The crime [of Article 300 of the CL] is 'using an evil cult to impede the implementation of the law'. The object protected here is the implementation of the law. But how can the implementation of the law be impeded here [by someone practicing their faith in private] – what law, precisely? And if it cannot be, why even bother about the definition of 'evil cult'? It is really a case of 'where there is no hide, there can be no hair.'[103]

Reflecting the connection between the freedom of religion and that of expression and other civil and political rights, some rights lawyers have emphasised that defending freedom of religion is not the same as defending a particular religion; few of those taking Falun Gong cases, for example, are particularly sympathetic to Falun Gong as a faith.[104] An experienced rights lawyer without any religious faith urged fellow lawyers to make this aspect clear in an electronic communication to a group of some 130 fellow lawyers in late 2013:

> Those lawyers who are able to should get more involved in cases concerning faith and ethnic minority issues; and clarify in their [criminal] defence that they are helping others to fight for their rights as opposed to debating the merits or demerits of a particular religion.[105]

Others have emphasised the special importance of taking up the cases of religious persecution of ethnic minorities, in essence making the same point – that rights advocacy must not be ethnically or religiously partisan.[106] While this message is not, apparently, shared by all rights lawyers, interlocutors central to human rights defence for Tibetan and Uighur communities both cited cases where (resisting pressure from the authorities) 'Han' Chinese lawyers had tried to undertake criminal defence for members of their communities.[107]

---

103 #3 2012-1.
104 I am aware of four or five, two of whom were interlocutors in the context of this project. According to the conversations led for this book it seems that rights lawyers have diverse personal attitudes to communities of faith and religions: some are Christians (mostly belonging to different Protestant house-churches), some Buddhist (i.e. belonging to one of the various groups of Buddhism), some Baha'i, some Falun Gong, some belong to indigenous religions close to Taoism. Some have sympathy and interest for communities of faith and religious practices without belonging to any, whereas others express some irritation with faith-based groups and the supposed privileges membership in some of them, such as Protestant Christianity, afford in their view; e.g. #25 2010-2. Some Protestant Christians believe that Christianity and rule of law are intrinsically connected; e.g. #15, 2011-1, 2.
105 #25 2013-6. In a different conversation, one of the interlocutors approached for this project took the view that Christian rights lawyers should focus on the cases of Christian clients. #29 2012-1. This lawyer emphasised that he did not mean other people were not equally deserving of defence of their rights.
106 #2 2013-1b.
107 In 2008, 18 lawyers publicly offered legal assistance to Tibetans who had been detained on suspicion of crimes during the March 2008 Lhasa riots. Teng Biao et al., '我们愿意为被捕藏

The abovementioned criminal provisions and their selective implementation could not be effective without self-censorship induced by fear, induced in an assumed relationship between the system and its subjects. Attempts to direct and control ideas and their expression use methods ranging, to use expressions often used in Chinese, from 'soft' to 'hard;' and many (if not all) deprivations of personal liberty and even forms of torture purport to be for the purpose of educating and reforming those it targets. Whereas soft measures of 'thought work' can include putting pressure on colleagues or relatives to talk to the control target, as well as informal invitations to 'chat' with representatives of the authorities, hard measures are those that affect liberty and bodily integrity of the person and that include torture, as an important tool of what is often called 'thought reform'.

While therefore the right of expression (closely connected to thought, conscience and association), on the one hand, and the right to life, to personal liberty and physical integrity, on the other, are distinct ideas that have generated complex theories and doctrines of their own, their violation can be part of one natural process from the disciplinarian, 'educational' perspective of the authorities intent on making a person comply. Just as positive 'public opinion guidance' complements efforts to censor online speech for the wider population, individuated 'thought work' and similar measures may target specific groups such as the prison and detention centre population, prospective evictees, workers, pregnant women and their relatives. It may be for this reason that there is fluidity to some of these measures, reflected in a euphemistic official vocabulary. 'Persuasion to return' can be forceful repatriation to one's hometown; 'study class' detention; 'thought reform' torture.[108]

Restriction of personal liberty by the State occurs in a variety of contexts, sometimes but not always based in law; and the roles lawyers play in their context differ depending on rules and practices governing detainees' access to lawyers. In the formal criminal justice process, the detention of criminal suspects is common. Both the 1996 and the 2012 Criminal Procedure Law (CPL) provide that it can last for up to 37 days, at the end of which period there must be a decision to recommend indictment or not, followed by the People's Procuracy's

---

民提供法律帮助 [We are willing to provide legal assistance to criminally arrested Tibetans]', 2 April 2008 at Boxun, at http://www.peacehall.com/news/gb/china/2008/04/200804022305. shtml. They encountered retaliation. A Tibetan rights defender mentioned 10 attempts of non-Tibetan, Chinese lawyers to take on Tibetans' criminal defence cases; in only three cases were the lawyers allowed to provide defence. #96 2013-1. An Uighur rights defender mentioned two cases, in both of which the families eventually declined assistance after initial contact with rights lawyers, due to government pressure. #91 2013-1. This interlocutor added that despite these rights lawyers' positive example, bias against Uighurs could be found even among rights lawyers; and noted that no indigenous rights lawyers had emerged in the Uighur community, as repression was too bad there. In 2014, when Uighur scholar Ilham Tohti and others were charged with the crime of separatism, the authorities 'persuaded' one rights lawyer to withdraw from Ilham Tohti's defence and pressurised other suspects' families not to appoint rights lawyers. Rights lawyers Li Fangping and Liu Xiaoyuan were able to act as Tohti's criminal defence lawyers. #115 2014-1.

108 On 'persuasion to return', see Flora Sapio, 'Legal erosion and the policing of petitions', in McConville and Pils, *Comparative Perspectives on Criminal Justice in China*, Edward Elgar Publishing, Cheltenham: 2013.

decision on indictment; but there are various ways of extending criminal investigation detention in accordance with rules, e.g. by sending a case back 'for further investigation;' and investigation detention may be followed by detention awaiting trial after the indictment. Nominally an alternative to investigation detention and detention awaiting trial, 'residential surveillance' can under the 2012 CPL also become the basis for *de facto* detention and, indeed, forced disappearance under international criminal law definition,[109] since the authorities can lock suspects up in holding places not their own residence, and there are no notification requirements and no requirement to give access to lawyers in certain types of case, namely those concerning State security, terrorism, and major corruption.[110] The longest period for such non-residential residential surveillance is twice six months, according to the rules, and it has been used to make certain 'suspects' 'disappear' for lengthy periods.[111] While the 2012 CPL 'guarantees' access to criminal suspects within 48 hours from the time of detention, and despite some evidence to the effect that access to suspects in detention has improved,[112] obstruction especially in 'sensitive' cases remains common.

Then there are a number of forms of detention, whose imposition is not premised on a decision by a judicial institution and which are outside the criminal process, and therefore do not satisfy the requirement of Article 37 of the Constitution in conjunction with Articles 8 and 9 of the 2000 Legislation Law,[113] for deprivation of liberty to be based on NPC law and premised on a judicial or procuratorial decision.[114] (I will here refer to them as 'extrajudicial' detention systems.) The oldest of these extrajudicial systems, the so-called 'Re-education Through Labour' or RTL system, was in use during most of the time during which conversations for the purpose of this book were led, and remains in force as

---

109 Universal Declaration of Human Rights, Article 9; International Covenant on Civil and Political Rights, Article 9; International Convention for the Protection of All Persons from Enforced Disappearances, Article 1; Joshua Rosenzweig, Flora Sapio, Jiang Jue, Teng Biao and Eva Pils, 'The 2012 revision of the Chinese Criminal Procedure Law: (mostly) old wine in new bottles (17 May 2012)', *CRJ Occasional Papers Series* (May 2012), and in Mike McConville and Eva Pils (eds.), *Comparative Perspectives, supra*.

110 Rosenzweig et al., *ibid*.

111 An interlocutor described the case of a client held in a 'legal education centre' (see below) under the rules for 'residential surveillance' for a year, for example. #93 2013-1.

112 Li Wen (李文), 律师刘卫国指警方禁探访许志永违法 [Liu Weiguo points out that the authorities' obstruction of a meeting with Xu Zhiyong is unlawful], 20 July 2013, at http://www.bbc.co.uk/zhongwen/trad/china/2013/07/130720_xuzhiyong_lawyer.shtml, accessed 29 December 2013; Liu Weiguo's open letters, see http://www.hrichina.org/en/content/6841, accessed 29 December 2013.

113 中华人民共和国立法法 [PRC Law on Legislation], promulgated by the Standing Committee of National People's Congress, 15 March 2000, effective July 1, 2000, at http://www.gov.cn/test/2005-08/13/content_22423.htm, accessed 29 December 2013.

114 For a discussion of the arguments challenging the constitutionality of the now-abolished custody and repatriation system, see Keith Hand, 'Using law for a righteous purpose: the Sun Zhigang Incident and evolving forms of citizen action in the People's Republic of China', 45 *Columbia Journal of Transnational Law* (2006) 138, at http://librarysource.uchastings.edu/repository/Hand/45ColumJTransnatlL114.pdf, accessed 29 December 2013. Hand thinks that it is easier to argue such systems violate the Legislation Law, than that they violate the Constitution.

of this writing, even though its abolition has been announced.[115] It is based in a set of State Council and other public rules whose constitutionality has always been persuasively contested, because these rules have not been issued by the only entity authorised to restrict personal liberty, as well as for other reasons.[116] It allows the police on their own authority to imprison a person for up to four years. Targeted groups have involved persons designated as petty criminals, persons who, like petitioners, are deemed socially harmful, and prostitutes. When the abolition of RTL was announced, new concerns arose regarding systems that might come to replace RTL, not least because such systems may be operating in secret. Other forms of extrajudicial detention include drug rehabilitation (used for those designated as drug addicts), shelter for education (used for those designated as prostitutes), and shelter for education and formation (used for juveniles).[117] Challenges to these measures are at least theoretically available, in the form of legal complaints against the authorities that imposed them, also against 'administrative detention' and 'judicial detention', which is in essence an administrative punishment, is imposed by a court as a penalty, but not on the basis of a court process.[118]

Virtually outside the scope of any regulations that lend at least an appearance of lawfulness to such practices and connect them to legally available channels to challenge their imposition lie other forms of detention that do not even purport to have a basis in State law. These include black (i.e. unofficial or illegal) jails, used mostly to detain petitioners, facilities and mechanisms usually called legal education centres (used mostly to detain Falun Gong members) and legal study classes (used to detain petitioners, Falun Gong members and others); and a system

---

115 In November 2013 the Party announced that China would 'put an end to the re-education through labor system, perfect laws on the punishment and correction of crimes and violations, [and] complete the system of community corrections.' See 'CPC Central Committee Decision on Several Major Issues of Deepening Reform', 12 November 2013, translation at http://chinalawtranslate.com/en/cpc-central-committee-decision-on-several-major-issues-of-deepening-reform/ and 全国人大常委会关于废止有关劳动教养法律规定的决定, passed by the Sixth Plenary Meeting of the Standing Committee of the National People's Congress, (第十二届全国人民代表大会常务委员会第六次会议通过) promulgated and effective 28 December 2013, at http://news.xinhuanet.com/legal/2013-12/28/c_118749199.htm, accessed 29 December 2013.

116 For critical discussion and appeals to abolish RTL see e.g. Mao Yushi and others, 'Open letter suggesting the abolition of Re-education Through Labour' (2007), at http://www.aboluowang.com/2007/1204/65722.html, accessed 29 December 2013; Reuters, 'China's Re-education Through Labour system', 20 December 2007, at http://www.reuters.com/video/2007/12/20/chinas-re-education-through-labour?videoId=73011, accessed 29 December 2013; Fu Hualing, 'Re-education Through Labour in historical perspective', *China Quarterly* (2005) 811–830, at http://www.jstor.org/stable/20192540, accessed 29 December 2013.

117 'Statement on abolition of RTL and related problems by Chinese lawyers for the protection of human rights', 19 November 2013, at http://www.siweiluozi.net/2013/11/statement-on-abolition-of-re-education.html; Amnesty International, 'Changing the soup but not the medicine? Abolishing Re-education Through Labour in China', 17 December 2013, at http://www.amnesty.org/en/library/asset/ASA17/042/2013/en/f7e7aec3-e4ed-4d8d-b99b-f6ff6ec860d6/asa170422013en.pdf.

118 Teng Biao, Presentation on the topic of 'Extra-judicial detention', copy on file with author. Sarah Biddulph, 'The production of legal norms: a case study of administrative detention in China', 20 *UCLA Pacific Basin Law Journal* (2003) 217–277.

known by the abbreviation *shuanggui* which is used to detain members of the Party, often prior to handing them over into the criminal process of the State.[119] In addition, incarceration in psychiatric institutions is used, e.g. on diagnoses such as 'litigation mania' or 'paranoia' for 'treatment' sometimes including the forced treatment with drugs.[120] These detention systems are bureaucratised and, as far as it is possible to ascertain, internally well documented; but they are run in secret. Only rarely does documentary evidence of them become publicly available, as in a notice concerning a petitioner sent to 'study class' informs the petitioner, who complained, that he was detained under the authority of a *'secret'* Party document. This detention is in violation of Articles 37 of the Constitution and the legislation law, as well as of the principle that laws must be publicised, and of petitioners' right to go to Beijing to petition, as Don Clarke points out.[121] Although theoretically, the imposition of such forms of detention should be actionable as a concrete administrative act,[122] lawyers generally report that it can only be opposed by bringing complaints about the crime of 'false imprisonment' and by trying to expose such wrongs. While there is one known case of criminal prosecution of operators of a large black jail in Beijing,[123] there is no known case in which rights lawyers successfully initiated a criminal investigation into such detention facilities.

The operation of most detention systems make use of them in its origins Maoist idea of 'thought reform' (*sixiang gaizao*);[124] which typically includes getting the targeted person to confess to their wrongs or crime(s), and/or making them promise that they will change.[125] To judge by lawyers' descriptions and their own experiences, 'hard' methods to achieve the goal of thought reform include not only incarceration but torture.

---

119 Teng Biao, *ibid.*
120 Teng Biao, *ibid.* Human Rights Watch, 'An alleyway in hell: China's abusive "black jails"', 12 November 2009, at http://www.hrw.org/en/reports/2009/11/12/alleyway-hell-0, accessed 29 December 2013; Jane Parry and Weiyuan Cui, 'China's psychiatric hospitals collude with officials to stifle dissent say civil rights groups', 28 June 2010, http://www.bmj.com/content/340/bmj.c3371.extract, accessed 29 December 2013; CHRD, 'The darkest corners: abuses of involuntary psychiatric commitment in China' Report, 22 August 2012, copy on file with author, at http://www2.amnesty.org.uk/blogs/countdown-china/%E2%80%9C-darkest-corners%E2%80%9D-abuses-involuntary-psychiatric-commitment-china, accessed 29 December 2013; Eva Pils, 'Taking *yuan* (冤) seriously: why the Chinese government should stop suppressing citizen protests against injustice', 25 *Temple International and Comparative Law Journal* (2011) 285–327.
121 Donald Clarke, 'Why Chinese needs a good word for "irony", and why it's too soon to bid farewell to re-education through labour', Chinese Law Prof Blog, 28 November 2013, at http://lawprofessors.typepad.com/china_law_prof_blog/2013/11/why-chinese-needs-a-good-word-for-irony-and-why-its-too-soon-to-bid-farewell-to-re-education-through.html, accessed 29 December 2013.
122 Article 11 (2) Administrative Litigation Law.
123 Wang Xing (王星), '北京"黑监狱"截访案 10 人获刑, [10 persons criminally punished in the case of the Beijing "Black Prison" for retrieving petitioners]', *Southern Metropolis Daily*, (南方都市报), 6 February 2013, at http://news.sohu.com/20130206/n365654524.shtml, accessed 29 December 2013.
124 In Chinese characters, 思想改造.
125 See Chapter 6. Falung Gong practitioners were reportedly required to sign three statements.

Torture is outlawed in the criminal process (as *xing xun bi gong*)[126] and is a criminal offence; and there have been continuous and elaborate efforts to stem its use in the criminal process through legislative and other measures, such as the introduction of exclusionary rules, and the use of video- and audio-recording equipment in interrogation rooms.[127] Torture has nevertheless by some been described as a common feature of criminal investigation detention.[128] According to one study, over 50% of persons detained for criminal investigation report having suffered torture at the hands of the police; and torture is most commonly used to extract a confession.[129] A lawyer who would not describe himself as a rights defence lawyer remarked that the police were often right in beating suspects (*da de dui*)[130] and only sometimes made a mistake (*cuoda*).[131] This view reflects what others have characterised as a predominantly held view among the law enforcement authorities; namely the view that uses of torture are legitimate means of disciplining those who refuse to confess to their crimes.[132]

Asked about cases involving torture, rights lawyers tended to address the topic in terms of how bad torture had been on a comparative range, and pay attention to evidential issues, characterising beatings with mineral water bottles and slaps in the face as 'just average' and 'nothing out of the ordinary', for example.[133] Almost always, they spoke with the clinical, professional detachment characteristic of surgeons:

> That client is dead now. He was executed. At the time when I handled the case, I had to go to the provincial authorities [in the place of detention] to get permission to meet the client. When we met, the police were [illegally] filming us and taking photographs. But they did not interfere, they let the defendant talk. (. . .) The defendant had been tortured and he talked about it. In the cases we handle we often encounter police torture. Regarding the degree of the torture in this case, the torture my client endured in this case would count as comparatively light (. . .). They had used a plant from the Northeast that is like pepper. They had put that in powdered form in a plastic bag and put the bag over my client's head. And they had also used

---

126 In Chinese characters, 刑讯逼供.
127 Flora Sapio, 'Coercive interrogation', in Sapio, *Sovereign Power and the Law in China*, Brill, Leiden: 2010; Margaret K. Lewis, 'Controlling abuse to maintain control: the exclusionary rule in China', *International Law and Politics* (2011) 629, at http://www.usasialaw.org/wp-content/uploads/2011/07/NYI303-lewis.pdf, accessed 29 December 2013; Ira Belkin, 'China's tortuous path toward ending torture in criminal investigation'.
128 E.g. #22, #9, #23, #21, #14, #6, #25, #20, #26, #28,#17, #30; Chen Youxi, 'Torture in China – fact or fiction?', translated by Duihua Foundation, 2 August 2010, at http://www.duihuahrjournal.org/2010/08/translation-commentary-torture-in-china.html (with link to Chinese original).
129 McConville *ibid.*, at p. 69; Ira Belkin, 'China's tortuous path toward ending torture in criminal investigation'; Flora Sapio, 'Coercive interrogation', *supra*.
130 In Chinese characters, 打得对.
131 In Chinese characters, 错打. #69 2012-1.
132 See Chapter 6.
133 #26 2010-1.

electric shocks – electric rods on him. It *was* very cruel; but even so, the torture had not left any obvious outer scars.[134]

The lawyer proceeded to provide examples to illustrate more cases of torture he considered more serious, because scars had been left:

> In another case I handled, a robbery and murder case in X [further details omitted], the clients had been beaten very badly; and when we took the case, it was ten years after the case had been opened, but you could see scars all over [my client's] body from the torture.[135]
>
> In a rape and murder case in Y, when I took on the case, a police bureau head had already lost his job due to botched handling of this case, and the newly incoming head officer was absolutely bent on 'solving' it. They used shackles to suspend the suspects [by their wrists]. Even after five to six years all the defendants still had very deep, clearly visible scars on their hands and wrists. Not just scars that had healed over. In addition, because it was in the South, where the suspects did not wear shoes, they [the police] had used leather shoes to squash their feet. Their feet were really just rotting away when we saw them.[136]

In both of the cases involving more serious torture, the defendants retracted their confessions later and their lawyers had good and well-documented reasons to believe that their clients were innocent – in both cases, the real perpetrator was thought to have been identified (he had in one case confessed to the crime) – but they were not successful in achieving their release, let alone getting justice for them, at the time of this writing.

Torture can never be regarded as a likely means of identifying the guilty: 'The police said to me, "There is no confession that we cannot obtain".'[137] For this reason, it is plausible that the numerous efforts to reduce and eliminate uses of torture are based also in a perception that its use does not lead to credible results, especially in criminal justice, and a need to prevent further cases of blatant injustice,[138] countering the officials' efforts to evade accountability for torture. Against this background, maintaining even a conviction that has been publicly exposed as wrong and a result of torture indicates a remarkable degree of systemic intransigence to such facts; yet such cases continue to occur.

Whereas torture in criminal investigation mainly serves to obtain a 'confession', the authorities use torture in other contexts purportedly to 'reform' their victim.

---

134 #6 2010-1.
135 #6 2010-1.
136 #6 2010-1.
137 #95 2013-3.
138 A 2013 SPC opinion makes this connection very clear. 关于建立健全防范刑事冤假错案工作机制的意见 [Opinion on establishing a healthy work mechanism for the prevention of wrongful criminal cases], promulgated by the Supreme People's Court on 21 November 2013, at http://www.chinanews.com/fz/2013/11-21/5530039.shtml, accessed 29 December 2013. The utilitarian philosopher Bentham argues against torture on these grounds.

This kind of torture is reported to happen especially in extrajudicial and illegal or criminal forms of Party–State detention, such as 'study classes'. In both instances, the use of torture appears to become a process essentially dissociated from the person it targets, however. This person becomes a tool serving a certain bureaucratic goal, such as a written confession to be used at criminal trials, or statements of guilt, repentance, and willingness to renounce previous beliefs and practices and to reform (in the context of detention facilities used, e.g. for petitioners, Falun Gong practitioners).

Thus, for example, a letter from a city-level Government Office for the Prevention of Evil Sects to a Party Committee for the Prevention of Evil Sects in the same city, sending a new 'student' to a sojourn in 'study class', simply states that he was found in possession of Falun Gong materials, investigated by the police 'on suspicion of crimes', and (apparently because the investigation yielded no satisfactory result) is sent there for 'education and conversion', in conformity with 'the requirements of the city- and district-level Public Security Bureau', without mentioning any time limit of the 'study' imposed.[139] Asked what was studied in 'study classes' and 'legal education centres', rights lawyers were universally contemptuous, indicating that so far as any 'study' took place at all it consisted in learning texts by heart, and that 'thought reform' was successful in producing the required documents because it relied on keeping inmates for as long as it took, and on the use of torture, to 'convert' (*zhuanhua*)[140] them.[141]

In sum, the utilitarian and post-totalitarian traits of the system, which are only imperfectly reflected in the PRC Constitution and formally so designated laws, and directly in tension with some of the constitutional and other legal safeguards for basic rights, nevertheless appear to supply the authorities with 'justifications' for its systemic rights violations in a variety of different contexts. Together with Party loyalty and the seeking of personal advantages, they constitute factors contributing to major grievances. If it appears that lawyers gave accounts of cases of major injustice with detachment, this is not to say that they were indifferent to their clients' experiences; rather, they had come to accept encountering victims as part of their professional routine in criminal cases. These at times harsh experiences constitute the background for lawyers' own professional activities. Their own encounter with the authorities is – with the exception of those disbarred – centred in the legal process and interaction with the authorities of the police, procuracies, and courts in handling cases.

The institutions to address injustices

There are connections between the utilitarian and post-totalitarian traits of the system that lead to certain kinds of grievance, and the mechanisms in place

139 Copy on file with author.
140 In Chinese characters, 转化.
141 E.g. #28 2013-1.

to address such grievances. For one thing, Party–State authorities generally welcome and promote the perception that they can deal with complaints and 'solve' (unspecified) 'problems;'[142] but its institutions are also used as tools for preventing the handling of cases that must remain un-addressed in order to protect certain powerful entities, cases generally referred to as '(politically) sensitive cases'. For another, the approach to the handling of certain cases has become strictly focused on the consequences a case might have for social stability, as the 'New Mass Line' propaganda emphasises.[143] Consequentialist social stability considerations can determine the outcome of a case regardless of what the law would require. The fact that such considerations naturally favour non-adjudicative means of dispute resolution, as well as syste-matic 'supervision' of and incidental interference with adjudicative processes, influences the role and status of lawyers in the legal process.

The Chinese judiciary in some ways resembles western systems of the continental European model. It requires professionally trained judges to adjudicate cases in accordance with the laws and the Constitution. It requires that courts (not individual judges) adjudicate cases independently,[144] and decide on the basis of the facts and the law. The judicial process envisages legal advocacy and adopts a broadly adversarial trial system. It safeguards the right to appeal first-instance decisions to higher courts; it also provides for broad grounds for the application for a retrial.

Despite its outward similarities with western models, the judiciary also retains features of the Soviet model that shaped it in the Mao era. Judges are subjected to the authority of their court president, of the adjudication committee within their court, and of various authorities outside, including notably the 'political and legal committees' of the Party; and adjudication is supposed to occur under the supervision of a number of entities, including in particular the People's Congresses. Various regulations envisage disciplinary punishments for many infractions including corruption, 'wrong' judgements, 'offending public morality' and 'violating political discipline'; and like other officials, judges are subject to an annual performance evaluation system that comprises criteria such as political probity and the question of how many of one's decisions have been overturned and effectively penalises independent judgement.

Judges are moreover required to study doctrines enjoining Party loyalty. Since 2008, the 'Three Supremes' doctrine articulates the principle, supposed to guide judges in their work, that 'upholding the Party's cause is supreme, the people's interests are supreme, and the constitution and laws are

---

142   See above on the use of *fumuguan*, 'father and mother official', 7.
143   Huang Zhaolin (黄兆麟), 找准法院践行党的群众路线的着力点, [Identifying key points in the judiciary's practice of the Party's mass line], 28 November 2013, at http://court.gmw.cn/html/article/201311/28/144212.shtml, accessed 29 December 2013.
144   Art 126 PRC Constitution (cited above). See Benjamin Liebman, 'China's courts: restricted eform', 20, *Columbia Journal of Asian Law*, 2, at http://www.law.columbia.edu/null?exclusive=filemgr. download&id=15116, accessed 29 December 2013.

supreme.'[145] 'So who is supreme?', a liberal legal scholar asked pointedly.[146] The Three Supremes doctrine provided judges with an added reason for obeying orders from superiors.[147] From 2013, after Xi Jinping assumed the offices of Party Secretary General and President, the leadership increasingly used political slogans explicitly drawing on the Mao Zedong era, such as the 'New Mass Line'. These slogans, on the one hand, enjoin judges to be closer to 'the people',[148] de-emphasising adversarial adjudicative procedures in favour of other mechanisms for the resolution of disputes. On the other, they emphasise discipline, and have been used to justify the practice of 'self-criticism' sessions, so as to be able to undergo correction;[149] and an anti-corruption campaign conducted by the Party's Discipline and Inspection Committee, which selects whom to investigate for corruption.

As in continental European systems, adjudication mechanisms follow different rules for civil, administrative and criminal litigation, with differences affecting the burden of proof, among other things. In civil litigation, the plaintiff generally bears the burden of proof to support the claims stated.

An advantage in administrative litigation (formalised since 1990) is that the burden of proof for the legality of administrative actions or decisions lies with the defendant, which must show what law or regulation such action is based in; however, 'normative document' cannot as such be an object of administrative litigation, according to Article 12 of the Administrative Litigation Law. This means that opportunities for challenging norms of law, however low ranking,[150] on account of its incompatibility with higher ranking law, are very limited; and in practice, documents issued by Party organisations or jointly by State and Party

---

145 He Weifang (贺卫方), '"No-trinity-theory" – debating professors Jia Yu, Wang Zhenmin, Guo Feng, Han Dayuan, Zhuo Zeyuan, Zhang Zhiming, Ma Huaide, Fu Zitang, Wang Limin and Zhu Jiping' ['三位一体论——与贾宇、李林、王振民、郭峰、韩大元、卓泽渊、张志铭、马怀德、付子堂、王立民、朱继萍教授商榷]', 22 July 2009, at http://blog.sina.com.cn/s/blog_488663200100emaw.html, accessed 29 December 2013.

146 He Weifang (贺卫方), 三个之上, 谁之上? [Who is supreme of the Three Supremes], 27 August 2008, at http://blog.sina.com.cn/s/blog_488663200100atga.html, accessed 29 December 2013.

147 It drew scornful criticism from lawyers. One commented, 'Even friends of mine in the judiciary – they, too, said that the "Three Supremes" was the worst mistake so far. You can *act* like that, but should by no means *talk* like that – it affects your place in history! But they [the leadership] apparently felt they actually had to say it.' #52 2011-1.

148 The language of the New Mass Line reintroduces Mao era vocabulary. See also '10 名优秀基层人民法院法官谈落实群众路线, [10 Outstanding basic-level court judges discuss how to realise the mass line]', 人民法院报, 22 November 2013, at http://www.chinapeace.org.cn/2013-11/22/content_9571432_4.htm, accessed 29 December 2013.

149 The 'New Mass Line' also calls for uses of mediation in handling cases, and for solving the problems of the poor and vulnerable groups in society. See, for example, a discussion of the meaning of the 'New Mass Line', Yang Zhengsen (杨政森), '司法如何走群众路线 [How can the judiciary practice the mass line]', China Party Member Net (共产党员网), 6 November 2013, at http://qzlx.12371.cn/2013/11/06/ARTI 1383702705976452_2.shtml, accessed 29 December 2013 (for courts) and Xu Jianbo, Luo Xin and Li Yujun, (徐建波、罗欣、李郁军), 用精细司法和服务创新诠释群众路线精髓, [Using precise adjudication and creativeness in service to interpret the essence of the mass line], Procuracy Daily (检察日报), 28 November 2013, at http://big5.qstheory.cn/zl/bkjx/201311/t20131128_296870.htm (for procuracies).

150 The 2000 Law on Legislation sets out a norm hierarchy.

agencies are equally considered exempt from review by the courts.[151] At best, courts may in cases of inconsistency between lower and higher ranking legal rules ignore the lower ranking ones in deciding a case.

In all kinds of litigation, the scope of judicial review is further limited by a widely held view, supported by certain Supreme People's Court Judicial Interpretations, to the effect that the courts may not base their decisions directly on the Constitution.[152] In the liberalising years under SPC President Xiao Yang, a SPC response to a lower court in the Qi Yuling case raised hopes that the judiciary could evolve into an institution conducting judicial review;[153] or that the Constitution could be 'judicialised'.[154] But after SPC President Xiao Yang's tenure ended and after the SPC Justice most directly associated with the Qi Yuling Interpretation, Huang Songyou, was ignominiously removed and later convicted of corruption, the SPC officially revoked its Judicial Interpretation given in this case.[155]

In criminal cases, certain – albeit imperfectly articulated – liberal principles have in theory established the requirement for the prosecution to prove the guilt of the defendant,[156] since the 2012 revision of the CPL 'beyond reasonable doubt'.[157] The 1997 CL recognised a principle of *nulla poena sine lege*;[158] and Article 12 of the 1996 CPL reads 'no one shall be found guilty without being judged to be guilty by a People's Court.'[159] The 1996 CPL also recognised the right to legal counsel in criminal cases, as well as the principle of public trials. The

151 The problem of 'red letterhead documents' is discussed in Eva Pils, 'Land disputes, rights assertion and social unrest: a case from Sichuan', 19 *Columbia Journal of Asian Law* (2006) 365.
152 最高人民法院关于在刑事判决中不宜援引宪法作论罪科刑的依据的批复 [SPC Answer regarding the non-application of the Constitution as a basis for criminal liability or sentencing decision]', Judicial Interpretation 1955 no. 11298, 30 July 1955; 最高人民法院关于人民法院制作法律文书应如何引用法律规范性文件的批复[SPC Answer regarding the question of how the courts when issuing legal documents should cite to normative documents]', Keith Hand, 'Resolving constitutional disputes in contemporary China', 7 EALR (2011) 125, at http://www.pennealr.com/archive/issues/vol7/EALR7(1)_Hand.pdf, accessed 29 December 2013; 'Keith Hand, 'Using a law', *supra*; Thomas E. Kellogg, 'Constitutionalism with Chinese characteristics', 7 *International Journal of Constitutional Law* 2 (2009) 215–246, at http://icon.oxfordjournals.org/content/early/2009/03/16/icon.mop001, accessed 29 December 2013.
153 See Huang Songyou (黄松有), 宪法司法化及其意义—从最高人民法院今天的一个 "批复" 谈起), (人民法院报 [The judicialisation of the Constitution and its significance – a discussion proceeding from the SPC's approving response today]', 13 August 2013, available at http://www.gongfa.com/huangsyxian fasifahua.htm, accessed 29 December 2013.
154 *Ibid.*
155 Kellogg, *supra*, and 'The death of constitutional litigation in China?', 9 *China Brief* 7 (2009), at http://www.jamestown.org/uploads/media/cb_009_7_02.pdf, accessed 29 December 2013.
156 Donald Clarke and James V. Feinerman, 'Antagonistic contradictions: criminal law and human rights in China', 141 *China Quarterly* (1995) 135–154.
157 Joshua Rosenzweig et al., *supra*.
158 Article 3 of the 1997 Criminal Law: 'For acts that are explicitly defined as criminal acts in law, the offenders shall be convicted and punished in accordance with law; otherwise, they shall not be convicted or punished', at http://www.cecc.gov/resources/legal-provisions/criminal-law-of-the-peoples-republic-of-china, accessed 29 December 2013.
159 The currently valid CPL has been revised in March 2012; revisions were to come into effect in 2013.

2012 revision of the CPL further consolidated these changes, and explicitly protected the accused person's right not to incriminate himself.[160] Most recently in November 2013, the SPC has exhorted the judiciary to acquit those whose guilt has not been proved.[161]

One can today find numerous books dealing with courtroom advocacy skills on the shelves of the law sections of major Chinese bookshops. 'The courtroom, the lawyer's major battlefield', according to one such book, is where law is dramatically enacted, and where cases are decided one way or another. Case examples described by the author, a practising criminal defence lawyer and member of the ACLA Criminal Defence Committee, include a courtroom dialogue in which the lawyer skilfully interrogates a witness to uncover the fact that he was bribed by the police to make a false statement incriminating the defendant, and this revelation leads to acquittal of the defendant.[162] But no name or citation is given for this case, and it is left unclear if it was modelled on actual experience, or whether it is another exercise in the 'as if' technique.

In practice, the challenges all criminal defence lawyers face in helping clients to get access to justice begin with getting access to the client, and such difficulties also arise when the client is held under some other form of detention; whereas in other cases, the chief challenge is to get one's case into the court – to get the authorities to initiate a judicial process. These difficulties are further discussed in the following chapter; below I point out a few general features.

Assuming that a letter of appointment can be obtained and that the client can be 'located' in a police detention centre (both can be difficult), permission to visit the client may be denied, e.g. on the grounds that lawyers must first obtain local authorisation.[163] If the lawyer eventually gets access, the meeting with the client may be monitored by the detention centre police officers (through physical presence of an officer, for example), and during monitored meetings, the police may stop lawyers from discussing certain details of a case. In 2013, there was some indication that access to suspects in 'ordinary' context had improved due to the revision of the CPL,[164] for instance on account of the rule now requiring that a meeting with the lawyer be arranged within 48 hours from the detention; but the 2012 CPL revision has added to this problem because the authorities are not

160 2012 CPL Article 50.
161 Zhang Xianming (张先明), 最高法院发布意见防范刑事冤假错案 [SPC issues Opinion on preventing wrongful criminal cases], People's Court Gazette (人民法院报), 22 November 2013, at http://www.chinacourt.org/article/detail/2013/11/id/1148623.shtml, accessed 29 December 2013.
162 Duan Jianguo (段建国), 大律师法庭攻守之道 [*The Barrister's Offence and Defence Strategies in the Courtroom*], Law Press (法律出版社), Beijing: 2010, at p. 140.
163 An audio-recorded example of an altercation with officials at a detention centre is provided in He Yang's (何杨) documentary, '专访朱明勇律师—黑打 [Conversation with Lawyer Zhu Mingyong – Torture]', August 2010, at http://vimeo.com/13706954.
164 The pre-revision rules of the CPL and especially of the Law on Lawyers do not allow for any of the specific measures of obstruction just mentioned, but it could be argued that they failed to ban them. The 2012 CPL now provides explicitly for the possibility of family or friends to appoint defence lawyers and obligates the authorities to pass on the suspect's request for a lawyer. Article 33 2012 CPL. Also, for the first time the CPL stipulates a time limit of 48 hours within which a meeting with the lawyer must be arranged. Article 37 2012 CPL.

obligated even to notify lawyers or families of the detention in cases of State security and certain other crimes; and in cases of extra-residential 'residential' surveillance, the suspect may effectively be disappeared for a period of up to six months with no access to a lawyer.[165] And even in a case where none of these exceptions from the normal process applied, a lawyer who ultimately abandoned criminal defence of his client because he was not allowed to see him for months, reported:

> The first time I went round [for a meeting with the detained client] they told me I had to wait because there 48 hours had not passed yet . . . but then we got no notification for over a day. So I knew there clearly was problem. They were trying to trick us. I went over again after 48 hours had passed. That time, the detention centre just adopted a thuggish stance. They told me there was a notice from the case-handling unity [saying I could not see the client]. I exploded (. . .) but he just said that they had orders from higher levels.[166]

Further main problems arise from limitations of access to the case files and from limitations on lawyers' ability to engage in their own criminal investigation.

In many administrative and civil litigation cases, rights lawyers represent the plaintiff, for instance in land expropriation and forced eviction cases, in complaints against the imposition of RTL or other administrative detention forms (i.e. cases in which detention has been imposed without criminal trial),[167] and in employment discrimination cases. In cases in which it is a potential defendant, rights' lawyers' first objective is to get the court to 'file the case' (*li'an*)[168] in order to get into a process in which decisions can be judicially reviewed. Lawyers asked about this process reported difficulties which can be explained from the perspective of 'the system' and its requirements:

> In China, even though it should only be a formal process, they actually conduct a substantive review. The judge who is in charge of filing the case is not the adjudicating judge, but that judge may nevertheless say, for example, 'this claim here is not ok, you can't include this claim here.' They may require you to change your application. According to the law you could refuse to revise your materials. But then they will generally not just act in accordance with law. If you refuse to revise the statement then maybe they won't take

---

165 Joshua Rosenzweig et al., *supra*.
166 #88 2013-3. The authorities allowed two other lawyers to take over.
167 Zheng Jianwei and Cang Hai ('郑建伟, 沧海'), 行政诉讼是首选—郑建伟律师谈上海童国菁被劳教案 [Administrative litigation is the first choice – Lawyer Zheng Jianwei discusses the RTL case of Tong Guoqing]', 28 February 2010, at http://boxun.com/news/gb/china/2010/02/201002180325.shtml, accessed 29 December 2013.
168 In Chinese characters, 立案. Thus the lawyers for Lawyer Tang Jingling, detained in 2014 on charges of a national security crime, were denied access to their client for months.

your submitted materials at all or they will harass you in other ways.[169] . . .
The judge will sometimes take the law into consideration [when rejecting
the application to file a case] but very often they will consider the law. Rather
they will consider if they could get into trouble if they accepted the case. For
example they will consider that there hasn't been such a case [handled by
the courts] before – it is bad if I accept it? Or how about the superior
levels – because, you see, the superior authorities' instructions are of greater
importance in the eyes of some case filing division judges than the law. So
the judge will ask very carefully about what the superior authorities think.
If they consent to his accepting the case, then the judge is not taking a risk
accepting it.[170]

Even if cases get into court, decisions can go against the complainant even when
the complaint is well founded; or, as we will see, judicial decisions have no effect
on the reality of rights infringements.

Beyond and outside what is sometimes termed the 'formal legal process', there
is the institution called 'Letters and Visits', a particularly widely used mechanism[171] that is connected to the judicial process, but in was not allowing lawyers
any institutionalised role as rights advocates. State and Party authorities at all
levels of the administration of the State are required to establish 'petitioning
offices' in accordance with central and local-level administrative regulations.[172]
Petitioning offices established in all bureaux and offices of the State, as well as
of the Party, receive a citizen's complaint and scrutinise it for its reasonableness.
If the complaint is considered well founded, the petitioning office may write a
letter instructing the Party–State entity or official in charge of the issue to solve
the problem. Petitioning has its place also inside the judiciary – courts, too, run
petitioning offices, and those who cannot get justice through the judicial process,
petition. Petitions not only seek the protection of their legal rights, but quite often
also the correct handling (correction) of criminal cases they consider to have been
decided unjustly or to have been ignored; or the imposition of punishment or
disciplinary measures on officials perceived to be corrupt.

Yu Jianrong and others have shown that the petitioning system is not really
a viable avenue to redress any grievances. Petitioners in larger cities may spend
weeks, months or even years seeking to present their case and get a resolution.[173]

---

169 #50 2011-1. In another case, the lawyers for Lawyer Chang Boyang, criminally detained in 2014,
   had been denied access to him for over 80 days, at the time of writing, without any reasons given.
170 #50 2011-1.
171 Carl Minzner makes this point in his 'Xinfang: an alternative to the formal Chinese legal system',
   42 *Stanford Journal of International Law* (2006) 103.
172 In accordance with Article 41 of the Constitution and the 中华人民共和国国务院信访条例
   [State Council Regulation on Letters and Visits], promulgated on 10 January 2005, effective
   as of 1 May 2005, at http://theory.people.com.cn/GB/41179/41181/3127789.html, accessed
   5 January 2014.
173 Zhao Ling (赵凌), 'China's first report on *Xinfang* work receives high-level attention' (国内首份信
   访报告获高层重视) NFZM 4 and 22 November 2004, at http://www.aisixiang.com/data/
   detail.php?id=4693, accessed 29 December 2013. In 2005 I met a petitioner who had been

Since their activities can be disruptive of the Party–State bureaucracy's normal work, a bureaucratic system of controlling petitioning and of awarding merits and demerits to officials has been developed;[174] and the fact that officials are held responsible in this way explains many of the abuses against petitioners.[175] As a consequence of such repression, complaints surge not only into channels the system provides – court adjudication, mediation, and petitioning – but also into other, unofficial channels such as street protest, where they generate further opportunities for repression in the name of 'social stability preservation'.

It is in these contexts that rights lawyers encounter petitioners: helping them with the cases they complain about (such as eviction cases), helping them when they have been detained or suffered other abuses, and at times, trying to persuade them to stop petitioning in order to escape the vicious cycle of persecution that engenders further grievances to petition about.[176] Rights lawyers consistently report that because they are so marginalised and frustrated in their quests for redress, petitioners are likely to become critics of the legal and political system; this can result in further marginalisation, as well as in stronger identification and organised protest among those marginalised:[177]

> The fact that the petitioners are now getting more organized is the result of years, perhaps even decades of going back and forth [petitioning in their particular cases]. The petitioners have been raised up to being to what they are through oppression. They now know that they cannot possibly resolve their own case. So if they cannot each resolve their own problem, they want to resolve the system.[178]

In sum, available institutional channels are ill equipped to protect substantive and procedural rights which, as a consequence of legal reforms, have been introduced; and as a result the system is institutionally intolerant toward many kinds of complaint. Its judicial procedures are closed to certain types of complaint

---

complaining about his wrongful conviction and imprisonment in the late 1950s, since his release from prison in the early 1980s. Copy of written complaint on file with author.

174 Minzner, 'China's turn against law', 59 *American Journal of Comparative Law* (2011) 935; Flora Sapio, 'Legal erosion', *supra*.

175 Discussed in Minzner, *supra*; Pils, 'Taking *yuan* (冤) seriously', *supra*.

176 E.g. #88 2013-2.

177 Identification occurs around symbolic figures such as that of Yang Jia, a petitioner thought to have staged a revenge attack by fatally stabbing six police officers in 2008 with a butcher's knife. Eva Pils, 'Yang Jia and China's unpopular criminal justice system', 1 *China Rights Forum* (2009) 59–66. I regret that I realised only after publication of this article that there are reasons to doubt that Yang Jia was the killer at all, in addition to other travesties of justice in the judicial process. Yang Jia nevertheless continues to be mourned and celebrated as a hero of the popular rights defence movement for 'killing' the six police officers, and to be a byword for the oppressed victim of injustice turning violent. Cp. Wang Rongfen (王容芬), '公,检,法,辩, 合谋构陷——杨佳案剖析 [The police, procuracy, defence and court collude in framing [the defendant] – a study of the case of Yang Jia]', 25 November 2011, at http://www.duping.net/ XHC/show.php?bbs=11&post=1174333, accessed 4 January 2014. I would like to thank Frank Münzel for sharing his insights on this point. See also #44 2011-1, #20 2011-1, #22 2010-2.

178 #52 2011-1.

and its judicial process is controlled, closed, and routinely unfair in certain types of case. Its petitioning system is repressive. The judiciary's systemically programmed inadequateness in this regard is in all respects compounded by the fact that the most important political power holder, the Party, has no clearly defined and consequently no clearly limited role in the constitutional framework, and is widely understood to be exempt from judicial review of its decisions. Although the adjudicative system has to some degree opened up to rights arguments, general legal practices that determine the ordinary handling of legal disputes have sought to absorb and accommodate the language of rights and law without fundamentally upsetting the system; and as is discussed in the following chapter, the renewed emphasis on 'mediative' dispute resolution avenues can become a tool for excluding lawyers from judicial processes, or for fundamentally changing the role they may take in such processes.

In the ordinary legal process, lawyers are expected to adapt and submit to the serious obstacles to access to justice outlined above, both by compromising and at times cooperating with the authorities,[179] even against the interests of their clients, and, as research into the judiciary has suggested and some lawyers confirmed, potentially also by participating in corruption.[180] It is in part because they often do not conform to such expectations that rights lawyers and other lawyers can feel at some distance from one another.

Marginalisation and identification

> The reputation of Chinese lawyers among the people at the moment is actually not very good, and there are some differences between them and human rights lawyers because these at least have a function in restraining public power . . . When human rights lawyers are one day vilified, perhaps it will mean that this society has matured . . . The fact that society puts more hope in human rights lawyers now actually shows that society is abnormal, because in a normal society, human rights lawyers would mostly defend persecuted social minorities and be criticised by society.[181]

Some tentative conclusions may be drawn from the above initial assessment of the Chinese system, regarding the place of rights, rights advocacy and rights lawyers in it. First, since legal advocacy requires lawyers to act as if the law were taken seriously in confronting the rights abuses by the (Party–)State, advocacy can be subversive of power structures by insisting on adherence to the law. This is especially obvious when it comes to opposing rights violations that occur at the order of powerful authorities within the Party–State structure, including

---

179 Elisa Nesossi, 'Compromising for "justice"? Criminal proceedings and the ethical quandaries of Chinese lawyers', in McConville and Pils, *Comparative Perspectives, supra*.
180 Li Ling, 'The "production" of corruption in China's courts – the politics of judicial decision-making and its consequences in a one-party state', *Journal of Law & Social Inquiry* (2011), at http://ssrn.com/abstract=188014; also e.g. #23, 2010–3; #78 2013-1.
181 #28 2013-2.

the organisations of the Party itself; rights violations whose 'justification' lies in authoritarian (totalitarian), rather than utilitarian considerations on the part of the authorities; and rights violations perpetrated against those whom the system has already collectively marginalised, e.g. due to ethnic status, faith, engagement in rights defence or political conviction.

Second, as the system has a tendency to marginalise those who challenge it, rights lawyers are likely to be marginalised, too. From these lawyers' perspective, the institutions of the Party–State fail to respect the State laws and legal ideals to which the lawyers feel committed in an abstract way. As a further consequence, while the demands of the system operate against the formation of a professional community and common professional ethics amongst lawyers and other legal professionals,[182] they strengthen the tendency for rights lawyers pushed 'outside the system' to identify experientially with their clients, whose numbers keep rising.

Bibliography

International law instruments

International Convention for the Protection of All Persons from Enforced Disappearances, at http://www.ohchr.org/EN/HRBodies/CED/Pages/ConventionCED.aspx, accessed 4 January 2014.
International Covenant on Civil and Political Rights, adopted and opened for signature, ratification and accession by General Assembly resolution 2200A (XXI) of 16 December 1966, entry into force 23 March 1976, at http://www.ohchr.org/en/professionalinterest/pages/ccpr.aspx, accessed 4 January 2014.
Universal Declaration of Human Rights, proclaimed by the United Nations General Assembly in Paris on 10 December 1948, at http://www.ohchr.org/en/udhr/pages/introduction.aspx, accessed 4 January 2014.

Constitution and NPC laws

PRC Administrative Litigation Law [中华人民共和国行政诉讼法], passed and promulgated on 4 April 1989, and effective as of 1 October 1990, at http://www.gov.cn/flfg/2006-10/29/content_1499268.htm.
PRC Constitution [中华人民共和国宪法], promulgated and effective as of 4 December 1982, last revised on 14 March 2004, at http://www.people.com.cn/GB/shehui/1060/2391834.html.
PRC Criminal Law [中华人民共和国刑法], passed on 1 July 1979, promulgated on 6 July 1979, and effective as of 1 January 1980, last revised on 25 February 2011, at http://www.moj.gov.cn/Prison_work/content/2013-05/07/content_4436670.htm?node=43130. For an English translation, see http://www.cecc.gov/resources/legal-provisions/criminal-law-of-the-peoples-republic-of-china.

---

182 Cp. Nina Jorgensen, 'Lawyer independence in criminal proceedings: a most professional virtue', *Legal Ethics* (forthcoming).

PRC Criminal Procedure Law [中华人民共和国刑事诉讼法], passed on 1 July 1979, promulgated on 7 July 1979, effective as of 1 January 1980, last revised on 14 March 2012, at http://www.gov.cn/flfg/2012-03/17/content_2094354.htm, CECC translation at http://www.cecc.gov/resources/legal-provisions/criminal-procedure-law-of-the-peoples-republic-of-china.

PRC Law on Legislation [中华人民共和国立法法], promulgated 15 March 2000, effective July 1, 2000, at http://www.gov.cn/test/2005-08/13/content_22423.htm.

Rules and regulations

Ministry of Civil Affairs, Provisional Measures on Banning Illegal Social Organisations, [取缔非法民间组织暂行办法], 10 April 2000, available in Chinese and English translation at http://www.chinadevelopmentbrief.cn/?p=712, accessed 26 December 2013.

State Council Regulation on Letters and Visits [中华人民共和国国务院信访条例], promulgated on 10 January 2005, effective as of 1 May 2005, at http://theory.people.com.cn/GB/41179/41181/3127789.html, accessed 5 January 2014. An English translation is available at http://unpan1.un.org/intradoc/groups/public/documents/UN-DPADM/UNPAN039990.pdf.

State Council Regulation on Compensation for Expropriation of Buildings on State-owned Land [国有土地上房屋征收与补偿条例], promulgated and effective as of 21 January 2011, at http://www.gov.cn/zwgk/2011-01/21/content_1790111.htm, accessed 4 January 2014.

Supreme People's Court Answer regarding the non-application of the Constitution as a basis for criminal liability or sentencing decision '[最高人民法院关于在刑事判决中不宜援引宪法作论罪科刑的依据的批复]', released on 30 July 1955, at http://www.law-lib.com/law/law_view.asp?id=1012, accessed 5 January 2014.

Supreme People's Court Answer regarding the question of how the courts when issuing legal documents should cite to normative documents [最高人民法院关于人民法院制作法律文书应如何引用法律规范性文件的批复], promulgated and effective on 28 October 1986, at http://china.findlaw.cn/fagui/p_1/134636.html accessed 5 January 2014.

Supreme People's Court Opinion on establishing a healthy work mechanism for the prevention of wrongful criminal cases [关于建立健全防范刑事冤假错案工作机制的意见], promulgated on 21 November 2013, at http://www.chinanews.com/fz/2013/11-21/5530039.shtml, accessed 29 December 2013.

Other official documents

Chinese Communist Party Central Committee, 'Decision on Several Major Issues of Deepening Reform [中共中央关于全面深化改革若干重大问题的决定]', 12 November 2013, translation at http://chinalawtranslate.com/en/cpc-central-committee-decision-on-several-major-issues-of-deepening-reform/.

National People's Congress Standing Committee Decision to annul legal regulations concerning Re-education Through Labour [全国人大常委会关于废止有关劳动教养法律规定的决定], promulgated and effective 28 December 2013, at http://news.xinhuanet.com/legal/2013-12/28/c_118749199.htm, accessed 29 December 2013.

Books and articles

ABC News, 'China eases one child policy and abolishes labour camps in reform package', 16 November 2013, at http://www.abc.net.au/news/2013-11-15/china-to-ease-one-child-policy3a-xinhua/5096380.

Ai, Xiaoming (艾晓明), '艾晓明访艾未未谈网络、艺术与公民问责 [Ai Xiaoming visits Ai Weiwei, discusses the internet, art and civic responsibility]', 25 November 2013, at http://canyu.org/n81956c9.aspx, accessed 26 December 2013.

Amnesty International, 'Changing the soup but not the medicine? Abolishing Re-education Through Labour in China', 17 December 2013, at http://www.amnesty.org/en/library/asset/ASA17/042/2013/en/f7e7aec3-e4ed-4d8d-b99b-f6ff6ec860d6/asa170422013en.pdf.

Amnesty International, 'Standing their ground: thousands face violent evictions in China', released October 2012, at http://www.amnesty.org/en/library/info/ASA17/001/2012/en, accessed 30 December 2013.

Arendt, Hannah, *The Origins of Totalitarianism*, Harcourt, Brace, Jovanovich, New York: 1973.

Bajoria, Jayshree, 'Access to justice in China', 16 April 2008, at http://www.cfr.org/china/access-justice-china/p15745.

Bandurski, David, 'What happened at the Beijing News', 15 September 2011, at http://cmp.hku.hk/2011/09/15/15432/, accessed 27 December 2013.

Bayefsky, 'The United Nations Human Rights treaties – China', as of 20 September 2011, at http://www.bayefsky.com/bycategory.php/state/36.

Béja, Jean-Philippe, *Civil Society against Democracy*, Conference paper on file with the author.

Belkin, Ira, 'China's tortuous path toward ending torture in criminal investigation', 24 *Columbia Journal of Asian Law* 2 (2011).

Bennet, Isabella, 'Media censorship in China', Council on Foreign Relations Website, 24 January 2013, at http://www.cfr.org/china/media-censorship-china/p11515, accessed 27 December 2013.

Biddulph, Sarah, 'The production of legal norms: a case study of administrative detention in China', 20 *UCLA Pacific Basin Law Journal* (2003) 217–277.

Bjoern, Ahl, 'Chinese law and international treaties', 39 *Hong Kong Law Journal* (2009), at http://www.cesl.edu.cn/eng/upload/201106214048086.pdf.

Bristow, Michael, 'China closes migrant worker schools', 1 September 2011, at http://www.bbc.co.uk/news/world-asia-pacific-14743222, accessed 27 December 2013.

Chang, Kai (常凯), '论中国的罢工权立法 [On the Legislation of Right to Strike in China]', 19 February 2011, at http://blog.sina.com.cn/s/blog_51bd78fc0100ogl9.html.

Charbonneau, Louis, 'China, Cuba, Russia, Saudi Arabia elected to UN Human Rights Council', *Reuters*, 12 November 2013, at http://www.reuters.com/article/2013/11/12/us-un-rights-council-idUSBRE9AB19E20131112.

Chen, Albert H.Y., 'Constitutions and values in three Chinese societies', working paper, 17 September 2009, at SSRN: http://ssrn.com/abstract=1474731.

Chen, Yongmiao (陈永苗), '大陆沦陷区的"民国党人" [The "Republicans" on the Occupied Territory of the Mainland]', 8 June 2012 at http://www.peacehall.com/news/gb/pubvp/2012/06/201206082208.shtml, accessed 25 December 2013.

Chen, Youxi, 'Torture in China – fact or fiction?', translated by Duihua Foundation, 2 August 2010, at http://www.duihuahrjournal.org/2010/08/translation-commentary-torture-in-china.html.

China Daily, 'Rural land disputes lead to social unrest in China', 6 November 2010, at http://www.chinadaily.com.cn/china/2010-11/06/content_11511194.htm, accessed 26 December 2013.

ChinaFile, 'Document No. 9', at http://www.chinafile.com/document-9-chinafile-translation, accessed 30 December 2013 (with further links).

Chinese Human Rights Lawyers (中国人权律师团), '中国人权律师团就保障人权完善宪法践行宪政的呼吁 [Chinese Human Rights Lawyers: Appeal to Safeguard Human Rights and Realise Constitutional Government]', 4 December 2013, at http://www.siweiluozi.net/, accessed 10 December 2013.

China Labour Bulletin, 'Wages in China', 10 June 2013, at http://www.clb.org.hk/en/node/100206, accessed 27 December 2013.

China Labour Bulletin, 'Unity is strength: the workers' movement 2–2011', 11 October 2011, at http://www.china-labour.org.hk/en/node/101134.

Chinese Lawyers for the Protection of Human Rights (中国保障人权律师团), '中国保障人权律师团律师对劳教制度废止相关问题的声明 [Statement on Abolition of RTL and Related Problems by Chinese Lawyers for the Protection of Human Rights]', 19 November 2013 at http://www.siweiluozi.net/2013/11/statement-on-abolition-of-re-education.html.

CHRD, 'The darkest corners: abuses of involuntary psychiatric commitment in China', Report, 22 August 2012, copy on file with author, at http://www2.amnesty.org.uk/blogs/countdown-china/%E2%80%9C-darkest-corners%E2%80%9D-abuses-involuntary-psychiatric-commitment-china, accessed 29 December 2013.

Chung, Dan and Branigan, Tania, 'China's migrant families suffer under hukou', 15 March 2010, at http://www.guardian.co.uk/world/video/2010/mar/15/china-migrant-workers, accessed 27 December 2010.

Clarke, Donald, 'Why Chinese needs a good word for "irony", and why it's too soon to bid farewell to re-education through labour', Chinese Law Prof Blog, 28 November 2013, at http://lawprofessors.typepad.com/china_law_prof_blog/2013/11/why-chinese-needs-a-good-word-for-irony-and-why-its-too-soon-to-bid-farewell-to-re-education-through.html, accessed 29 December 2013.

Clarke, Donald C., China Law Professor Blog, 'The famous Hukou editorial', 26 March 2010 at http://lawprofessors.typepad.com/china_law_prof_blog/2010/03/the-famous-hukou-editorial.html, accessed 27 December 2013.

Clarke, Donald and Feinerman, James V., 'Antagonistic contradictions: criminal law and human rights in China', 141 *China Quarterly* (1995)135–154.

Cook, Sarah and Lemish, Leeshai, 'The 610 Office: policing in the Chinese spirit', 11 *China Brief* 17 (2011), at http://www.jamestown.org/uploads/media/cb_11_43.pdf, accessed 27 December 2013.

Dong, Yunhu and Chang, Jian (董云虎, 常健) (eds.) *Six Decades of Building Human Rights in China* (中国人权建设 60 年), Jiangxi People's Press, Nanchang: 2009.

Duan, Jianguo (段建国), 大律师法庭攻守之道 [*The Barrister's Offence and Defence Strategies in the Courtroom*], Law Press, Beijing: 2010.

Fu, Hualing, 'Access to justice in China: potentials, limits, and alternatives, draft (September 2009)', at http://papers.ssrn.com/sol3/papers.cfm?abstract_id=1474073.

Fu, Hualing, 'Re-education Through Labour in historical perspective', *China Quarterly* (2005) 811–830, at http://www.jstor.org/stable/20192540, accessed 29 December 2013.

Gallagher, Mary, 'Legislating harmony: labour law reform in China', draft (2008) at http://www.erb.umich.edu/Research/Initiatives/colloquiaPapers/Gallagher RevisedPaperJan08.pdf, accessed 27 December 2013.

Gao, Zhisheng, *A China More Just*, Broad Press USA, New York: 2007.

Guangzhou Daily, '孟建柱赴乌鲁木齐指导维稳 强调当前新疆工作维稳压倒一切 [Meng Jianzhu travels to Urumqi to guide stability preservation, emphasises that in current work in China, stability preservation trumps everything]', 5 September 2009, at http://gzdaily.dayoo.com/html/2009-09/05/content_692660.htm, accessed 1 January 2014.

Guo, Guoting (郭国汀), '废除或修改煽动颠覆国家政权罪 [Abolish or revise the crime of inciting subversion]', at http://blog.boxun.com/hero/200811/guoguoting/3_2.shtm, accessed 27 December 2013.

Hand, Keith, 'Resolving constitutional disputes in contemporary China', 7 *University of Pennsylvania East Asia Law Review* 1 (2011) 51, at http://www.pennealr.com/archive/issues/vol7/EALR7(1)_Hand.pdf, accessed 29 December 2013.

Hand, Keith, 'Using law for a righteous purpose: the Sun Zhigang Incident and evolving forms of citizen action in the People's Republic of China', 45 *Columbia Journal of Transnational Law* (2006), 138, at http://librarysource.uchastings.edu/repository/Hand/45ColumJTransnatlL114.pdf, accessed 29 December 2013.

Hart, H.L.A., *The Concept of Law*, 2nd ed., Oxford University Press, Oxford: 1994.

He, Weifang (贺卫方), 'No-trinity-theory' – debating Professors Jia Yu, Wang Zhenmin, Guo Feng, Han Dayuan, Zhuo Zeyuan, Zhang Zhiming, Ma Huaide, Fu Zitang, Wang Limin, and Zhu Jiping ['三位不一体论——与贾宇、李林、王振民、郭峰、韩大元、卓泽渊、张志铭、马怀德、付子堂、王立民、朱继萍教授商榷]', 22 July 2009, at http://blog.sina.com.cn/s/blog_488663200100emaw.html, accessed 29 December 2013.

He, Weifang (贺卫方), '三个之上，谁之上？[Who is supreme of the Three Supremes]', 27 August 2008, at http://blog.sina.com.cn/s/blog_488663200100atga.html, accessed 29 December 2013.

He, Weifang, *In the Name of Justice: Striving for the Rule of Law in China*, Brookings Institute Press, Washington: 2013.

Hua, Xinmin (华新民), '华新民：土地私有产权从来就没有消失过, [Hua Xinmin: Private property in land has never vanished]', 29 June 2011, at http://news.qq.com/a/20110701/000579.htm, accessed 26 December 2013.

Huang, Songyou (黄松有), '宪法司法化及其意义—从最高人民法院今天的一个"批复"谈起, [The judicialisation of the Constitution and its significance – a discussion proceeding from the SPC's approving response today]', *People's Court Gazette* (人民法院报), 13 August 2013, at http://www.gongfa.com/huangsyxianfasifahua.htm, accessed 29 December 2013.

Huang, Yeqing; Guo, Fei and Tang, Yiming, 'Hukou Satus and social exclusion of rural-urban migrants in transitional China', 3 *Journal of Asian Public Policy* 2 (2010) 172–185, at http://www.tandfonline.com/doi/pdf/10.1080/17516234.2010.501160.

Huang, Zhaolin (黄兆麟), '找准法院践行党的群众路线的着力点, [Identifying key points in the judiciary's practice of the Party's mass line]', 28 November 2013, at http://court.gmw.cn/html/article/201311/28/144212.shtml, accessed 29 December 2013.

Human Rights in China, Liu Xiaobo's 1st and 2nd instance defence statements at http://www.hrichina.org/en/content/3206 and http://www.hrichina.org/en/content/3210, accessed 27 December 2013.

Human Rights in China, 'State secrets: China's legal labyrinth' (2009), at http://www.hrichina.org/sites/default/files/PDFs/State-Secrets-Report/HRIC_StateSecrets-Report.pdf, accessed 27 December 2013.

Human Rights Watch, 'An alleyway in hell: China's abusive "black jails"', 12 November 2009, at http://www.hrw.org/en/reports/2009/11/12/alleyway-hell-0, accessed 29 December 2013.

Jacobs, Andrew, 'Chinese professor who advocated free speech is fired', *New York Times*, 10 December 2013, at http://www.nytimes.com/2013/12/11/world/asia/chinese-professor-who-advocated-free-speech-is-fired.html?_r=0.

Jiang, Shigong (强世功), 'Written and unwritten Constitutions: a new approach to the study of constitutional government in China [中国宪法中的不成文宪法——理解中国宪法的新视角]', 36 *Modern China* 1 (2010) 12–46, at http://www.lishiyushehui.cn/modules/topic/detail.php?topic_id=282, accessed 27 October 2013.

Jiang, Shigong (强世功), '图施耐特和 "大众宪法", [Tushnet and the 'populist constitutional law]', 11 *Dushu* (读书 (2004) 122–131, at http://www.civillaw.com.cn/article/default.asp?id=55048, accessed 27 October 2013.

Jorgensen, Nina, 'Lawyer independence in criminal proceedings: a most professional virtue', *Legal Ethics*.

Kavanagh, Dennis and Riches, Christopher (eds.), *A Dictionary of Political Biography*, Oxford University Press, 2009, at http://www.oxfordreference.com/view/10.1093/oi/authority.20110803100155343, accessed 25 December 2013.

Kellogg, Thomas E., 'Constitutionalism with Chinese characteristics', 7 *International Journal of Constitutional Law* 2 (2009) 215–246, at http://icon.oxfordjournals.org/content/early/2009/03/16/icon.mop001, accessed 29 December 2013.

Kellogg, Thomas E., 'The death of constitutional Litigation in China?', 9 *China Brief* 7 (2009), at http://www.jamestown.org/uploads/media/cb_009_7_02.pdf, accessed 29 December 2013.

Lawrence, Susan and Martin, Michael S., 'Understanding China's political system', *Congressional Research Service Paper*, 20 March 2013, www.fas.org/sgp/crs/row/R41007.pdf.

Lewis, Margaret K., 'Controlling abuse to maintain control: the exclusionary rule in China', *International Law and Politics* (2011) 629, at http://www.usasialaw.org/wp-content/uploads/2011/07/NYI303-lewis.pdf, accessed 29 December 2013.

Li, Cheng, 'Hukou in a human rights perspective' (2008 Dissertation), at http://www.duo.uio.no/publ/jus/2008/77477/77477.pdf, accessed 26 December 2013.

Li, Raymond, 'Rights groups miss out on easing of registration rules for NGOs', *South China Morning Post*, 12 March 2012, at http://www.scmp.com/news/china/article/1188742/rights-groups-miss-out-easing-registration-rules-ngos, accessed 26 December 2013.

Li, Wen (李文), '律师刘卫国指警方禁探访许志永违法 [Liu Weiguo points out that the authorities' obstruction of a meeting with Xu Zhiyong is unlawful]', 20 July 2013, at http://www.bbc.co.uk/zhongwen/trad/china/2013/07/130720_xuzhiyong_lawyer.shtml, accessed 29 December 2013.

Lieberthal, Kenneth G. and Lampton David M., *Bureaucracy, Politics and Decision-making in Post-Mao China*, University of California Press, Berkeley: 1992, at http://publishing.cdlib.org/ucpressebooks/view?docId=ft0k40035t;brand=ucpress.

Liebman, Benjamin, 'China's courts: restricted reform', 20 *Columbia Journal of Asian Law* 2, at http://www.law.columbia.edu/null?exclusive=filemgr.download&id=15116, accessed 29 December 2013.

Lin, Ping (林坪), '中国首例户籍就业歧视案被法院驳回 [China's first hukou discrimination case rejected by the Court]', *Radio Free Asia*, 4 December 2013, at http://www.rfa.org/mandarin/yataibaodao/renquanfazhi/yl-12042013160724.html?searchterm:utf8:ustring=%E6%88%B7%E5%8F%A3, accessed 27 December 2013.

Liu, Jie, 'A biased view of China', *China Daily* of 30 January 2012, at http://www.chinadaily.com.cn/cndy/2012-01/30/content_14502312.htm.

Liu, Lee, 'Made in China: cancer villages', *Environment Magazine*, March/April 2010, at http://www.environmentmagazine.org/Archives/Back%20Issues/March-April%202010/made-in-china-full.html, accessed 26 December 2013.

Liu, Weiguo, Open letters, at http://www.hrichina.org/en/content/6841, accessed 29 December 2013.

Longanecker, Mindy Kristen, 'No room for dissent: China's laws against disturbing social order undermine its commitment to free speech and hamper the rule of law', 18 *Pacific Rim Law & Policy Review* 2 (2009).

Mao, Yushi et al., 'Open letter suggesting the abolition of Re-education Through Labour' (2007), at http://www.aboluowang.com/2007/1204/65722.html, accessed 29 December 2013.

Minzner, Carl, 'China's turn against law', 59 *American Journal of Comparative Law* (2011) 935.

Minzner, Carl, 'Xinfang: an alternative to the formal Chinese legal system', 42 *Stanford Journal of International Law* (2006) 103.

Mueller, Klaus, 'East European studies, neo-totalitarianism and social science theory', *TIPEC Working Paper 03/7*, at www.trentu.ca/tipec/3muller7.pdf, accessed 27 December 2013.

Nesossi, Elisa, 'Compromising for "justice"? – criminal proceedings and the ethical quandaries of Chinese lawyers', in McConville and Pils, *Comparative Perspectives on Criminal Justice in China*, Elgar Publishing, Cheltenham: 2013.

Parry, Jane and Cui, Weiyuan, 'Chinas psychiatric hospitals collude with officials to stifle dissent say civil rights groups', 28 June 2010, http://www.bmj.com/content/340/bmj.c3371.extract, accessed 29 December 2013.

People's Court Gazette (人民法院报), '10 名优秀基层人民法院法官谈落实群众路线 [10 Outstanding basic-level court judges discuss how to realise the mass line]', 22 November 2013, at http://www.chinapeace.org.cn/2013-11/22/content_9571432_4.htm, accessed 29 December 2013.

Pils, Eva, 'Taking *yuan* (冤) seriously: why the Chinese government should stop suppressing citizen protests against injustice', 25 *Temple International and Comparative Law Journal* (2011) 285–327.

Pils, Eva, 'Waste no land: property, dignity and growth in urbanising China', 11 *Asian-Pacific Law & Policy Journal* 2 (2010) 1–48, at http://blog.hawaii.edu/aplpj/files/2011/11/APLPJ_11.2_pils.pdf, accessed 26 December 2013.

Pils, Eva, 'Citizens? The legal and political status of peasants and peasant migrant workers in China', in Liu Xiangmin (ed.), 制度, 发展与和谐 [*System, Development, and Harmony*] Mingpao, Hong Kong, 2007, 173–243; draft available at http://papers.ssrn.com/sol3/papers.cfm?abstract_id=1563724.

Pils, Eva, 'Contending conceptions of property and ownership in urbanising China', in Fu Hualing and John Gillespie (eds.), *Resolving Land Disputes in East Asia*, Cambridge University Press: forthcoming.

Qian, Yanfeng, '"Most homes" to be demolished in 20 years', *China Daily*, 7 August 2010, at http://www.chinadaily.com.cn/china/2010-08/07/content_11113982.htm, accessed 26 December 2013.

Radio Free Asia (Mandarin Desk), '中国多位学者,律师联署呼吁消除计生与户籍捆绑政策 [Several scholars and lawyers in China sign joint statement calling for abolition of restrictive birth control and *hukou* policies]', 5 December 2013, at http://www.rfa.org/

mandarin/Xinwen/huji-12062013101031.html?searchterm: utf8:ustring=%E6%88%B7%E5%8F%A3, accessed 27 December 2013.

Reuters, 'China's Re-education Through Labour system', 20 December 2007, at http://www.reuters.com/video/2007/12/20/chinas-re-education-through-labour?videoId=73011, accessed 29 December 2013.

Rosenzweig, Joshua D., 'China's battle over the right to criticise', *Far Eastern Economic Review*, 5 May 2009.

Rosenzweig, Joshua, Sapio, Flora, Jiang, Jue, Teng, Biao and Pils, Eva, 'The 2012 revision of the Chinese Criminal Procedure Law', in McConville, Mike and Pils, Eva (eds.), *Criminal Justice in China: Comparative Perspectives*, Elgar Publishing, Cheltenham: 2011.

Sapio, Flora, 'Legal erosion and the policing of petitions', in McConville and Pils, (eds.) *Comparative Perspectives on Criminal Justice in China*, Elgar Publishing, Cheltenham: 2013.

Sapio, Flora, 'Coercive interrogation', in Sapio, Flora, *Sovereign Power and the Law in China*, Brill, Leiden: 2010.

Seppänen, Aaro Samuli, *Useful Paradoxes: Ideological Conflicts in the Chinese Rule of Law Discourse*, PhD dissertation, Harvard, September 2012; draft on file with author.

Simon, Karla, *Civil Society in China: The Legal Framework from Ancient Times to the 'New Reform Era'*, Oxford University Press, Oxford: 2013.

Simon, Karla, 'The regulation of civil society organisations in China', (2011), at http://ssrn.com/abstract=1781075.

Teng, Biao, (滕彪), 'The political meaning of the crime of "subverting state power"', in Béja, Fu and Pils, *Liu Xiaobo and Challenges of Constitutional Reform in China*, Hong Kong University Press, Hong Kong: 2013.

Teng, Biao, 'The political meaning of the crime of "subverting state power"', translated from the Chinese by Pinky Choy and Eva Pils, in Jean-Philippe Béja, Fu Hualing and Eva Pils, *Charter 08 and Challenges to Constitutionalism in China*, Hong Kong University Press, Hong Kong: 2012.

Teng, Biao et al., '我们愿意为被捕藏民提供法律帮助 [We are willing to provide legal assistance to criminally arrested Tibetans]', *Boxun*, 2 April 2008, at http://www.peacehall.com/news/gb/china/2008/04/200804022305.shtml.

Tong, Lihua (佟丽华), 为了正义 [*Strive for Justice*], Law Press (法律出版社), Beijing: 2009.

Wang, Rongfen (王容芬), '公、检、法、辩，合谋构陷——杨佳案剖析 [The police, procuracy, defence and court collude in framing [the defendant] – a study of the case of Yang Jia]', 25 November 2011, at http://www.duping.net/XHC/show.php?bbs=11&post=1174333, accessed 4 January 2014.

Wang, Tiancheng (王天成), 大转型—中国民主化战略研究框架 [*The Great Transition – a Framework for Studying Strategies of Democratisation in China*], Greenfield Bookstore, Hong Kong: 2012.

Wang, Xing (王星), '北京"黑监狱"截访案10人获刑 [10 persons criminally punished in the case of the Beijing "Black Prison" for retrieving petitioners]', *Southern Metropolis Daily*, (南方都市报), 6 February 2013, at http://news.sohu.com/20130206/n365654524.shtml, accessed 29 December 2013.

Webster, Timothy, 'Ambivalence and activism: employment discrimination in China', 44 *Vanderbilt Journal of Transnational Law* 643 (2011), at http://digitalcommons.law.yale.edu/cgi/viewcontent.cgi?article=1000&context=ylas, accessed 13 November 2013.

Wee, Sui-lee, 'Thousands being moved from China's Three Gorges – again', Reuters, 22 August 2012, at http://www.reuters.com/article/2012/08/22/us-china-threegorges-idUSBRE87L0ZW20120822.

Wu, Fengshi and Chan, Kin-man, 'Graduated control and beyond: the evolving government–NGO relations', 3 *China Perspectives* (2012) 9.

Wu, Tiaohe (吴调和), '党是人民利益的代表 [The party is the representative of the people's interests]', *Shi Dai Chao Magazine* (时代潮)', Issue 3, 2006, at http://www.people.com.cn/GB/paper83/16850/1480483.html, accessed 22 December 2013.

Xi Wang (希望, a pen name), '中国 14 名律师要求审计署公布社会抚养费的去向 [14 lawyers seek public disclosure on where social welfare fees have gone from the National Audit Bureau]', 2 September 2013, at http://www.rfa.org/mandarin/yataibaodao/renquanfazhi/nu-09022013155348.html.

Xiao, Gongqin (萧功秦), 'Re-establishing civil society: a brand new phrase in China's turn-of-the-century reform [重建公民社会：走向 21 世纪中国大转型新阶段]', *Southern Metropolis Daily* (南方都市报), 10 January 2010, at http://www.usc.cuhk.edu.hk/PaperCollection/Details.aspx?id=7423.

Xinhua Net, '科学发展观 [Scientific Development Perspective]', at http://news.xinhuanet.com/ziliao/2005-03/16/content_2704537.htm.

Xu, Jianbo, Luo, Xin and Li, Yujun, (徐建波, 罗欣, 李郁军), '用精细司法和服务创新诠释群众路线精髓, [Using precise adjudication and creativeness in service to interpret the essence of the mass line]', *Procuracy Daily* (检察日报), 28 November 2013, at http://big5.qstheory.cn/zl/bkjx/201311/t20131128_296870.htm.

Yang, Guobin, *The Power of the Internet in China: Citizen Activism Online*, Columbia University Press, Columbia, OH: 2009.

Yang, Ming (杨明), '北京华远集团董事长任志强: 不存在非公共利益拆迁 只要是城建都是公共利益 [Ren Zhiqiang, Chairman of the Board of Beijing Yuayuan Group, comments that there is no such thing as demolition and relocation not in the public interest]', *Liaowang Dongfang Zhoukan* [瞭望东方周刊], 10 February 2012, at http://finance.ifeng.com/opinion/zjgc/20100210/1822226.shtml, accessed 26 December 2013.

Yang, Zhengsen (杨政森), '司法如何走群众路线 [How can the judiciary practice the mass line]', China Party Member Net (共产党员网), 6 November 2013, at http://qzlx.12371.cn/2013/11/06/ARTI1383702705976452_2.shtml, accessed 29 December 2013.

Yi, Xing (易兴), '论公众人物的隐私权 [On the Right to Privacy of Public Figures]', 6 June 2009, at http://www.civillaw.com.cn/article/default.asp?id=44964, accessed 27 December 2013.

Yu, Nayang (于呐洋), '人大：单独两孩非放弃计划生育 要与二胎政策衔接 [The new policy that allows couples to have two children is not an abandonment of the one child policy, to be linked to two-child policy]', *Legal Daily*, 25 December 2013, at http://www.chinanews.com/gn/2013/12-25/5659946.shtml.

Zhang, Boshu (张博树), '中共党专制逻辑的 28 个命题 [28 Propositions concerning the CCP's Dictatorship]', *Human Rights in China Biweekly*, (中国人权双周刊) Issue 109, 12 July–25 July 2013, at http://city.mirrorbooks.com/news/?action-viewnews-itemid-95190, accessed 25 December 2013.

Zhang, Qianfan (张千帆), *宪法学讲义* [*Lectures on Constitutional Law*], Peking University Press, Beijing: 2011.

Zhang, Qianfan, *The Constitution of China. A Contextual Analysis*, Hart Publishing, Oregon: 2012.

Zhang, Xianming (张先明), '最高法院发布意见防范刑事冤假错案 [SPC issues Opinion on preventing wrongful criminal cases]', *People's Court Gazette* (人民法院报), 2 November 2013, at http://www.chinacourt.org/article/detail/2013/11/id/1148623.shtml, accessed 29 December 2013.

Zhang, Xiong, 'Yu Jianrong is all the rage', *Nandu Zhoukan*, 8 December 2010, http://
www.nbweekly.com/magazine/cont.aspx?artiID=12431, accessed 27 December 2013;
translated by Stacy Mosher, in Marina Svensson and Eva Pils, *An Anthology of writings by
Professor Yu Jianrong of the Chinese Academy of Social Science in English Translation* [working
title], ME Sharpe, forthcoming.

Zhang, Xuezhong (张学忠), '新常识：一党专政的性质与后果 [The new common
sense: the nature and effects of one-party dictatorship]', 2013, electronic publication,
copy on file with author.

Zheng, Jianwei and Cang, Hai (郑建伟, 沧海), '行政诉讼是首选—郑建伟律师谈上海童
国菁被劳教案 [Administrative litigation is the first choice – Lawyer Zheng Jianwei
discusses the RTL case of Tong Guoqing]', 28 February 2010, at http://boxun.com/
news/gb/china/2010/02/201002180325.shtml, accessed 29 December 2013.

Zhou, Ruiping (周瑞平), '中国首例艾滋病就业歧视案详情披露 [Details of China's
first AIDS discrimination case disclosed]', *Legal Weekend (法治周末)*, 12 January
2011, at http://news.sina.com.cn/c/sd/2011-01-12/004521799440.shtml, accessed
27 December 2013.

Zhu, Suli (朱苏力)，波斯纳及其他——译书之后 [*Posner and other matters – after translating
his book*], Law Press, Beijing: 2004.

Documentaries and multimedia sources

Chinese People's Liberation Army National Defence University (中国人民解放军国防大
学), '较量无声 [Silent Contest]', at http://www.youtube.com/watch?v=M_8lSjcoSW8,
accessed 31 December 2013.

He, Yang (何杨), documentary, '专访朱明勇律师—黑打 [Conversation with Lawyer
Zhu Mingyong –Torture]', August 2010, at http://vimeo.com/13706954, accessed
5 January 2104.

Websites, blogs and microblog entries

Beijing Cailiang Law Firm (北京市才良律师事务所) at http://www.cai-liang.com/,
accessed 30 December 2013.

'Cancer villages' Google Maps, at https://maps.google.com/maps/ms?msa=0&msid=10
4340755978441088496.000469611a28a0d8a22dd&dg=feature, accessed 26 December
2013.

China Against Death Penalty (北京兴善研究所) at http://www.cadpnet.org/en/show.
asp?ID=146, accessed 31 December 2013.

China Labour Bulletin (中国劳工通讯) at http://www.clb.org.hk/en/, accessed
31 December 2013.

Dagongzu Service Centre (广东番禺打工族服务部) at http://blog.sina.com.cn/dgzngo.

4 Courtroom advocacy

To the extent that the authorities rely on a State judicial system created in the image of liberal justice, they nurture a popular vision of courts as open, independent, fair and strong institutions capable of protecting the rights of the weak and of handling and punishing criminals in accordance with law (*yifa*).[1] The image modern court buildings generally present is one of order and power; and court hearings use the global trappings of judicial justice, a continental trial courtroom design and seating order with the judge, prosecutor and lawyer wearing western-style robes and the presiding judge equipped with a gavel to keep order at trial.[2]

In many instances, however, due to features of the system discussed in the previous chapter, Chinese courts are places of Party–State control and exclusion. Despite the judiciary's impressive institutional development and its significant role in resolving civil disputes, courts routinely block certain kinds of case from entering a court procedure. Some court hearings, especially in criminal trials, adopt practices designed to prevent issues of central importance from coming up. Such measures of control and exclusion extend beyond the gates, sentries, entry controls and safety checks used to protect court buildings; they rely in part on tacit compliance by the professional actors central to court processes, including lawyers, and are hidden from public view.

Rights lawyers make use of the vision of fair and open courts to oppose the restrictions, controls, and measures of exclusion. Their practices and experiences in some respects challenge the perceived understanding that Chinese lawyers are ordinarily compliant and passive at trial.[3] The lawyers who discuss their

---

1 In Chinese characters, 依法.
2 These images contrast with the reality of the rural judiciary, however. Cp. Stéphanie Balme, 'Local courts in western China', in Randall Peerenboom (ed.), *Judicial Independence in China: Lessons for Global Rule of Law Promotion*, Cambridge University Press, Cambridge: 2009; Frank Upham, 'Who will find the defendant if he stays with his sheep? Justice in rural China', 114 *Yale Law Journal* (2005) 1675.
3 There is good empirical evidence to support this. McConville et al. write that 'retained lawyers [i.e. those lawyers generally more likely to exert themselves on behalf of their clients] are generally inactive at the trial stage, ask few questions, make few objections and in the most usual case direct their efforts towards making a plea in mitigation.' Michael McConville et al., *China's Criminal Justice: An Empirical Enquiry*, Edward Elgar Publishing, Cheltenham: 2011, at p. 318.

experiences with judicial processes and courtroom advocacy here are aware of the existing constraints and tacit conventions, but in many instances choose not to comply with them, instead insisting on adherence to the public rules and principles of State law. Their experiences can help us to understand some of the techniques used to scare off, keep out, shout down, or more permanently professionally silence lawyers who try to engage in authentic courtroom advocacy. They also show if – or to what extent – they can make courtrooms places of genuine advocacy on behalf of the most vulnerable parties, and how – on what limited terms, really – they can sometimes succeed.[4] Lastly, rights lawyers' testimonies shed light on what remains ordinary about trials in which rights lawyers play an extraordinary part; it helps to understand and explain the routine which rights lawyers to some extent disrupt and challenge. It is these challenges that drive them out of State-provided institutional spaces (including courtrooms and mechanisms such as 'unconstitutionality review' by the National People's Congress Standing Committee) and into new alternative spaces, including the internet and the street. The drama of their exclusion can give them opportunities to articulate more explicitly political demands.

Rules and practices limiting courtroom advocacy

At a training session for judges in May 2012, the Supreme People's Court Vice President Zhang Jun observed that because Chinese judges were still used to an 'inquisitorial' mode of trial hearings, trials did not generally involve much conflict (*maodun*)[5] and were quite 'orderly' (*you zhixu*).[6] Only in some cases, SPC Vice President Zhang Jun continued:

> [D]ue to some procedural injustice, something should have been done but was not done. And then this gets hyped up. This includes some situations in which lawyers have been treated unfairly. A very few unscrupulous lawyers will then accuse the Court during the court hearing of serious violations of procedure; and once this gets published, no one trusts the judges anymore, no one has faith in the courts. They only trust those lawyers' rubbish . . . [W]hen they encountered situations in which the lawyers *made trouble in the courtroom* [*nao ting*],[7] such as in Beihai in Guangxi,[8] . . . our judges at the time were outwitted; they really didn't know what to do. (emphasis added)[9]

---

4 The discussion here is based largely in conversations with lawyers and nonprofessional rights defenders about their experiences of courtroom advocacy. Because of the particularly constrained nature of these cases, reliance on lawyers' direct testimony is necessary to understand what happens in these trials.
5 In Chinese characters, 矛盾.
6 In Chinese characters, 有秩序.
7 In Chinese characters, 闹庭.
8 Aspects of the Beihai case are discussed in Chapters 5 and 6.
9 Shen Nianzu (沈念祖), '法院副院长们的压力 [Pressure on Court Vice Presidents]', originally published in *Economic Observer*, (经济观察报), 19 May 2012, at http://www.eeo.com.cn/2012/0519/226779.shtml, accessed 7 November 2013. See also Kai Wen (凯文), '副院长与正律师：一场不对称战争 [Court Vice President and Righteous Lawyers: battle between unequal

The expression *nao ting*, 'making trouble in the courtroom,' likens lawyers engaging in forceful rights advocacy to other perceived 'troublemakers', notably petitioners, who are customarily described using the word *nao*.[10] By describing certain lawyers in this way and grouping them with those whom rights lawyers frequently represent in court, this judge signals effectively that lawyers can create 'conflict' at trial if they do not submit to what he conceives of as an 'orderly trial'. He does not further discuss in what ways such lawyers may violate courtroom order; but pointing out procedural rights violations, and creating 'conflict' (*maodun*) appear to be on his list of 'troublemaking' courtroom advocacy, requiring disciplining measures.

In fact, there is an impressive arsenal of measures the system can take to suppress courtroom advocacy.

Constraints arising from public legal rules, in particular rules of procedural law

According to Article 36 (1) of the 2007 Law on Lawyers, 'The rights of lawyers who are engaging in legal representation or criminal defence to present a criminal defence and to engage in criminal defence must be safeguarded in accordance with law'; and 'The personal rights [safety and liberty] of a lawyer engaged in practising law shall not be infringed upon. The representation and defence statements presented in court by a lawyer shall not be subject to legal prosecution, except for statements compromising the national security, maliciously defaming others or seriously disrupting the court order.'[11] The courtroom rules articulate further requirements of courtroom order, including, predictably, rules against shouting, applauding, and similar conduct in the courtroom,[12] and the rule that members of the audience are not allowed to audio- or video-record the proceedings.[13] While

opponents]', 24 May 2012, at http://boxun.com/news/gb/pubvp/2012/05/201205240034. shtml, accessed 7 November 2013; for an essay arguing that lawyers' *nao ting* results from lack of fairness in the court process, see Mao Lixin (毛立新), '律师"闹庭"与"辩审"冲突 [Lawyers' trouble-making in court and the conflict between the advocacy and the judiciary]', at http://police.fyfz.cn/b/739166, accessed 7 November 2013.

10 For an official court report on successfully handling a *nao ting* (the 'troublemaking' party kneels in front of the court building), see People's Court of Xiangtan County (湘潭县人民法院), '青山桥法庭妥善处理一起闹庭事件 [Qingshan Bridge Court Properly Handled a Nao Ting Incident]', 26 August 2013, at http://xtxfy.chinacourt.org/public/detail.php?id=632.

11 中华人民共和国律师法 [PRC Law on Lawyers] passed on 28 October 2007, effective as of 1 June 2008. For the Chinese text, see http://www.gov.cn/flfg/2007-10/28/content_788495.htm, and for an English translation http://www.cecc.gov/pages/newLaws/lawyersLawENG.php.

12 Article 8 of 中华人民共和国人民法院法庭规则 [SPC PRC People's Court Rules on Courtroom Proceedings], passed on 26 November 1993, promulgated on 1 December 1993, effective as of 1 January 1994, at http://old.chinacourt.org/flwk/show.php?file_id=76042, accessed 7 November 2013.

13 Article 9 of 中华人民共和国人民法院法庭规则 [PRC People's Court Rules on Courtroom Proceedings]; see also Article 19 of 律师和律师事务所违法行为处罚办法 [Ministry of Justice, Regulation on Punishments for Law-Violating Conduct on the Part of Lawyers and Law Firms], passed on 7 April 2010, promulgated on 8 April 2010, effective as of 1 June 2010, at http://www.gov.cn/gongbao/content/2010/content_1713712.htm, accessed 7 November 2013; 中华人民共和国行政处罚法 [PRC Law on Administrative Punishment], adopted on 17 March 1996, promulgated on 17 March 1996, and effective as of 1 October 1996, at http://www.gov.cn/banshi/2005-08/21/content_25101.htm, accessed 7 November 2013.

this is no different from standards in other jurisdictions, special problems arise with regard to this rule in China.

In addition to requirements affecting legal representation and defence at court, some general rules limiting access to justice in criminal, civil and administrative procedure, and therefore putting lawyers in human rights cases at a disadvantage, have already been discussed in Chapter 3. In the criminal process, lawyers' access to suspects or defendants and to case files is a problem in the pre-trial phase. Trials, while designed to be open and to allow for a reasonable process of engagement with the evidence and both sides' arguments (inclusive of opportunities for prosecution and defence to question witnesses and debate the evidence), are further negatively affected by the fact that witnesses appear so rarely. The criminal provision of Article 306 the Criminal Law moreover, overshadows the criminal trial with a threat of prosecution for the presentation of evidence in discrepancy with that of the police or procuracy.[14]

The 2012 Criminal Procedure Law revision has created some rules that on the surface would appear to extend the opportunities for rights advocacy, including for instance the accused person's right not to incriminate themselves. The operation of these new rules is tangential to the current study, but the discussion below justifies doubts about their ability to change actual practice.[15]

In civil and administrative litigation, rules indirectly constraining courtroom rights advocacy include the rules limiting the scope of judicial review; the fact that litigation against administrative acts generally does not stay the enforcement related proceedings; and bad-faith applications of the procedural requirement of 'filing cases' for civil or administrative litigation.

Further practices and measures limiting the role of independent legal advocacy in courtroom hearings include the pre-trial suppression of unwelcome advocates, the prevention of trials by and refusing to file cases and non-adversary (conciliation, mediation) mechanisms, the restrictive rules governing settings in the courtroom and courtroom behaviour, threats of disciplinary measures and deregistration, and criminalisation of courtroom advocacy, as well as uses of threats and violence to intimidate courtroom advocates' performance in court.[16]

---

14 McConville sums up the constraints ordinarily affecting the defence in criminal trials thus: 'The risk of prosecution of the lawyer if defence witnesses give evidence that is different from their statements they gave to the police; the reluctance of witnesses to become involved in criminal cases; the lack of resources available to lawyers; the exclusion of lawyers from the interrogation stage; the lack of early and full disclosure of the prosecution case; the absence of prosecution witnesses from the trial and hence to inability to cross-examine witnesses and test evidence by forensic processes; the fact that in almost all cases the prosecution will have extracted one or, frequently, more statements of confession from the defendant.' Mike McConville et al., *An Empirical Enquiry*, at p 317.

15 Joshua Rosenzweig, Flora Sapio, Jiang Jue, Teng Biao and Eva Pils, 'The 2012 revision of the Chinese criminal procedure law', in Mike McConville and Eva Pils (eds.), *Criminal Justice in China: Comparative Perspectives*, Edward Elgar Publishing, Cheltenham: 2011.

16 The SPC even considered introducing a rule (in the form of a judicial interpretation) that would have allowed courts to ban troublemaking lawyers who had been subject to a fine or judicial detention from attending trials for six months. Chen Hongwei (陈虹伟), '律师"闹庭"引出规制 [Lawyers' "troublemaking" in the courtroom triggers regulation]', *Legal System and News* (法制与新闻),

Obstruction and intimidation before criminal trials

Because they expect that other lawyers could be made to comply with certain tacit or explicit instructions from the authorities regarding their role in the trial process, the authorities have an interest in preventing human rights lawyers from taking on cases in which they could act in 'disruptive' ways. To achieve this goal, they have on various occasions taken measures to prevent particular lawyers from being involved in a case or to prevent lawyers from attending court hearings in cases in which they have already been appointed as lawyers.

Attempts to prevent particularly combative and independent lawyers from being hired, especially in sensitive cases, are frequently mentioned by lawyers, and in cases that have attracted some public attention such efforts are also recorded in the media. Widely reported attempts included the cases of rights advocate Chen Guangcheng (tried for obstructing traffic in 2005),[17] rights lawyer Gao Zhisheng (tried for inciting subversion in 2006),[18] Tibetans after the 2008 unrest in Tibet,[19] the Uighur journalist Hairat Niyaz in 2009 after unrest in Xinjiang (tried for inciting subversion),[20] Yang Jia (an unemployed petitioner, tried for murder in 2009), Zhao Lianhai (a middle-class parent turned rights defender in the 'tainted milk powder' incident, tried for creating a social disturbance in 2009),[21] Chen Kegui (Chen Guangcheng's nephew, tried for assault in 2012), rights advocate Xu Zhiyong[22] and rights advocate Guo Feixiong.[23]

In the case against lawyer Gao Zhisheng, tried for inciting subversion in 2006, for example, his wife was put under informal house-arrest together with their children and they were prevented from signing an appointment form;[24] and it took his family several weeks before they were able to hand deliver a form signed

19 October 2012, at http://news.sina.com.cn/c/sd/2012-10-19/120825394306.shtml, accessed 1 January 2014. This rule was not ultimately adopted. Cp. 中华人民共和国最高人民法院司法解释法释[Supreme People's Court, PRC SPC Judicial Interpretation on the Criminal Procedure Law], passed on 5 November 2012, promulgated on 20 December 2012, effective as of 1 January 2013, at http://legal.people.com.cn/n/2012/1224/c42510-20000004.html, accessed 1 January 2014.
17 Jerome A. Cohen, 'China trips up its barefoot lawyers', *Far Eastern Economic Review* (November 2005) 168.
18 Discussed below.
19 Teng Biao et al., '我们愿意为被捕藏民提供法律帮助 [We are willing to provide legal assistance to criminally arrested Tibetans]', 2 April 2008, at http://www.peacehall.com/news/gb/china/2008/04/200804022305.shtml. See also Chapter 3.
20 Amnesty International, 'China holds Uighur journalist over Xinjiang unrest remarks', 30 October 2009, at http://www.amnesty.org/en/news-and-updates/news/china-holds-uighur-journalist-over-xinjiang-unrest-remarks-20091030, accessed 1 January 2014. #91 2013-1.
21 Amnesty International, 'Against the law, crackdown on China's human rights lawyers deepens', June 2011, at http://www.amnesty.nl/sites/default/files/public/china_-_against_the_law.pdf, accessed 1 January 2014, at p. 31.
22 Human Rights in China, 'Xu Zhiyong's lawyer Liu Weiguo in custody, rights group is shut down', 18 July 2013, at http://www.hrichina.org/en/content/6825, accessed 1 January 2014. Also #19 2013-1.
23 China Change, 'Denied meetings, advocates fear for activist Guo Feixong', 18 October 2013, at http://chinachange.org/2013/10/18/denied-meetings-lawyers-fear-for-advocate-guo-feixiong/, accessed 1 January 2014. Also #88 2013-1, 2.
24 Laojoh (pen name), '高智晟侄子试找人签律师委托书受阻 [Gao Zhisheng's nephew obstructed when trying to get letter of attorney signed]', 6 September 2006, at http://boxun.com/forum/zongjiao/12033.shtml, accessed 1 January 2014.

by Lawyer Gao's older brother from rural Shaanxi to the lawyer in Beijing. When he promptly presented it to the authorities, the letter 'disappeared' in the bureaucratic apparatus supposed to facilitate the lawyer's access to his client for several days, resurfacing only after public protest.[25]

In the 2008 case of Yang Jia, the unemployed, apparently mentally disturbed young man who had allegedly stabbed six police officers in a revenge attack in Shanghai in 2008,[26] the authorities detained his mother in a psychiatric hospital and then produced her 'letter of appointment' for an obedient lawyer chosen by the authorities, at the same time declaring that the lawyer appointed by Yang Jia's father was ineffective, since a lawyer had already been appointed. The lawyer 'appointed' by the mother publicly predicted that 'in such an aggravated case' his client was likely to receive the death penalty, and indeed, by the time his mother was released, her son had already been executed.[27] She had been allowed to see him one last time, but not been told at the time that he was about to be killed.

Lawyers' testimony suggests that in many of these cases, obstruction and inter-ference with the appointment of lawyers ultimately takes the form of an unequal bargain in which the authorities use their factual (albeit unlawful) control of access to the criminal suspect in detention to 'persuade' a team of preferred lawyers not to take on a particular case, and to discuss alternative appointments. This was the case, for instance, when rights defender Guo Feixiong was not allowed to see the two lawyers he had designated prior to his criminal detention. They protested in a series of open letters, but were unable to obtain the authorities' 'approval'. As anxiety about Guo Fexiong's wellbeing rose (he had been tortured on previous occasions), it was considered that perhaps another lawyer should take over.[28] The lawyers ultimately allowed to meet the client brought back a report about his 25-day hunger strike in detention.[29] In other cases, it appeared that suspects were successfully persuaded to 'dismiss' their lawyer while in detention and to confess, in exchange for the offer of 'lenient' treatment.[30]

If the process of seeking access to their client and exercising the right to repre-sent this client can be trying, rights lawyers may face further difficulties when they have been successfully retained. Resourceful authorities unable to prevent them from being hired have on other occasions successfully prevented them from appearing in court or taken measures to intimidate them just before the trial. Thus two criminal defence lawyers were criminally detained 'on suspicion of

---

25 Hu Jia(胡佳), '高智晟大哥签署委托书; 中共享黑帮手段胁迫撤销委托书 [Gao Zhisheng's older brother signs letter of attorney, CCP uses thugs to force lawyers' dismissal]', letter to the editor, *Epoch Times* (大纪元) 14 October 2006, at http://www.epochtw.com/6/10/14/38774g. htm, accessed 1 January 2014. On Gao Zhisheng, see also Eva Pils, 'Asking the tiger for his skin: rights activism in China', 30 *Fordham International Law Journal* (2007) 1209–1287.

26 See also Chapter 3.

27 Eva Pils, 'Yang Jia and China's unpopular criminal justice system', in 1 *China Rights Forum* (2009) 59–66. See Chapter 3 on arguments suggesting Yang Jia was not the killer.

28 #88 2013-1,2.

29 Verna Yu, 'Detained Guo Feixiong tells lawyer of hunger strike', *South China Morning Post*, 14 November 2014.

30 Keith Zhai, 'Rights advocate Wang Gongquan latest to give video confession', *South China Morning Post*, 6 November 2013.

theft' of a wallet the day before the trial of Chen Guangcheng in Linyi, Shandong, in 2005.[31] In another case, a lawyer was told that 'a provincial level document' stipulated that in Falun Gong cases, 'the defendant must not be represented by outside [non-local] lawyers', held against his will and deprived of his mobile phone before he was sent back.[32] In certain instances, lawyers were physically assaulted shortly before the court hearing. In one such case, local police officers attacked a young lawyer with fists right outside a court building. His description captures the embarrassment and muted outrage the attack produced.

> A woman judge saw us. She lowered her head; I think she was ashamed. Then an elderly woman came along, just an ordinary elderly woman, and she was the only one who said something. She said, 'How can you beat this person, *several* police officers at a time!'[33]

In another case in 2011, the criminal defence lawyer in a Falun Gong case was assaulted while asleep in a hotel. Purporting to be robbers, the two attackers removed the lawyer's computer, mobile phone and shoes, forcing him to appear in court in hotel slippers the next morning. He published an online account of his experience entitled 'Account of a curious robbery – deeply thanking my robbers for taking no valuables.'[34] His computer was returned to his hotel room the following day, infected by malware, making a simple robbery or the intention seriously to fake one appear unlikely.

In cases of violent assaults such as those described above, the absence of official explanations is hardly surprising. When asked about reasons given for non-criminal obstruction measures, lawyers at most report vague references to 'the upper levels'.[35] Thus the authorities' silence on the sources and basis of such measures suits the system: on the one hand, it would gain nothing from exposing the working of those of its parts, which are not part of the framework of publicly enacted laws, or of what Ernst Fraenkel would have called the 'State of norms'.[36] On the other, allowing lawyers glimpses of the powers and practices that explain decisions to disregard the law when expedient may serve as a useful reminder of the presence of powers which the law of the State cannot reach.

31 Joseph Kahn, 'Advocate for China's weak crosses the powerful', *New York Times*, 20 July 2006, at http://www.nytimes.com/2006/07/20/world/asia/20blind.html?_r=1&ex=1154059200&en=f468ddc24bc80f6d&ei=5070, accessed 9 November 2013.

32 Voice of America (Mandarin Desk), '吉林 610 办公室阻挠律师依法辩护 [A Jilin 610 Office obstructs lawyer's lawful criminal defence]', 13 September 2010, at http://www.voanews.com/chinese/news/china/20100913-lawyer-harassed-102769329.html, accessed 9 November 2013. Also #55 2011-1.

33 #7 2011-1.

34 Li Jinglin (李静林), '记我被抢的奇遇, 真切感谢劫匪不贪财 [Account of a curious robbery – deeply thanking my robbers for taking no valuables]', 26 April 2011, at http://www.peacehall.com/news/gb/china/2011/04/201104260023.shtml, accessed 9 November 2013.

35 Chapter 3 describes the experience of one lawyer trying to see his client under the new rules of the 2013 CPL.

36 Ernst Fraenkel, *The Dual State. A Contribution to the Theory of Dictatorship*, translated by E.A. Shils, Oxford University Press, New York: 1941.

'Managing' the trial

Trials that include rights lawyers must, from the authorities' perspective, be managed as well as possible, in order to ensure what is characterised as a 'smooth' (*shunli*),[37] or orderly running of the trial. This is the case especially with criminal trials, which are essential to support the claim that criminals are handled and punished in accordance with law (*yifa*).[38] The meaning of these expressions may be explained as 'following the procedure set up by relevant laws and regulations', with an emphasis on visible obedience to the rules, but potential disregard for their purpose:

> I am not sure about ordinary cases but in the kinds of case we handle it is like this: The judge anyway can't decide the case. S/he must just turn up and go through this procedure, holding the trial in a way that complies with formal requirements.[39]

In order to secure what they regard as a 'smooth' trial process, judges are understood to seek the defence's compliance in advance of the hearing in some non-routine cases. Thus in the first-instance retrial (on appeal) of a complicated drug-related case, in which two of the three defendants were facing the death penalty, two lawyers involved commented as follows:

> Just before the court hearing began, the judge called us outside the courtroom, where he said, 'Gentlemen, I hope we can run this hearing in a smooth way and finish by the end of the day, without any disruptions.'[40]
>
> We nodded and assented, but of course we were not going to be influenced by this.[41]

Before this, in the first (first-instance) trial, one of the defendants had been approached by the trial judge, according to what he told his defence lawyer at the retrial stage:

> In this case the judge in the first instance trial[42] was called [X]. When he first saw [the defendant] he said to him 'At trial, you've got to testify in accordance with what you told the police. You can't just say whatever you want. If not, I will send the case back [for further investigation].' This would have been possible in accordance with our Criminal Procedure Law ... Of course it would have meant that the defendant [who had been tortured very cruelly] might be beaten again, and perhaps even worse than the first time. [Judge X] said that to [the defendant] before the trial hearing. 'Second, you must dismiss the [local] lawyer you had hired in this case

---

37 In Chinese characters, 顺利.
38 In Chinese characters, 依法.
39 #2 2012-5.
40 #69 2012-1.
41 #2 2012-5.
42 The case was tried twice in first instance.

[i.e. not one of the later *weiquan* lawyers]. Third, you mustn't let your [two relatives] submit complaints in all sorts of places.'[43]

It appears clear, from the course this case took, that the judge's communications were effective and that only after rights lawyers got involved in second instance (retrial), the defendant felt emboldened to retract his 'confession'.

The lawyer further explained trial judges' practice of communicating with defendants in advance. Given that the trial judge was not allowed to decide the case, he pointed out, this practice made some sense, and indeed might be expected from a conscientious trial judge – even though as just seen, the judge in the case here discussed acted in violation not only of rules disallowing ex parte contact, but also in flagrant violation of the procedural rules protecting the accused against threats (e.g. through Article 43 CPL):[44]

> Of course, in western law this is not allowed, due to the presumption of innocence.[45] . . . It is of course easy to understand that the [trial] judge can't see the defendant prior to the trial, that the judge must listen to both sides' arguments at the trial and make a decision [based on the trial]. But in China, the case is decided by the Political–Legal Committee or an even higher authority. Now of course, these authorities will need to listen to the views of the judge in charge and also of the police officers in charge – the police president may well be the Political–Legal Committee president. So, they must understand more about the case from the judge in charge. It therefore makes perfect sense for the judge in charge to go and meet the defendant prior to the trial, and then to report to the Political–Legal Committee.

To secure a 'smooth process', many efforts may be made to control the course of the trial through direct interventions during trial. Most commonly, judges may interrupt lawyers and their clients (criminal defendants or complainants) in order to stop them from mentioning points which in their view ought not to be part of the trial process, such as allegations of torture or references to human rights violations inherent to substantive criminal law. For example, in a courtroom in Luzhou in 2009 Lawyers Liu Wei and Tang Jitian, defending a Falun Gong practitioner, were instructed by the presiding judge that:

> [We] were not allowed to engage in an analysis of the nature of the crime, and we were not allowed to analyse the application of the law to that

---

43 #2 2012-5.
44 Gong Ting, 'Dependent judiciary and unaccountable judges: judicial corruption in contemporary China', 4 *China Review* 2 (2004); Li Ling, 'The "production" of corruption in China's courts – the politics of judicial decision-making and its consequences in a one-party state', 5 July 2011, *Journal of Law & Social Inquiry*, 2011, at http://ssrn.com/abstract=188014.
45 In continental European systems, trial judges are no longer able to access the accused before trial. In Germany, the office of *Untersuchungsrichter* has been abolished; French law distinguishes between jurisdiction over investigation and adjudicative decision processes; (even so, the office of the *juge d'instruction* continues to be criticised).

case . . . I think that's really strange: If they can't analyse the nature of the crime or the application of the law to the case, what are lawyers supposed to say [in defence of their client]? These are the key issues in a criminal case! . . . The judge kept hammering his gavel. He did that to keep Tang Jitian and me from speaking. The moment we started discussing the application of the law or the nature of the crime, he hammered wildly. He hammered so furiously that it hurt our ears. Before he started hammering in this way there was a preparatory signal that went like this: Right beneath his desk there sat a man who looked like a government official, and he would exchange glances with this man, or sometimes this man would cough. Then the judge would immediately interrupt us and follow with pounding the gavel, once, then a second time if Lawyer Tang or I did not stop speaking; And if we still didn't stop, he went *bang bang bang bang*, like this.[46]

In another case, Lawyer Wang Quanzhang's efforts to present his criminal defence statement – according to his later description, he had merely raised his voice when meeting with similar obstruction from the judge – resulted in his 'judicial detention' for a number of days at the conclusion of the trial hearing.[47]

Reducing the public nature of trials

Despite some important exceptions, including cases affecting national security the law generally requires trials to be public; this means that any Chinese citizen may enter on the strength of their national ID card. In fact, however, the authorities screen some trials from the public scrutiny they ought to receive by blocking certain persons from attending. This practice is to some extent supported by the PRC People's Courts' Rules on Courtroom Order,[48] whose Article 8 states that minors, mentally disabled people and 'other people whose attendance would be inexpedient' may not attend; and whose Article 9 provides for the use of 'attendance permits' or *pangtingzheng*.[49] The legitimacy of these rules created by the judiciary itself is in doubt, since they undermine the principle of public trials.

The ability of the authorities to screen out would-be audiences in hearings deemed sensitive significantly reduces the value of trials with selectively assembled audiences. Such trials are not genuinely public even though they are officially called public trials. Courtrooms are packed so that 'no more seats were available'; undesirable individuals seeking admission to the courtroom are simply denied an attendance permit. Foreigners are on occasion allowed to attend court hearings, but attendance in a politically sensitive case is usually impossible. In addition to

---

46 Liu Wei in He Yang, [independent documentary film] *Disbarment* (吊照门, 2010). Contrast with #3 2012-1: 'Here [in the south], the 610 office will merely send someone round to attend the trial; but there will not be any [direct] interference.'
47 As discussed in Chapter 7.
48 *Supra*, note 3.
49 In Chinese characters, 旁听证.

the exclusion from the actual courtroom, the authorities take further measures in some cases. In some cases, moreover, persons planning to attend are house-arrested or detained to prevent them from even getting close to the court building.[50]

In addition to these extensive opportunities to control public access to trials, they are also managed to allow for the 'participation' of those who are an essential part of the proceedings, such as the Adjudication Committee or Political and Legal Committee, who in some cases are actually in control of the process but cannot be seen to be part of it. Measures taken to allow them to monitor the proceedings include the use of video cameras – thus in the Luzhou trial just mentioned, an unidentified man was seen to film the proceedings, according to Liu Wei.[51] Some rights lawyers have expressed the belief that sometimes a trial is even video-streamed into a separate room in which the higher political leadership watches the proceedings, so as to be able to give instructions in real time:

> The reason for this is that they may fear being recognized. If they are recognized then others may think that their presence has influenced the way the judge holds the trial . . . Of course, the judge is in fact influenced by them. But they still don't want others to see that.[52]

Such reports and concerns cannot be further investigated. The fact that lawyers are exposed to experiences (e.g. the video-recording in the Luzhou trial) that justifiably give rise to these doubts is by itself significant. The purpose of public trials is to allow for public scrutiny, not least because this protects against undue interference with weaker parties in the trial process. To install or even institutionalise video-monitoring of the trial proceedings is to create a positively intimidating atmosphere of constraint and Party–State control. In an apparent effort to create an even more controlled environment, some officially 'public' court hearings were reportedly held in places of pretrial detention instead of in court buildings in some individual cases, possibly due to consideration of expediency:

> Once I went to a prison in X district [of a large city] and they had a court-room there [inside the prison] to try people who commit offences while in prison . . . The law makes provisions for [holding trials in improvised courtrooms in] remote places, and so on. But it certainly doesn't

---

50 For instance, several individuals were prevented from attending the trial of rights defender Wang Lihong. Charles Hutzler, 'Wang Lihong, Chinese online activist, sentenced to prison for staging protest', 9 September 2011, at http://www.huffingtonpost.com/2011/09/09/wang-lihong-prison_n_955226.html, accessed 9 November 2013; 'Chinese activist Wang Lihong's trial "not fair" says lawyer', *NTDTV*, at http://www.youtube.com/watch?v=pbOs4aQ1UVw, accessed 9 November 2013.

51 Liu Wei in He Yang (*supra* note); Committee to Support Chinese Lawyers 'Letter to Director Yu Hongyuan of Beijing Municipal Bureau of Justice', 21 April 2010, at http://www.csclawyers.org/letters/CSCL%20Letter%2004.21.2010%20BJJB.pdf, accessed 9 November 2013.

52 #2 2012-5. For an account of CCP influence on trials, see also Li Ling, *supra*, especially at pp. 10 ff.

allow for court hearings to be held in the [police] detention centre or in the prison![53]

The circumstances reported by another lawyer suggested that the chosen venue served the purpose of minimising public scrutiny:

> In one case concerning Article 300 of the Criminal Law [i.e. an 'evil cult' crime], the trial was held right inside the police detention centre ... The detention centre only has interrogation rooms, meeting rooms for lawyers and for family members. Those are in the front part, in the back part there are the cells, and a courtyard. There is no courtroom there because [the meeting rooms] are also within the closed area and outside people can't enter. So this entirely fails to meet the requirements for a courtroom. This is clearly a serious violation of the law. The problem is that just as in other cases of Chinese law, there is nothing that stipulates the legal consequences of a violation of the rules by public power ...[54]

Obstructing cases against the authorities

In recent years, the Party–State has made considerable efforts to prevent certain cases from going to court, and to control the ability of lawyers to become active in cases. Some of these efforts, such as the 2006 ACLA Guidelines on mass litigation and sensitive cases and intervention on the part of judicial bureaux, lawyers' associations and law firm heads to stop lawyers from taking on certain cases, or to request advance copies of criminal defence statements from lawyers identified as 'sensitive', shall be discussed in the next chapter. Additional ways of preventing court litigation from happening include not filing cases, and an increased use of mechanisms to avoid litigious decision processes in favour of settlements, where this is possible.

The problem of courts not filing cases, especially cases of administrative litigation, but also civil litigation cases brought against State or other powerful entities,[55] explains in part why so many petitioners seek justice through the Letters and Visits system; it also explains how human rights lawyers are prevented from engaging in courtroom advocacy outside the criminal process. Regarding certain types of dispute, there are reports of directions given to judges not to file particular kinds of cases, and while there have been public instructions from the SPC not to handle particular kinds of case.[56] More common are local-level

---

53 #7 2011-2.
54 #21 1108 34:00.
55 Eva Pils, 'Land disputes, rights assertion and social unrest: a case from Sichuan', 19 *Columbia Journal of Asian Law* (2006) 365; reprinted as Hauser Global Law School Working Paper 07/05 and in Perry Keller (editor), *Obligations and Property Rights in China*, Ashgate, Aldershot: 2012.
56 E.g. 最高人民法院关于受理虚假陈述的证券民事纠纷的通知 [SPC Notice on Relevant Issues Concerning the Acceptance of the Issue of Accepting Cases of Securities Markets Civil Tort Dispute Cases Caused by False Statements in the Securities Markets], 15 January 2002,

directions not to file certain cases may generically affect a particular group of cases and general reluctance to file cases in which the defendant would be the government. Decisions not to file cases may also be taken in cases where an unwelcome complainant has become active:

> Initially I thought that case filing was not a problem. But [in one case] there was even a judge who when refusing to file a case threw the materials out of the room into the corridor. That was in 2008. We even recorded this, at the time. . . . If the judge takes a case and the result is bad, this will affect the judge's performance record. Only entirely ordinary cases will not raise a problem with filing the case. Hep B cases are not the worst. At least initially, it was not so much because particular interests were affected, but rather that these cases were so new. There are, of course, also cases where the problem is whose interests are affected.[57]

Several lawyers approached in the context of this project expressed the view that in certain types of case it had become harder in recent years to file cases. Not filing cases is an effective means of suppressing courtroom litigation especially where the complainant is in a particularly weak position – for instance, because they are in detention, or because they have been subjected to extra-legal harassment. One such type of case is administrative litigation against a police decision to impose Re-education Through Labour (RTL) – this measure allows for detention of a person for up to four years without any trial, albeit with a chance of bringing administrative litigation against the decision once it has been taken and the would-be complainant having been detained:

> Most judges will listen to the Party and Government; but there are still some judges with a conscience and these might decide that the imposition of RTL was illegal. That's the reason they now want to cut off the litigious avenue completely, and not let cases get into court.[58]

This view is supported by academic studies on the disposition of cases according to statistical information and administrative court division judges' performance evaluation criteria. According to one scholar, these suggest that in administrative litigation, performance criteria requiring courts to file large numbers of cases first drove up the numbers of litigation, but that subsequently, further instructions caused high rates of 'settled' cases to avoid high percentages of administrative litigation cases supporting the complainant. As the proportion of settled cases increased, that of cases won against the government decreased. This suggests that

at http://www.law-lib.com/law/law_view.asp?id=16956, accessed 4 January 2014; Secret China（看中国）'最高法内部文件被泄露 网络审查纠纷不立案   [SPC internal document on not filing cases concerning internet censorship revealed]', 25 April 2012, at http://www.secretchina.com/news/12/04/25/449323.html, accessed 1 January 2014.
57 #50 2011-1.
58 #52 2011-1.

judges might be reluctant to decide against patently well-founded complainants and push parties to settle in such cases:[59]

> Now there is this great problem with not filing cases. Including even simple land conflicts, cases about residential plots in rural areas, and so on; the judge will just not file the case saying, 'this case is a bit too complicated.' There used to be target quota such as for filing [administrative litigation] cases, disposition of cases and so on; but I think that these kinds of requirement have become fewer, because complying with them is no longer practicable . . . It really is as though the courts had begun to withdraw from litigious court procedures altogether. . . . When you get to court, they just refuse to file cases without any written explanation. And this problem affects more and more cases. The moment they have accepted a case the conflict in question has come to their court and they are responsible for it, and they don't want that. The conflicts are becoming more and more obvious.[60]

The same lawyer narrated a particular case of an attempt to file administrative litigation against a decision to impose RTL. The application for filing the case and initiate a court litigation process had been sent to the court by (registered) speed-mail, and the sender, the lawyer, had been duly notified of its receipt by the recipient:

> 'For instance in the RTL case that I was just mentioning, I speed-mailed the letter to the court. It initially received it, but then it immediately sent it back. Just like that.'[61]

The lawyer produced the envelope he had sent to the court for illustration. It was unopened and showed a stamp that read 'reject and send back (*tuihui*)',[62] making it apparent not only that the court had thought better of even opening the envelope addressed to it, but also that, so enmeshed in its own procedures, there was a required bureaucratic need for a stamp to 'reject and send back'.

Judges will rarely be fully open about the reasons why they do not want to 'file' particular cases; but occasionally provide a direct explanation under pressure from the parties. In one case, according to a lawyer's report, the parties went to the court to try and negotiate for the filing of their case:

> They said, the Party and Government won't allow this case to be filed. They said that right in the parties' faces. The parties actually have an audio-

---

59 He Haibo (何海波), '没有判决的诉讼: 行政诉讼撤诉考 (1987–2008) [Litigation without decision: on withdrawal of complaints in administrative litigation (1987–2008)]', 4 *Peking University Law Review* (北大法律评论) 2 (2002), at http://article.chinalawinfo.com/Article_Detail.asp?ArticleID=23443, accessed 9 November 2013.
60 #52 2011-1.
61 #52 2011-1.
62 In Chinese characters, 退回.

recording of that. . . . At the time they first demanded that the clients hand over all phones and things to avoid recording. Then they just said it like that: 'the Party and Government don't allow the filing of this case.'[63]

The unopened envelope sent back to the lawyer in the abovementioned RTL case, and the conduct of the judge 'who threw the application materials out into the corridor' in the Hepatitis B discrimination case capture official anxieties about filing certain cases better than spoken words. The hidden rules governing the conduct of trials and attitude toward defendants and defence lawyers in court, the rules and practices that characterise the Party–State's handling of petitioners, as well as the explicit political rhetoric developed by the political leadership of the Chinese judiciary indicate that a mental division has been established between regular and irregular, troublemaking citizens. Members of the latter category are not meant to get access to justice; and in cases of doubt or 'newness' of a complaint, it is safest not to admit that complaint. The unopened envelope is a reflection, ultimately, of the recently revived theory of contradictions,[64] according to which contradictions between the people and its enemies must be handled in different ways from ordinary conflicts; patently, recalcitrant petitioners are 'enemies'.

'Harmonising' the judicial process

While the Party–State has an interest in holding but also tightly controlling court hearings in criminal cases, where the trial process as such is expected to increase its legitimacy, a different dynamic applies in other kinds of case, where lawyers act on behalf of persons seeking redress for human rights violations. As discussed in Chapter 3, complainants routinely turn to the petitioning system, as well as to the courts; and indeed, those who feel wronged by the courts, may engage in 'litigation-related petitioning', i.e. complaints by litigants or would-be litigants about the courts.[65] Petitioners have played a major role in challenging the courts, as is discussed further below; and the example of the 100 evictees turning up for a court hearing in Beijing cited above illustrates the ability they

---

63 #52 2011-1. See also He Haibo, *supra*, for similar examples.
64 Mao Zedong (毛泽东), 1957, 'On the correct handling of contradictions among the people', (translation) in Selden, Mark, *The People's Republic of China: A Documentary History of Revolutionary Change*, New York Monthly Review Press, New York: 1979. See Chapter 2.
65 Minzner, Carl F., 'Xinfang: an alternative to the formal Chinese legal system', 42 *Stanford Journal of International Law* (2006) 103; Li Li, 'Judicial independence should come first', 10 November 2005 interview with Professor He Weifang, at http://chinadigitaltimes.net/2005/11/judicial-independence-should-come-first-li-li/, accessed 10 November 2013; Yu, Jianrong, 'The petitioners' dilemma and the way out [中国信访制度的困境和出路]', 1 *Strategy and Management* (2009), at http://theory.rmlt.com.cn/2012/1126/54714.shtml, accessed 10 November 2013. It must be noted that the popularity of *she sushangfang* (in Chinese characters, 涉诉上访), litigation-related petitioning, is also due to the fact that court decisions can be challenged easily – and this, in turn, is due to the fact that the courts are so controlled.

have to 'disrupt the script' and protest in a highly vocal manner. The fact that this has led to further pressure on them as well as on the courts is ultimately a consequence of political decisions against further openness and for 'social stability'. Public dissatisfaction with the justice system has led to a number of policies and directives seeking to address dissatisfaction. Among these there have been policies ordering courts to take popular sentiment into account in deciding criminal cases.[66] In 2011 this led, among other things, to the death sentence for a young student from a supposedly middle-class background, and to a young migrant worker being spared the death penalty.[67]

On the other hand in the name of 'harmony (*hexie*)',[68] 'stability preservation (*weiwen*)'[69] and 'social management (*shehui guanli*)',[70] an increasing number of judicial policies and un-official practices have aimed to effectively eliminate trials and court hearings by resolving disputes in alternative ways or suppressing them. 'Harmonious society' was propagated in a Party Central meeting of October 2006.[71] 'Harmony' was widely understood as another expression for 'social stability' and, in that meaning, it soon came to be associated with repression of public dissension. Being 'harmonised', in the Chinese slang of bloggers and microbloggers, came to mean having one's posts deleted by censors. Popular uses in judicial contexts can be similar, as when citizens complain that their citizen's right to attend a public trial has been 'harmonised'.[72]

Following the announcement of 'harmonious society,' official calls for 'harmonious adjudication'[73] soon triggered a move away from adversarial court processes. From 2008, the judiciary's political leadership encouraged the use of judicial mediation, in the name of 'Great Mediation' (*da tiaojie*)[74] and 'harmonious adjudication' (*hexie shenpan*)[75] campaigns. Individual courts were praised for

---

66 Notably, courts were instructed in 2008 to pay attention to popular sentiment in applying the death penalty, for example. For a discussion of this instruction see McConville, *supra*, p. 396; Jerome A. Cohen, 'Body blow for the judiciary', *South China Morning Post*, 18 October 2008, at http://www.cfr.org/publication/17565/body_blow_for_the_judiciary.html?breadcrumb=%2Fbi os%2F14%2Fjerome_a_cohen, accessed 10 November 2013.

67 Susan Trevaskes compares the criminal cases of Yao Jiaxin and Li Changkun in 'The ideology of law and order', (2012), http://www.thechinastory.org/wp-content/uploads/2012/07/ChinaStory2012.pdf, accessed 1 January 2014.

68 In Chinese characters, 和谐.

69 In Chinese characters, 维稳.

70 In Chinese characters, 社会管理.

71 See Xinhua News, 'Party Central resolution on the construction of a socialist harmonious society', [中共中央关于构建社会主义和谐社会若干重大问题的决定], passed on 11 October 2006, at http://news.xinhuanet.com/politics/2006-10/18/content_5218639.htm, accessed 14 November 2013.

72 Zhongyizhe (忠义者, a pseudonym), '6月8日被"被和谐"的法院旁听 [A "harmonised" attendance at trial]', 8 June 2012 at http://hd3g.gxnews.com.cn/viewthread.php?t=7103215, accessed 1 January 2014.

73 Luo Gan (罗干), '政法机关在构建和谐社会中担负重大历史使命和政治责任 [The political and judicial authorities' historic mission and political responsibility for constructing a harmonious society]', 3 *Qiushi Journal* (求是) (2007), at http://theory.people.com.cn/GB/49169/49171/5355912.html, accessed 10 November 2013.

74 In Chinese characters, 大调解.

75 In Chinese characters, 和谐审判.

achieving a '100% mediation rate' through the institution of 'social' courts in one year.[76]

In administrative and criminal litigation, the settlement process is referred to as 'reconciliation'. While the 1990 Administrative Litigation Law explicitly disallows administrative mediation, 'reconciliation' was allowed in Supreme People's Court Judicial Interpretations;[77] and the 2012 Criminal Procedure Law has adopted provisions introducing 'reconciliation' in criminal justice processes.[78] In 'criminal reconciliation', the suspect or defendant and the victim are 'persuaded' to negotiate a settlement, or indeed to accept a settlement imposed by the State official in charge. The law requires that the suspect or defendant admit guilt and be 'remorseful', and that the victim be a 'voluntary' participant in criminal reconciliation. If on this basis 'forgiveness' by the victim can be achieved, charges against a criminal suspect may be dropped or a defendant may be given a more lenient sentence.[79]

To judge by the changes in procedures and by what rights lawyers report of their work, the impact of 'harmony' on judicial practice/the administration of justice appears to have been profound. In criminal trials, a settlement can be achieved through the use of 'criminal reconciliation', a procedure formally recognised in the 2012 Criminal Procedure Law revision, or similar techniques sometimes referred to as 'reducing punishment by paying compensation' [to the alleged victim]. For instance, at the suggestion of the court, there can be an offer of compensation by the alleged perpetrator to the victim or the victim's family; 'in exchange' for this the court can undertake to reduce the sentence. The relevant negotiations are undertaken between the victim's family, the lawyer, and the court.[80] The uses of 'mediation' and 'reconciliation' and of adjudication styles aimed at achieving 'mediated' results has origins in the Mao era, in which it was associated with Mao's Theory of Contradictions. These techniques suit the power distribution in the legal–political system better than adversarial court processes. As 'mediation' and 'reconciliation' have been given clearer statutory bases, e.g. in the criminal process, continued use of these techniques seems assured as long as official campaigns reviving Mao Zedong thought and practices under the new Party leadership of Xi Jinping continue.

76 Cheng Yuanjing and Cao Tianxiang (程远景,曹天祥), '河南方城县社会法庭受理案件调解率达100% [Mediation rate in Henan Facheng Social Court hits 100%]', 19 August 2011, at http://court.gmw.cn/html/article/201108/19/76103.shtml, accessed 1 January 2014.
77 See最高人民法院关于执行〈中华人民共和国行政诉讼法〉若干问题的解释[Supreme People's Court, Interpretation on Several Issues concerning the Implementation of the PRC Administrative Procedure], promulgated on 8 March 2000, effective as of 10 March 2000, at http://www.pkulaw.cn/fulltext_form.aspx?Gid=26982, accessed 10 November 2013; 最高人民法院〈关于行政诉讼证据若干问题的规定 [Supreme People's Court Regulations on Several Issues concerning Evidence in Administrative Procedures, promulgated on 24 July 2002, effective as of 1 October 2002, at http://www.jincao.com/fa/22/law22.14.htm, accessed 10 November 2013.
78 Article 277, 2012 CPL.
79 Jiang Jue, 'The practice of "criminal reconciliation" (*xingshi hejie*) in the PRC criminal justice system', PhD dissertation at the Chinese University of Hong Kong (2012).
80 Joshua Rosenzweig et al., 'The 2012 revision', *supra*.

Empirical research on criminal reconciliation pilot projects in recent years suggests that even in cases perceived to have gone well and in accordance with designated procedure, reconciliation consists mainly in a bargaining process about the compensation amount, sometimes without the suspect or defendant even being present. 'Reconciliation' – or the result of a bargain – may be imposed, however, because it is in the interests of the State to avoid disgruntled (putative) victims, and because judges may be given 'reconciliation quota' they have to fulfil. Moreover, despite its statutorily limited scope 'reconciliation' is, in effect, used, for example, through a mechanism known as 'paying money to avoid/lower punishment', in extremely serious cases including cases of homicide and death penalty cases.[81] The issues discussed above affect all lawyers. Not all lawyers are likely to be reluctant to adapt to the judicial practices and trends mentioned; and from the perspective of this study the potential usefulness of mediation and reconciliation processes in some cases cannot be disputed. One of the reasons why lawyers, 'rights lawyers' included, often welcome the availability of mediation and reconciliation as an option is that it can help to mitigate problems arising in ordinary adjudication process, in particular, the harshness and frequent unfairness of criminal trials.[82]

However, under 'criminal reconciliation', lawyers run the obvious risk of being co-opted into a practice that transforms their function to one of ultimately dispensable 'facilitation' rather than rights defence. The changing function of court hearings affects rights lawyers and the human rights movement in a particular way. The rise of rights lawyers was due in part to their ability to make the court hearing an opportunity for genuine rights advocacy for criminal defence lawyers who come to the courtroom well prepared to plead not guilty on behalf of their clients. In the cases in which rights lawyers have been active, even highly flawed trials have still given them an opportunity to expose these flaws, and publicly to challenge the way in which cases are decided.

Limited achievements in courtroom advocacy

The fact of intense efforts to keep human rights lawyers out of courtrooms testifies to their perceived ability to disrupt routines and irritate the authorities. Despite the numerous constraints and efforts to eliminate trials outlined above, courtroom advocacy takes place and is meaningful, not only in the Party–State tolerated zones of advocacy on behalf of specific causes outlined below, but also and especially outside these zones of toleration. It is meaningful to advocates themselves, because it provides for a special setting in which they can 'speak truth' to the power of the Party–State – and in which the State's (and the Party's) representatives must hear them, even though they may choose not to listen or, if they listen, may not be able to respond in positive ways. As shown below, this has great significance for the advocates' (so easily endangered) sense of self-worth and personal resilience.

---

81 Jiang Jue, *supra*; Joshua Rosenzweig et al., 'The 2012 revision', *supra*.
82 # 56 2012-1.

It is also meaningful politically, for other trial participants and for the community that learns about such rights advocacy, even though straightforward legal victories through courtroom advocacy are extremely rare. The political significance of courtroom advocacy rests to some extent in the importance of collective memories created through advocacy; in the fact that cases, even if they superficially 'fail', can contribute to an intellectual as well as emotional archive of contention with the Party–State. In this context, the emotions of individuals involved in these processes have political significance as much as the rational argument and written and unwritten rules do.

The anxiety, fear, frustration, despair and anger felt by various participants of such comparatively extraordinary trials help to complement accounts of more subdued ordinary trials, allowing us better to understand the normalcy of control and suppression in ordinary court adjudication.

Advocacy inside tolerated zones

Observers suggest that certain areas of advocacy – such as disability rights, LGBT rights, and labour rights more readily promise success and the possibility of meaningful reform as a result of such advocacy.[83] Employment discrimination litigation in which the litigant has been a confirmed carrier of the contagious disease Hepatitis B is among the more promising rights defence cases.[84] The facts supporting such complaints are usually clear, the law is clear, and lawyers and groups specialising in employment discrimination tend to pick private entities, not government agencies as defendants in these cases, as discussed earlier.[85] In addition to these advantages, a lawyer explained, official support for protection of the Hepatitis B carriers has a direct impact on the courts' willingness to 'file' such cases – a precondition for the adjudication of the case by the court, as was seen in Chapter 3.

> In Hepatitis B [employment discrimination] cases, the judges [initially] felt that these cases could not be accepted so they would find all sorts of problems with your application. But . . . it has become comparatively speaking a bit easier to get such cases filed now, *because the policy environment has changed . . . and there have been many official statements confirming that Hep B carriers should be protected.* Last year, for example, we would bring [supporting] materials with us [for filing case]: some media reports where you did not see much [critical] official voices, and we would print out the laws and regulations for them, and also show them some decided cases which had been won, to show them that it

83 Thomas E. Kellogg, 'Western funding for rule of law initiatives in China: the importance of a civil society-based approach', *China Perspectives* (2012/3) 53–59, at http://chinaperspectives.revues.org/5954, accessed 14 November 2013.
84 Timothy Webster, 'Ambivalence and activism: employment discrimination in China', 44 *Vanderbilt Journal of Transnational Law* (2011) 643, at http://digitalcommons.law.yale.edu/cgi/viewcontent.cgi?article=1000&context=ylas, accessed 13 November 2013.
85 See Chapter 3. Also, #23 2011-4.

was possible to accept to file such a case and that other people [judges] who had accepted them hadn't run into any trouble, either. That was quite effective, because this way the judge could accept the case *feeling quite safe*.[86] (emphases added)

In such Hepatitis B-based employment discrimination cases, lawyers could successfully sue employers on the basis of detailed new legislation that prohibits such discrimination[87] and sometimes win compensation for their clients:

[In] my very first case of Hep B discrimination . . . the judge gave a definition, saying that no matter where you are discriminated against while seeking employment or after having got employment, both will count as employment discrimination. This was the first time ever that a judge said that. And *so far there hasn't been any other judge who has dared to say so*. You might think from looking at it that it was a very simple decision, but in China, this is quite unique; it gave me a real feeling of achievement. When the decision came out, it felt great even though [the Court] did not award much compensation. The client had hoped to get more, but they had also wanted an acknowledgement, and at least they got that.[88] (emphasis added)

The lawyer did not offer any particular comment on the court hearing as such, but noted that it had been adjudicated in a province outside Beijing where judges appeared less distrustful, and gave the impression that it was the submission of written materials, including in particular the argument that 'the State' supported these kinds of case, that had played a decisive role in persuading the court to decide in the client's favour in these kinds of case.

The very specificity of this, by itself certainly significant, area of rights defence (there are thought to be some 130 million Hepatitis B carriers in China)[89] explains what rights advocacy against discrimination is 'up against'. Discrimination on the basis of household registration, gender, regional provenance or ethnicity and illness that cause greater social embarrassment, such as AIDS, remain harder to address.[90] Even as employment discrimination lawyers and NGOs seek to expand the scope of their advocacy, for instance by 'branching out' into litigation against gender-based discrimination, there is an implicit recognition of the official endorsement that is required for litigation success.

---

86 #50 2011-1.
87 In Chinese characters, 很安心得受理. For an extended discussion of such policies, see also #23 2011-4.
88 #50 2011-1.
89 Melissa Chan, '"Hepatitis B carriers need not apply": discrimination in China', *Al Jazeera*, 1 September 2011, at http://wp.hepb.org/2011/09/01/hepatitis-b-carriers-need-not-apply-hbv-discrimination-in-china/, accessed 13 November 2013.
90 See Chapter 3. Also #23 2011-4.

Advocacy outside tolerated zones

In areas of rights defence in which the 'policy environment' is unfavourable, the function of courtroom advocacy is limited and altered in complex ways. Thus, in cases of evictees seeking redress against urban governments, there is a wide assumption that no litigation against an eviction or expropriation decision as such is possible, even though, theoretically, courts should be able to reject the legality of expropriations (both rural and urban) on the grounds of lack of public interest.[91] Litigation in such cases usually does not challenge the expropriation as such but, rather, aims at improving the terms on which people are forced to move, such as compensation:

> In demolition and relocation [eviction] cases it is really a matter of compensation amounts. And so the proper method and the lawyers' attitudes will not be the same as in other matters. It is the same with the client. They just want to maximize what they get.[92]

The closer rights lawyers' advocacy gets to representation of central concerns of groups and individuals who already have a suspect status in the eyes of the Party–State, the less likely they are to win cases. An example for this are petitioners who, as explained in the previous chapter, seek to use avenues of redress outside the formal legal system but who, if they persist, can incur punishment. Many are given 'RTL' sentences, which, in turn, may lay the ground for further challenge.

In administrative litigation against decisions to impose detention, such as for instance Re-education Through Labour (RTL), rights lawyers' advocacy may address a number of issues beyond the immediate object of obtaining release of the client, such as the rights-based, constitutional and international treaty-based arguments against detention mechanisms.[93] However, while such arguments have been presented in petitions to the National People's Congress and articulated in scholarly discussions as well as journalistic outlets, it is widely believed in China that such arguments would be useless in court because, as noted in the previous chapter, a widely accepted doctrine prohibits judges from striking down laws or regulations on the ground that they violate higher ranking law. (Petitions to the NPC Standing Committee which would have the formal authority to strike down the regulations in question have thus far been unsuccessful.) Commenting on this issue in the context of RTL, a rights lawyer explained:

---

91 Eva Pils, 'Contending conceptions of ownership and property in urbanising China', in Fu Hualing and John Gillespie (eds.), *Resolving Land Disputes in East Asia*, Cambridge University Press (forthcoming).
92 #2 2011-5. Similarly, #39 2011-1.
93 Discussed in Chapter 3.

In my view, you should do things that you have the ability to influence, in order to affect that which you have no power to control. For example, we do not have the ability to abolish RTL. But here is what we can do: we can bring litigation against RTL imposed on a person found on board a train without a railway ticket worth just one Yuan RMB, and draw attention to the issue of RTL in this way.[94]

The case referred to was one of three petitioners who had travelled from their hometown in Jiangsu to Beijing, where they had boarded a bus without buying tickets valued at 1 yuan Renminbi (ca. 12 US cents) each. For this infraction, the authorities of their hometown imposed a one-year RTL sentence on each of them. Human rights lawyers took up the case and fought it through instances of the administrative litigation system. The decision to impose RTL was upheld in both instances by the Jiangsu courts; but the lawyers were eventually able to negotiate their clients' early release and, as indicated by the lawyer just quoted, to draw public attention to the issue.[95]

In the majority of cases of this nature, however obvious the appropriate result may seem, neither the lawyers nor their clients expect a formal win in court:

My client said right in the courtroom – the client was illiterate but understood very well – 'I don't blame my lawyer one bit. I knew I couldn't possibly win and he has already done so much for me. I don't blame him.' The client said that right in court. To receive such confirmation from her was great.[96]

While no systematic empirical research exists on this point, it is not difficult to understand why courts might find it harder than, say, in Hepatitis B employment discrimination cases, to find for the complainant in such cases: litigation of necessity targets not only the State but a particularly powerful entity within it – the Public Security Bureau; and there is no 'policy environment' supporting the protection of the rights of detainees in such extrajudicial, let alone extra-legal or criminal detention systems. In cases that get to the adjudication stage and in which rights lawyers are active, therefore, there is a certain likelihood that, even if the argument is substantively persuasive, the judge will come under pressure to reject the challenge:

'After the trial hearing, the judge actually also expressed his agreement. But when the written decision came out it wasn't like that at all. . . . A case of personality split!'[97]

---

94 #39 2011-1.
95 '江苏三访民因一元车票被劳教 [Three petitioners in Jiangsu sent to RTL over one-yuan bus ticket]', *Epoch Times*, 19 July 2011, at http://epochtimes.com/gb/11/7/19/n3319533.htm, accessed 13 November 2013.
96 #39 2011-1.
97 #39 2012-1 (web chat).

Any victories achieved could also prove pyrrhic in cases in which lawyers had challenged the government for infringement of power. Both in eviction and RTL cases, accounts of persons 'winning' their case without benefiting from this 'victory' are not infrequent. In eviction cases, this can be due to the fact that litigation against eviction does not stay the execution of an eviction and demolition order for a building:

> For instance in that case I handled, last year this petitioner was sent to RTL and we litigated and ultimately negotiated a settlement [whereby the party got compensation.] The party went petitioning again immediately after he got out. And then he was sent to RTL again straightaway.[98]

Despite their structural difference, cases related to police-administered detention are similar to criminal cases in that they pit rights lawyers against the generally powerful security apparatus. In a system in which conviction rates tend to be over 99% defence lawyers cannot realistically work to achieve an acquittal of their client. Commenting on his experience with Falun Gong cases, in which acquittal is particularly unlikely, a lawyer acknowledged this:

> [The Procuracy] know themselves that what they say doesn't make sense. But they also know that no matter how well we defend the client, the Court cannot possibly acquit the defendant; and that even if they themselves don't speak a single word, the Court will find the defendant guilty anyway.[99]

In criminal cases there is an especially wide range of influences on the 'judicial' decision to be made. Cases are according to the Constitution 'decided independently by *courts*', not individual judges – this justifies the role of the courts' adjudication committees. In fact, as is widely understood, court decisions in non-routine cases are influenced by a wider range of entities including but not limited to the Party's political and legal committees:

> The system in China is one of adjudication committees and not of panels of judges deciding cases [at trial]. The authority to decide is with the adjudication panel . . . so the Presiding Judge is not allowed just to announce the verdict without having liaised previously . . . If he does, it means that the decision was made in advance anyway.[100]
> In totally un-influential cases it really is the judicial panel [that holds the trial] that decides the case; but even in those the decision will not necessarily be announced right at the end of the trial.[101]

---

98 #52 2011-1. Similarly: 'Once they get to being tried in Court, they will invariably be found guilty. However, the Procuracy can engage in minor acts of resistance by for instance not approving the arrest.' #3 2012-1.
99 #3 2012-1. Several rights lawyers report being told that defendants in Falun Gong cases must not be acquitted, according to an 'internal directive'.
100 #26 2010-1. See also Li Ling, *supra*.
101 #2 2012-5 (July).

Yet lawyers make it clear that they regard the presentation of arguments at trial, regardless of whether the argument is going to persuade anyone (as in the cases of the petitioner sent to RTL and the journalist sent to prison), and regardless of whether it affects the verdict, as valuable, even when all she can give their client is moral support, and all they can try to do in speaking to trial judges is present their case as they see it.

Advocacy between 'speaking truth' and negotiation

There is no doubt that rights lawyers, like their colleagues, engage in negotiation on behalf of their client, and that sometimes, such negotiation contributes to the corrosion of roles that public legal rules purport to ascribe to the actors in the judicial process. While engaging in negotiation, rights lawyers emphasise principles they will refuse to undermine, and show themselves at times willing to abandon their 'collaborative' stance and become confrontational:

> I found a witness to certify that my defendant had [tried to 'enforce' a debt by beating the victim, and] given money to a third person *they* did not owe money to [but who was owed money by the victim]. I did not dare [*sic*] to produce this witness statement in court, because of Article 306 – you know.[102] But I gave it to the prosecutor [in advance]. But then, the prosecutor refused to show it to the Court at trial! So I protested during the trial hearing. I said that this was really unfair – I had tried to support the prosecutor by finding him evidence, and the prosecutor had a duty to look into incriminating as well as exonerating [mitigating] evidence. Eventually he said, 'ok, then I'll show it.'[103]

In the case of a well-known human rights defender who had permitted herself to be addressed as '*Lawyer* Ni Yulan,' and been charged with fraudulently obtaining donations by purporting to be a licensed lawyer, her defence lawyers were able to provide conclusive witness statements by the donors showing that whether or not she had held a lawyer's licence, she had not been given any money *on the strength of* being thought to be a licensed lawyer. In fact, she had received donations after her case was publicised in documentary films and opinion pieces documenting her experiences of police torture and other cruelties, and because she had no home at the time. In this case, too, the defence decided to submit new evidence to the court, which passed it on to the prosecution, in advance; and a solution was negotiated: at the trial hearing, the prosecution 'no longer mentioned' the issue of fraud.[104]Although the charges concerning fraud were not formally dropped, Ni was convicted 'only' of creating a disturbance, but not of fraud.

102 Article 306 Criminal Law, CECC, at http://www.cecc.gov/resources/legal-provisions/criminal-law-of-the-peoples-republic-of-china, accessed 13 November 2013.
103 #69 2012-1.
104 Author interview with person close to the case (2012).

A trial's irrelevance to the outcome of the case does not diminish the rights' lawyers recourse to legal advocacy, and indeed can increase rights lawyers' opportunities to engage in advocacy. Thus in the case of a journalist put on trial for blackmail, after the defendant had exposed corrupt links between local government and business, he was charged with blackmail in circumstances suggesting he had been 'framed,' and put in detention, where according to the defence lawyer, he was tortured.[105] Even though, in the opinion of the defence lawyer, the outcome was predetermined, the trial still gave him an important opportunity to argue the case. Unable to speak to the judge *qua* adjudicator representing and exercising State power, he spoke to the judge, other officials and the general audience as arbiters in a fictional (constructed) court of his and the defendant's imagination, a court whose conventional social reality lay primarily in being able to be a forum able to receive such arguments and in whatever 'verdict' these powerless arbiters could express. In his function as 'presiding' official the presiding judge, however weak, could choose to cooperate in minimal and crucial ways with this advocacy so that the persuasiveness of the argument could be appreciated by the audience – and even, perhaps, re-enforced by the required and predicted outcome:

> There were over a hundred persons at the trial, and they locked the gate of the courthouse to prevent more people from getting in. The trial went on from 9 am to past 9 pm, over twelve hours, with a one-hour break for lunch. The right to present a criminal defence was still basically respected at that trial. It deserves to be said that the judge in that case, as a person, he understood the technical complexity of this case. He wasn't bad as a person.[106]

On being asked how his assessment came to be so positive, the lawyer replied that what was significant, from his perspective, was that some officials' covertly expressed recognition of the lawyer's efforts: one social reality had succeeded in the face of one whose failure had been predetermined:

> At least he [the judge] still allowed those attending the trial to learn the truth about this case. I was also deeply impressed by the fact that after the trial, quite a number of judicial staff [i.e. staff from the Court, Procuratorate, Justice Bureau, or from the police] came over to speak to me. One amongst them, a young person from the Justice Bureau, who introduced us to a number of his colleagues, very much approved – he actually agreed with our defence![107]

---

105 #26 2010-1.
106 Conversation #25 2010-1.
107 Conversation #25 2010-1.

If the judge in the RTL case mentioned above had invited the lawyer involved to the indulgent comment 'a case of personality split!', the judge in this criminal trial of a journalist was put in an even more conflicted, and potentially humiliating, situation. Having appreciated the arguments of the defence, and seen other State officials go so far as to congratulate the defence on its performance, he must yet proceed to deliver a scripted guilty verdict, according to the lawyer's narrative (which is to some extent corroborated by NGO and media reports). The guilty verdict could only reinforce the impression of its injustice on spectators, while possibly unsettling the system's officials.[108]

In another case, a rights lawyer (commenting on a case he had not directly handled but understood well) described the fact that there was practically no hope of saving the defendant from the death penalty as a reason for using this particular case for vocal and open protest. It was 'safest' to expose police abuses – in this case, very brutal torture – and demand accountability in cases which were already lost, he said.[109] All that remained was to seek 'justice' for a defendant certain to be wrongfully convicted. Fan Qihang was a Chongqing entrepreneur caught up in the Chongqing anti-mafia campaign, tortured to obtain a (according to the defence lawyers) false confession to instigating murder.[110] Calling for a criminal investigation of his torturers was considered 'safe' because as the rights lawyer just mentioned put it:

> No matter what was done, [the defendant's] life could not be saved … because it was a political case. In China we call that 'doctoring a dead horse as though it were still alive'.[111] In his case, there was just no hope.[112]

Human rights lawyers may use the trial to expose the truth as best they can, and to present their arguments, and in some trials, this is the most important or perhaps the only aim of criminal defence they can point to, beyond a 'hope beyond hope' that may be felt strongly – as in the just mentioned case of Fan Qihang, whose

---

108 #9 2012-5 expresses scepticism as judges 'have already become inured'.
109 'If there is a strong desire to pursue the responsibility of the prosecution officials or police officers this will affect the chances of the family member to get out. If you do pursue that responsibility then this will generally not be conducive to handling their case successfully.' #2 2011-5.
110 See He Yang (何杨), 专访朱明勇律师—黑打 [*Conversation with Lawyer Zhu Mingyong – torture*], August 2010 on a case involving torture in the case of Fan Qihang (樊奇杭), at http://www.vimeo.com/13706954, accessed 13 November 2013. To quote the defendant, filmed secretly by his defence lawyer, Zhu Mingyong: 'They shackled my hands behind my back and hung me by my wrists from an iron window grille, so that my toes just barely touched the ground, and they never took me off. The longest they did that was for five [consecutive] days before they took me off . . . The shackles ate into the flesh [of my wrists]; they became embedded so deeply that when they were taken off, it was all blood and pus.' *Ibid.* Also, Wang Gong (王工) et al., '敦请最高人民检察院立即对重庆打黑运动中的刑讯逼供问题依法调查的公开信 [Open letter requesting Supreme People's Procuracy immediately to open an investigation into the use of torture in the Chongqing anti-mafia campaign]', published 23 August 2010, at http://www.gongfa.com/html/gongfaxinwen/201008/23-1347.html, accessed 13 November 2013.
111 In Chinese characters, 死马当做活马医.
112 #2 2011-5.

defence lawyer was devastated by the defendant's execution[113] – but be, in fact, elusive.

Genuine courtroom advocacy

Only in some cases does genuine courtroom advocacy seem possible; and whether there is a chance to engage in it does not solely depend on the lawyers. In these cases, lawyers are able to do more than just 'speak truth'; and they can obtain improved results for their clients without engaging in demeaning (and potentially unlawful) negotiations. It is perhaps from these experiences that lawyers get the most profound sense of achievement; and it is in these cases that they exhibit the strength that so dismayed SPC Vice President Zhang Jun, whose comments on 'courtroom troublemakers' engaging in *nao ting* were quoted at the outset.

In one death penalty case, a human rights lawyer explained that at the public trial, the lawyers insisted the court should initiate a procedure for investigating allegations of torture on the part of the defendant, who according to the lawyers had been framed by one of the persons he had worked for. The defendant had been a driver working for a group of drug dealers, some of whom had originally worked in the local Public Security Bureau's drug enforcement division. The defence team thought this defendant had been framed by some members of this group. The defendant had been sentenced in first instance, but once human rights lawyers took over his defence in second instance, they gained a quashing of the conviction and order for a retrial; and they participated in the second first-instance hearing (retrial). In this retrial, the lawyers were seeking to exclude a 'confession' obtained by torture; and they invoked new rules issued in 2010 by the SPC and other authorities on the possibility of initiating a special investigation procedure in death penalty cases in which doubts about the admissibility of evidence could be substantiated.[114]

> We needed to make the point about starting an investigation of the legality of the evidence before entering into the stage of evaluating evidence at the trial. So we kept saying that we demanded such a procedure; whereas the judge wanted to move on with the trial . . . Whenever it was our turn to speak we just came back to the issue of initiating the torture investigation procedure. The judge got very unnerved.[115]

The official rationale given for such interruptions is that the lawyers are 'making trouble';[116] and admonitions to behave correctly may be accompanied by threats.

---

113 Zhu Mingyong (朱明勇), '一路走好 [Farewell]', (poem published after Fan Qihang's execution), at http://renminbao.com/rmb/articles/2010/10/3/53303b.html, accessed 13 November 2013.
114 For a discussion of these rules, see Ira Belkin, 'China's tortuous path toward ending torture in criminal investigation'.
115 #9 2012-5.
116 #2 2012-5: 'If only the judge does not want us to continue speaking and we persist in speaking, then from their perspective, it is *nao*.'

We had an intense clash with the judge . . . Eventually he asked, 'can you or can't you exercise your right of criminal defence in a correct manner?' This was a covert threat: if we did not exercise our right of criminal defence in a 'correct' manner he could have the court police take us out.[117] . . . Whenever we had spoken a few words, the moment he understood that we wanted to talk about torture, he would pound the gavel and interrupt us. He said innumerable times that we were not to raise the issue of torture again, that 'you must exercise your right of criminal defence in a correct manner,' and 'pay attention to your status as defenders.' During lunch we thought that there was a great likelihood that if he lost patience he would have us dragged out by the court police; but in the afternoon, we continued to engage in the same vigorous defence. We weren't concerned at all about being dragged out. At least this would have helped disclose the injustices in the case more effectively.[118]

In this case, the lawyers eventually succeeded in persuading a co-defendant to retract an incriminating statement he had made in court and in getting the court to hear two of the fourteen proposed witnesses testifying to his treatment while in detention:

Due to our arguments it was possible for two witnesses to come forth and testify at trial. We had prepared for them to wait outside. Often they don't allow any witnesses. That they did this time, may have counted as a concession on their part. The witnesses testified to [the defendant] having been tortured. The judge didn't interrupt them too much. They were former inmates locked up together with him who had been released. He had been beaten on the head leaving open wounds and been electro-shocked, so [they could testify that] he had had wounds on his whole body.

The lawyers also encouraged the defendant to talk about torture:

The defendant did talk about all the forms of torture he was subjected to.[119] The defence lawyer will instruct the defendant prior to the trial that they should persist in saying it all. Even if the judge interrupts them, asking the defendant to make it shorter, we tell the defendant that he should say OK, but just go on to say exactly what he had planned to say. Sometimes

---

117 Cp. Article 161 CPL (1996), CECC translation, *supra*.
118 #2 2012-5.
119 According to the lawyer, the defendant detailed eight forms of torture inflicted on six or seven different occasions: 'They used torture six or seven times. There were three kinds of hanging the defendant up (吊法), one hanging him up with both feet not touching the ground, one like this [diagonal suspension, presumably from a grille, with one hand pointing upward and one downward] with only one foot touching the ground; and one hanging by the hands/wrists with both soles touching the ground; use of electro-shocks; use of plastic bags to choke him; use of pepper; use of cigarette stubs to scald him; and a method by which the victim's hands are fastened to his back and then they use their fists to squeeze the victim's bones.' [#2 2012-5.]

> the defendant will say he has scars on his body and will try and take off his clothes to show them but the judge won't allow this. That's what happened in [this] case. We told him, even with handcuffs on – no matter how – you've got to try and take off your trousers to show [your scars from torture] to the judge! But the judge wouldn't let him.[120]

And even after they had failed to persuade the judge that an investigation procedure ought to be initiated, they persisted with raising the topic of torture.[121]

Summing up these experiences, a lawyer suggests that it is only in a minority of cases that criminal defence has no chance whatsoever of affecting the results of the trial in some way, however indirect:

> In cases like that of Gu Kailai[122] or Liu Xiaobo,[123] no lawyer can change the result. But in a case like that of Ni Yulan, although there is no chance of an acquittal, at least they can through their efforts get a reduced sentence. Also in ... the death penalty case [discussed above, a case in which two clients faced the death penalty] – if the families [of the defendants] had all along only hired obedient lawyers, they could not have changed the death sentence; but this way the two death sentences were changed into one life sentence and one fifteen year one. If it becomes clear that there just isn't enough evidence to sentence someone then they [the authorities] may be prepared to make some concessions.[124]

Curiously echoing SPC Vice President Zhang Jun's observations on 'trouble-making' lawyers, this lawyer continued by aligning his own experience to that of another social group understood to be widely marginalised, petitioners:

> There are no statistics on how many can succeed in achieving some improvement for their clients. I am not sure if this is an appropriate comparison but it is rather like petitioners – only a tiny percentage of them succeed, but because these successful cases exist, they will persist in petitioning.[125]

---

120 #2 2012-5.
121 #2 2012-5. 'There were over ten defendants in this case. Apart from one other local lawyer the other lawyers, local ones and one designated by the authorities, they did do their best on behalf of the client but they did not dare to raise the issue of torture.'
122 Gu Kailai is the wife of former Chongqing Party Secretary Bo Xilai. She was tried in August 2012 for the murder of a British businessman. Tania Branigan, 'Gu Kailai murder trial ends in China', *Guardian*, 9 August 2012, at http://www.guardian.co.uk/world/2012/aug/09/gu-kailai-murder-trial-begins?newsfeed=true, accessed 13 November 2013.
123 Liu Xiaobo, the literary critic and activist, was sentenced to 11 years' imprisonment for 'inciting subversion' in 2009, and awarded the Nobel Peace Prize in 2010.
124 #2 2012-5.
125 #2 2012-5.

In sum, it is perceived as important to 'fight' (*zhengqu*)[126] for clients through courtroom advocacy, even though crucially important facts or legal arguments may be suppressed, though negotiation may be necessary, and though no fully just verdict is expected.[127] Despite great flaws and iniquities, rights lawyers are able through courtroom advocacy to achieve some improvements in the lot of their clients in the majority of cases they take on.[128] But it is not always such concrete improvements that they or their clients most value; and rights advocacy is meaningful, even where no such concrete improvements are achieved:

> Once you realise [the power structures], then in your choices in the process of rights-defence, you can no longer just focus on losing the case or on wanting so and so much compensation ... You mustn't make them think that you focus too much on very tangible gains. The moment you do, they have a way to get at you. Instead you should concentrate on revealing the truth, exposing contradictions, and providing people with a convincing argument.[129]

The dispersal of rights advocacy into the wider community

Pushed out of the courts, rights advocacy is not silenced; instead it acquires a stronger political focus, toward the articulation of wider political demands through individual cases and grievances. Because lawyers understand the attractiveness of legal ideals, the lawyers' activism is never a turn against the law. Rather, the law, and the demands of justice which it ideally represents, is externalised and dispersed in order to further the demand for internal reform of the justice process. Their activism often consists in disobedience to extra-legal orders and 'hidden rules'.

As they have been pushed out of the courts, lawyers have increasingly become aware of the potential of using community power (or 'people power'), and increasingly seen strength in numbers. This has led to the related phenomena of using the courtroom 'as street' and of expanding rights advocacy into spaces where rights advocates can compensate for the constraints and deficiencies of court trials, while at the same time re-articulating, concentrating, and sharpening their political demand for a better justice system.

Courtroom as street and social media happening

It was shown above that litigation in non-endorsed zones, such as for instance in demolition and land-grab cases, is far from addressing the great underlying

---

126 In Chinese characters, 争取.
127 #2 2012-5.
128 Zhang Xueran, 'China's all-star legal team pleads for defendants' rights on social media', *Tea Leaf Nation*, 25 July 2012, at http://tealeafnation.com/2012/07/bilingual-brew-chinas-all-star-legal-team-pleads-for-defendants-rights-on-social-media.
129 #25 2010-2.

problems that arise from demolitions and land-grabs, issues equally affecting tens (if not hundreds) of millions of people. It is not surprising, against this background, that the social tension around evictions, demolitions and land-grabs can be at times transported into courtrooms and even court buildings, when eviction protesters try to express grievances that cannot be heard in the formal court process.

A nonprofessional rights defender acting as 'agent ad litem' explained that court hearings in eviction cases can turn tense when they involve sympathetic crowds:[130]

> Many evictees in the whole of Beijing are in touch. There is a silent agreement amongst us. Say my case will be heard in court. Then I will get in touch with many other evictees [from different districts all over the city] and they will all show up for the court hearing. Each time there is such a court hearing there will be at least a hundred people. A while ago we went to a court hearing, over a hundred people and Sister X [another rights defender] and I went. It was a pretty lively hearing; the effect was not bad! At the time we pointed out some illegalities of the other side. And they had to answer us but they had nothing to say. The petitioners were quite loudly critical. The judge couldn't fully control the situation. And then we also pointed out some unreasonable things the judges had done.
>
> Actually at the time I said a few words . . . not directly insulting the judges but, well, criticising them. Well, here, I have got a copy of what I [read out] at the time.[131]

The document read:

> Some of today's judges don't respect the higher-ranking law and disrupt the implementation of the law. Some judges use illegal judicial interpretations, laws and regulations as a shield to counter-act the State Council and the Party Central. These forms of conduct are criminal and entirely contemptuous of the State, society, and the people. We hope that the Judge deciding this case will not stand on the side of corrupt officials but on the side of the people. [The judge] should stand on the side of the laws of the State and strike hard against all corrupt officials who commit crimes.
>
> Their illegal conduct is trampling the law of the State and the people's masses underfoot. It is like sitting on the parties' heads and playing around, or like crapping on Hu Jintao's head. The local level is openly challenging the Centre, cloaking itself in the name of the government and making deals with underworld rogues. We demand that the Court uphold justice. We trust

130 #51 2011-2. '[In the hearing in 2006] they had to break off the public hearing because there was so much protest [against corruption and power abuse] that they had to break off. Then in 2010 April we received a forced eviction notice.'
131 #51 2011-2.

that the Judge in this case will tear off their cover. We trust that the Judge will uphold justice, protect the parties' legal rights and safeguard the dignity of the law.[132]

The rights defender added that the judge had interrupted her many times, trying (apparently unsuccessfully) to stop her from reading her statement.

In one sense, this form of 'advocacy' seems far removed from lawyers' professional and sophisticated arguments. Although brave and disputatious, it is inelegant and crude and it would trigger attempts to enforce order in court in most jurisdictions. Yet it does effectively convey several messages of central concern to human rights defenders: protest against corruption, appeal to the individual judges' sense of professional honour despite general reasons for distrust of the judiciary; the claim that official decisions, including laws and regulations, can be in violation of higher law as well as of justice; and a crafty portrayal of corrupt judges as enemies of the Party–State. The statement would be quite understandable, indeed, against the background of the rights defender's full personal story of years of brutality and indignity in a common land expropriation and forced eviction case[133] and taking into account that eviction cases almost invariably end in the destruction of the home(s) being fought for.[134]

In numerous conversations, rights lawyers have shown their awareness of the importance of such popular voices, and expressed the view that the force they represent would be instrumental in promoting their own, the lawyers', advocacy – both in the sense that petitioners should be trained up to engage in courtroom representation of clients as civil representative,[135] and in the sense that collective protest actions might in some situations have to replace rights advocacy through litigation. It testifies to the importance of these suggestions that the lawyer who was perhaps most involved in efforts to coordinate petitioners' and lawyers' rights advocacy was among those worst affected by the 2011 Jasmine Crackdown, discussed in Chapter 6.

In an ironic way, then, the labelling of rights lawyers as troublemakers who engage in *nao*, like petitioners, is being confirmed by lawyers who feel disempowered as they are deprived of fair opportunities to advance their arguments, in the courtroom and also beyond; and they may come to endorse behaviour that would be regarded as disreputable and inappropriate in a fairer courtroom setting. For example, in efforts to reinforce the effect of expositions of absurdities in trial proceedings, they may resort to secretly recording such proceedings; and in cases where they feel deprived of any opportunity to defend their client, they may resort to walking out of the courtroom, as lawyers Liu Wei and Tang Jitian did in the 2009 Luzhou trial (after handing copies of their written defence statements to

132 #51 2011-2; copy on file with author.
133 #51 2011-2.
134 Eva Pils, 'Contending conceptions', *supra*.
135 Pan Xuanming, 'Non-lawyers as legal resources for the State: issues, institutions and implications for China's legal reform', PhD dissertation, the Chinese University of Hong Kong (2012), discusses the institution of civil representatives at length.

the presiding judge). Increasingly lawyers also use social media to provide updates on the progress of a trial, where possible in real time. This was done to great effect in a Guiyang trial, which involved 57 defendants, in 2012. To quote:

> On Weibo [the Chinese version of Twitter], the lawyers acted like professional journalists, covering all sorts of relevant information from details like 'the prosecutors' microphones are louder than the defense's', to typos in the indictment, to overall analyses of the case. Throughout the 47-day trial, the defense posted more than 1,000 tweets in total, some even giving real-time updates during the sessions. . . . During the court debate, many even published their speeches of defense on Weibo.
>
> For many netizens, following the case every day became a habit . . . [and] because of the influence of social media, scholars, lawyers and netizens went to Guiyang to observe the trial one after another, and also tweeted their observations on Weibo.[136]

To the extent that they refuse to conform to expectations, the lawyers are genuinely subversive; but they are only subversive of a courtroom 'order' largely established by pressure and tacit convention.

Alternative spaces for rights advocacy

As courtroom advocacy is eliminated, obstructed, and suppressed, advocacy as resistance conquers new spaces outside the Party–State-controlled courtrooms and government offices. Increasingly, advocacy moves to the internet, into artistic expression, and onto the streets. There, it is in one sense weaker than the kinds of advocacy that can take place in courtrooms, because it cannot directly affect a court process; because speech deemed to be harmful to the national interest can be easily deleted or taken away or destroyed;[137] and because those who challenge the Party–State can be prosecuted, for instance for 'inciting subversion'.

Yet in another sense, the dislocation of rights advocacy can also make it stronger. Many criminal trials have involved crowds not admitted to the court hearing gathering outside the court building, chanting slogans and ensuring the visibility of their exclusion from the trial, usually supposed to be 'public'. Lawyers not allowed to present their arguments in court have presented them to wider and more receptive online publics. Freed from the need to persuade Party–State officials they have become bolder, more creative and freer in their language, and struck up associations with various groups in society they would not otherwise have reached out to.

---

136 See Zhang Yueran, *supra*.
137 'Rights lawyer held for four hours over T-shirt, police destroy garment with political slogans', *South China Morning Post*, 12 October 2009, at http://www.scmp.com/article/695107/rights-lawyer-held-four-hours-over-t-shirt, accessed 14 November 2013.

The dispersal of courtroom rights advocacy into the wider community has become a common feature of certain kinds of protest that allow for the mobilisation of large groups of people. As seen in the report by a human rights defender above, groups of victims and rights defenders have begun to organise themselves in flexible ways, allowing them to arrange for 100 or more people to show up in front of the court building at the time of the trial hearing. They can become participants, if not of any action inside the courtroom, then at least of dramatic enactments of their exclusion from it:[138]

> Definitely [the situation for victims of forced evictions and land-grabs] is much better now because it is at least possible for people to defend their rights. Before, people would simply be kicked out and there was almost nothing they could do. Nowadays at least people can engage in rights defence.[139]

The same interlocutor described a scene in which an angry crowd of petitioner–protesters gathered inside a court building chanting 'we want to see the Court President' until this individual appeared to speak to them.[140] Gatherings of petitioners, evictees, sympathisers at the site of Party–State activities to protest and show solidarity, generally referred to as 'surrounding and watching' or *weiguan*,[141] have become common in recent years, as it has become easier to organise such gatherings using social media, and hard for the authorities to suppress *weiguan* activities.

A relatively early example of this trend was the 2010 trial of three internet activists, charged with defamation due to their calls for the police to investigate the death of a young woman, Yan Xiaoling, who had died under circumstances suggesting that she had been raped and murdered. The authorities had refused to investigate. After initial support, the state media stopped reporting the alleged crime. The three activists (the 'Three Netizens of Fujian') who had supported the young woman's mother in her appeals to the authorities and to society were prosecuted and convicted of defamation of the police. After they went to prison, their own cases became causes of further activism, organised mainly through the internet; various actions to help the 'Three Netizens of Fujian' are portrayed in the film *Herzog's Days*.[142] On the day of the activists' trial, activists from all over China came to Fuzhou and gathered outside the court building, waiting for one of the three defendants, You Jingyou, to be conveyed to the courtroom.

---

138 I have witnessed such exclusion during the trial of a rights defender and petitioner in 2010. Petitioners gathered outside the court building and were not admitted.
139 #51 2012-2.
140 *Ibid.*
141 In Chinese characters, 围观.
142 He Yang (何杨), '赫索格的日子 [Herzog's Days]', independent documentary film, August 2010, available at http://vimeo.com/12938865, accessed 1 January 2014.

As the van with You inside drew up in front of the building, they chanted:

> You Jingyou – innocent!
> We love you
> We support you
> Fairness! Justice!
> You Jingyou!
> Wu Huaying!
> Wu Huaying – innocent!
> You Jingyou – innocent!
> Fan Yanqiong – innocent![143]

Their protest, which was soon stopped by police who forcefully dispersed the protesters, was filmed by a professional documentary filmmaker. The film included comment from scholar Cui Weiping:

> The Fujian Three Netizens case in essence was a protest. In this protest, on the one hand you have an authoritarian, closed, ossified system of power, and on the other hand is society. Authorities, to the largest extent possible have tried to disregard the part of society in this, to keep them out of the information loop. Yet then you have this protest here in support of the netizens being falsely charged – an independent social force, the independent [expression of] public opinion. It has two dimensions, on the one hand an online component, provision of background information on the case and various public appeals; and on the other hand an offline component with people articulating constructive and rational demands on the ground right outside the courtroom.[144]

Cui's analysis well captured the two aspects of dislocation or sublimation that transpose the drama of the courtroom into spaces less well controlled by the Party–State than courtrooms themselves. It also helps to understand in what way protest in the Fujian Netizens case was unprecedented. It was a coming together not of resident petitioners who had spent years bonding in their joint efforts to redress grievances but, rather, of online activists gathering in order to engage in political protest, crucially supported by persons with different kinds of skill: legal scholars and lawyers, activists, and independent filmmakers. Cameras, in particular, have been used by protesters chanting 'I want to file my case' outside court building in Shanghai;[145] and a would-be litigant was captured kneeling naked on the steps of a Shanghai court building trying to

---

143   *Ibid.*
144   *Ibid.*
145   '我要立案 [I Want to File My Case]' 12 August 2011, at http://www.youtube.com/watch?v=MckgKZJl0g8, accessed 13 November 2013.

attract attention to the fact that she was unable to file her case.[146] This new form of mobilisation across different professional and social groups appeared to alter the dynamics of contention between Party–State and citizens, and presented an especially great challenge to it.[147]

Lawyers themselves also started using the *weiguan* idea of showing solidarity by attending court hearings and public hearings in their own cases; thus many lawyers came to or tried to attend the public hearing in the disbarment of Tang Jitian and Liu Wei. Several lawyers travelled to Tianjin from Beijing to show solidarity with a lawyer being tried there in a case in which it was thought she had been framed after challenging public security officials;[148] and it became *de rigueur* that sympathising rights lawyers would try to show up, along with other friends of the *weiquan* community, outside the court building for trials of rights defenders.

Concurrently, several NGOs began increasingly to rely on cooperation from and organisation by lawyers, taking up the cases of various vulnerable groups such as the disabled, persons with mental disabilities or persons who had suffered retaliatory psychiatric incarceration, death row prisoners.[149] Lawyers gathered more frequently and became better versed in the organisational skills required to run NGOs, communication with the public, and organising small protest actions such as 'performance art' to draw public attention to particular causes. Many of these efforts relied on the internet. (For instance, a small performance art action involving a disabled person holding up an oversized railway ticket to demonstrate against the refusal to let disabled persons travel for free, as the law required, was disrupted very quickly by the police; but less than a minute was required to produce a photograph that could be used in online communications.)[150]

It did not take the Party–State long to respond to the threat it apparently saw in these developments. The case of the 'Three Netizens of Fujian' can serve as an example. Persons involved in it were affected by the 'Jasmine Crackdown' of 2011. Rights defender Wang Lihong, who is also in the film, was prosecuted for 'creating a social disturbance' in the course of the same crackdown; the main charges against her were connected to her role in the 'Fujian Netizen' case. Wang Lihong was sentenced to a short prison term in August 2011; but

---

146 Zhuang Jinghui and Gaelle Faure, '77-year-old woman strips to protest the demolition of her home', *France 24*, 7 September 2011, at http://observers.france24.com/content/20110907-china-77-year-old-woman-strips-down-shanghai-courthouse-protest-land-grab, accessed 13 November 2013.

147 Teng Biao, 'Video cameras break official monopoly: video plays a notable role in citizen movements', 4 *China Rights Forum* (2010), at http://www.hrichina.org/content/4961, accessed 13 November 2013.

148 #23 2010-3.

149 #23 2010-3.

150 Beijing Yirenping (北京益仁平), Anti-discrimination Bulletin no. 19 (反歧视通讯第19期), http://www.yirenping.org/admin/edit/editor.htm?id=content&ReadCookie=0" \l "_Toc28143 铁道部门口上演行为艺术 肢残人呼吁火车票半价 [Performance art piece staged by disabled calling for half-price railway tickets in front of Railway Ministry],' 13 April 2014 at http://www.yirenping.org/zlxzx.asp?ID=1355&typeNumber=0011.

even as she was convicted, the authorities had to confront a new 'stability preservation' issue, in the form of the people who came to 'surround and watch' her trial:

> Civic consciousness is very strong now, I think. I went to the Wang Lihong court hearing. There were many people who came and who just knew about Wang Lihong and that was the reason they came. They want to express their solidarity. Just standing there to 'surround and watch' is a sort of force.[151]

In conclusion, even though the odds are stacked against them, and although they rarely 'win' cases (in the formal sense), rights lawyers can engage in politically meaningful rights advocacy that unsettles the entrenched judicial process, exposes its iniquities, and sometimes allows lawyers to obtain better results for their clients. If we may say, as suggested earlier, that legal reform in China has had unintended consequences for the Party–State, the discussion here has shown that such trials are one of the settings in which officials of the system may be confronted with these consequences. Pushed out of the courts, rights advocacy is not silenced; instead it acquires a stronger political focus, toward the articulation of wider political demands through individual cases and grievances. Because lawyers understand the attractiveness of legal ideals, the lawyers' activism is never a turn against the law, rather, legal action is externalised in order to further the demand for internal reform of the justice process though disobedience to extra-legal orders and 'hidden rules'.

Bibliography

NPC laws

PRC Criminal Law [中华人民共和国刑法], passed on 1 July 1979, promulgated on 6 July 1979, and effective as of 1 January 1980, last revised on 25 February 2011, at http://www.moj.gov.cn/Prison_work/content/2013-05/07/content_4436670. htm?node=43130. For an English translation, see http://www.cecc.gov/resources/ legal-provisions/criminal-law-of-the-peoples-republic-of-china.

PRC Criminal Procedure Law [中华人民共和国刑事诉讼法], passed on 1 July 1979, promulgated on 7 July 1979, effective as of 1 January 1980, last revised on 14 March 2012, at http://www.gov.cn/flfg/2012-03/17/content_2094354.htm, accessed 4 January 2014.

PRC Law on Administrative Punishment [中华人民共和国行政处罚法], adopted on 17 March 1996, promulgated on 17 March 1996, and effective as of 1 October 1996, at http://www.gov.cn/banshi/2005-08/21/content_25101.htm, accessed 7 November 2013.

PRC Law on Lawyers [中华人民共和国律师法], passed on 28 October 2007, effective as of 1 June 2008. For the Chinese text, see http://www.gov.cn/flfg/2007-10/28/

151 #52 2011-1.

content_788495.htm, and for an English translation http://www.cecc.gov/pages/newLaws/lawyersLawENG.php.

Rules and regulations

Ministry of Justice, Regulation on Punishments for Law-Violating Conduct on the Part of Lawyers and Law Firms [律师和律师事务所违法行为处罚办法], passed on 7 April 2010, promulgated on 8 April 2010, effective as of 1 June 2010, at http://www.gov.cn/gongbao/content/2010/content_1713712.htm, accessed 7 November 2013.

Supreme People's Court, Interpretation on Several Issues concerning the Implementation of the PRC Administrative Procedure [最高人民法院关于执行〈中华人民共和国行政诉讼法〉若干问题的解释], promulgated on March 8, 2000, effective as of 10 March 2000, at http://www.pkulaw.cn/fulltext_form.aspx?Gid=26982, accessed 10 November 2013.

Supreme People's Court, Notice on Relevant Issues Concerning the Acceptance of the Issue of Accepting Cases of Securities Markets Civil Tort Dispute Cases Caused by False Statements in the Securities Markets [关于受理虚假陈述的证券民事纠纷的通知], 15 January 2002, at http://www.law-lib.com/law/law_view.asp?id=16956, accessed 4 January 2014.

Supreme People's Court, PRC People's Court Rules on Courtroom Proceedings [中华人民共和国人民法院法庭规则], passed on 26 November 1993, promulgated on 1 December 1993, effective as of January 1 1994, at http://old.chinacourt.org/flwk/show.php?file_id=76042, accessed 7 November 2013.

Supreme People's Court, PRC SPC Judicial Interpretation on the Criminal Procedure Law, [中华人民共和国最高人民法院司法解释法释], passed on 5 November 2012, promulgated on 20 December 2012, effective as of 1 January 2013, at http://legal.people.com.cn/n/2012/1224/c42510-20000004.html, accessed 1 January 2014.

Supreme People's Court Regulations on Several Issues concerning Evidence in Administrative Procedures [最高人民法院〈关于行政诉讼证据若干问题的规定], promulgated on 24 July 2002, effective as of 1 October 2002, at http://www.jincao.com/fa/22/law22.14.htm, accessed 10 November 2013.

Other official documents

Chinese Communist Party, 'Party Central Resolution on the Construction of a Socialist Harmonious Society', [中共中央关于构建社会主义和谐社会若干重大问题的决定], passed on 11 October 2006, at http://news.xinhuanet.com/politics/2006-10/18/content_5218639.htm, accessed 14 November 2013.

Books and articles

Amnesty International, 'Against the law, crackdown on China's human rights lawyers deepens', June 2011, at http://www.amnesty.nl/sites/default/files/public/china_-_against_the_law.pdf, accessed 1 January 2014, at p. 31.

Amnesty International, 'China holds Uighur journalist over Xinjiang unrest remarks', 30 October 2009, at http://www.amnesty.org/en/news-and-updates/news/china-holds-uighur-journalist-over-xinjiang-unrest-remarks-20091030, accessed 1 January 2014.

Balme, Stéphanie, 'Local courts in eastern China', in Peerenboom, Randall (ed.), *Judicial Independence in China: Lessons for Global Rule of Law Promotion*, Cambridge University Press, Cambridge: 2009.

Beijing Yirenping (北京益仁平), Anti-discrimination Bulletin no. 19 (反歧视通讯第19期), '铁道部门口上演行为艺术 肢残人呼吁火车票半价 [Performance art piece staged by disabled calling for half-price railway tickets in front of Railway Ministry],' 13 April 2014 at http://www.yirenping.org/zlxzx.asp?ID=1355&typeNumber=0011.

Branigan, Tania, 'Gu Kailai murder trial ends in China', *Guardian*, 9 August 2012, at http://www.guardian.co.uk/world/2012/aug/09/gu-kailai-murder-trial-begins?newsfeed=true, accessed 13 November 2013.

Chan, Melissa, '"Hepatitis B carriers need not apply": discrimination in China', *Al Jazeera*, 1 September 2011, at http://wp.hepb.org/2011/09/01/hepatitis-b-carriers-need-not-apply-hbv-discrimination-in-china/, accessed 13 November 2013.

Chen, Hongwei (陈虹伟), '律师"闹庭"引出规制 [Lawyers' "troublemaking" in the courtroom triggers regulation]', *Legal System and News* (法制与新闻), 19 October 2012, at http://news.sina.com.cn/c/sd/2012-10-19/120825394306.shtml, accessed 1 January 2014.

Cheng, Yuanjing and Cao, Tianxiang (程远景,曹天祥), '河南方城县社会法庭受理案件调解率达100% [Mediation rate in Henan Facheng Social Court hits 100%]', 19 August 2011, at http://court.gmw.cn/html/article/201108/19/76103.shtml, accessed 1 January 2014.

China Change, 'Denied meetings, advocates fear for activist Guo Feixong', 18 October 2013, at http://chinachange.org/2013/10/18/denied-meetings-lawyers-fear-for-advocate-guo-feixiong/, accessed 1 January 2014.

Cohen, Jerome A., 'Body blow for the judiciary', *South China Morning Post*, 18 October 2008, at http://www.cfr.org/publication/17565/body_blow_for_the_judiciary.html?breadcrumb=%2Fbios%2F14%2Fjerome_a_cohen, accessed 10 November 2013.

Cohen, Jerome A., 'China trips up its barefoot lawyers', *Far Eastern Economic Review* (November 2005 issue) 168.

Committee to Support Chinese Lawyers, 'Letter to Director Yu Hongyuan of Beijing Municipal Bureau of Justice', 21 April 2010, at http://www.csclawyers.org/letters/CSCL%20Letter%2004.21.2010%20BJJB.pdf, accessed 9 November 2013.

Epoch Times, '江苏三访民因一元车票被劳教 [Three petitioners in Jiangsu sent to RTL over one-yuan bus ticket]', *Epoch Times*, 19 July 2011, at http://epochtimes.com/gb/11/7/19/n3319533.htm, accessed 13 November 2013.

Fraenkel, Ernst, *The Dual State. A Contribution to the Theory of Dictatorship*, translated by E.A. Shils, Oxford University Press, New York: 1941.

Gong, Ting, 'Dependent judiciary and unaccountable judges: judicial corruption in contemporary China', 4 *China Review* 2 (2004).

He, Haibo (何海波), 'The scope of case filed in administrative litigation [行政诉讼受案范围– 一页司法权的实践史 (1990–2000)]', 4 *Peking University Law Review* (《北大法律评论》) 2 (2002), at http://article.chinalawinfo.com/Article_Detail.asp?ArticleID=23443, accessed 9 November 2013.

He, Haibo (何海波), 'Litigation without decision: on withdrawal of complaints in administrative litigation [没有判决的诉讼：行政诉讼撤诉考(1987–2008)]', 2 *Peking University Law Journal*, (《中外法学》) (2001), at http://article.chinalawinfo.com/Article_Detail.asp?ArticleID=41944, accessed 9 November 2013. Conversation #2011-1.

Hu, Jia (胡佳), '高智晟大哥签署委托书，中共享黑帮手段胁迫撤销委托书 [Gao Zhisheng's older brother signs letter of attorney, CCP uses thugs to force lawyers' dismissal]', letter to the editor, *Epoch Times* (大纪元) 14 October 2006, at http://www.epochtw.com/6/10/14/38774g.htm, accessed 1 January 2014.

Human Rights in China, 'Xu Zhiyong's lawyer Liu Weiguo in custody, rights group is shut down', 18 July 2013, at http://www.hrichina.org/en/content/6825, accessed 1 January 2014.

Hutzler, Charles, 'Wang Lihong, Chinese online activist, sentenced to prison for staging protest', 9 September 2011, at http://www.huffingtonpost.com/2011/09/09/wang-lihong-prison_n_955226.html, accessed 9 November 2013.

Jiang, Jue, 'The practice of "criminal reconciliation" (*xingshi hejie*) in the PRC criminal justice system', PhD dissertation at the Chinese University of Hong Kong (2012).

Kahn, Joseph, 'Advocate for China's weak crosses the powerful', *New York Times*, 20 July 2006, at http://www.nytimes.com/2006/07/20/world/asia/20blind.html?_r=1&ex=1154059200&en=f468ddc24bc80f6d&ei=5070, accessed 9 November 2013.

Kai, Wen (凯文), '副院长与正律师：一场不对称战争 [Court Vice President and Righteous Lawyers: battle between unequal opponents]', 24 May 2012, at http://boxun.com/news/gb/pubvp/2012/05/201205240034.shtml, accessed 7 November 2013.

Kellogg, Thomas E., 'Western funding for rule of law initiatives in China: the importance of a civil society-based approach', 3 *China Perspectives* (2012) 53–59, at http://chinaperspectives.revues.org/5954, accessed 14 November 2013.

Laojoh (pen name), '高智晟侄子试找人签律师委托书受阻 [Gao Zhisheng's nephew obstructed when trying to get letter of attorney signed]', 6 September 2006, at http://boxun.com/forum/zongjiao/12033.shtml, accessed 1 January 2014.

Li, Jinglin (李静林), '记我被抢的奇遇，真切感谢劫匪不贪财 [Account of a curious robbery – deeply thanking my robbers for taking no valuables]', 26 April 2011, at http://www.peacehall.com/news/gb/china/2011/04/201104260023.shtml, accessed 9 November 2013.

Li Li, 'Judicial independence should come first', 10 November 2005 interview with Professor He Weifang, at http://chinadigitaltimes.net/2005/11/judicial-independence-should-come-first-li-li/, accessed 10 November 2013.

Li, Ling, 'The "production" of corruption in China's courts – the politics of judicial decision-making and its consequences in a one-party state', 5 July 2011, *Journal of Law & Social Inquiry* (2011), at http://ssrn.com/abstract=188014.

Luo, Gan (罗干), 'The political and judicial authorities' historic mission and political responsibility for constructing a harmonious society [政法机关在构建和谐社会中担负重大历史使命和政治责任]', 3 *Seeking Truth* (《求是》) (2007), at http://theory.people.com.cn/GB/49169/49171/5355912.html, accessed 10 November 2013.

Mao, Lixin (毛立新), '律师"闹庭"与"辩审"冲突 [Lawyers' trouble-making in court and the conflict between the advocacy and the judiciary]', at http://police.fyfz.cn/b/739166, accessed 7 November 2013.

Mao Zedong (毛泽东), 1957, 'On the correct handling of contradictions among the people', (translation) in Selden, Mark, *The People's Republic of China: A Documentary History of Revolutionary Change*, New York Monthly Review Press, New York: 1979. See Chapter 2.

Minzner, Carl F., 'Xinfang: an alternative to the formal Chinese legal system', 42 *Stanford Journal of International Law* (2006) 103.

Pan, Xuanming, 'Non-lawyers as legal resources for the State: issues, institutions and implications for China's legal reform', PhD dissertation, the Chinese University of Hong Kong (2012).

People's Court of Xiangtan County (湘潭县人民法院), 'Qingshan Bridge Court properly handled a Nao Ting incident' (青山桥法庭妥善处理一起闹庭事件), 26 August 2013, at http://xtxfy.chinacourt.org/public/detail.php?id=632.

Pils, Eva, 'Yang Jia and China's unpopular criminal justice system', 1 *China Rights Forum* (2009) 59–66.

Pils, Eva, 'Asking the tiger for his skin: rights activism in China', 30 *Fordham International Law Journal* (2006) 1209–1287.

Pils, Eva, 'Land disputes, rights assertion and social unrest: a case from Sichuan', 19 *Columbia Journal of Asian Law* (2006) 365; reprinted as Hauser Global Law School Working Paper 07/05 and in Perry Keller (ed.), *Obligations and Property Rights in China*, Ashgate, Aldershot: 2012.

Pils, Eva, 'Contending conceptions of ownership and property in urbanising China', in Fu Hualing and John Gillespie (eds.), *Resolving Land Disputes in East Asia*, Cambridge University Press (forthcoming).

Rosenzweig, Joshua, Sapio, Flora, Jiang, Jue, Teng, Biao and Pils, Eva, 'The 2012 revision of the Chinese Criminal Procedure Law', in McConville, Mike and Pils, Eva (eds.), *Criminal Justice in China: Comparative Perspectives*, Edward Elgar Publishing, Cheltenham: 2011.

Secret China (看中国), '最高法内部文件被泄露 网络审查纠纷不立案 [SPC internal document on not filing cases concerning internet censorship revealed],' 25 April 2012, at http://www.secretchina.com/news/12/04/25/449323.html, accessed 1 January 2014.

Shen, Nianzu (沈念祖), '法院副院长们的压力 [Pressure on Court Vice Presidents],' originally published in *Economic Observer*, (经济观察报), 19 May 2012, at http://www.eeo.com.cn/2012/0519/226779.shtml, accessed 7 November 2013.

South China Morning Post, 'Rights lawyer held for four hours over T-shirt, police destroy garment with political slogans', *South China Morning Post*, 12 October 2009, at http://www.scmp.com/article/695107/rights-lawyer-held-four-hours-over-t-shirt, accessed 14 November 2013.

Teng, Biao, 'Video cameras break official monopoly: video plays a notable role in citizen movements', 4 *China Rights Forum* (2010), at http://www.hrichina.org/content/4961, accessed 13 November 2013.

Teng, Biao, et al., '我们愿意为被捕藏民提供法律帮助 [We are willing to provide legal assistance to criminally arrested Tibetans]', 2 April 2008, at http://www.peacehall.com/news/gb/china/2008/04/200804022305.shtml.

Trevaskes, Susan, 'The ideology of law and order', 2012, http://www.thechinastory.org/wp-content/uploads/2012/07/ChinaStory2012.pdf, accessed 1 January 2014.

Upham, Frank, 'Who will find the defendant if he stays with his sheep? Justice in rural China', 114 *Yale Law Journal* (2005) 1675.

Voice of America (Mandarin Desk), '吉林610办公室阻挠律师依法辩护 [A Jilin 610 Office obstructs lawyer's lawful criminal defence],' 13 September 2010, at http://www.voanews.com/chinese/news/china/20100913-lawyer-harassed-102769329.html, accessed 9 November 2013.

Wang, Gong (王工) et al., '敦请最高人民检察院立即对重庆打黑运动中的刑讯逼供问题依法调查的公开信 [Open letter requesting Supreme People's Procuracy immediately to open an investigation into the use of torture in the Chongqing anti-mafia campaign],' published 23 August 2010, at http://www.gongfa.com/html/gongfaxinwen/201008/23-1347.html, accessed 13 November 2013.

Webster, Timothy, 'Ambivalence and activism: employment discrimination in China', 44 *Vanderbilt Journal of Transnational Law* (2011) 643, at http://digitalcommons.law.yale.edu/cgi/viewcontent.cgi?article=1000&context=ylas, accessed 13 November 2013.

Yu, Jianrong (于建嵘), 'The petitioners' dilemma and the way out [中国信访制度的困境和出路]', 1 *Strategy and Management* (2009), at http://theory.rmlt.com.cn/2012/1126/54714.shtml, accessed 10 November 2013.

Yu, Verna, 'Detained Guo Feixiong tells lawyer of hunger strike', *South China Morning Post*, 14 November 2014.

Zhai, Keith, 'Rights advocate Wang Gongquan latest to give video confession', *South China Morning Post*, 6 November 2013.

Zhang, Xueran, 'China's all-star legal team pleads for defendants' rights on social media', *Tea Leaf Nation*, 25 July 2012, at http://tealeafnation.com/2012/07/bilingual-brew-chinas-all-star-legal-team-pleads-for-defendants-rights-on-social-media.

Zhu, Mingyong (朱明勇), '一路走好 [Farewell]', (poem published after Fan Qihang's execution), at http://renminbao.com/rmb/articles/2010/10/3/53303b.html, accessed 13 November 2013.

Zhuang, Jinghui and Faure, Gaelle, '77-year-old woman strips to protest the demolition of her home', 24 *France* (7 September 2011), at http://observers.france24.com/content/20110907-china-77-year-old-woman-strips-down-shanghai-courthouse-protest-land-grab, accessed 13 November 2013.

Documentary and multimedia sources

'我要立案 [I Want to File My Case]', 12 August 2011, at http://www.youtube.com/watch?v=MckgKZJl0g8, accessed 13 November 2013.

He, Yang (何杨), *Conversation with Lawyer Zhu Mingyong on black-strike/torture* (专访朱明勇律师—黑打), 21 September 2010, at http://www.vimeo.com/13706954, accessed 13 November 2013.

He, Yang (何杨), '赫索格的日子 [*Herzog's Days*],' independent documentary film, August 2010, at http://vimeo.com/12938865, accessed 1 January 2014.

He, Yang, '(何杨) [*Disbarment*]', independent documentary film, 2010.

NTDTV, 'Chinese activist Wang Lihong's trial "not fair" says lawyer', at http://www.youtube.com/watch?v=pbOs4aQ1UVw, accessed 9 November 2013.

Websites, blogs and microblog entries

Zhongyizhe (忠义者, a pseudonym), 6月8日被"被和谐"的法院旁听, 8 June 2012, at http://hd3g.gxnews.com.cn/viewthread.php?t=7103215, accessed 4 January 2014.

5   Bureaucratic control of the legal profession

The signs of control

Judging by the external appearance of their offices and working lives, Chinese lawyers today in many ways resemble their counterparts around the world. They are professionally trained and they command a vocabulary of legal terms and procedures many of which would be easily understood in other countries. They must satisfy rigorous professional qualification conditions to enter the legal profession, including a Chinese national legal exam. Their profession is economically self-reliant, dependent primarily on their own initiatives to find clients and create business; and they normally expect to make an income from their cases. The majority of lawyers work in law firms with partners and associates, whose external structure will appear familiar to foreign lawyers.[1]

But there are important signs of difference, in all firms but especially in firms that have human rights lawyers working in them. If you go to such a lawyer's office you may find a guard stationed in the lobby of the building, declaring that all visitors must register, or enquiring why a foreigner is visiting.[2] Inside the office, a plaque might announce the existence of a Party branch office the firm was forced to establish.[3] Even uniformed police may be temporarily stationed inside the offices of a law firm.[4] Practically always, the lawyer's office is assumed to be under electronic surveillance from the security apparatus.[5] You will sometimes be asked by the lawyer to remove the battery and SIM card from your mobile

---

1 Three structures for law firms continue to be recognised in accordance with the 2007 Law on Lawyers (Articles 14–20 Law on Lawyers). Cp. Xueyao Li and Sida Liu, 'The learning process of globalisation: how Chinese law firms survived the financial crisis', 80 *Fordham Law Review* (2012) 2850.
2 #24 2011-1.
3 *Ibid.*
4 *Ibid.*
5 A few of the conversations were held in lawyers' offices and some in the offices of an NGO. Occasionally (#26 2011-1 or 2; #62 2012-1) the interlocutor explicitly commented on the likelihood of electronic surveillance of the conversation. On one occasion an interlocutor, having just emerged from a period of forced disappearance, pretended barely to know me ('I think we've met') although we had known each other for years; later he took me outside to provide a full account of his recent experience.

phone to avoid tracking via the GPS system.[6] More often, the meeting will take place in a coffee shop, teahouse, restaurant or public park. Once one gets talking, it will become apparent that some of the lawyers interact frequently yet reluctantly with Justice Bureau and Lawyers' Association officials. At some point in their professional lives, finally, human rights lawyers are likely to experience the pressure of expulsion from the licensed legal profession.

The symbols of Party supremacy, the lawyer's licences with their 'annual assessment' stamps and the fact of surveillance and coerced interaction with the authorities are signs of the bureaucratic control discussed here. Control is associated primarily with the justice bureaux and the lawyers' associations, as well as with law firms and, as always, the Party; and it is in part exerted through mechanisms resembling professional self-regulation. While control is invasively manifest in the lives of human rights lawyers, it also reaches pervasively into the wider legal profession; but this wider bureaucratic control is less easy to notice, and its success is not assured since its effects are limited.

In many places, the discussion here consciously adopts the term 'control' in preference over 'regulation'. 'Regulation' would suggest that the purpose of the authorities was to ensure that the legal profession worked in accordance with public rules expressing standards of rightness that could be rationally understood and strive for coherence and predictability in the way they exercised their powers. A survey of the authorities' actual measures taken against individual law firms and lawyers, however, indicates that the authorities themselves have been frequently unwilling to acknowledge the force of the rules to which they are subject, in so far as any rules are discernible; that they are making use of the dualism of a 'State of norms' and 'State of measures'.[7]

The control complex of justice bureaux, lawyers' associations and the Party

The 'two conjoined' and the Party

Since the creation of the All China Lawyers' Association ('ACLA') in 1986,[8] the justice bureaux and the lawyers' associations have operated what has been characterised in official jargon as the 'two conjoined' management system for lawyers. As one of the 'two conjoined' entities, ACLA's stated goals according to its website are to:

> Unite and educate members to maintain the dignity of the Constitution and laws, be faithful to the legal profession, abide by standards of professional

---

6 #62 2012-1.

7 Ernst Fraenkel, *The Dual State. A Contribution to the Theory of Dictatorship*, translated by E.A. Shils, Oxford University Press, New York: 1941. See also Chapter 1.

8 See 中华全国律师协会 [All China Lawyers' Association] or 全国律协 [ACLA] introduction at http://www.acla.org.cn/about.jhtml, accessed 17 February 2013.

ethics and discipline, defend members' lawful rights and interests, raise members' professional competence, strengthen professional self-regulation in order to promote the healthy development of the profession and to struggle for the establishment of rule by law (*yi fa zhi guo*),[9] a state under socialist rule of law, and a more civilized and progressive society.[10]

ACLA characterises itself as a social organisation with legal personality (Article 2 of the ACLA Charter, last revised in 2011).[11] In accordance with Article 45 of the Law on Lawyers, Lawyers' Associations are responsible for protecting the rights and interests of lawyers, for educational, training and internship activities, for the maintenance of a self-discipline system that includes the possibility of imposing punishment (but not disbarment), for taking complaints against lawyers and for mediating disputes among lawyers. Membership in the local lawyers' association where one is registered, entailing automatic membership in ACLA, is compulsory for all licensed lawyers according to the 2007 Law on Lawyers.[12] While there are one-person firms,[13] this means that no lawyer may practise outside the reach of the lawyers' associations.

The Ministry of Justice as the other one of the 'two conjoined' entities and the justice bureaux subordinate to it, according to Article 4 of the Law on Lawyers, is in charge of 'supervision' and 'guidance' of the legal profession. They also have responsibility for the licensing or 'registration' system, what Article 52 characterises as 'day-to-day supervision and management' of the work of law firms and lawyers,[14] and the power to impose the sanction of suspension or disbarment on lawyers. The justice bureaux have offices specifically responsible for lawyers.[15]

Sida Liu mentions that a judicial administration official once likened the principle of the 'two conjoined' to 'two skins' – one can wear either one as needed. This simile would indicate that neither of the 'two conjoined' had full institutional agency – that neither of them was the person inside either skin. Liu also notes that sometimes the departmental head responsible for 'lawyer management'

---

9 In Chinese characters, 依法治国.
10 *Ibid.*
11 中华全国律师协会章程 [ACLA Charter] (last revised on 26 December 2011), Article 3, available at http://www.acla.org.cn/zhangchen.jhtml, accessed 17 February 2013.
12 中华人民共和国律师法 [PRC Law on Lawyers], passed 2007, in effect since June 2008. For the Chinese text, see http://www.npc.gov.cn/npc/xinwen/2012-10/27/content_1741052.htm and for an English translation http://www.cecc.gov/pages/newLaws/lawyersLawENG.php.
13 The Beijing Lawyers Association (北京律师协会) lists a few one-person law firms as having passed the latest 2012 assessment exercise at its website http://www.beijinglawyers.org.cn/qtmodel/lxgg.htm, for example.
14 Article 52, Law on Lawyers.
15 For example, as of November 2013, three of the Beijing Justice Bureau's sub-offices are primarily concerned with lawyers: these are 律师业务指导和执业监管处 [Office for Professional Task Guidance and Supervision and Management of Lawyers], 律师行业综合指导处 [Office for Comprehensive Guidance of the Legal Profession], 律师和律师事务所执业许可处 [Office for Professional Licensing of Lawyers and Law Firms]. Their websites can be accessed through http://www.bjsf.gov.cn/publish/portal0/tab97/, accessed 31 December 2013.

within the justice bureau will often be the general secretary of the lawyers' association at a corresponding level of administration. The subordination of the lawyers' associations to the justice bureaux is given expression in various ways. Thus the Beijing Justice Bureau at its website links the Beijing Lawyers' Associations as a 'subordinate agency'; and in many locations, the head of the relevant justice bureau sub-office(s) will be the general secretary of the lawyers' association.[16]

If there is a person inside the 'two skins', it must be the Party, as it has ultimate agency and control. Neither the 2007 Law on Lawyers nor the Ministry of Justice's 'Regulation on the Legal Profession' mentions the Party in any way; but in recent years the authorities have begun to promote the role of the Party with regard to the legal profession in a public way, in apparent reaction to a 2004 decision made at the highest political level. The Party Central Committee's Leading Group on Judicial System Reform, in a document called 'Preliminary Opinions on the Reform of the Judicial System', distributed to all Party committees in central State agencies and in all 'people's organisations' called on:

> [A]ll departments in all areas [to] pay attention to and conscientiously study new situations and problems that have arisen in the process of judicial reform, report on their experiences in a timely manner, and safeguard the realisation of all reform agenda items.[17]

The 2004 Preliminary Opinions contain one important paragraph on 'reform and perfection of the lawyer system', phrased in the subjectless and characterless, elliptical language typical of bureaucratic documents:

> Reform and perfect the structure and form of lawyers' organisations to establish a lawyer system that is suited to socialism with Chinese characteristics. Perfect the conjoined legal systems of administrative management and professional self-regulation for lawyers, strengthen management efficiency, strictly examine professional status, standardise professional behaviour, and punish illegal conduct. Strengthen the establishment of basic-level Party organisations in the legal profession, raise the legal profession's political and professional quality and its quality with regard to professional ethics, uphold the principle of serving the People, and safeguard judicial justice.[18]

This, at the time, was still merely a bureaucratic command without clear origins, setting in motion an as yet non-detailed programme of reinforced control. It

---

16 *Ibid.*
17 中央司法体制改革领导小组关于司法体制和工作机制改革的初步意见 [Preliminary Opinions on the reform of the Judicial System and Working Mechanisms of the Party Central Committee Leading Group on Judicial System Reform], dated 1 December 2004, reprinted in 中华人民共和国监察部办公厅 (PRC Ministry of Supervision), 行政监察工作文件选编 2004 年 [Selected Administration and Supervision Work Documents, 2004 Issue], Beijing, 2005, at p. 626 ff.
18 *Ibid.*, at p. 633.

was not until Zhou Yongkang had assumed the position of head of the central Political and Legal Committee and became a member of the Politburo Standing Committee that the Party–State proceeded to implement this programme. A hardliner whose political credentials had been established as Sichuan Party Secretary (1999–2002) and Public Security Minister (2003–2007),[19] Zhou had now acquired a position of sufficient power to tighten control of the legal system; and this he accomplished during his tenure, leaving behind bureaucratic institutions more closely connected to and more directly compliant with instructions from the security apparatus, usually given in the name of 'stability preservation', 'social management', etc.

In May 2008, just prior to the 2007 Law on Lawyers coming into effect (in June 2008), the Party's Central Organisation Department and the Ministry of Justice jointly issued a document called 'Notice of the Central Organisation Department and Ministry of Justice on further Strengthening the Establishment of Party Organisations in the Legal Profession'.[20] It called for improving lawyer Party members' education, management and service and said:

> All locations must in accordance with the number and distribution of Party members in the legal profession strengthen categorized guidance and work hard to increase coverage of Party organizations and Party work. (. . .) Making law firms that are run in a fairly standardised manner and have a certain social influence our priority, [we shall] strive within about one year to get to a point at which Party organisations cover, and Party work unfolds, wherever a law firm has been established.[21, 22]

The announced goal became known as 'total coverage'[23] through 'professional Party-building work'.[24] In November 2008, a speech by Zhou Yongkang delivered

---

19 A short profile of Zhou Yongkang is available, e.g. at 'Zhou Yongkang', *South China Morning Post*, at http://www.scmp.com/topics/zhou-yongkang, accessed 25 December 2013. Official profiles formerly available at http://chinese-leaders.org/zhou-yongkang/ are no longer available as of December 2013. Jonathan Ansfield and Chris Buckley, 'China focusing graft inquiry on ex-official', *New York Times*, 15 December 2013, at http://www.nytimes.com/2013/12/16/world/asia/china-presses-corruption-inquiry-of-powerful-former-security-official.html?_r=0. On the further downfall of Zhou Yongkang, see Jerome A Cohen, 'Zhou Yongkang case shows China's rule of law still good only in theory,' *South China Morning Post*, 18 August 2014.

20 See 中组部、司法部关于进一步加强和改进律师行业党的建设工作的通知 [Central Organisation Department and Ministry of Justice's Notice on Further Strengthening the Establishment of Party Organisations in the Legal Profession], dated 8 May 2008, at http://www.acla.org.cn/hydjzd/2878.jhtml, accessed 11 February 2013, copy on file with author; 全国律协关于深入学习贯彻全国律师工作会议和全国律师行业党的建设工作会议的意见 [ACLA Opinion on Conscientiously Studying and Implementing the Establishment of Party Organisations in the Legal Profession], 30 December 2012, at http://www.acla.org.cn/fazhixinwen/617.jhtml, accessed 11 February 2013, copy on file with author.

21 Central Organisation Department and Ministry of Justice's Notice on Further Strengthening the Establishment of Party Organisations in the Legal Profession, *ibid*.

22 *Ibid*. See also http://politics.people.com.cn/GB/14562/13260124.html, accessed 25 December 2013.

23 Quanfugai, quanmianfugai, 全覆盖、全面覆盖.

24 *Hangyedangjiangongzuo*, 行业党建工作.

to ACLA officials reinforced the message that the central leadership was 'paying attention' to the legal profession. Zhou said that lawyers were duty bound toward society to maintain social stability, adding:

> [Lawyers must] develop their strengths, provide legal services so that the Party and the Government can deal with public emergencies, do targeted mass work, and jointly safeguard the social order. [They must] be highly vigilant and take strict precautions against trouble-making (*daoluan*)[25] and sabotaging activities under the banner of 'defending rights'. [They must] of their own accord safeguard national security and social and political stability.[26]

Never before, human rights lawyers have commented, had the head of the powerful Political and Legal Committee condescended to speak to an ACLA meeting in person.[27] His presence and comments, as well as a number of subsequent speeches, work meetings, and 'visits',[28] made it clear that there was a 'problem' that needed to be addressed.

According to the ACLA's Annual Report, by the end of 2011, all provincial level and 360 municipal lawyers' associations had established Party organisations within themselves; and among a total of 18,235 law firms, 4,855 had established their own Party organisation while 8,668 law firms had established altogether 2,886 joint 'Party branches' together with other law firms. So-called 'Party-building work guidance officers' or 'Party-building work liaison officers' had been despatched to 4,085 law firms that did not have Party members. Thus, 17,608 law firms nationwide had been subjected to some sort of Party 'coverage' at the end of 2011, leaving a mere 627 firms nationwide 'uncovered'.[29]

Since its revision in December 2011, moreover, the ACLA Charter states upholding Party leadership as the first in a list of ACLA goals;[30] and the Ministry

---

25 In Chinese characters, 捣乱.
26 Zhou Yongkang (周永康),在第七次全国律师代表大会上的讲话 [Speech at the Seventh National Lawyers' Congress], 25 October 2008, at http://news.xinhuanet.com/legal/2008-10/26/content_10257859.htm.
27 Comments by #62. #24 2011-1.
28 Thus on 18 May 2009, Zhou Yongkang gave another, widely noted speech, later published in the Magazine *Qiushi*. Zhou Yongkang (周永康), '全面推进社会治安综合治理工作确保人民安居乐业社会和谐稳定 [Safeguard Social Equality and Justice; Uphold Social Harmony and Stability]', 12 *Qiu Shi [Seeking Truth] Magazine* (2009), available at http://www.mps.gov.cn/n16/n894593/n895609/1953766.html, accessed 18 November 2013. See also '周永康在全国律师工作会议上的讲话 [Zhou Yongkang's speech at All China Lawyers' Delegates Meeting]', November 2010, at http://cpc.people.com.cn/GB/64093/64094/13402392.html, accessed 18 November 2013.
29 全国律协 (ACLA), '中国特色社会主义法律工作者的生动实践 [The real life practice of socialist-with-Chinese-characteristics legal workers]', Annual Report, 1 November 2012, at http://www.acla.org.cn/industry/4179.jhtml.
30 ACLA Charter (last revised 26 December 2011), Article 3, available at http://www.acla.org.cn/zhangchen.jhtml.

of Justice requires all lawyers taking up their licence to practise to swear an oath of loyalty that included the Party:

> I volunteer to become a practising lawyer of the People's Republic of China and promise to faithfully perform the sacred duties of a socialist-with-Chinese-characteristics legal worker; to be faithful to the motherland and the people; to uphold the leadership of the Chinese Communist Party and the socialist system; to safeguard the dignity of the Constitution and the law; to practise on behalf of the people; to be diligent, professional honest, and corruption-free; to protect the legitimate rights and interests of clients, the correct implementation of the law, and social fairness and justice; and diligently strive for the cause of socialism with Chinese characteristics![31]

This means that at least to outward and symbolic purposes, 'total coverage' has been very nearly achieved, even though according to official statistics, the number of lawyers who are members of the Party is just around one-third of the total.[32]

Yet, despite copious references to supervising the work of 'lawyer Party members', 'clarifying work responsibilities' and so on, publicly available documents are unclear as to the underlying rules and principles, if any, of 'leadership' and 'work guidance' to be provided to its Party members, and on how such leadership and guidance might affect the operation of the law firms overall. While there is a sense that the Party is the person inside the skins of the 'two conjoined' entities – that it alone has the power to make any major decisions – this agent lacks public personality. Its structure and mechanisms are obscure; its obscurity secures omnipresence. It is clear neither to what extent, if at all, Party organisations set up within law firms or groups of law firms affect these firms' professional operation – their work as lawyers; nor who or what specific entity within the Party exerts control on lawyers or law firms.

The website of ACLA contains a regulation on Party organisations in basic level administrative departments,[33] which emphasises that Party organisations must operate on Leninist principles – they are strictly hierarchical; and members must uphold the principle of 'democratic centralism' as interpreted by the Party

---

31 Translation by Siweiluozi Blog, 'New pledge of allegiance for Chinese lawyers', 3 March 2012, at http://www.siweiluozi.net/2012/03/new-pledge-of-allegiance-for-chinese.html (English translation and link to original); see also 关于印发《关于建立律师宣誓制度的决定》的通知 [Notice on Issuance of 'Decision on Oath System for Lawyers'], dated 3 February 2012, at http://baike.baidu.com/view/8206917.htm?fromTaglist (both accessed 31 December 2013). The phrase translated as 'socialist-with-Chinese-characteristics legal workers' is 中国特色社会主义法律工作者 in Chinese.

32 全国律协 (ACLA), '中国特色社会主义法律工作者的生动实践 [The real life practice of socialist-with-Chinese-characteristics legal workers]', 1 November 2012, at http://www.acla.org.cn/industry/4179.jhtml accessed 2 January 2014.

33 中国共产党党和国家机关基层组织工作条例 [Chinese Communist Party Regulation on the Work of Basic Level Party and State Organisations], promulgated by the Central Committee of Chinese Communist Party on 30 March 1998, at http://www.acla.org.cn/hydjzd/2222.jhtml, accessed 2 January 2014; http://www.bjsf.gov.cn/publish/portal0/tab97/info9120.htm, accessed 22 February 2013.

(e.g. Article 7 (3)). The 'Three Supremes' as a maxim touted for judges have also been applied to lawyers;[34] and the regulation also mentions 'the nature and characteristics of the Party' or more loosely translated, 'Party spirit' (*dangxing*),[35] (cp. Articles 13 and 24). 'Nurturing Party spirit' was reportedly one of the subjects of a speech by Xi Jinping in August 2013,[36] and the Party's Third Plenary Session in November 2013 was described as 'releasing Party spirit and the feelings of the people'[37] (sometimes also called 'people spirit'), which as Willy Lam has noted, must be 'always uniform and united'.[38] Local lawyers' associations have promptly devoted spaces on their websites to soul-searching discussions of what 'Party spirit' means and how best to nurture it.[39]

Publicly available reports on the role of the Party in the legal profession, etc., focus on innocuous promotional and public service-related activities. An example is the just mentioned ACLA report. It provides a number of photographs depicting the Party organisations in action, including three lawyers described as '18th Party Congress Party Representatives';[40] a stall displaying the banner 'Ten Thousand Lawyer Party Members Serve the People for One Hundred Days' (the photo depicts lawyers behind the stall, handing out leaflets to some women passers-by); a 'Party History Knowledge Contest'; and the opening of a Party school for lawyers aspiring to join the Party.

Glimpses of how the triadic complex of Party, Ministry of Justice and ACLA really affect and control lawyers and law firms (and of how law firms at times sometimes pass pressure on to individual lawyers working with them) can be gained by studying the concrete measures and mechanisms at their disposal and these measures' and mechanisms' day-to-day uses. The mechanisms of registration and annual re-registration, requirements to make reports about individual cases to the justice bureaux, and various broadly speaking 'educational' activities,

34 E.g. by Zhou Yongkang in his speech to ACLA in 2010 (*supra*).
35 In Chinese characters, 党性.
36 Qiu Shi (秋石), '革命理想高于天——学习习近平同志关于坚定理想信念的重要论述 [Revolutionary ideals are higher than heaven – studying Comrade Xi Jinping's important discourse on strengthening ideals and beliefs]', 1 November 2013, at http://big5.qstheory.cn/zxdk/2013/201321/201310/t20131030_284176.htm, accessed 1 January 2014; available in translation at *China Copyright and Media*, http://chinacopyrightandmedia.wordpress.com/2013/11/, accessed 23 December 2013.
37 Shu Sheng (舒升), '三中全会释放的是党性和民心 [The Third Plenary has released Party spirit and popular feelings]', 13 November 2013, at http://blog.people.com.cn/article/1384356795570.html. See also Zhang Feng (张峰), '宣传思想工作要坚持党性和人民性的统一 [Propaganda and thought work must maintain that Party spirit and people spirit are united]', video-recorded lecture dated 28 October 2013, at http://www.71.cn/2013/1028/742244.shtml, accessed 23 December 2013.
38 Willy Lam, 'Xi Jinping's crackdown could in effect destroy China's economy', *Jamestown Foundation*, 4 October 2013, at http://www.asianews.it/news-en/Xi-Jinping%E2%80%99s-ideological-crackdown-could-destroy-China%E2%80%99s-economy-29192.html.
39 E.g. Shenzhen City Lawyers' Association website, essay by Wan Yanping (完颜平), '党性"四问 [Four questions concerning *Dangxing*]', Guangming Daily, undated, at http://www.szlawyers.com/info/619e760cb38945c9c57817e7b22361a4, accessed 23 December 2013.
40 Among them the public interest lawyer Tong Lihua (佟丽华) who heads a network of legal aid stations helping migrant workers run as a subordinate agency of the justice bureaux. See http://www.zgnmg.org/, http://www.zgnmg.org/a/10gywm/ and Chapter 3.

as well as informal 'chats' with particular individuals are part of an increasingly finely meshed net that serves the authorities' purpose of control.

Control mechanisms (1): the licensing, registration and assessment systems

The justice bureaux run the professional licensing system for lawyers, and the lawyers' associations and justice bureaux are jointly responsible for the running of the annual assessment system.

The registration and licensing system, which governs those who want to enter the profession, as well as those who hold licences, ensures that minimum conditions of professional competence are satisfied. In order to obtain a licence under the 2007 Law on Lawyers, one must have passed the national judicial/bar exam, have been a trainee lawyer in a firm for two years, and be 'a person of good character and conduct'. This requirement can be used to exclude politically undesirable would-be lawyers. In recent years the justice bureaux have begun to require assessment interviews with the local lawyers' association in the case of first-time applicants. Having been assessed as 'in accordance with standards' (*hege*)[41] by the Beijing Lawyers' Association, for example, is a requirement for getting a lawyer's licence in Beijing. In his 2010 speech to ACLA delegates, Zhou Yongkang had said that those 'of bad political quality, professional quality, or with bad legal ethics could not be lawyers'.[42] Human rights lawyers report that this system has given the authorities opportunities to reject entrants to the legal profession for political reasons:

> For instance, A had only just met with us a few times and was visited by the *guobao*[43] police straightaway; and as a result she cannot get her lawyer's licence now. . . . She had not really been involved in the handling of any cases yet. She was only just completing her traineeship, and she was really just concerned about this area [of rights defence], and especially interested in [the work of a well-known rights defender]; and she had participated in a few of our meetings.[44]

In recent years, some localities such as Beijing have begun further to restrict access to the local profession to persons with a local *hukou* or household registration, even though the 2007 Law on Lawyers prohibits regional (local) registration systems (Article 10). Widely interpreted as a measure of economic protectionism, this provision can also serve to enhance bureaucratic control of politically sensitive

---

41 In Chinese characters, 合格.
42 周永康在全国律师工作会议上的讲话 [Zhou Yongkang's speech at All China Lawyers' Delegates Meeting], November 2010, at http://cpc.people.com.cn/GB/64093/64094/13402392. html. In the same speech, Zhou praised as model public interest lawyers the lawyers Tong Lihua (佟丽华, mentioned above), and Zhao Chunfang (赵春芳).
43 In Chinese characters, 国保.
44 #20 2010-2; #23 2013-1 (further examples).

lawyers. It has left some human rights lawyers in limbo after the law firm they were registered with ceased to exist, as they feel compelled to contemplate a move away from the capital to obtain a lawyer's licence.[45]

Once licensed, lawyers remain subject to annual reassessments of their professionally licensed status, required under rules and regulations of the 'two conjoined' entities. The so-called *annual examination (nianjian)*[46] system attracted criticism for its apparent violation of the 2004 Administrative Licensing Law;[47] and the 2007 Law on Lawyers was silent on *nianjian*. In July 2008, however, the Ministry of Justice issued its new 'Regulations on the Management/Administration of Lawyers' Professional Licences' and the 'Regulation on the Management/ Administration of Law Firms' Registration'.[48] The system formerly known as *annual examination (nianjian)* was replaced with a system called *annual assessment (niandu kaohe)*.[49] In 2010, the Ministry of Justice and ACLA issued supplementing regulations on the assessment of law firms and lawyers, respectively.[50,51] In essence, the system has not changed much.

According to the rules and regulations now in place, both law firms and individual lawyers must undergo an annual assessment exercise. The justice bureaux are primarily responsible for the annual assessment of law firms, and the lawyers associations are primarily responsible for individual lawyers' assessment. Both of the 'two conjoined' entities are expected to coordinate their work and report to one another.

An individual lawyer will be assessed as to whether he or she fulfils the requirement of 'competence' (*chengzhi*),[52] and if a lawyer is deemed to be 'competent' or 'basically competent',[53] the lawyers' association will report this result to the judicial bureau and the lawyer's professional licence booklet will receive a stamp

45 #14 2012-1.
46 In Chinese characters, 年检.
47 #25 2010-1a (written communication on file with author).
48 #25 2010-1a (written communication on file with author); '律师事务所管理办法 (司法部111 号令) [Regulation on Management of Law Firms (Ministry of Justice edict no. 111)]', dated 18 July 2008, at http://www.chinanews.com/gn/news/2008/07-21/1319598.shtml, accessed 11 February 2013; '律师执业管理办法 (司法部 112 号令) [Regulation on Management of Lawyers (Ministry of Justice edict no. 112)]', at http://www.moj.gov.cn/2008zcfg/2008-07/22/content_906514.htm, accessed 11 February 2013.
49 In Chinese characters, 年度考核. #25 2010-1a. ('Assessment' is the term used in the 2007 Law on Lawyers in its Articles 23, 24, and 46 and the two aforementioned 2008 Regulations, which refer to 'daily assessment' 'annual assessment' and 'annual examination and assessment'.)
50 律师事务所年度检查考核办法 [Regulation on Annual Law Firm Assessment], promulgated by the Ministry of Justice on 8 April, 2010, effective from 8 April, 2010, at http://www.legalinfo.gov.cn/index/content/2010-04/09/content_2108819.htm, accessed 24 November 2013. 律师执业年度考核规则, [Regulation on Annual Assessment of Lawyers], promulgated by All China Lawyers Association on 13 August, 2010, effective from 1 January 2011, at http://2009.lawyers.org.cn/profile/info.jsp?id=12f438db9a4fbb68482443a568fa6448, accessed 24 November 2013.
51 Events and experiences described in the following occurred in the time period between 2004 and now; and different rules were being applied at different times.
52 In Chinese characters, 称职.
53 Article 9 of the Regulation.

recording this result.[54] A lawyer's assessment as 'incompetent'[55] will also be recorded in the lawyer's licence booklet,[56] which has to be used, e.g. when seeking to meet a client in police detention. The lawyer assessed as 'incompetent' will receive a written instruction for 'correction' and be enrolled for training and educational activities:

> You can still use the licence, as long as there is any stamp in it. But if your stamp says 'incompetent' people may ask you about that, for example in the police detention centre [when you try to meet a client]. And, well, it looks really bad toward clients![57]

If they have been found 'incompetent' for two years in succession, the lawyers' association may impose the disciplinary measures of issuing a criticism or a public reprimand. 'In serious cases', it may also 'suggest' to the judicial bureau that it impose an appropriate administrative punishment; or it may 'suggest' to the law firm at which the lawyer in question is working that it dissolve the employment relationship with this lawyer or that it expel the lawyer from the partnership through a resolution of the law firm's partners.[58] Administrative punishments to be given to lawyers and law firms by the justice bureaux, in turn, are dealt with by the 2010 Ministry of Justice Regulation on Administrative Punishments for Lawyers and Law Firms;[59] and they include, as the severest form of punishment, permanent disbarment.

The 2010 Ministry of Justice Regulation on the Annual Assessment of Law Firms details as criteria of the assessment their performance in 'lawyer team building', which includes 'thought and political education' and 'education on professional ethics and discipline', and 'Party-building work in the legal profession';[60] 'professional practice activities' including 'guidance and supervision of lawyers' work on major cases and cases of a mass nature', and 'praise or complaints of their professional practice activities by the clients, concerned departments or the masses'; 'professional performance as lawyers' and 'internal management'

---

54 Article 19. *Ibid.*
55 Article 12 describes situations in which a lawyer is deemed incompetent, including 'violation of professional discipline' and 'other conduct in contravention of the law, regulations, or duties of the members that produces a negative social impact'.
56 Picture of a licence booklet with 'incompetent' stamp, on file with author.
57 #23 2013-1.
58 Article 22 of the 2010 ACLA Rules on Assessment of Lawyers, *supra.*
59 Although it is difficult to know how many lawyers are penalised every year and why, the judicial authorities at different levels regularly publish reports about the number of law firms that have been 'stopped for rectification' (*tingye zhengdun*/停业整顿), de-registered (*zhuxiao*/注销), or issued administrative warnings (*bei xingzheng jinggao*/被行政警告); and about lawyers who have had their licences withdrawn (*diaoxiao*/吊销), or have been suspended for a period of time (*tingzhi zhiye*/停止执业), have been 'issued criticisms' (*tongbao piping*/通报批评), or temporarily de-registered (*bei zanhuan zhuce*/被暂缓注册). Human Rights Watch, 'A great danger for lawyers: new regulatory curbs on lawyers representing protesters', December 2006, at http://www.hrw.org/reports/2006/china1206/4.htm#_Toc153174877, accessed 24 November 2013.
60 In Chinese characters, *dangjiangongzuo*, 律师党建工作.

[of the firm].[61] Article 12 of this Regulation provides that the annual assessment exercise can result in assessment of being 'in accordance with standards' or 'not in accordance with standards'.[62]

If a law firm is deemed to be 'in accordance with standards', it will receive a stamp recording this in a copy of its licence to practise.[63] If a law firm is deemed 'not in accordance with standards', the judicial bureau will, 'depending on the nature and detailed circumstances of its illegal conduct [sic] and the degree of danger [it posed] impose a suspension of activity for one month to six months in accordance with law',[64] instruct it to make 'corrections' and 'give appropriate punishments' to persons held responsible within the firm. 'In extremely serious cases, its practice licence shall be permanently revoked in accordance with law.'

Before and after the 2010 Ministry of Justice Regulation was issued, various local justice bureaux at provincial level and below created their own regulations and forms setting out more detailed schemes for the law firm assessment exercises.[65] The form used by Jiangsu Province, for example, contains rubrics largely reflecting the assessment criteria mentioned above, and stipulates a maximum number of one to two points to be obtained for each sub-criterion (such as 'Party organisation establishment work'), and requires firms to engage in 'self-assessment' by grading their own performance, which is juxtaposed with the official assessment. The form also shows that there is a procedure of initial assessment by a low-level local justice bureau which reports both to the lawyers' association and to the next higher justice bureau, before assessment can be finalised.[66]

In the view of one rights lawyer, two main reasons explain why the authorities (judicial bureaux and lawyers' associations) continued to require the annual stamp affixed to the lawyer's licence as a precondition of 'legal' exercise of the lawyer's profession. First, he said, the lawyers' associations wanted to continue to take membership fees, for which he thought there was no legal basis: 'If they did not have the re-assessment system, there would be no way they could operate the fees system. Second, they need a means of political control of lawyers and law firms.'[67]

The annual assessment exercise and the annual examination exercise preceding it have indeed been used to put pressure on lawyers and firms. This was especially evident in 2009, when over 20 human rights lawyers reported having difficulties passing the annual examination exercise. Some of them were later able to pass

---

61 Articles 7–9 of 律师事务所年度检查考核办法 [MoJ Regulation on Annual Law Firm Assessment].
62 *'Hege' he 'buhege' liangge dengci*, 合格和不合格两个等次.
63 Article 22 of 律师事务所年度检查考核办法 [MoJ Regulation on Annual Law Firm Assessment].
64 Article 25 of the MoJ Regulation on Annual Law Firm Assessment [律师事务所年度检查考核办法].
65 Cp. 江苏省律师事务所年度检查考核办法(试行), 江苏省律师事务所年度检查考核细则 (试行), [Jiangsu Province Measures on the Annual Assessment and Examination of Law Firms (Provisional)], [Jiangsu Province Implementation Regulations on Law Firms' Annual Assessment and Examination (Provisional)], promulgated by Jiangsu Province Justice Bureau on 3 April 2009, http://www.jssf.gov.cn/skywcm/webpage/iframe/zwgk_detail.jsp?infoId=5606, accessed 3 December 2013.
66 *Ibid.*
67 *Ibid.*

and get the all-important stamp in their lawyer's licence booklets; but for several lawyers this took months, and in some cases, the licence was at some point permanently revoked. Among over 80 interlocutors who held a licence to practise law at one time, at least 27 reported encountering difficulties with their annual 'assessment' or 'examination'. Eight more are no longer licensed lawyers because they have had their licences provisionally or permanently revoked (*zhuxiao* or *diaoxiao*);[68] this list is not identical with the persons widely reported to have encountered problems in 2009.[69]

The case of Liu Wei and Tang Jitian is well documented.[70] Their disbarment was in reaction to their forceful attempts to present a defence in the court of Luzhou in 2009, as discussed earlier.[71] While Liu and Tang describe a trial process in which the presiding judge and an unidentified person apparently giving instructions to the judge severely disrupted their criminal defence, the official investigator states during the Beijing Justice Bureau hearing on this case:

> We believe this case, in terms of both the facts and the law, is quite clear in respect of facts. As this investigation report puts it, at the trial at Luzhou Intermediate Court on 27 April 2009, the lawyers Tang Jitian and Liu Wei failed, during the trial proceedings, to comply with the instructions from the judge. They did not obey when the judge stopped them, and they withdrew from the courtroom during the criminal defence statement stage of the trial. This was a severe disruption; it impaired the power of the judge to give instructions, and affected the normal progress of the litigation. We think this was an especially serious case.[72]

The later decisions to disbar Liu Wei and Tang Jitian in essence reiterate this assessment.[73] Teng Biao comments that:

> The Beijing Justice Bureau's reasoning is very confused. It contains a number of leaps, huge leaps in logic. They began by treating the withdrawal from the

---

68 In Chinese characters, 注销或吊销.

69 A Human Rights Watch report in 2009 names the following lawyers as having encountered threats regarding the licence: (Beijing-based) Li Heping, Cheng Hai, Jiang Tianyong, Li Xiongbing, Li Chunfu, Wang Yajun, Tang Jitian, Yang Huimin (Huiwen?), Xie Yanyi, Li Dunyong, Wen Haibo, Liu Wei, Zhang Lihui, Peng Jian, Li Jinglin, Lan Zhixue, Zhang Kai and Liu Xiaoyuan; Wei Liangyue, Yang Zaixin and Human Rights Watch, 'China: leading civil rights lawyers face threats to licences', 26 May 2009, at http://www.hrw.org/news/2009/05/26/china-leading-civil-rights-lawyers-face-threats-licenses, accessed 3 December 2013. See also Human Rights Watch, *Walking on Thin Ice* (2008), at http://www.hrw.org/reports/2008/04/28/walking-thin-ice-0, accessed 3 December 2013.

70 See also Elizabeth Lynch, 'China's rule of law mirage: the regression of the legal profession since the adoption of the 2007 Lawyers Law', 42 *Georgetown University International Law Review* (2010) 535, pp. 562 ff. at pp. 558 ff.

71 In Chapter 4 (Liu Wei's account of her courtroom experience).

72 The investigator in *Disbarment, supra*.

73 '北京市司法局行政处罚决定书京司罚决 [2010] 2, 3号 [Beijing Municipal Justice Bureau Administrative Punishment Decision (2010) nos. 2 and 3]', dated 7 May 2010, available at http://www.bjsf.gov.cn/sy/sytztg/201005/t20100507_1279393.html and http://www.bjsf.gov.cn/sy/cxjl/cxjllsgl/201005/t20100507_1279438.html respectively, accessed 10 May 2010.

courtroom as withdrawal without adequate reason. Then they treated it as withdrawal of criminal defence without adequate reason. Then they treated that as a disruption of the order of the court, and in a further step as a serious disruption. On that basis they announced that they were revoking the licences. Logically, this simply cannot be established. Withdrawing from the courtroom is relinquishing one's right to engage in criminal defence. It has nothing to do with disrupting the order of the court.[74]

In another case, a lawyer had discovered his name listed online (at the website of the local Lawyers' Association) among lawyers whose licence had been provisionally revoked (*zhuxiao*)[75] just before a scheduled meeting with me. He was stunned, and said he had received no prior notification whatsoever of this measure, but subsequent events made it clear that the licence had indeed been revoked and that as of this writing, there is no chance of getting it back.[76]

In its daily operation, pressure can be exerted in subtle ways, sometimes by indicating specious 'reasons' for potential trouble:

> They know how to give us trouble. For instance in this year's re-registration round, they said it was necessary to 'investigate *in situ*' whether our law firm qualified [for reassessment]. So they sent round some people; but they couldn't find anything wrong. Eventually they said that our office space 'was not sufficiently large to comply with the requirements of the development of the legal profession', and that we would have to change to another place next year. This had absolutely no basis in law![77]

Since law firms must separately pass the annual assessment exercise, moreover, the fate of a law firm and all those who work in it can depend on the actions of a single lawyer in it and law firm colleagues and bosses therefore have a strong incentive to control any human rights lawyers in their midst. Current regulations, indeed, envisage and encourage such control, to the point of containing a provision allowing the lawyers' association to 'suggest' a lawyer's dismissal, as noted above.

In conversation, lawyers told many stories about pressurised law firm heads and colleagues passing on that pressure. One of the earliest occurred at the end of 2004, when a human rights lawyer was requested, first by the local justice bureau and then by his own law firm head, to cancel a proposed trip to visit a prospective client in the provinces. The law firm head told him blandly that he had just received another call from the local justice bureau, and that there was simply no alternative to cancelling the trip.[78]

---

74 Teng Biao in *Disbarment, supra*.
75 In Chinese characters, 注销.
76 A similar experience is described by #29 2011-1.
77 #52 2011-1. Also #3 2012-1. Local justice bureaux use assessment systems purporting to be a 'legal basis' for such requirements. E.g. 怀化市司法局办公室文件 [Huaihua City Justice Bureau Document, edict no. 6 (2012)], obtained 11 February 2013, on file with author.
78 #9 2010-1.

This episode, among others, also shows that the justice authorities and the security apparatus started collaborating early on, even though in earlier years, their collaboration may have been less evident to lawyers and less widely noticed. According to another lawyer, the head of his law firm had frequently received visits from two sub-offices of the department for managing lawyers of the local justice bureau. Here, too, the justice bureau officials identified numerous 'problems', he said, among them that the firm had taken fees that might be in excess of the stipulated rates, and that the firm was employing lawyers on open-term contracts: 'My law firm head said to me, "if you weren't in our firm, the justice bureau wouldn't even know me!"'[79]

The lawyer believed that in reality, these visits were due to the fact that he had handled Falun Gong cases, and because he had tried (unsuccessfully) to sue the justice bureaux of two urban districts in the context of trying to get his permission to practise back. Some months later, this lawyer was, at the 'suggestion' of the justice bureau, asked to provide a written assurance that he would transfer to another law firm within six months, in order to enable this law firm to pass its own annual assessment.[80] Of course, it then became extremely difficult for the lawyer to find a firm that would agree to take him on.[81]

Numerous other lawyers have commented on the use of divisive strategies by the judicial bureaux; and one lawyer commented after having been disbarred: 'What tires me most is not even the disbarment . . . it is that the justice bureau is sowing discord among us colleagues to further hurt us and trigger recriminations among colleagues.'[82]

Specific control mechanisms of daily supervision and management and of various kinds of 'ethics', 'guidance' and 'discipline' etc. thus must be discussed on the understanding that not only the most immediately responsible 'two conjoined' entities, namely the justice bureaux and lawyers' associations, and the Party in their background, are made 'responsible' for the control of individual (human rights) lawyers. To the extent that law firms, law firm heads and colleagues are also used to pass on pressure, they can become (reluctantly) collusive.

Control mechanisms (2): 'daily supervision and management' and enforcement of 'ethics' and 'discipline'

From a bureaucratic control standpoint, the licensing, registration and annual assessment system creates almost perfect conditions for the enforcement of 'professional discipline' and 'professional ethics', which are the task of the lawyers' associations, and for the implementation of 'day-to-day supervision and management' of law firms by the lowest level justice bureaux (Article 52 Law on Lawyers).

79 #21 2011-5.
80 #21 2011-6. The author was shown a copy of this document during a meeting.
81 #21 2011-1 to 6. At one point, his own case became such a highly energy-consuming task that the lawyer appeared obliged to spend a large part of his time on this increasingly labyrinthine effort, over a period of more than three years.
82 #20 2010-2.

These interlocking systems give the authorities many opportunities to influence what kinds of client lawyers take on, how they handle their cases, and how they interact with the authorities. Some aspects of such influence have already been critically discussed elsewhere, including in media reports and reports by human rights organisations. From the perspective of the authorities in charge, however, control is their bureaucratic duty, and it is appropriate for law firms to help them exercise control.

The Law on Lawyers in its provision on 'daily supervision and guidance' provides a general basis for these sorts of requirement; and there are a number of more specific textual bases for it. Local regulations such as for instance the 1999 Beijing Justice Bureau Regulation on Beijing Law Firms Seeking Instruction and Reporting When Handling Major Tasks contain further rules.[83] Its Article 2 requires the Beijing Justice Bureau to 'establish a Major Cases Guidance Group, with the Justice Bureau Vice President in charge of lawyer management work acting as Head of the Group, and related responsible persons from the Lawyer Management Office, the Municipal Lawyers' Association and other chambers and offices as Members of the Group', defines its responsibilities as follows:

(1) To hear requests for instruction and reports concerning major cases from lawyers
(2) To gain a good grasp of the principles for handling major cases, negotiate the principles of handling major cases, and help lawyers liaise with relevant departments in the handling of cases
(3) To unify opinions when there is disagreement within a law firm and to produce guiding opinions
(4) To undertake follow-up work on how to understand the further development of major cases.[84]

Its Article 3 states that Beijing Law Firms 'have the responsibility to seek instruction on and report all major cases to the Guidance Group'; and its Article 4 defines 'major cases for which the seeking of instruction or reporting is required':

(1) Seeking instruction
  1. Cases related to crimes endangering State security
  2. Criminal and civil cases that have a major influence on society, criminal cases with a foreign element.

83 北京市司法局关于北京市律师事务所承办重大法律事务请示报告的制度 [Beijing Justice Bureau Regulation on Beijing Law Firms Seeking Permission and Reporting (*qingshibaogao*) When Handling Major Tasks], 14 January 1999, available at http://www.beinet.net.cn/policy/wbj/sfj/200508/t35645.htm, accessed 15 December 2013.
84 *Ibid.*

(2) Reporting
    1. Group litigation cases
    2. Cases concerning government authorities and cases concerning cadres from *ju* level upward
    3. Cases [related to] major national construction programmes
    4. Cases concerning people's Congress or Consultative Congress delegates at all levels or concerning well-known figures in society
    5. Other legal work and tasks for which there is a need to report are to be reported after the law firm has confirmed [the need to report].[85]

According to human rights lawyers, such a requirement is routine in all criminal defence cases concerning Falun Gong, for example. A 2006 ACLA 'Guiding Opinion on Handling of Mass Litigation' required lawyers and law firms to 'report to' and 'liaise with' the 'two conjoined' entities about their legal representation in such cases.[86] It triggered public criticism;[87] but in substance it was nothing new. A human rights lawyer who has now lost permission to practise commented that:

> [Initially] we didn't think much about having to submit a report and request permission prior to handling a particular case. We just didn't do it. One would just go and handle the case. And if they didn't know about it, that was that. Only from about 2006 did we strongly object to having to request permission and reporting. We asked, on the basis of what should we have to do that? . . . Thus, later (too), we did not report or request permission. So a group of people in the Bureau of Justice took a dislike to the lawyers in our circle. They felt that we were picking a fight with the government.[88]

Another lawyer commented:

> This document [2006 mass litigation cases Opinion] itself hasn't had any effect but speaking of my personal experience, what happens is that there may be pressure from the justice bureau; they contact us and put pressure on us. . . . We now sometimes cooperate with the justice bureau by 'reporting cases for filing'.[89]

85 *Ibid.*
86 中华全国律师协会关于律师办理群体性案件指导意见 [Guiding Opinion of the ACLA on the Handling of Mass Litigation], promulgated on and effective from 20 March 2006, available http://www.legaldaily.com.cn/ecard/content/2011-04/08/content_2586358.htm?node=23949, accessed 15 December 2013.
87 Human Rights Watch, 'A great danger for lawyers: new regulatory curbs on lawyers representing protesters', *supra.*
88 #9 2010-1.
89 #52 2011-1.

This lawyer added that in the view of a more experienced colleague, a few compromises should be made so as to ensure a few lawyers would still be able to take on clients.[90]

While no publicly available rules exist detailing this possibility, the various systems for reporting and filing 'major' or (otherwise) 'sensitive' cases serve not only the purpose of giving the authorities an opportunity to influence how lawyers handle their work but also lead to authorities' interference with taking certain cases on at all. One lawyer detailed the experience of their law firm when two lawyers working in this firm took on a land-grab case in a suburban or rural district of another city. In this case, local authorities went to particularly great lengths; but the attitudes and arguments on both sides resemble those in many other cases:

> In the spring of 2007 in X Area of Y District of Z City, we had taken on a big case litigating on behalf of 40,000 peasants [number changed], a case where the ordinary people's land had been occupied by the government, and the people demanded reasonable compensation. Local lawyers were not allowed to defend these ordinary people's rights. So they asked some of our lawyers, who were more combative. Two lawyers from our firm went there. After that the local government authorities turned to the C Justice Bureau [where the law firm was located], and they then called us and said we must report on cases, and asked us if we could just not take on this one.[91]

The head of the law firm refused to drop the case, pointing out that the firm had already signed a contract with the clients:

> Then (. . .) in May 2008, the secretary of the political and legal [Party] committee of Y District – altogether seven [government] heads [of Y District] – the head of the Disciplinary Bureau, the head of the Justice Bureau, the head of the Financial Bureau, the head of the Land Administration Bureau, as well as the head of the Letters and Visits Bureau and the President of the Lawyers' Association, travelled to the C Justice Bureau. The C Justice Bureau then arranged for a dialogue between them and [our] Law Firm. . . . They demanded that we firstly 'emphasise politics' and secondly 'protect social stability' and 'ensure the opening of the Olympic games' [note: the city in which the land-grab took place was not Beijing, where the 2008 Olympic games were held]. . . . They said that because of our representation of the peasants in this case, we had produced disharmony and instability in their locality. They really 'put a big hat on our heads!'
>
> My answer lasted for about ten minutes. He had said we must emphasise politics. I said, 'the Secretary of the Political and Legal Committee is right, we absolutely need to emphasise politics. But what is "politics"?' I shared my

90 #70 2012-1. See also #9 2012-4.
91 *Ibid.* 'Since 1949 no such dialogue had happened.'

view with them. I said, our NPC General Secretary, Qiao Xiaoyang, once at an NPC assembly gave a speech in which he said the following. 'The Party leads the people in passing laws, and it leads the people in following the laws. And Article 5 of the PRC Constitution says that the Party and public bodies uphold the rule of law and must act within the law. If anyone violates the law their legal responsibility will be pursued. So, what does it mean to "emphasise politics"? The laws made by the Party and the laws made by the people under the Party's leadership are the greatest "politics" of the People's Republic of China. The politics you are talking about are "politics" [of this kind] if they are in compliance with those; but if not they are merely small "politics". And if they are anything to do with your own interests, then we are really only talking about [the "politics" of] a small [interest] group.' That is what I said to them. 'So, what does it mean to "emphasise politics"? We lawyers must just remain within the frame of the Constitution and the law, pursue our tasks in accordance with law then that is "emphasising politics". If we lawyers violate the law, you should detain us, because lawyers must not violate the law.'

He added:

'You are the "father-and-mother-officials",[92] you have an obligation to protect the legal rights and interests of vulnerable groups in your place . . . You should be thanking us, not blaming us . . . we are helping you do your job. Second, if we don't help the peasants protect their rights in accordance with law, social instability may arise from that. Because our way of defending rights through the legal process is the most rational and peaceful and secure method. If we use this process and if the court decides in accordance with justice there won't be one peasant who will make trouble. And anyway, you should trust your courts. They are under the leadership of your Party. They are implementing *your* "politics". They are safe . . . Third, you are misunderstanding us lawyers. Our lawyers, when they went to your place, were beaten [by local people]. Next time our lawyers go there, you must protect their personal safety.' When I had finished, the officials didn't really know what to say.[93]

The officials in this case proceeded to some extent to 'flatter' the lawyer, according to his account, without however indicating that they would make any concessions.

What emerges from this account is a picture that well reflects the terms the Law on Lawyers uses to describe the justice bureaux' duties for 'day-to-day super-vision and management', a form of management extending to trivial aspects of the size of a law firm's office, but also to central ones, such as what cases and clients a lawyer takes on. Through both kinds of aspects, the system projects

---

92 *Fumuguan*, 父母官. This expression is briefly discussed in Chapter 3.
93 *Ibid.* Claims, 'Since 1949 no such dialogue had happened.'

managerial omnipresence and an absence of boundaries. The authorities meddle; but it is implicitly understood that their meddling serves – sometimes unspecified – official purposes.

Control mechanisms (3): educational and committee activities – the example of the 'Warning and Education' campaign 2010–11

Compared to licensing and assessment and daily supervision and management, 'educational' activities – for which lawyers' associations are responsible – are both more subtle and less immediately coercive in their effects. They are also potentially much further reaching, as they can serve to marginalise and stigmatise rights lawyers socially and professionally as well as politically, and create fear among a large range of lawyers. Marginalisation was manifest in some early decisions driving lawyers out of certain ACLA expert committees. The story of the ACLA Constitutional Law Committee is perhaps the best known among these:

> For instance the Constitutional Law Committee of the ACLA used to have all those who were progressive in it. But then the old one got dissolved and they founded a new one. For the new one, they set very high thresholds for membership, so they could tell you that you didn't fulfil the criteria for being a member.[94]

Another problem, this lawyer added, was this:

> [T]he Lawyers' Association has now blacklisted some lawyers, not allowing them to attend certain meetings. For instance, yesterday, there was a meeting related to the currently ongoing 'Warning and Education' campaign. Lawyer A tried to go but they wouldn't let him; and [official X] 'asked him to tea' [to prevent him from attending]. They have also stopped posting information about [certain] meetings online – they no longer want civil society or international society to find out about these (. . .) A person like me wouldn't be able to participate in a 'Warning and Education' meeting any longer.[95]

The 'Warning and Education' campaign the lawyer referred to, according to Chinese government information,[96] unfolded in March 2010. It specifically targeted a criminal defence lawyer's performance in the case of the alleged mafia boss Gong Gangmo.[97] Lawyer Li Zhuang was an experienced criminal defence

94 #25 2010-2.
95 *Ibid.*
96 Zhou Bin (周斌), 司法部向各地司法行政机关就李庄违法违纪案件发出通报 [Ministry of Justice issues notice on Li Zhuang's case of violation of the law and discipline to all justice administration authorities], 18 March 2010, at http://www.gov.cn/gzdt/2010-03/18/content_1558826.htm.
97 For a discussion of the 'Li Zhuang' case, see Lan Rongjie, 'Killing the lawyer as the last resort: the Li Zhuang case and its effects on criminal defence in China', in Mike McConville and

lawyer but not considered a *weiquan* lawyer; rather, he was widely regarded as a lawyer with high professional standards, as well as official connections. He had conducted the defence of Gong Gangmo, accused and later convicted of mafia-related crimes in Chongqing in the context of the 'Strike Black' campaign under now disgraced Party Secretary Bo Xilai and Police Chief Wang Lijun. In his defence, Lawyer Li Zhuang had alleged that his client had been tortured to extract a confession. Under rules then in place,[98] his allegations, reportedly supported by the fact that Gong had torture scars on his wrists, appeared to warrant an investigation into the alleged illegality of evidence for the prosecution case. Later, similar allegations were made by a co-defendant in the same case,[99] who (through his lawyer) not only alleged torture by hanging from his wrists, beating, sleep deprivation and starvation, but also had scars on his wrists to prove it. This co-defendant was secretly photographed and filmed by the defence lawyer, Zhu Mingyong, who went public with the detailed torture account (filmed) and further photographic evidence in an effort to save his client's life.[100]

Although Gong Gangmo, too, bore the scars that could serve as evidence of the torture he had been subjected to, Li Zhuang's arguments were not considered sufficient grounds for an investigation into the torture allegations. In a sadly classic use of Article 306 of the Criminal Law,[101] the authorities instead detained, prosecuted and convicted Lawyer Li Zhuang of the crime of falsifying evidence as a lawyer (Article 306 CL – see also Chapter 6); the conviction led to his subsequent disbarment. At a later stage in the criminal process, Li Zhuang's client stated that his defence lawyer had incited him to make false torture allegations.[102] Gong Gangmo, described as 'number one defendant' in this case, was convicted but spared execution. By contrast, the aforementioned co-defendant (described as 'number two defendant') by his earlier account and by his lawyer and was given the death sentence and executed. At the time of this writing, Li Zhuang (who had falsely 'confessed' in second instance in order to be able to get out of prison and back to work on his case) is seeking rehabilitation.[103] The purpose of detaining Li Zhuang was:

> To scare everybody else. [Li Zhuang] was the only one to raise the issue of torture during the first instance trial. By detaining [Li Zhuang] they could

Eva Pils (eds.), *Criminal Justice in China: Comparative Perspectives*, Edward Elgar Publishing, Cheltenham: 2014; Elizabeth Lynch, *supra*, at pp. 562 ff.

98 关于办理死刑案件审查判断证据若干问题的规定 [Rules Concerning Questions about Examining and Judging Evidence in Death Penalty Cases], at http://www.spp.gov.cn/site2006/2010-06-25/0005428111.html; English translation by Duihua Foundation available at http://www.duihuahrjournal.org/2010/06/translation-chinas-new-rules-on.html.

99 #79 2013-1; #17 2013-1.

100 He Yang (何杨), 专访朱明勇律师:黑打 [Interview with Lawyer Zhu Mingyong: torture], Beijing (2010), at http://vimeo.com/13706954. #17 2013-1.

101 Discussed in Cheung Yiu-Leung, 'Between a rock and a hard place: China's criminal defence lawyers', Mosher and Poon (2009).

102 Lan Rongjie, *supra*, at p. 306 (note 5).

103 #79 2013-1.

shut up all the other lawyers [acting as defence lawyers in this case]. After that, no other lawyer ever raised the issue of torture again [in this case].[104]

In fact, as has been seen in Chapter 4, criminal defence lawyers have (especially in recent years) alleged police torture and sought the exclusion of illegally obtained evidence in a number of cases; and they have generally met with passivity, if not active obstruction or retaliation, when doing so. In this case, the authorities decided to retaliate and make an example of Li Zhuang. According to an official report, the Ministry of Justice's notice in March 2010:

> [P]oints out that under the leadership and care of Party Central and the State Council, the national system for socialist lawyers has been perfected day by day, the corps of lawyers has developed incessantly, and the professional abilities of lawyers are on display every day. The vast majority of lawyers holds high the great banner of socialism with Chinese characteristics, maintains excellent professional ethics, provides legal services in accordance with law, implements the basic strategies of Ruling the Country in Accordance with Law, and makes an active contribution to the promotion of economic and social development. Practice has shown that the mainstream of our country's corps of lawyers is good, that it is a corps the Party and the People can rely on. The case of Li Zhuang was merely an individual case and we must distinguish it from the overall corps of lawyers. The Justice Administration and Lawyers' Associations at all levels and the generality of lawyers shall understand the harm done by Li Zhuang's crime with perfect clarity and draw a proper lesson from it, understand the warning sounded by it and hear the alarm bells rung by it.[105]

Expressions such as 'corps' (*duiwu*)[106] to describe lawyers testify to Statism and militarism in the bureaucratic language used to integrate lawyers into the wider workings of the Chinese system; as does the phrase 'socialist-with-Chinese-characteristics legal workers' (already encountered in the Lawyers' Oath):

> [A]t all times keep in mind that they are socialist-with-Chinese-characteristics legal workers, and from beginning to end spontaneously maintain the supremacy of the Party's cause, the supremacy of the People's interests, and the supremacy of the Constitution and the laws; maintain and protect the leadership of the Party, the socialist system, and the Constitution.[107]

---

104 #79 2013-1.
105 Zhou Bin (周斌), 司法部向各地司法行政机关就李庄违法违纪案件发出通报 [Ministry of Justice issues notice on Li Zhuang's case of violation of the law and discipline to all justice administration authorities], 18 March 2010, at http://www.gov.cn/gzdt/2010-03/18/content_1558826.htm.
106 In Chinese characters, 队伍.
107 *Ibid.*

A rights lawyer close to the underlying events commented:

> They showed me a document, quite short, perhaps a hundred characters or so; in it the phrase 'with-Chinese-characteristics' appeared six times. I thought it was absurd. Those 'Chinese characteristics' destroyed the fairness of the law. They meant that 'Chinese characteristics' could supersede the law.[108]

The Ministry of Justice notice went on to observe that 'education, management and supervision' would have to be 'comprehensively strengthened':

> The justice administration authorities and lawyers' associations at all levels shall, using the case of Li Zhuang, conscientiously hold warning and education campaigns for the lawyer corps. They shall engage in profound analysis of the causes of the Li Zhuang case, develop a correct understanding of the nature of the problem and the harm done by the Li Zhuang case, and draw profound lessons from the Li Zhuang case, to achieve unity of thought and understanding.

According to a 'Plan for the Warning and Education Campaign of the Beijing Justice Bureau' available online,[109] this campaign was led by the (Party) Political and Legal Committee of the Beijing Justice Bureau. The just mentioned 'Plan' is in its language and structure sufficiently similar to the report made at the government website to give it credibility, even though its provenance cannot be confirmed:

> The Li Zhuang case shall be distinguished from the Beijing legal profession's overall situation. Full trust and reliance should be placed in the lawyers' corps in general; the generality of lawyers shall be encouraged spontaneously and enthusiastically to participate in study and education . . . Each unit shall, in the course of this round of Warning and Education activities for the lawyer corps, resolutely start from practice and efficiency, and shall both put its full and undiminished effort into carrying out the activities mandated by higher levels, and at the same time also connect to practise and adopt flexible and manifold forms of education to render educational activities both serious and lively, and to increase the emotional impact and attractiveness of educational activities. They shall solve the problem of 'reaching eyes, ears, brains and hearts.' (*ruyan, ru'er, runao, ruxin*).[110]

---

108 #79 2013-1.
109 Beijing Justice Bureau Lawyer Corps Warning and Education Campaign Plan [北京市律师队伍警示教育工作方案], promulgated on 19 March 2010, at http://wenku.baidu.com/view/e629b883ec3a87c24028c42e.html.
110 In Chinese characters, 入眼、入耳、入脑、入心.

Acting on this last instruction, the Beijing Lawyers Association (BLA) reportedly arranged 'Warning and Education' meetings at which other lawyers considered deviant and in violation of discipline were publicly exposed.

An older colleague commented as follows on a lawyer thus victimised for similarly spurious reasons:

> 'I heard that A had to make a 'self-criticism' in public before the entire city's law firm heads and administrative leaders [of the BLA] in the context of the 'Warning and Education' campaign, about his defence of X. (. . .) It was not publicized, so far as know. But B's law firm head went [and participated in the meeting and later told B].

He added:

> This has been a big psychological assault on [A]. The problem isn't whether you've actually done right or wrong – it's about subduing you psychologically or in other ways. The Party has a very deep understanding of people's hearts; they know how to use people's weak points. (. . .) It is just like at the time of June Fourth. I remember at the time in X City [while the interlocutor was working in a legal service station connected to the government], there was a [colleague] who had previously been labelled a 'rightist'. We had a meeting and he persistently refused to 'show [the correct] attitude (*biaotai*)';[111] he insisted on the view that suppression [of June Fourth] had been wrong. He refused to change his views . . . He [and people like him], they were all disbarred later. Reverting to these old methods is quite helpful to them.[112]

The 'Warning and Education' campaign around the Li Zhuang case is perhaps an extreme – as well as a particularly well-known – example. Many of the lawyers' associations' educational and training activities may be as innocuous as the pictures on the 'Warning and Education' campaign available at the BLA's official website. They show about 100 young lawyers from over 50 Beijing-based law firms planting trees in the rain, in the context of an oath ceremony for new lawyers described as part of the BLA's 'Warning and Education Activities Series'.[113] But, no number of innocuous tree-planting activities could undo the effect, however subtle and obscure, of a campaign such as the 2011 'Warning and Education' one.[114]

---

111 In Chinese characters, 表态.
112 #21 2010-2. The lawyer went on to explain the proverb 'pointing to a deer and calling it a horse' discussed in Chapter 2.
113 '北京律协举办警示教育系列活动之新执业律师宣誓仪式 [BLA holds New Lawyers Oath Ceremony as Part of the Warning and Education Campaign]', 23 April 2010, at http://www.beijinglawyers.org.cn/cac/1024.htm, accessed 15 December 2013.
114 One reporting form mentions the number of prevented mass incidents as 'criterion' of assessment, a negative hypothetical. On file with author.

Lessons of the struggle of X Law Firm

The authorities have used control mechanisms and measures in a variety of scenarios when lawyers appeared to show recalcitrance or resistance. A particularly 'provocative' attempt on the part of a handful of Beijing-based human rights lawyers to gain greater freedoms for themselves and their colleagues in the period between 2008 and 2010 can best explain the full force of their convictions that they need to manage and control lawyers. These years saw an attempt to liberate the organisation of the legal profession 'from within', beginning with the creation of law firms that could serve as bases for human rights lawyering, and continuing with an attempt to democratise the official lawyers' associations.

The setting up of a 'human rights' law firm

It has become apparent from the above discussion that bureaucratic control makes extensive use of law firms, law firm colleagues and (especially) law firm heads to put pressure on individual human rights lawyers, and that one easily available form of pressure is to withdraw cases from the lawyer in question, endangering their livelihood.

The account presented in the following is in essence a story of a firm that tried to evade some of the system's bureaucratic control. Part of its effort consisted in getting involved in efforts to change, albeit in minor ways, the governance system of the Beijing Lawyers' Association.[115] For the sake of preserving the integrity of the story, it is told here in full:

> In 2007 I opened a law firm called X Law Firm [name changed]. . . . I had two goals. First, we wanted to solve the economic problem and second, we wanted to create a platform [for lawyers]. At the time our law firm's motto was, 'providing legal help to vulnerable groups and pursuing fairness and justice'. [For the first two years] I was the law firm head . . . We quickly grew to 24 lawyers [number changed]. Well, then something rather big happened. That was the scheduled elections for positions in the Beijing Lawyers Association. Around that time I made the acquaintance of A, B and C.[116]

He went on to explain that his previous professional experience had included advising villagers in village elections, under China's system for village level 'self-governance': 'I felt that if peasants can elect their own representative, then there

115 Jerome A. Cohen, 'The struggle for autonomy of Beijing's public interest lawyers', *China Rights Forum*, (1 April 2009), at http://www.hrichina.org/content/3692. See also Donald C. Clarke, 'Tempest in the Beijing Lawyers' Association', 11 September 2008 at http://lawprofessors. typepad.com/china_law_prof_blog/2008/09/tempest-in-the.html; Human Rights in China (tr.), 'Keep pace with the course of history, implement lawyers association direct election: an appeal to all Beijing lawyers, the Beijing Municipal Bureau of Justice, and the Beijing Municipal Lawyers Association', 31 October 2008, at http://www.hrichina.org/public/ contents/press?revision_id=149319&item_id=149292.
116 #62 2012-1.

was no reason why we lawyers could not; and the law allows [for such elections], too.'[117]

In August 2008, 35 lawyers took the unusual step of releasing a signed open letter in which they called for democratisation of the Beijing Lawyers' Association (BLA). Through this letter and by contacting lawyers individually via text messages, etc., they proposed new procedures for holding elections in the BLA, and stated that the BLA was not capable of protecting lawyers' rights while it was not made accountable to its members through a democratic election process.[118] This elicited a response from the Beijing Justice Bureau that insisted on its status as 'a legally constituted social organization, an autonomous professional organization representing the interests of all Beijing lawyers', and portrayed the 35 campaigning lawyers as people unlawfully stirring up trouble;[119] the call for changed election procedures was unsuccessful.

In the context of this campaign, however, some Beijing lawyers announced that they would stand as independent candidates in the upcoming election round:

> D publicly declared that he would stand for head of the local lawyers' association. From 1949 up to now there had been not a single other lawyer publicly to declare his intention to stand for election – and in writing, too! [D and his supporters] produced leaflets. They went to a meeting place where lawyers had been invited and distributed the leaflets, together with friends. I heard that at the time the [official] instructed the security guards to beat them – not badly, but in a way that hurt their dignity.[120]

A lawyer who had participated in the leaflet action in another conversation, confirmed this experience.[121] The former law firm head went on explaining that the elections were announced 'suddenly, giving us only a few days to prepare'; and that in addition to D, Lawyer E, also working at his law firm, decided to stand for the position of representative at the Lawyers' Association as well. The candidates decided to seek endorsement as candidates from several other law firms, even though technically only two firms were required for endorsement of a candidate.

Despite these precautions, the authorities refused to put the independent candidates (including D and E) on the official list of candidates:

> We held a meeting including me, A, E and D (who participated via telephone from HK). We decided to stand up together at the same time and to tell other lawyers, 'I want to be a representative.' We (A and his assistant visited the other law firms at the time, as I was rather busy) told the other lawyers, 'You

117 #62 2012-1.
118 Human Rights in China, *supra*.
119 China Free Press (tr.), 'The Beijing Bar Association's response to a small number of lawyers and their so-called call for direct elections to the Beijing Bar Association', 10 September 2008, at http://archive.is/ezYHY.
120 #62 2012-1.
121 #29 2011-1.

must elect us four, because we dare really to speak for the lawyers – we dare to, and we want to speak for them.' That was how we put it at the time: we dared and we really wanted to speak up.[122]

Eventually, the independent lawyers were amongst the top candidates. A second round of voting, however, failed to include them on the list of candidates and left no option to vote for them:

> In the first round, at the bottom of the ballot, there had been an empty box saying 'If you are not happy with these [listed] candidates, you can propose another person.' And in the first round, that was how the four of us were able to get any votes. But in the second election round, the empty box was gone. They also spoke to [the electors] and told them, 'If you propose a person other than one of the designated candidates, your ballot will be invalid.'

Even though this meant that the independent candidates had lost: 'We felt that we had actually won. We *were* the lawyer representatives! They just didn't let us act as representatives.'[123]

In a variety of ways, the lawyers in X Law Firm had tried to break through systemic obstacles hindering the development of an independent legal profession (or of a legal profession with some level of independence). They had acted with strategic foresight in choosing their election agenda by connecting their wider democratic goals to the immediate problem of high fees taken by the local lawyers' association; and they successfully mobilised the opinions of their professional colleagues. Another lawyer in that firm commented:

> Some colleagues who in 2008 and 2009 used to be quite friendly and warm have not become cold and distanced . . . [Yet] in terms of their innermost thoughts these lawyers who now keep at a distance and avoid contact may not have changed.[124]

The phases of bureaucratic annihilation of X Law Firm

Tellingly, while the matter of how to deal with X Law Firm's recalcitrance was in the hands of the 'two conjoined', nothing much happened:

> In May 2009, the time of annual assessment came round. Initially it did not seem so serious. Initially the [District] Justice Bureau merely required us to make some changes to our system [of operation]. They meant by that, for example, that we must submit reports regarding all the sensitive cases we handled to the Justice Bureau. . . . It was just a demand for self-discipline.

122 #62 2012-1.
123 #62 2012-1.
124 #25 2010-2.

They also said that the law firm's current sign was not in accordance with standards because we had put up two signs, and only one was allowed.

But after 10 June 2009, their attitude changed.

On 10 June 2009 a speech was made by the then head of the Political and Legal Committee, Zhou Yongkang:[125]

> [After 10 June] They made two demands: first that we expel, or persuade to leave, the sensitive lawyers from our firm – namely A, D and E – the ones who had participated in the direct election campaign. I said to the Justice Bureau head, 'While I am the law firm head, I am also their colleague. If I dismiss them, that would really not be decent, it would be immoral![126] Also, assuming that they are deemed to be sensitive this year, what would it be like next year? This makes no sense.' I refused to fire them, and I wrote a report to the other partners. I said that I did not have the ability to ensure that X Law Firm could pass the annual assessment, and so I had decided to step down as head of the Firm. We got an old Party cadre, a really 'red' old guy, to be head of the Firm instead.
>
> But then the next thing was that they said that our name was 'sensitive' and that we must change our name. Then we could re-register under a new name. I said, 'in the *Stories from the Water Margin* it is written, "All things should be done above-board and in the proper way."[127] If you ask me to change our name, that is just not right!' We insisted on not changing the name. (. . .) Well, then they really went for us and 'forcibly demolished' our firm. They called all of our lawyers [i.e. including associates] in for a chat, one by one, and asked them, 'Do you want to be a lawyer or not? If yes, then if you leave X Law Firm I can put your stamp certifying that you have passed the assessment in your lawyer's licence right now! But if you want to stay in X Law Firm, you will find you are no longer able to handle any cases in future.' This is how they 'forcibly demolished' X Law Firm.

In a further step, the authorities told the 'red guy' who had been selected as law firm head that he would not have his licence extended unless he left X Law Firm:

> After this 'demolition round', only we four partners were left, plus the [other] three 'sensitive' lawyers and one assistant, altogether eight persons. Next, they demanded that the [other] partners also leave the firm. There was one partner called Lawyer Li [name changed], he was asked to leave and wanted

125 Zhou Yongkang, 'Safeguard social equality and justice', *supra*.
126 In Chinese characters, 我不仁不义, 我不道德!
127 In Chinese characters, e/行不更名, 坐不改姓 'do not change your name after doing something, and do not change your surname after sitting down.' http://www.chazidian.com/r_ci_25ac540f4782dd180c2f178ad6a45fd The allusion to this particular work can be taken as an indication of rebelliousness.

to leave; he said, 'I can no longer take on cases.' We thought, if just three partners remain, that is enough to satisfy the legal requirements. The two other partners (. . .) did not want to leave. But then the Justice Bureau sent for them. One afternoon, a car came for them and took them to the District Justice Bureau for a 'chat'. In that chat, according to our analysis, they must have carried out 'thought work' on them. As a result of their 'thought work', these two wrote a report to the Lawyers' Association requesting the de-registration of X Law Firm.

In the view of X Law Firm's former head, the partners who had thus been put under pressure could not 'just leave' by writing a report to the justice bureau, but would have had to dissolve the partnership, and then request de-registration. By writing a report to the lawyers' association, however, they enabled the association to forward their report to the justice bureau at the next higher administrative (City) level, explaining 'that these lawyers wanted to leave X Law Firm, and said that the Firm was not letting them go'. Within the same day, the justice bureau forwarded instructions to the local-level justice bureau, which produced a 'judicial notice' [addressed to X Law Firm] on the same afternoon, stating that the two lawyers in question had left the firm, and requesting X Law Firm to find two new partners (since at least three partners per firm are required) within four days from the date of the notice:

> That was going to be really difficult! We decided to make D and A partners. But when we reported our selection of new partners, the Justice Bureau refused to file them. First, they imposed an administrative punishment on D because he had at one point accepted a 4500 RMB/month salary from [an NGO] while concurrently working as a lawyer, without reporting this to the Justice Bureau as required. I hadn't known about that. They made this a basis for an administrative punishment and said that because of this, D could not be a partner. (. . .) We wrote a report saying the punishment was unjustified. We insisted that we had three partners and that there was no reason for refusing us re-registration.[128]
>
> Then the next thing that happened was that in early 2010, they went for A.[129]

In the following, the lawyer told the story of his colleague A's (unjustified) disbarment. Resuming the narrative about X Law Firm's 'forced demolition', he continued:

> Around March 2010, the lease term for our office right next to the local Court expired. The landlord called me and said he was unable to renew the lease. He said, 'You must move out immediately.' We had had a good relationship; so I asked him if he had been given pressure. Through a

128 *Ibid.*
129 *Ibid.*

middle-man, he told us, 'It is not that we don't want to lease the offices to you, but that certain leaders got in touch with us [i.e. instructed us not to extend].' [The middleman] explained that a vice president of the local Justice Bureau had (. . .) required the landlord not to extend our lease.[130]

Eventually forced to move from their old office, they had some difficulty finding a new office; but when they eventually found one:

We tried to register it; but now that local justice bureau [in another district of Beijing] refuses to register our new offices. As long as they keep refusing to do this, we can't hang a sign outside of our offices. At the time I wrote a [blog] post saying, 'X Law Firm – Gone Missing!' So, now, because we still have not obtained our registration, which became necessary because they introduced a new registration, we have neither a sign, nor a licence. I suppose we're now just a group of people [laughs].[131]

Serious bureaucratic harassment has affected different law firms differently. Some have been placed in a situation 'in limbo' similar to that of X Law Firm; some have been forced to expel or sidetrack lawyers and change their name; some have been forced to move offices and accept humiliating symbolic constraints, such as the already mentioned temporary stationing of police in the firm's offices. Some have been given temporary suspensions; and some are no longer in existence. Firms that have been affected by such persecution include, in alphabetical order, Anhui Law Firm,[132] Globe Law Firm,[133] Mo Shaoping Law Firm,[134] Shengzhi Law Firm[135] and Yitong Law Firm.[136]

130 *Ibid.*
131 *Ibid.* This lawyer also narrated how, as the firm encountered financial difficulties after no longer being allowed to hang its sign outside the office, a wealthy friend from another part of China tried to donate money to the firm to allow it to continue paying rent. This friend abandoned his attempt to help after being sent to two weeks' administrative detention. Lawyers #25, #29; and also #14, #22 and others have also commented on the story of X Law Firm.
132 Xia Yu (夏雨), '行政干预密令房主不续约, 北京安汇律师事务所陷入绝境 [Landlord does not extend lease following secret order by administrative intervention; Beijing Anhui Law Firm in critical state]', at http://boxun.com/news/gb/china/2010/03/201003252229.shtml.
133 Bai Mei (白梅), '中共利用律师事务所打压维权律师高博隆华所屈服 [CCP uses law firms to suppress lawyers, Globe Law Firm caves in]', 31 May 2009, at http://www.ntdtv.com/xtr/gb/2009/06/01/a302005.html.-%E4%B8%AD%E5%85%B1%E5%88%A9%E7%94%A8%E5%BE%8B%E5%B8%88%E4%BA%8B%E5%8A%A1%E6%89%80%E6%89%93%E5%8E%8B%E7%BB%B4%E6%9D%83%E5%BE%8B%E5%B8%88-%E9%AB%98%E5%8D%9A%E9%9A%86%E5%8D%8E%E6%89%80%E5%B1%88%E6%9C%8D.html.
134 Radio Free Asia (Mandarin Desk), '莫少平律师事务所被迫搬迁 [Mo Shaoping Law Firm forced to move office]', 10 June 2010, at http://www.rfa.org/mandarin/yataibaodao/mo-06102010103435.html.
135 Cp. Liu Sida and Terence Halliday, 'Dancing handcuffed in the minefield: survival strategies of defense lawyers in China's criminal justice system', 14 May 2008, Center on Law and Globalization Research Paper No. 08–04, at http://ssrn.com/abstract=1269536 or http://dx.doi.org/10.2139/ssrn.1269536; Eva Pils, 'Asking the tiger for his skin: rights activism in China', 30 *Fordham International Law Journal* (2006) 1209–1287.
136 Xin Yu (心语), 北京忆通律师事务所遭打压,被停六个月 [Beijing Yitong Law Firm encounters repression, is suspended for six months]', 18 February 2009, at http://www.rfa.org/mandarin/yataibaodao/yitong-02182009085956.html.

Dimensions and limitations of bureaucratic control

Invasive and pervasive dimensions of control

The new oath for lawyers requiring lawyers to swear allegiance to the Party, the forced display of Party plaques in law firms' offices and various other by themselves innocuous activities may put us in mind of Vaclav Havel's famous greengrocer, forced to display a Communist Party of Czechoslovakia slogan in his shop window. Since the slogan is by itself unobjectionable, it allows him some semblance of freedom that would not be possible were he instructed to display an explicit comment on his unquestioning submission to Party control, no longer allowing him 'to conceal from himself the low foundations of his obedience'. The use of such symbols and measures is also reminiscent of the system of the (East) German Democratic Republic, where control and terror were characterised as 'silent', 'soft' and 'subtle'.[137] This form of control cannot be fully understood as long as the role of the security apparatus has not been discussed in detail; but the preceding discussion requires some comment on its combination of invasive and pervasive measures.

The invasive effects of bureaucratic control are easily understood. So far as the justice bureaucracy is concerned, the possibility of disbarment, for example, is a highly invasive measure of retaliation for advocacy. Lawyers who have been disbarred are no longer allowed to take fees for legal services. Even though procedure laws recognise the possibility of acting as a 'civil representative' (*gongmin daili*)[138] in litigation, such representatives will face further difficulties trying to get access to clients under detention as criminal suspects, or to get access to criminal case files. Disbarment is also a measure that can deeply damage a (usually already marginalised) lawyers' feeling of self-worth:

> It is a problem of status/identity (*shenfen*),[139] not just about what society thinks. You simply are no longer a lawyer if you have lost the licence. Even though it is true that the licence was taken away illegally . . . Imagine a university professor has their status taken away. They can no longer continue to be a professor. Perhaps others will continue to respect them and continue saying 'Professor Wang' and 'Professor Li'. Similarly, people continue saying 'Lawyer X' to me. But I still can't claim to be a lawyer on public speaking occasions and so on.[140]

---

137 Jürgen Fuchs, 'Unter Nutzung der Angst – Die "leise Form" des Terrors – Zersetzungsmaßnahmen des MfS [Making use of fear – the "soft form" of Terror]', *BF informiert* Nr. 2, Berlin 1994; Cornelius Janzen, 'Subtiler Terror: die Opfer von Stasi-Zersetzungsmethoden [Subtle terror: the victims of Stasi disintegration methods]', *3Sat*, 27 July 2009, at http://www.3sat.de/page/?source=/kulturzeit/themen/136072/index.html.
138 In Chinese characters, 公民代理.
139 In Chinese characters, 身份.
140 #20 2010-2.

To understand the pervasive effects of control, we may remind ourselves of the nameless colleagues mentioned in the X Law Firm story above – the colleagues who quit under pressure, having been asked to have 'chats' – and of the participants in the 2010–11 'Warning and Education' campaigns throughout the country. Pervasive control primarily creates a climate of 'having taken warning' in which the law firms heads called to attend the abovementioned BLA meeting, say, will take their own steps to ensure as best they can that the lawyers in their firms will not do anything that could bring similar humiliation and potential loss on themselves, passing pressure on to individual lawyers, who may in turn opt for *peihe*, compliance, obedience and support toward the authorities. It might be seen as a challenge to understanding this dimension fully, that we cannot know the number of people who have been affected by such measures as a 'Warning and Education' campaign; or exactly how it affected them. However, the uncertainty this creates is part of this form of control's pervasive dimension; as long as it can be reasonably assumed that everybody will give some thought to the 'warnings' the authorities must consider that they have reached their goal; and it is understood that further, invasive measures are available to deal with the recalcitrant.

In the above two examples, uncertainty resulting from the obscurity of repressive measures could add to their pervasive terrors. It is in this context noteworthy that the lawyer chosen to 'set an example' in the Li Zhuang 'Warning and Education' campaign was an established, well-known and generally highly regarded member of the profession, not somebody who had already suffered years of persecution and marginalisation. His vilification could hardly have been more public and overt. But, as was seen above, official notices did not actually describe what Li Zhuang was supposed to have done in refutable detail. Instead, they merely produced platitudes that could not easily be rejected. The vilification of human rights lawyers following the BLA democratic election campaign appears to have followed a similar pattern.[141] The prospect of harsh punishment for having committed an infraction that is only described as a vague abstraction is very unsettling; more unsettling perhaps than punishment for a clearly defined 'crime'. Obscurity and moral confusion are features of the kind of bureaucratic control that is needed to achieve pervasive effects – to 'reach', in the words of the BLA document quoted above, 'the eyes, ears, brains and hearts' of all Chinese lawyers.

Even though the authorities did not propagate the cases of human rights lawyers who had daringly raised issues such as torture for years and been subjected to particularly invasive persecution not only in the form of criminal prosecution, scarce information about their even worse persecution could also have intimidating effects; and as will be discussed later, the ability to communicate widely and independently about such persecution disrupts the goals of

141 #25 2013-2.

pervasive control. A lawyer who had only recently begun to be in contact with rights lawyers commented in 2012:

> A few years ago I was still too afraid to participate, I admired people like Teng Biao; but mainly wanted to make money at that time (. . .).[142] Even when in 2008 I had just met people in this circle I was still rather fearful. So we can learn from this that a precondition of terror is secrecy.[143]

More widely, pervasive control makes use of techniques of obscurity that render it difficult not only to understand the consequences of rule infraction, but also the nature of any rules not to be infracted or lines not to be crossed. For instance, there is an assumed 'rule' that one must not take on Falun Gong cases; yet what it amounts to is only a vague understanding that doing so could get one into trouble:

> A while ago I decided to take on a Falun Gong [criminal defence] case and I mentioned it to a friend who teaches at [a famous university]. [My friend] was really shocked and urged me sincerely not to do this; he couldn't understand it and just kept saying, 'you can't do this, you can't do this!'[144]

The lack of boundaries in this particular bureaucratic control system leads to a situation where there never was neither will there ever be a line of transgression at the far side of which punishment will be incurred. It is a system that well precludes the creation of zones of liberty understood negatively in the sense coined by Isaiah Berlin.[145]

Problems with modernisation and institutional liberalisation narratives

Liberalisation narratives as understood here combine a stated adherence to liberal ideas, such as independent legal advocacy, with an historicist commitment to the idea that economic change produces political or ideological change in societies. For the realm of Chinese legal studies, this approach is represented by the work, for instance, of Randall Peerenboom, who considers rule of law development to be correlated to economic development.[146] In the present context,

---

142 #73 2012-1, also #25 2010-1.
143 #73 2012-1.
144 # 73 2012-1.
145 Isaiah Berlin, *Two Concepts of Liberty*, Oxford University Press, Oxford: 1958.
146 Randall Peerenboom characterises rights lawyering as an exceptional and distinct area the suppression of which does not hinder 'modernisation' (e.g. see Randall Peerenboom, 'Economic development and the development of the legal profession in China', 13 February 2009, at http://ssrn.com/abstract=1342287 or http://dx.doi.org/10.2139/ssrn.1342287; and argues that 'Authoritarianism in China is not the result of legal reforms . . . the ruling regime would be even more authoritarian in the absence of legal reforms.' See also Randall Peerenboom, 'Statement before the Congressional-Executive Commission on China', 1 April 2003, at http://scholarship.law.georgetown.edu/cgi/viewcontent.cgi?article=1081&context=cong.

modernisation narratives would suggest a gradual convergence of the legal profession in China with other legal professions in modernised countries, while liberalisation narratives would suggest that the legal profession as such, by virtue of its institutional function in the legal process (representation of clients and protection of their rights), was a force for greater rights orientation of the overall legal system.

From the perspective of their proponents, liberalisation narratives are left largely undisturbed by the invasive dimension of control; by the handful – or let it be a few dozen – individual lawyers (and other rights defenders) who fall victim to repression, because of their seemingly insignificant number and because they can be regarded as the price of incremental liberation of the legal profession through institutional reform. Because there is such a strong belief that the – demonstrably occurring – economic development (growth) will result in greater political freedoms eventually, it becomes imperative not to endanger this process but instead to provide institutional support for it. A host of institutions, organisations and foundations appear to be committed to this view and operating on the basis of its precepts. For example, in 2007 an American Bar Association official commented that, taking into account that ACLA and its members were under 'Chinese central government' supervision (there is no direct mention of the Party, as though this would be politically incorrect – outside entities collaborating with the moderately liberal elements of the establishment generally absorb their practice of referring to institutions of the State only, a practice also advocated by many rights lawyers, as discussed):

> Within the parameters in which it operates, ACLA has been instrumental in a number of ways in promoting the development of the legal profession and the substantive law of China. ACLA committees have not only played an important role in China's economic reform and opening but have also become influential, particularly over the last five years, in advocating for an enhanced role for lawyers' participation in such areas as environmental protection, criminal justice, children's rights, and death penalty administration (. . .) ACLA, on behalf of the legal profession in China, is unambiguously and understandably proud of its increasing openness and participation with its counterparts in the international community. Such participation is welcomed by the ABA and the national bars of the world, for many reasons. Foremost among these reasons is the great potential presented for a united legal profession in all nations to serve as a strong force for advancing and protecting the rule of law throughout the world.[147]

On its website, ABA continues to convey essentially the same message as of this writing, reporting on events including representatives of the justice bureaucracy,

---

147 'The ABA-ACLA memorandum of understanding: a strong step forward for the rule of law', 1 March 2007, at http://www.metrocorpcounsel.com/articles/7990/aba-acla-memorandum-understanding-strong-step-forward-rule-law, accessed 20 December 2013.

and noting that 'with funding from various sources, the Asia Division has . . . supported Chinese partners' efforts in the areas of criminal defence, property rights, legal aid, legal ethics, women's rights, environmental public interest litigation, migrant workers' rights, and children's rights.'[148]

In their self-presentations at international level, the authorities themselves have so far tended to confirm the liberalisation narrative to the extent possible, although internally, expressed commitments to rule of law have been increasingly supplemented by expressions of Party loyalty, as seen above. The self-description of ACLA, for example, places much emphasis on 'the dignity of the Constitution and laws', 'professional ethics', 'self-regulation', 'members' rights and interests' and the principle of rule of law (or rule by law). When one visits the only official website that contains information about ACLA in English language, this is the message one will see – under 'Brief Introduction' we find a translation of the text passage using all these terms (already cited above) – [149] but in contrast to the Chinese-language site, there is no mention whatsoever of the Party on the English-language website, let alone any attempt to explain its role and function within ACLA, as the Chinese-language website does.

The consequences and potential benefits of rule of law programmes operating on the premise of liberalisation narratives are complex and hard to assess.[150] But prima facie, statements like these should give pause against the background of what has been discussed in this chapter, given the pervasiveness of control through officially recognised associative structures, including ACLA and (in general) law firms.

The phenomenon of pervasive control disturbs the liberalisation narrative. The assumption underlying rule of law programmes of this kind, namely that the legal profession and its representation have an inherent tendency to strive for independence, suggests a too facile inclination to regard control as necessarily connected to 'the State', understood in juxtaposition with the legal profession as part of civil society (broadly speaking). In a liberal system, self-regulation does mean giving the so-called 'liberal professions' greater autonomy. But, as has been argued extensively with regard to the role of NGOs in authoritarian or neo-totalitarian systems, social organisations can mean acquiring additional tools of control. Some have contrasted 'Tocquevillean' with 'corporatist' understandings of civil society along these lines. In a 'corporatist' organisation of social life organ-isations that in a Tocquevillean democracy would be seen as part of the sphere of

---

148 American Bar Association, 'China background', at http://www.americanbar.org/advocacy/ rule_of_law/where_we_work/asia/china/background.html, accessed 25 December 2013.

149 ACLA webpage http://chineselawyer.com.cn/html/union/englishunion/briefintroduction.html; screenshot on file with author, dated 17 February 2013, 'undergoing reconstruction' as of December 2013.

150 For further discussion of such programmes, see e.g. Sophia Woodman, 'Driving without a, ap: implementing legal projects in China aimed at improving human rights', in Daniel A. Bell and Jean-Marc Coicaud (eds.), *Ethics in Action*, Cambridge University Press, Cambridge: 2006, http://ebooks.cambridge.org/chapter.jsf?bid=CBO9780511511233&cid=CBO97805115112 33A017, accessed 30 December 2013.

civic responsibilities are instruments of control by the authoritarian State.[151] The evidence of the current chapter suggests that while some individuals seek independence, no such tendency can be clearly ascribed to ACLA, or to the majority of law firms and lawyers, and that these organisations can indeed become agents of control. Organisations that continue their engagement in projects with them are at risk of becoming victims of the control they congratulate their partners on – gradually – overcoming. Their risk of being implicated in this way increases along with repression of independent advocacy and human rights defenders through now established control mechanisms. The more pervasive and invasive control systems are perfected, the harder it is to defend collaboration with those responsible. It is all the more important to resist the argument that control of the kind discussed in this chapter could be acceptable for the official purpose of 'preserv[ing] social stability', be it even only 'when absolutely necessary'.[152]

Acceptance of the liberalisation narrative can also obscure the true grounds of optimism that consist in the formation of independent lawyer organisations.[153]

Limitations of bureaucratic control

The fact that bureaucratic control of the legal profession relies in many ways on psychological effects makes them harder to manage from the perspective of the controller. As control makes use of fear techniques, it is subject to the vagaries and uncertainties of its targets' psychological reactions; and the person trying to understand fear techniques, even if only in the role of an 'observer', can be drawn into the circle of those affected by these techniques. Both observation and comments suggest that the effects of control by fear techniques were wearing off because people simply have got used to them, and that there might be a tipping point of rebellion. The effect of deciding that one will no longer heed a threat or constraint that has until this point made one refrain from saying or doing what one really wanted to say or do is invariably liberating and constitutes a threat to the controlling bureaucracy. This explains why almost invariably lawyers comment that the more pervasive control (at least bureaucratic control of the kind discussed here) becomes – the more it tries to affect all lawyers, use irregular, informal techniques on everyone – the more likely it is to be discounted:

> I think that the number of those who 'have been spoken to' (*bei tan hua*)[154] by the Municipal Justice Bureau keeps steadily rising. But once this one and then that one and then yet another is talked to – if *everybody* were to be 'talked to', they could not handle it, it would be too many to be dealt with. Also, in the process of 'being talked to', we are getting to know each other and realising

---

151 Anthony Spires, 'Contingent symbiosis and civil society in an authoritarian state: understanding the survival of China's grassroots NGOs', 117 *American Journal of Sociology* (2011) 1–45, at p. 2.
152 Cp. Melissa S. Hung, 'Obstacles to self-actualisation in Chinese legal practice', *Santa Clara Law Review* (2008) 239.
153 See Chapter 7.
154 In Chinese characters, 被谈话.

that we have some common, if not convictions, then at least views; and that there is actually no need to be too fearful.[155]

And, once a feared 'tea invitation' takes place, it may be experienced as not as frightening as the time spent fearing that it might occur.[156]

Rights lawyers take satisfaction in observing that control does not work and feel encouraged by these observations. Sometimes they also observe that their own informal getting organised has been a reaction to the official bureaucracy 'failing them'; and this at some point prompts their own efforts to come together in various kinds of shadow structure to help one another.[157] Even the most invasive bureaucratic measure, disbarment, is not necessarily fully successful. If in a different system disbarment would be the end of a human rights lawyer's existence as a problem for the authorities, this is not quite so in China, not only because of the mechanism of 'civil representatives' (*gongmin daili*) and the ability to conduct criminal defence without being a licensed lawyer.[158] In fact, while by a lawyer's expulsion from the professional community of licensed lawyers the justice bureaucracy can successfully remove the lawyer from the realm of their responsibility, the system in its most impersonal and largest sense loses a means of control over this lawyer,[159] who may in turn gain in standing within the rights lawyer community and its looser alternative structures. Therefore, expulsion from the legal profession is a serious threat to professional licensed lawyers; but when it comes, it may be experienced as also a form of liberation from one of the layers of Party–State control. One interlocutor, an NGO worker, who had obtained all the required qualifications to become a lawyer, even explained carefully why he had chosen never to become a licensed lawyer: this made it easier to avoid control efforts by the justice bureaucracy.[160]

Officials in the 'two conjoined' entities discussed here (and in the Party organisations connected with them), in turn, work with bureaucratic limitations that are important to how they understand their duty. They may be eager to suppress rights advocacy within their own sphere of responsibility, but unconcerned with responsibility beyond that sphere. Once a lawyer is removed from this sphere they do not need to care and may be pleased not to care; after all, lawyers' comments suggest that often, officials take no personal interest in their bureaucratic control duties.

By the time bureaucratic control by the justice bureaux and lawyers' associations comes to an end, however, control by the security apparatus, discussed in the next chapter, will already have started.

---

155 #52 2011-1.
156 *Ibid.* also e.g. #77 2013-1.
157 Discussed in Chapter 7.
158 In Chinese characters, 公民代理.
159 It is not clear if functionaries of the justice bureaucracy will themselves be given demerits when lawyers are disbarred.
160 #54 2011-1.

Bibliography

NPC laws

PRC Law on Lawyers [中华人民共和国律师法], passed on 28 October 2007, effective as of 1 June 2008. For the Chinese text, see http://www.gov.cn/flfg/2007-10/28/content_788495.htm, and for an English translation http://www.cecc.gov/pages/newLaws/lawyersLawENG.php.

Rules and regulations

Beijing Justice Bureau Lawyer Corps Warning and Education Campaign Plan [北京市律师队伍警示教育工作方案], promulgated on 19 March 2010, at http://wenku.baidu.com/view/e629b883ec3a87c24028c42e.html.

Beijing Justice Bureau Regulation on Beijing Law Firms Seeking Permission and Reporting When Handling Major Tasks [北京市司法局关于北京市律师事务所承办重大法律事务请示报告的制度], 14 January 1999, at http://www.beinet.net.cn/policy/wbj/sfj/200508/t35645.htm, accessed 15 December 2013.

Beijing Justice Bureau Rules for the Implementation of Beijing Justice Bureaux' Measures on the Management of Lawyers [北京市司法局律师执业管理办法实施细则], 2 December 2009, at http://hdsfj.bjhd.gov.cn/falvfagui/lsfw/2013-08-23/928.html.

Jiangsu Province Measures on the Annual Assessment and Examination of Law Firms (Provisional) [江苏省律师事务所年度检查考核办法(试行)], Jiangsu Province Implementation Regulations on Law Firms' Annual Assessment and Examination (Provisional) [江苏省律师事务所年度检查考核细则(试行)], promulgated by Jiangsu Province Justice Bureau on 3 April 2009, at http://www.jssf.gov.cn/skywcm/webpage/iframe/zwgk_detail.jsp?infoId=5606, accessed 3 December 2013.

Ministry of Justice Notice on Issuance of 'Decision on Oath System for Lawyers' [关于印发《关于建立律师宣誓制度的决定》的通知], dated 3 February 2012, at http://baike.baidu.com/view/8206917.htm?fromTaglist, accessed 31 December 2013.

Ministry of Justice Regulation on Annual Law Firm Assessment [律师事务所年度检查考核办法], promulgated on 2010, effective from 8 April, 2010, at http://www.legalinfo.gov.cn/index/content/2010-04/09/content_2108819.htm, accessed 24 November 2013. Ministry of Justice Regulation on Management of Law Firms (Ministry of Justice edict no. 111) [律师事务所管理办法 (司法部111号令)], 18 July 2008, at http://www.chinanews.com/gn/news/2008/07-21/1319598.shtml, accessed 11 February 2013.

Ministry of Justice Regulation on Management of Lawyers '(Ministry of Justice edict no. 112) [律师执业管理办法(司法部112号令)]', at http://www.moj.gov.cn/2008zcfg/2008-07/22/content_906514.htm, accessed 11 February 2013.

Supreme People's Court, Supreme People's Procuratorate, Ministry of Public Security, Ministry of State Security, and Ministry of Justice Rules Concerning Questions about Examining and Judging Evidence in Death Penalty Cases [关于办理死刑案件审查判断证据若干问题的规定], at http://www.spp.gov.cn/site2006/2010-06-25/0005428111.html; English translation by Duihua Foundation available at http://www.duihuahrjournal.org/2010/06/translation-chinas-new-rules-on.html.

Other official documents

All China Lawyers' Association Charter [中华全国律师协会章程] (last revised on 26 December 2011), at http://www.acla.org.cn/zhangchen.jhtml, accessed February 2013.

All China Lawyers' Association Guiding Opinion on the Handling of Mass Litigation [中华全国律师协会关于律师办理群体性案件指导意见], promulgated on and effective from 20 March 2006, at http://www.legaldaily.com.cn/ecard/content/2011-04/08/content_2586358.htm?node=23949, accessed 15 December 2013.

All China Lawyers' Association Opinion on Conscientiously Studying and Implementing the Establishment of Party Organisations in the Legal Profession [全国律协关于深入学习贯彻全国律师工作会议和全国律师行业党的建设工作会议的意见], dated 30 December 2012, at http://www.acla.org.cn/fazhixinwen/617.jhtml, accessed 11 February 2013; copy on file with author.

All China Lawyers' Association Regulation on Annual Assessment of Lawyers [律师执业年度考核规则], promulgated on 13 August 2010, effective from 1 January 2011, at http://2009.lawyers.org.cn/profile/info.jsp?id=12f438db9a4fbb68482443a56 8fa6448, accessed 24 November 2013.

Chinese Communist Party Central Committee Leading Group on Judicial System Reform Preliminary Opinions on the reform of the Judicial System and Working Mechanisms [中央司法体制改革领导小组关于司法体制和工作机制改革的初步意见], dated 1 December 2004, reprinted in 中华人民共和国监察部办公厅 (PRC Ministry of Supervision), 行政监察工作文件选编 2004 年 [Selected Administration and Supervision Work Documents, 2004 Issue], Beijing, 2005, at p. 626 ff.

Chinese Communist Party Central Organisation Department and Ministry of Justice's Notice on Further Strengthening the Establishment of Party Organisations in the Legal Profession [中组部、司法部关于进一步加强和改进律师行业党的建设工作的通知], dated 8 May 2008, at http://www.acla.org.cn/hydjzd/2878.jhtml.

Chinese Communist Party Regulation on the Work of Basic Level Party and State Organisations [中国共产党党和国家机关基层组织工作条例], promulgated by the Central Committee of Chinese Communist Party on 30 March 1998, at http://www.acla.org.cn/hydjzd/2222.jhtml, accessed 2 January 2014.

Huaihua City Justice Bureau, 怀化市司法局办公室文件 [Huaihua City Justice Bureau Document, edict no. 6 (2012)], obtained 11 February 2013, on file with author.

Books and articles

All China Lawyers' Association (全国律协), '徐州市律师事务所党建工作纪实 [Record on Party-Building work in Law Firms of Xuzhou City]', 7 December 2012 at http://www.acla.org.cn/lvshifengcai/4743.jhtml, accessed 11 February 2011.

All China Lawyers' Association (全国律协), '中国特色社会主义法律工作者的生动实践 [The real life practice of socialist-with-Chinese-characteristics legal workers]', Annual Report, 1 November 2012, at http://www.acla.org.cn/industry/4179.jhtml.

American Bar Association, 'The ABA-ACLA memorandum of understanding: a strong step forward for the rule of law', 1 March 2007, http://www.metrocorpcounsel.com/articles/7990/aba-acla-memorandum-understanding-strong-step-forward-rule-law, accessed 20 December 2013.

American Bar Association, 'China background', at http://www.americanbar.org/advocacy/rule_of_law/where_we_work/asia/china/background.html, accessed 25 December 2013.

Ansfield, Jonathan and Buckley, Chris, 'China focusing graft enquiry on ex-official', *New York Times*, 15 December 2013, at http://www.nytimes.com/2013/12/16/world/asia/china-presses-corruption-inquiry-of-powerful-former-security-official.html?_r=0.

Bai, Mei (白梅), '中共利用律师事务所打压维权律师高博隆华所屈服 [CCP uses law firms to suppress lawyers, Globe Law Firm caves in]', 31 May 2009, at http://www.ntdtv.com/xtr/gb/2009/06/01/a302005.html.-%E4%B8%AD%E5%85%B1%E5%88%A9%E7%94%A8%E5%BE%8B%E5%B8%88%E4%BA%8B%E5%8A%A1%E6%89%80%E6%89%93%E5%8E%8B%E7%BB%B4%E6%9D%83%E5%BE%8B%E5%B8%88-%E9%AB%98%E5%8D%9A%E9%9A%86%E5%8D%8E.E6%89%80%E5%B1%88%E6%9C%8D.html.

Beijing Lawyers' Association, '北京律协举办警示教育系列活动之新执业律师宣誓仪式 [BLA holds New Lawyers Oath Ceremony as Part of the Warning and Education Campaign]', 23 April 2010, at http://www.beijinglawyers.org.cn/cac/1024.htm, accessed 15 December 2013.

Berlin, Isaiah, *Two Concepts of Liberty*, Oxford University Press, Oxford: 1958.

China Free Press (tr.), 'The Beijing Bar Association's response to a small number of lawyers and their so-called call for direct elections to the Beijing Bar Association', 10 September 2008, at http://archive.is/ezYHY.

Cohen, Jerome A., 'The struggle for autonomy of Beijing's public interest lawyers', *China Rights Forum*, 1 April 2009, at http://www.hrichina.org/content/3692.

Cohen, Jerome A., 'Zhou Yongkang case shows Chinas's rule of law still good only in theory', *South China Morning Post*, 18 August 2014.

Feng, Haiming and Gao, Aiping (冯海明, 高爱萍), '公民代理打官司不得收入"律师费" [Civil Representatives must not take lawyers' fees]', at http://zzfy.hncourt.org/public/detail.php?id=8401, accessed 26 December 2013.

Fraenkel, Ernst, *The Dual State. A Contribution to the Theory of Dictatorship*, translated by E.A. Shils, Oxford University Press, New York: 1941.

Fuchs, Jürgen, 'Unter Nutzung der Angst – Die "leise Form" des Terrors – Zersetzungsmaßnahmen des MfS [Making use of fear – the "soft form" of Terror]', *BF informiert* Nr. 2, Berlin 1994.

Havel, Václav, *Moc Bezmocných* [*The Power of the Powerless*], Prague, 1978; published in translation by Jan Vladislav (ed.) *Living in Truth*, Faber & Faber, London and Boston: 1986.

Human Rights Watch, 'China: leading civil rights lawyers face threats to licences', 26 May 2009, at http://www.hrw.org/news/2009/05/26/china-leading-civil-rights-lawyers-face-threats-licenses, accessed 3 December 2013.

Human Rights Watch, *Walking on Thin Ice*, 2008, at http://www.hrw.org/reports/2008/04/28/walking-thin-ice-0, accessed 3 December 2013.

Human Rights in China (tr.), 'Keep pace with the course of history, implement lawyers association direct election: an appeal to all Beijing lawyers, the Beijing Municipal Bureau of Justice, and the Beijing Municipal Lawyers Association', 31 October, 2008, http://www.hrichina.org/public/contents/press?revision_id=149319&item_id=149292.

Human Rights Watch, 'A great danger for lawyers: new regulatory curbs on lawyers representing Protesters', December 2006, at http://www.hrw.org/reports/2006/china1206/4.htm#_Toc153174877, accessed 24 November 2013.

Hung, Melissa S., 'Obstacles to self-actualisation in Chinese legal pactice', *Santa Clara Law Review* (2008) 239.

Janzen, Cornelius, 'Subtiler Terror: die Opfer von Stasi-Zersetzungsmethoden [Sutble terror: the victims of Stasi disintegration methods]', *3Sat*, 27 July 2009, at http://www.3sat.de/page/?source=/kulturzeit/themen/136072/index.html.

Lam, Willy, 'Xi Jinping's ideological crackdown could destroy China's economy', *Jamestown Foundation*, 4 October 2013, at http://www.asianews.it/news-en/Xi-Jinping%E2%80%99s-ideological-crackdown-could-destroy-China%E2%80%99s-economy-29192.html.

Lan, Rongjie, 'Killing the lawyer as the last resort: the Li Zhuang case and its effects on criminal defence in China', in McConville, Mike and Pils, Eva (eds.), *Criminal Justice in China: Comparative Perspectives*, Edward Elgar Publishing, Cheltenham: 2014.

Li, Xueyao and Liu, Sida, 'The learning process of globalisation: how Chinese law firms survived the financial crisis', 80 *Fordham Law Review* (2012) 2850.

Liu, Sida and Halliday, Terence, 'Dancing handcuffed in the minefield: survival strategies of defense lawyers in China's criminal justice system (14 May 2008)', Center on Law and Globalization Research Paper No. 08–04, at http://ssrn.com/abstract=1269536 or http://dx.doi.org/10.2139/ssrn.1269536.

Lynch, Elizabeth, 'China's rule of law mirage: the regression of the legal profession since the adoption of the 2007 Lawyers Law', 42 *Georgetown University International Law Review* (2010) 535.

Peerenboom, Randall, 'Economic development and the development of the legal profession in China (13 February, 2009)', at http://ssrn.com/abstract=1342287 or http://dx.doi.org/10.2139/ssrn.1342287.

Pils, Eva, 'Asking the tiger for his skin: rights activism in China', 30 *Fordham International Law Journal* (2006) 1209–1287.

Qiu, Shi (秋石), '革命理想高于天——学习习近平同志关于坚定理想信念的重要论述 [Revolutionary ideals are higher than heaven – studying Comrade Xi Jinping's important discourse on strengthening ideals and beliefs]', 1 November 2013, at http://big5.qstheory.cn/zxdk/2013/201321/201310/t20131030_284176.htm, accessed 1 January 2014; available in translation at *China Copyright and Media*, http://chinacopyrightandmedia.wordpress.com/2013/11/, accessed 23 December 2013.

Radio Free Asia (Mandarin Desk), '莫少平律师事务所被迫搬迁 [Mo Shaoping Law Firm forced to move office]', 10 June 2010, at http://www.rfa.org/mandarin/yataibaodao/mo-06102010103435.html.

Shu, Sheng (舒升), '三中全会释放的是党性和民心 [The Third Plenary Has Released Party Spirit and Popular Feelings]', 13 November 2013, at http://blog.people.com.cn/article/1384356795570.html.

Southern Daily (南方日报), '惠州 "红色律师" 实践: 治理 "黑律师" 党建是剂良方' [To make 'red lawyering' a reality, is Party-Building work the right way to control 'black lawyers'?], 19 November 2010, at http://politics.people.com.cn/GB/14562/13260124.html, accessed 25 December 2013.

Spires, Anthony, 'Contingent symbiosis and civil society in an authoritarian state: understanding the survival of China's grassroots NGOs', 117 *American Journal of Sociology* (2011) 1–45.

Wan, Yanping (完颜平), '"党性" 四问 [Four questions concerning Party ppirit]', *Guangming Daily*, undated, at http://www.szlawyers.com/info/619e760cb38945c9c57817e7b22361a4, accessed 23 December 2013.

Wang, Qi (汪旗), '北京市限制外地律师进京执业 [Beijing restricts out-of-town lawyers from coming to Beijing to practise]', at http://www.cesl.edu.cn/upload/201204205275010.pdf, accessed 21 December 2013.

Woodman, Sophia, 'Driving without a map: implementing legal projects in China aimed at improving human rights', in Daniel A. Bell and Jean-Marc Coicaud (eds.), *Ethics in Action*, Cambridge University Press, Cambridge: 2006; http://ebooks.cambridge.

org/chapter.jsf?bid=CBO9780511511233&cid=CBO9780511511233A017, accessed 30 December 2013.

Xia, Yu (夏雨), '行政干预密令房主不续约, 北京安汇律师事务所陷入绝境 [Landlord does not extend lease following secret order by administrative intervention; Beijing Anhui Law Firm in critical state]', at http://boxun.com/news/gb/china/2010/03/201003252229.shtml.

Xin, Yu (心语), '北京忆通律师事务所遭打压, 被停六个月 [Beijing Yitong Law Firm encounters repression, is suspended for six months]', 18 February 2009, at http://www.rfa.org/mandarin/yataibaodao/yitong-02182009085956.html.

Zhou, Bin (周斌), '司法部向各地司法行政机关就李庄违法违纪案件发出通报 [Ministry of Justice issues notice on Li Zhuang's case of violation of the law and discipline to all justice administration authorities]', 18 March 2010, at http://www.gov.cn/gzdt/2010-03/18/content_1558826.htm.

Documentary and multimedia sources

Zhang, Feng (张峰), '宣传思想工作要坚持党性和人民性的统 一 [Propaganda and thought work must maintain that Party spirit and people spirit are united]', video-recorded lecture dated 28 October 2013, at http://www.71.cn/2013/1028/742244.shtml, accessed 23 December 2013.

Websites, blog and microblog entries

All China Lawyers' Association [中华全国律师协会] Introduction of ACLA, at http://www.acla.org.cn/about.jhtml, accessed 17 February 2013.

Beijing Justice Bureau [北京市司法局], 'Party committees and organisations' website, at http://www.bjsf.gov.cn/publish/portal0/tab97/info9120.htm, accessed 22 February 2013.

Beijing Justice Bureau [北京市司法局], Beijing Justice Bureau's website at http://www.bjsf.gov.cn/publish/portal0/tab97/, accessed 18 November 2013.

Beijing Justice Bureau's sub-offices, sub-offices structure, at http://www.bjsf.gov.cn/publish/portal0/tab97/, accessed 31 December 2013.

Beijing Lawyers Association [北京律师协会], List of one-person law firms that have passed the latest 2012 assessment exercise, at http://www.beijinglawyers.org.cn/qtmodel/lxgg.htm, accessed 31 December 2013.

Clarke, Donald C, 'Tempest in the Beijing Lawyers' Association', 11 blog entry, September 2008, at http://lawprofessors.typepad.com/china_law_prof_blog/2008/09/tempest-in-the.html.

Lawyer Tong Lihua (佟丽华)'s website at http://www.zgnmg.org/.

Liu, Sida (刘思达), 中国律师行业管理体制批判 [A critique of the management system for the legal profession], blog entry, 1 July 2011, at http://blog.sina.com.cn/s/blog_6d33e7f5010186rn.html, accessed 17 February 2013.

South China Morning Post, A short profile of Zhou Yongkang, at http://www.scmp.com/topics/zhou-yongkang, accessed 25 December 2013.

Recorded speeches

Zhou, Yongkang (周永康), '周永康在全国律师工作会议上的讲话 [Zhou Yongkang's speech at All China Lawyers' Delegates Meeting]', November 2010, at http://cpc.people.com.cn/GB/64093/64094/13402392.html, accessed 18 November 2013.

Zhou, Yongkang (周永康), '全面推进社会治安综合治理工作确保人民安居乐业社会和谐稳定 [Safeguard Social Equality and Justice; Uphold Social Harmony and Stability]', 12 *Qiu Shi [Seeking Truth] Magazine* (2009), at http://www.mps.gov.cn/n16/n894593/n895609/1953766.html, accessed 18 November 2013.

Zhou, Yongkang (周永康), 在第七次全国律师代表大会上的讲话 [Speech at the Seventh National Lawyers' Congress], 25 October 2008, at http://news.xinhuanet.com/legal/2008-10/26/content_10257859.htm.

Administrative and judicial decisions

北京市司法局行政处罚决定书京司罚决 [2010] 2, 3号 [Beijing Municipal Justice Bureau Administrative Punishment Decision (2010) nos. 2 and 3]', dated 7 May 2010, at http://www.bjsf.gov.cn/sy/sytztg/201005/t20100507_1279393.html and http://www.bjsf.gov.cn/sy/cxjl/cxjllsgl/201005/t20100507_1279438.html, accessed 10 May 2010.

6 Relationship with the security apparatus

Once they cross a certain threshold of rights advocacy and publicly effective criticism of the system, human rights lawyers are bound to encounter the Party–State's security apparatus. 'The security apparatus' is a network of collaborating agencies and individuals – the police or public security, State security, and various other, flexibly established Party–State offices and bureaux dealing with 'factors of social instability', such as the so-called 'stability preservation offices'.

The creation of the last likely date back to 2004, when the government decided to establish 'stability preservation offices' at each level of the administration down from the Party Central Stability Preservation Office. During most of the time period in which conversations for the purpose of this book were held, it was headed by Politburo member and Political and Legal Committee President Zhou Yongkang. The details of its creation and organisation have not been publicised, but it is staffed with personnel drawn from the judicial organs (comprising the police, procuracies and courts); the State Security Department; and the Propaganda or Publicity Department.[1] Around 2012 offices and individuals formerly designated as serving 'stability preservation' were being integrated in a wider 'social management' programme with a further expanded network.[2] In November 2013 the Party announced the creation of a 'National Security Committee'; while its role and powers were left open, it was probably to be controlled directly by the Party Secretary General and Premier Xi Jinping, and would henceforth be responsible for internal stability preservation as well as

---

1 See '"维稳办" 走上前台 ["Stability preservation" offices come to the fore]', Nanfengchuang (南风窗), 14 April 2009 at http://www.nfcmag.com/articles/1463/page/2, accessed 25 December 2013.
2 See e.g. Tyler Thompson, 'Reviving the Cultural Revolution – China's social management campaign targets "radical thought"', 1 April 2011, at http://chinaelectionsblog.net/?tag=social-management, accessed 4 January 2014. China Digital Times, 'New social management grids to preserve stability', 24 January 2011, at http://chinadigitaltimes.net/2011/02/new-social-management-grids-to-preserve-stability/, accessed 25 December 2013; Zhou Benshun (周本顺), '走中国特色社会管理创新之路 [The path to innovation of social management with Chinese characteristics]', Seeking Truth (求是), 16 May 2011, at http://www.qstheory.cn/zxdk/2011/2011010/201105/t20110513_80501.htm, accessed 25 December 2013; for a translation, see Flora Sapio Forgotten Archipelagos blog, entry of 6 July 2001, at http://florasapio.blogspot.hk/2011/06/belated-translation-zhou-benshun-road.html, accessed 25 December 2013.

external State security.[3] As establishment scholars observed that the National Security Committee would be 'coordinating the police, the Foreign Service, military, defence, economic security and maritime affairs',[4] rights lawyers generally expressed the expectation that this concentration of responsibilities and powers would strengthen 'stability preservation' and by implication make their lives more difficult.[5] Such concentration of responsibilities would also be in line with more general efforts to draw on China's Mao era past.[6]

The security forces have always collaborated with other authorities: the lawyer's associations and judicial bureaux as well as the people's procuracies and the people's courts; and it has been in the nature of State security that membership may be a secret.[7] Moreover, as also in other areas of State administration, there is overlap with Party institutions, such as the political–legal committees.

Security apparatus individuals most frequently active in these contexts are officers of the public security bureaux, 'Internal National Security Protection Squad (*guonei anquan baowei zhidui*)', or for short, the *guobao* police:[8]

> Formerly only dissidents would have interaction with the *guobao* police, and they would still not really use this word. They would rather say, 'some mates', or 'the brothers', or 'a certain friend' (*gemenr, xiongdi, mouge pengyou*).[9] After [Charter] 08 they [the *guobao*] suddenly appeared in force and took care of various groups including the lawyers, petitioners, Falun Gong and so on. Later, it was also the grass-mud-horses [internet activists].[10]

Apparently in collaboration with 'stability preservation' offices, the *guobao* police maintain a system for classifying 'stability preservation' targets such as human rights lawyers according to different grades.[11] Occasionally, they may inform one of their targets that their ranking has been determined as '"A category"

---

3 Jane Perlez, 'New Chinese panel said to oversee domestic security and foreign policy', *New York Times*, 13 November 2013, at http://www.nytimes.com/2013/11/14/world/asia/national-security-committee-china.html?_r=0&pagewanted=all, accessed 3 January 2014.

4 Li Jie (李杰), quoted in Liu Junguo, Xiao Da, Wang Gang, Qing Mu, Yang Ming, Ji Shuangcheng, Yang Jingjie, Wang Xi and Liu Zhi (刘军国, 萧达, 王刚, 青木, 杨明, 纪双城, 杨静婕, 汪析, 柳直), '世界解读三中全会公报 感叹中国改革决心 [The world is analyzing the Third Plenary Meeting report, sighing over China's commitment to reform]', *Global Times* (环球时报), 13 November 2013, at http://world.huanqiu.com/depth_report/2013-11/4558902_2.html, accessed 3 January 2014.

5 #23 2013-4; observation of online chat group, 13 November 2013.

6 A rights lawyer pointed out that if the boundaries between *gong'an* (公安) and *guo'an* (国安) seemed at times unclear, this was unsurprising since they had originated from the same institution. 'Originally, state security/*guo'an* (国安) and internal security/*guobao* (国保) were all one entity – they belonged to *zhengzhi baowei* (政治保卫) [political security]; later they separated out into these different entities but they continue to be closely related.' #25 2011-2.

7 #25 2011-2: '*Guo'an* are more covert. E.g. you might have a guy in a travel agency or in Xinhua News Agency whose actual job and salary is from *Guo'an* (国安).'

8 In Chinese characters, 国内安全保卫制度 and 国保.

9 In Chinese characters, 哥们儿, 兄弟, 某个朋友.

10 #23 2011-2. On the expression 'grass-mud-horse', see Anonymous Contributor, Liz Carter, Anne Henochowitz and Xiao Qiang, *The Grass-Mud-Horse Lexicon*, Kindle Books: 2013; entry for 'grass-mud-horse' (in Chinese, 草泥马).

11 I have seen forms concerning 'stability preservation targets' reflecting such a complex grading system.

stability preservation target', for example, or that they have just been downgraded.[12] The grade a person has been given will determine the general level of attention they receive from *guobao* officers and the wider security apparatus.

The means of control available specifically to the security apparatus include the criminal process – criminal investigation, prosecution and punishment – and various forms of administratively imposed detention such as Re-education Through Labour. In addition to these, there is a range of measures without basis in public rules, sometimes described as 'extra-legal'. These include electronic surveillance outside criminal investigation contexts;[13] 'educational', 'warning' and 'investigatory' chats or 'tea-drinking' sessions; tracking and following; harassment; casual beatings; incarcerations; and torture. There can be overlap between 'legal' and extra-legal measures, not least because some of the laws used as a basis for 'legal' measures are in violation of higher ranking law, including the PRC Constitution (see Chapter 3). Overall, as noted in Chapter 1, there is some justification for using Fraenkel's distinction between a 'state of norms' and a 'state of measures' to understand the way in which legal norms and extra-legal measures interact, especially in the operation of the security apparatus.[14]

It is possible to describe a general progression from the lightest kinds of measure such as may potentially affect anyone to targeted severe rights violations such as enforced disappearances and torture. From the perspective of the controlling Party–State the goals pursued by these techniques are the same: 'educational' conversations and coercive interrogations, for instance, are essentially similar and can merge into one another. To comprehend this logic, it is necessary to understand how radically the rights of the security forces' targets are disregarded, and to understand how such disregard is also exacted from the victims of the measures and techniques discussed here.[15]

Police surveillance, 'chats', tracking and following and casual violence

Individuated interaction

The *guobao* police officer and other persons assigned to a particular rights lawyer can interact with the lawyer almost whenever they choose, without physically following them all the time. For example, it is possible to determine the location of the 'stability preservation target' through that person's mobile phone; and when

---

12 On different occasions, two rights lawyers mentioned such occurrences to me.
13 The 2012 Criminal Procedure Law revision legalises the use of electronic surveillance for criminal investigation, previously regulated in various ministerial regulations etc.
14 Ernst Fraenkel, *The Dual State. A Contribution to the Theory of Dictatorship*, translated by E.A. Shils, Oxford University Press, New York: 1941.
15 The present chapter is largely based on the accounts of lawyers affected by these various techniques, with a focus on forced disappearance and what happens in the course of it. The account amalgamates several interlocutors' individual descriptions as far as possible. This can be done easily because the various measures discussed here, while not being subject to legal norms, follow certain patterns and appear to be carefully calculated.

there is a congregation of several 'high-importance' targets in one particular place, the *guobao* police may appear and forcibly escort them back home, or instruct them by phone to come to a police station 'for a chat'.[16] The phone is also frequently used to send instructions to lawyers. Thus on the eve of an important meeting of high-level Party–State officials, a lawyer might be instructed to 'take a good rest': 'Look at this text message here. "You had best not work too much in the next few days. Take a good rest." How caring of him!'[17]

Or, the lawyer might receive a text message from one of 'his' *guobao* officers instructing him, somewhat cryptically but with clear intention: 'Be careful, don't say anything you ought not to say!' Or, hours before his participation in a research seminar outside of Mainland China,[18] a lawyer participating in a seminar out of town might be called and required to explain why he had not returned home yet.[19] Lawyers do sometimes choose not to answer such calls. They can attempt to ignore the text messages, or stop using their ordinary phones. However, they can only escape such 'attention' at the cost of cutting themselves off from most of their other contacts:

> [Right now] I have one phone for exclusive use to talk with my wife, and another one to talk about issues (*shuo shir de dianhua*),[20] and one public, general one. But [because the public one is turned off most of the time] people often can't 'find' me these days, except via Skype.[21]

As long as they remain in China, they can be almost certain that the security apparatus will find them if it chooses to do so. Some particularly important stability preservation targets, indeed, reported being told that their voice alone would be sufficient to recognise them if they used any telephone inside China. More generally, lawyers and anyone interacting with them will be conscious of the possibility of electronic surveillance, a consciousness that potentially affects any interaction, be it only by requiring lawyers to resist mentally:

> See, our conversation right now might be listened in on. But we don't need to take any counter-measure, such as taking the battery out of our phones, because we actually don't care, do we?[22]

16 #2 2011-3.
17 # 9 2011-3.
18 Observation (March 2012).
19 Observation (March 2012).
20 In Chinese characters, 说事儿的电话.
21 #9 2010-4.
22 #52 2011-1.

Where electronic surveillance and communication are deemed insufficient, a rights lawyer may be physically followed around to achieve a more intimidating effect:

> For example, the moment I speak to someone they consider a bit sensitive – like you, they might well start following me again. Never mind, I don't fear. If they want to follow me, just let them.[23]

Or the lawyer may be 'invited to tea', usually in a teahouse, coffee shop or police station. In the slang that has evolved around these practices, 'being asked to tea', or 'being asked for a chat' (*bei he cha; bei yuetan*)[24] indicates conversations with officers, often but not always of the *guobao* police, following an 'invitation' that – as everybody understands – cannot be refused without risk of unpleasant consequences.

In the context of interaction with the *guobao* police, 'tea drinking' and 'chatting' can be superficially innocuous, and there may even develop an appearance of friendliness; but rights lawyers consistently comment that they experience chats with *guobao* police as threatening at some level, even when no explicit threat is made. After all, having had exposure to criminal suspects and defendants and other vulnerable groups, they are well aware of what the security apparatus can do to their clients; and by the time they confront *guobao* police officers, they tend to know a lot about State-centred violence. Some lawyers have commented that violence inflicted on them personally tends to be less frequent and less severe than in the case of some of their clients, because of their higher social status.[25] But even rights lawyers who have not experienced any violence themselves are generally also aware of some instances of violence inflicted on their colleagues.

Tea drinking with the security apparatus, thus, sometimes merely serves to reinforce general intimidation. It can, however, also be used for 'interrogation' purposes, as when *guobao* officers seek to gather information about a lawyer's social environment. These goals can overlap, since one principal form of control is putting pressure on a person's friends, and *guobao* officers frequently impress on the targeted lawyer the possibility that s/he might be instrumental in harming a friend, colleague or relative:

> I used to think that people got entrapped by people consciously reporting on them. Like spies. But then I realized that probably, that was not how it really worked. What happens is that they call you in for questioning and then ask you many questions about another person. Maybe a hundred replies you give are favourable [to the person they ask you about]. But then you say

---

23 #23 2010-2. Similarly, #6 2011-1: 'Look, if you came more often [to see me] then perhaps later I would also be followed. And you might lose your visa.'
24 In Chinese characters, 被喝茶, 被约谈. #26 2011-2, 3.
25 E.g. #14 2011-3; #23 2011-6.

one unfavourable thing. They will be recording all of it but only use that one unfavourable reply later.[26]

In order to cope with these methods some lawyers try to make it a principle never to speak about what their friends do.[27] A Twitter user commented:

> Advisory for being asked to tea: don't remember your own affairs, be not sure about those of others, don't know about anything you're specifically asked about, and have no views.[28]

'Chat' sessions are also used to intimidate the target directly by threatening them:

> It wasn't that they said all that much to her . . . but in the end she still had to cry . . . She had merely participated in a very few gatherings with rights lawyers; and just because of that they came and talked to her.[29]

> The chat took only twenty minutes this time. I was just about to go. I was already at the door. Then he called me back and said, 'Hey, [name], assume one wants to criminally arrest a person in Beijing who is from outside [Beijing, i.e. not registered in Beijing]. How does one serve the arrest notice on their family?'[30]

Attribution of collective responsibility

It is an established practice for the security apparatus to target a person's social environment through 'chats': 'If they feel they can neither persuade you nor scare you *(quan ye quan bu liao, xia ye xia bu liao)*,[31] they will target your family'.[32]

On such occasions the authorities hold family, friends and colleagues responsible for the actions of the targeted individual. The traditional concept of *zhulian*, 'implication', 'guilt by association' or 'collective responsibility',[33] can help to explain this non-individuated approach. Historically, *zhulian* denotes a mechanism of criminal liability used for certain types of crime. The 'extermination of the nine family categories' meant that in certain types of crime, in particular treason, punishment would be meted out against not only the individual wrongdoer, but also his family.

26 #9 2011-1.
27 #9 2011-1.
28 Twitterer named 'bridgeduan', 17 April 2011, at http://twitter.com/#!/bridgeduan 110417; Bridgeduan (blogger pseudonym) (2011), (喝茶谈话守则普及: 自己的事不记得, 别人的事不清楚, 特定事件不了解, 没看法), 17 April 2011, available as retweet at https://twitter.com/#!/sanzuwu/statuses/59823408686448642, accessed 16 February 2012.
29 #20 2010-2.
30 #9 2011-1.
31 In Chinese characters, 劝也劝不了, 吓也吓不了.
32 #9 2011-1; continues: 'That started with Gao Zhisheng (高智晟). . . .'
33 In Chinese characters, 株连,株连九族.

The persecution of family members in contemporary China has been investigated and described as a phenomenon of 'relational repression' with regard to Party–State control of protesters (e.g. in the context of protests against rural land-grabs).[34] This analysis is helpful, as any analysis for such persecution and punishment must acknowledge the possibility that the target person's social environment is used, simply, to multiply the effect of fear of the security apparatus by adding to the fear experienced directly for oneself, fear experienced for others. However, there may be an additional layer of explanation reaching beyond treating relational repression descriptively as a phenomenon of social control. An attempt to justify such repression must work on the basis of an assumption that the individual at the centre of 'relational repression' committed wrong, *because* his or her social environment did not sufficiently influence his or her thoughts and actions to ensure correct conduct. This assumption would reject – or ignore – the moral autonomy of the target person. It would make the target person's decisions (thoughts and actions) someone else's moral responsibility, and go further by implying that these decisions (thoughts and actions) could be *legitimately* controlled by someone else, and that failure to control them was a failure of the target person's professional or social environment:

> Each person must ask themselves, not only how much they can do but also ... how much pressure they can accept to be put on their friends and family. You must explain things to them and you must make sure that you prepare any necessary documents [needed in case of detention or disappearance]. Most importantly, you must not worry too much that your family won't understand. Even if they don't understand, as long as they are mentally or physically not completely unable to deal with this, you have to explain what you are doing and explain that you are not harming anyone and not doing anything shameful. At the least, you mustn't let the *guobao* get hold of them and turn them into a force obstructing us or obstructing communication with them. There are some lessons to learn from this, because on many previous occasions the *guobao* or the 610 Office or the Justice Bureau ended up controlling the family – not in the sense of controlling them physically, but in the sense of controlling their thoughts. This turned them into collaborators and made matters a lot easier for the authorities.[35]

In the context of the Chinese security apparatus's attitudes toward wrongdoing, the term frequently used to capture the mechanism by which collective

---

34 Deng Yanhua and Kevin O'Brien, 'Relational repression in China: using social ties to demobilise protesters', 215 *China Quarterly* (September 2013) 533–552. To quote, 'When popular action breaks out, local officials, staff of public organisations (e.g. school teachers) and beneficiaries of government largesse (e.g. pensioners) with ties to protesters are assembled into a work team to conduct "thought work" (*sixiang gongzuo* 思想工作). Team members are then expected to use their influence to pacify and "transform" (*zhuanhua* 转化) activists, and to coax or pressure them into abandoning popular action' (at p. 2).
35 #25 2013-1.

responsibility is realised is *zuo [sixiang] gongzuo*,[36] 'working on someone' or 'doing thought work on someone', an expression that appears to have its most immediate origins in the Maoist ideology of thought reformation.[37] There are many accounts of this practice provided by rights lawyers who report that State security or the *guobao* police went to their hometown to speak to their parents, their former teacher, siblings, neighbours or people in their still wider social environment:

> These days, although originally State security (*guo'an*)[38] should only be taking care of issues concerning foreign involvement and operate in secret, they sometimes also send people to investigate one's background. (. . .) Guo'an in [two consecutive years] went to where I had studied and my home to investigate – just to ask questions about me. . . . At that time they actually weren't trying to act in secret. They were *hoping* that someone would inform me about that.[39]

Thought work is considered to be a legitimate means of ensuring 'correct' behaviour, and the notion of collective responsibility for correct behaviour entails that it is natural for thought work to be carried out by persons close to the target person. In the eyes of those who use it, the correctness of the attitude exacted by thought work appears to justify the means used for this purpose. Yet as is discussed with reference to some of these means below, it is hard to liken 'thought work' to co-optation of the target person or their social environment in cases where the pressure applied makes genuine assimilation impossible, or where the target person as well as their social environment are regarded as belonging to 'the enemy' and essentially put in fear in an effort to influence their minds:

> I was scared when I heard they had sent people to speak to my family. They operated very indirectly. They spoke to a colleague, who then spoke to my [family member]. Just to ask about my background. They did that to let me know that my family had come under pressure from the authorities.[40]

Soft detention and similar measures

If intimidating visits, chats and 'thought work' are thought not to have had the desired effect, however, the lawyer may 'be travelled' (*bei lüyou*)[41] – that is, forcibly

---

36 In Chinese characters, 做[思想]工作.
37 To quote Mao Zedong (毛泽东): 'It is man's social being that determines his thinking. Once the correct ideas characteristic of the advanced class are grasped by the masses, these ideas turn into a material force which changes society and changes the world.' Mao Zedong, 'Where do correct ideas come from?' (1963), at http://www.marxists.org/reference/archive/mao/selected-works/volume-9/mswv9_01.htm, accessed 25 December 2013.
38 In Chinese characters, 国安. The full name is 中华人民共和国国家安全部 [PRC Ministry for State Security]. See above on the creation of the National Security Committee.
39 #25 2011-3.
40 #20 2011-1. Also #21 2011-1.
41 In Chinese characters, 被旅游. #25 2011-2, #25 2010-2.

taken to a place in the countryside, often a holiday resort, in the company of two or more *guobao* officers.[42] Or the lawyer may be put under 'soft detention' (*ruanjin*),[43] a form of house-arrest without legal basis,[44] that may also affect the wider household (family) of the target person.

Numerous accounts of rights defenders illustrate how soft detention can be imposed, often without warning: on wanting to leave his or her home, the stability preservation target finds (usually) two or more *guobao* officers standing guard outside the door of the flats or outside the main entrance of the residential compound,[45] and is told she may not leave. Exactly how strict 'soft detention' is, whether, for instance, the lawyer might be allowed to leave home in the company of the *guobao* officers on certain occasions, or be allowed to receive visitors, is often left to the *guobao* officer's discretion. It consequently allows for negotiation that may be further used to control the lawyer. One lawyer explained that one might distinguish between two kinds of *guobao* officer, those ('the vast majority') who were not seeking personal advancement, who were just doing their job to put food on the table, for instance, because they were already approaching retirement, and those who had 'personal motivation' to be aggressive and eager on their job:

> Those others who have personal motives, they may want to seek personal advancement, and therefore, they're willing to do evil; and they will take the initiative in doing evil. For example, they may of their own accord gather more evidence that can put their target in prison ... they will be particularly zealous. Say their superior didn't explicitly say [your target] must not leave their home, following them around is enough. Well, then maybe that particular *guobao* will decide not to let you out of the house at all.[46]

Direct violence

The threat of violence is sometimes realised in casual, but still apparently calculated ways. Numerous lawyers have been beaten or otherwise attacked.[47] Attacks have included the case of Lawyer Zhang Kai who was attacked by unidentified men in several cars without number plates while driving in Beijing,[48]

---

42 E.g. #8 2010-1.
43 In Chinese characters, 软禁.
44 The authorities often do not claim that rights lawyers are under 'residential surveillance' when putting them under 'soft detention' except when the lawyer is to be detained in a place that is neither his residence nor an official police detention centre, as in the case of Lawyer Yang Zaixin in the Beihai case (Chapter 5). Residential surveillance (see Article 73, 2012 CPL) is a form of house-arrest while under criminal investigation.
45 Observation, e.g. 2011, 2007.
46 #2 2010-1.
47 See for an incomplete list of incidents He Yang (何杨), *Disbarment* (吊照门), documentary film, June 2010.
48 'Lawyer who had taken on legal representation in "My Father is Li Gang" case aggressively chased by unidentified individuals in middle of night' (代理过"我爸是李刚"案的张凯律师, 半夜突遭不明身份多人追杀)', China Aid, 14 December 2010, at http://www.chinaaid.net/2010/12/blog-post_14.html, accessed 26 December 2013.

at a time when he was handling a high-profile case, and beatings of lawyers outside courtrooms or court buildings mentioned in Chapter 4. The crackdown on lawyers that began in February 2011, too, was preceded by seemingly casual violence against individual lawyers:

> The *guobao* [name] from that Yangfangdian police station grabbed me by the collar right in front of police officer [name] and police officer[s] from the Yangfangdian police station; in a rage, he smashed my head against the wall. The police officers around at the time didn't care at all. I said I wanted to bring a complaint. A police officer said, 'they're not going to take your complaint if it concerns a police officer.' [49]

Lawyer Jiang Tianyong was 'disappeared' for two months only three days after this casual assault;[50] and numerous cases of beatings of lawyers continued to occur, especially since the beginning of the 2013 crackdown on movements involving lawyers.[51]

The unpremeditated or casual nature of assaults can increase the sense of insecurity resulting from them. A lawyer who was attacked by a police officer interrogating him for talking back explained:

> On the evening of the [date], I was in [another city] and my wife rang me up to let me know that they had again glued up the door of our flat while she took our child to school in the morning.[52]

Against this background consciousness of persecution, as it were, the lawyer went on to describe his fruitless efforts to visit a friend at that time constrained by the security apparatus on one of the following days. In the course of these efforts, he had temporarily taken the battery out of his phone:

> [Eventually] I gave up and walked out. Just as I was taking some pictures of the scene around me, police officer [V] turned up by my side. I had been prepared for this, because I had consciously turned my phone on again.

---

49 Tian Xi (田溪) '江天勇律师被海淀分局国保殴打 [Lawyer Jiang Tianyong beaten by Haidian branch police office guobao officers]', *Sound of Hope*, 16 February 2011, at http://www.soundofhope.org/node/69493/print, accessed 2 January 2014.

50 Prior to being 'disappeared' another lawyer, Liu Shihui, was assaulted by unidentified thugs outside his home in Guangzhou, leaving Liu with a broken leg and an apparently inflamed wound. Liu Shihui had left home with the – publicly stated – intention to participate in a 'jasmine rally' planned for that day. '刘士辉律师遭广州国保暴打骨折 [Lawyer Liu Shihui attacked by Guangzhou *guobao*, suffers bone fracture]', 20 February 2011, *Sound of Hope*, at http://soundofhope.org/programs/162/181866-1.asp, accessed 25 December 2013; picture of injury available at http://img.ly/33J1, accessed 25 December 2013.

51 Discussed in Chapter 7.

52 #103 2012-1.

I preferred being taken away from [that place] to being taken away from home. So, I knew what was going to happen.[53]

In the event, however, the *guobao* officers did not merely catch up with their surveillance target but also interrogated him, which resulted in an altercation:

V beating me – that was actually a sort of accident. It just happened because V got too angry. He had . . . taken twenty people out to look for me over several days. So he was really furious, and he swore at me really badly. He was also extremely angry because I had publicised the fact that they had tracked and followed me and he had threatened me at an earlier time . . . We yelled at each other and abused each other . . . 'Son of a b–!'

We were sitting opposite one another on two sofas with a small tea table between us, and there were just two other *guobao* officers in the room [shows that they were standing at a distance, one of them by the door]. Then, suddenly, he hit me, really fast. I immediately felt as though my eardrum had been burst. Three times, with his fists, on the ears . . . He had really lost control over himself because normally when they beat people they do it in a way that leaves no injuries . . . Then I realised that he was speaking to me but that I could no longer hear what he was saying. I just kept saying, 'I want to see a doctor. I want to see a doctor for a check-up.' And 'You have beaten me; I want to make a complaint.' I could still hear a little bit, actually, I could hear there was a sound, but couldn't understand what was said. But eventually I made it out: He was saying, 'I haven't beaten *a person*.'[54] What he meant was, 'beating *you* isn't beating a person.' And he also said, 'What evidence do you have that I've beaten you!' And then the young *guobao* officer also said – speaking in a very loud voice – 'Absolutely! Who can prove that we've beaten you! What evidence do you have!' A real rogue (*wulai*).[55]

Then they walked out and then they came back. I couldn't hear very clearly everything they said [to me], but they talked about 'cooperating' (*peihe*)[56] and about 'having crossed our bottom line' (*chu le dixian*).[57] I said, 'What bottom line! The only line between you and me is the law. You and I can respect law that's been published. But if you start wanting to determine any other line, we've got a problem, right? Then this person draws the line one way and that person another way, right?' We argued till after 2 am. Then we finally left that place. On walking out I said I wanted to see a doctor. But V said, 'You're not the one to decide where to go. If you want to go somewhere, now, you need our approval. Get into the car!'[58]

---

53 #103 2012-1.
54 In Chinese characters, 我没有打人.
55 In Chinese characters, 无赖.
56 In Chinese characters, 配合.
57 In Chinese characters, 触了底线.
58 #103 2012-1.

The lawyer was driven around for some time – possibly while the police officers negotiated a way of handling this incident with their superiors – before being taken back home. He was not allowed to see a doctor until several days later, and even then the doctor, who was from a military hospital, would not provide him with a diagnosis. A few days passed before a diagnosis confirmed that one eardrum had been burst and the other ear been injured.[59]

In this incident, the officer who dealt the blows that injured the lawyer was not acting in accordance with orders. But this does not mean that his actions could not be understood to be part of a system in which there is an overall point and purpose to such casually violent attacks. The lawyer, in drawing attention to the arbitrary nature of 'our bottom line' expresses the point concisely, and also accurately positions himself and the nature of the challenge that rights lawyers pose to the security apparatus. On the one hand, there is a force purporting to represent State power that can afford to be randomly and viciously violent, providing feeble references to 'our bottom line' *ex post facto*. On the other hand, there are rights lawyers insisting on respect for law that fulfils the minimum standards of a good legal order – one of these requirements, as Fuller and others have pointed out,[60] is that laws be publicised, of course. The 'justifications' offered by the police officer do not withstand scrutiny but they do illustrate that there is a method and system in such casual violence – that orders given or promises extracted months earlier can be used to 'justify' violent acts. There is a sense, albeit a very thin one, in which the officers seek justification by reference to rules: the police officer, having seriously injured the lawyer, claims that this was done because the lawyer had committed a transgression.

Combined effect of the measures

Taken together, these measures combine to create a profound sense of insecurity not only on the part of the target person but also on the part of their immediate social environment, especially their family. The security apparatus creates fear for others in the target person; it also directly targets family members, friends, etc., by humiliating or terrorising them in order to exert indirect influence on the target. The targeted person, in turn, may react by displacing their own fear and concern to others in his or her social environment; and such displacement may at times further strengthen the terrorising efforts of the security apparatus.

Even lawyers who had experienced particularly terrible torture have said that feelings about their families far exceeded any other cruelty they had experienced. In a private communication, Lawyer Gao Zhisheng wrote in 2008, while under strict house-arrest, that he felt that even being alive was 'an unexpected bonus' for him:

> [B]ut the fact that [my daughter] Gege cannot go to school, this inexorable reality, has made us despair. [My family] . . . have not done anything; yet

---

59 Diagnosis on file with author.
60 Lon Fuller, *The Morality of Law*, Yale University Press, New Haven, CT: 1969.

from 15 August 2006 they have been subjected to daily surveillance by no fewer than 20 secret police officers who have been harassing them in a savage and terrorizing manner that is frightening even just to hear about. [61]

Gao's wife and two children were able to leave China and settle abroad in early 2009. In 2012 his daughter, who had experienced great mental torment immediately after escaping from China, related how she had been ostracised at school when she was around 13 or 14 (ca. 2007):

> The teacher said very clearly to all the students in the class, 'Geng Ge has a political criminal in her family. You must be careful. If you speak to her, you may be sent to prison. Your teacher doesn't tell you a lot, or go into depth – you will understand that.' The teacher had asked me to leave the classroom to get a book and I overheard her when I returned. At the time, I felt ... I was thirteen or fourteen at the time and I don't know how to put it, I felt as though the whole world did not want me. And those police officers, they would every now and then beat me in front of the whole class. It felt as though one was not a person at all. It felt as though I was a dog, and not an ordinary dog, but one they used to flaunt their power.[62]

The fear created by the exposure of entire families to arbitrary violence is not often expressed directly but can be sensed from much of what the lawyers relate. Not infrequently they themselves seem to express themselves indirectly, through references to the friends that appear to displace their experiences to another person. Thus when lawyer Gao was able to meet friends and journalists during a brief period after an extended period of forced disappearance in 2010, he dwelt at length on concerns for the wellbeing of his family – then already safely out of China – and on his fears and concerns for the safety and health of these and several other friends. He was 'disappeared' again shortly afterward.[63]

A place of absolute safety becomes elusive and unreachable. A lawyer who had suffered abductions and violence himself and whose family had also been affected commented as follows:

> I heard that Chen Guangcheng had fled to the American Embassy. They said he was in an 'absolutely safe place', and when I heard that, I knew immediately that they could only mean the US Embassy. Not even the British Embassy – not even the Embassy of any smaller country would have been 'absolutely safe'. For after all, Chen Guangcheng had once been grabbed away from outside [Lawyer Jiang Tianyong's] home and his mother and child from outside [Lawyer] Teng Biao's home, and his wife had been

61 Private communication (December 2008), on file with author.
62 NDTV, '专访耿格(二)：迫害中像狗　来美挺胸做人　[Interview with Geng Ge (2) – being like a dog under repression, holding her head up like a person after coming to the U.S.]', posted 20 July 2012, at http://www.youtube.com/watch?v=xc-DLHS5fTc&feature=related, accessed 25 December 2013.
63 Observation (April 2010).

followed and grabbed away at the airport just after she left [rights defenders] Hu Jia's and Zeng Jinyan's home. Even if you go to any trusted friend's place in Beijing, none of those places will be safe.[64]

Limited uses of the formal criminal process

From the perspective of the authorities, uses of the formal criminal process to subdue rights lawyers or lay rights defenders have advantages in that they allow the State to claim it is acting 'in accordance with law'.[65] The trial by itself could also be used as a platform to expose political criminals and put them on show, such as was done in early decades of the PRC; but so far, the State has largely refrained from doing so. Lawyers have been charged with and some have been convicted of crimes affecting the integrity of the judicial process, public order and national security, including 'falsifying evidence', 'obstructing public office', 'gathering a crowd in a public place to obstruct order' and 'inciting subversion'. After all, from the perspective of the authorities, much of legal advocacy on the part of rights lawyers is viewed as subversive, even though the Criminal Law (CL) has excised certain clearly 'political' provisions such as 'counterrevolutionary activities' crime and replaced them with politically somewhat more neutral language such as 'inciting subversion of State power or overthrow of the socialist system'.[66]

> As long as you engage in rights defence, you may, superficially speaking, act within the law; but the government will never see it that way: for them, you attack them and shake their legitimacy (*dongyao ta de hefaxing*).[67]

However, by using laws that reflect liberal legal principles such as transparency, publicness and fairness of the legal process, in addition to many substantive rights, the authorities lay themselves open to criticism and exposure of any failure on their part to follow legal rules. The use of the formal criminal process therefore comes at a cost. The cost is especially high in those areas of 'criminality' in which the current legal and political system is especially conflicted, in particular, the 'crime' of political dissent.

Uses of the criminal process are therefore in some ways burdensome, especially when the target is relatively well known. For one thing, there is a general public expectation that criminal legal processes are open and adversarial, and follow the rules. They can be criticised for any rule violation that occurs. In none of the

---

64 #103 2012-1.
65 This point is also made in Elizabeth Lynch, 'China's rule of law mirage: the regression of the legal profession since the adoption of the 2007 Lawyers Law', 42 *Georgetown University International Law Review* (2010) 535, especially at p. 581.
66 Teng Biao, 'The political meaning of the crime of "subverting state power"', translated from the Chinese by Pinky Choy and Eva Pils, in Jean-Philippe Béja, Fu Hualing and Eva Pils, *Liu Xiaobo, Charter 08 and Challenges of Political Reform in China*, Hong Kong University Press, Hong Kong: 2012.
67 #21 2011-2 30. In Chinese characters, 动摇它的合法性.

well-known cases in which rights lawyers or lay rights defenders have been prosecuted, for instance, has the legal process been without major flaws. Where there is a judicial decision, as one rights lawyer put it:

> At least there will be a process. Each party has an opportunity to appear on stage. Say, if they detained [the suspect] and then the lawyer had problems meting the client, etc. then at various stages of the criminal process, there will be a platform for voicing these concerns.[68]

Also, while high-profile cases themselves may progress in an ordinary way, any 'ordinary' infraction of the rules within the criminal process can have extraordinary consequences if the target or sympathisers manage to put out an account; and this is becoming easier as communications techniques diversify.

One of the key provisions that has thus far served as the basis for retaliatory criminal prosecution of lawyers is Article 306 of the Criminal Law (CL).[69] It provides for criminal punishment of lawyers who falsify or suppress evidence or instruct their clients to falsify or suppress evidence. In practice, this translates into a risk of prosecution of the lawyer if defence witnesses give evidence that is different from their statements they gave to the police. The main problem with Article 306 CL has been the targeting of lawyers – not necessarily lawyers previously known as 'rights lawyers' – in a retaliatory way for trying to challenge the prosecution's evidence e.g. by producing witness statements contradicting those of the prosecution, or challenging the reliability of confessions. It is for this reason that in an uncharacteristically high number of cases lawyers detained on Article 306 charges were later not publicly indicted.[70]

68 #88 2013-2.
69 Article 306 CL: If, in criminal proceedings, a defender or agent ad litem destroys or forges evidence, helps any of the parties destroy or forge evidence, or coerces the witness or entices him into changing his testimony in defiance of the facts or give false testimony, he shall be sentenced to fixed-term imprisonment of not more than three years or criminal detention; if the circumstances are serious, he shall be sentenced to fixed-term imprisonment of not less than three years but not more than seven years. Where a witness's testimony or other evidence provided, shown or quoted by a defender or agent ad litem is inconsistent with the facts but is not forged intentionally, it shall not be regarded as forgery of evidence. CECC translation at http://www.cecc.gov/resources/legal-provisions/criminal-law-of-the-peoples-republic-of-china, accessed 25 December 2013. Article 307 CL (*ibid.*), addresses non-lawyers and stipulates different rules for charges against them, creating bias.
70 To quote, 'An All China Lawyers' Association officer, who asked not to be named, said in the 10 years after the clause was introduced in 1997, at least 200 lawyers had been detained under clause 306. At least half were proven innocent or not prosecuted, but those convicted faced jail terms and were disbarred for life.' Ng Tze-wei, 'Until clause goes, defence lawyers are just decoration', *South China Morning Post*, 7 July 2011, at http://www.scmp.com/article/972741/until-clause-goes-defence-lawyers-are-just-decoration, accessed 25 December 2013. Mao Lixin (毛立新), '律师伪证罪的追诉程序探析 [Analysis of the handling of crimes of falsification of evidence by lawyers]', 30 August 2011, at http://blog.sina.com.cn/s/blog_4e7afe890102dssf.html, accessed 25 December 2013; Ran Yanfei, 'When Chinese criminal defense lawyers become the criminals', (32) *Fordham International Law Journal* (2009) 986, at http://ir.lawnet.fordham.edu/cgi/viewcontent.cgi?article=2152&context=ilj, accessed 25 December 2013.

Notable recent cases of retaliatory prosecution have included that of Lawyer Li Zhuang (who was convicted under Article 306) and the 'Beihai Lawyers case'. In both cases, lawyers were tried on Article 306 charges after alleging torture of their clients in the criminal process. The case of Li Zhuang well illustrates the risks the Party–State takes if it opts to prosecute lawyers. The prosecution of Lawyer Li Zhuang attracted widespread and public critical comment from prominent legal academics such as Professor He Weifang of Peking University Law School and Professor Jiang Ping of the China University of Politics and Law.[71] It also drew attention to a considerable amount of evidence indicating that torture and other abuses in the context of the 'Chongqing Strike-Black' (anti-mafia) campaign orchestrated by the then Chongqing Party Secretary were common and systemic. Evidence of torture in a closely related context was also produced by a friend and colleague of lawyer Li Zhuang's who had acted as the criminal defence lawyer for another co-defendant in the same case. (The co-defendant alleged similar torture methods, supported by evidence such as deep scars on his wrists. While Li Zhuang's client was given a custodial sentence after alleging that Li Zhuang had induced him to make 'false' allegations of torture, the other co-defendant was given the death sentence and executed weeks later.)[72]

In the 'Beihai Lawyers' case, four criminal defence lawyers including one well-known 'rights lawyer', Yang Zaixin, conducted their own investigation of a murder case after learning that the defendants had been subjected to especially cruel torture, and forced to confess. They found witnesses whose statements, together with other evidence such as the empty state of the deceased's stomach, etc., amounted to strong evidence that the defendants could not be guilty as charged. As a result, the authorities charged these lawyers themselves with falsifying evidence under Article 306 CL and detained them. The Beihai Lawyers' case led to the formation of a team of prominent criminal defence lawyers, publicised information both on the original murder trial and on the case of their colleagues (three lawyers were soon released, but Yang Zaixin refused to collaborate and was not) via blogs, microblogs and the print media outside of Guangxi Zhuang Autonomous Region.[73] Their reports attracted wide attention, all the

---

71 Although his conviction triggered vocal protest from parts of the legal profession and academia persons close to this case hold the opinion that general public opinion has remained against Li Zhuang due to the 'bad press' he had domestically. Author conversations December 2011. See e.g. Xu Kai (徐凯), '李庄案第三季前传 [Prequel to third phase of the Case of Li Zhuang]', Caijing Net [财经网], 14 December 2011, at http://blog.caijing.com.cn/expert_article-151567-27454.shtml, accessed 25 December 2013. Cp. also Liu Sida and Lily Liang and Terence C. Halliday, 'The trial of Li Zhuang: Chinese lawyers' collective action against populism', 1 *Asian Journal of Law and Society* (2014), at http://ssrn.com/abstract=2333258, accessed 1 January 2014.
72 Lan Rongjie, 'Killing the lawyer as the last resort: the Li Zhuang Case and its effects on criminal defence in China', in Mike McConville and Eva Pils (eds.), *Criminal Justice in China: Comparative Perspectives*, Edward Elgar Publishing, Cheltenham: 2013.
73 Zhao Yanhong (赵艳红), '"北海律师伪证案" 追踪: 维权律师团成员称遭围攻　警方回应 [Follow-up on Beihai lawyers case: rights defence lawyers claims they were besieged and attacked, police responds]', People's net (人民网), 19 July 2011, at http://legal.people.com.cn/GB/15195351.html, accessed 2 January 2014.

more after members of the defence lawyer team were themselves brutally beaten by some 40 or 50 people of unknown identity, with Lawyer Li Jinxing knocked unconscious in a hotel room on the evening before the scheduled trial.[74] One of the Beihai lawyers was placed under 'non-residential residential surveillance' (police detention in an ordinary apartment that can amount to forced disappearance),[75] followed by informal house-arrest at home that also affected his family.[76] The eventual retrial of the murder case lasted several days and allowed the lawyers to challenge the use of confessions obtained under torture; eventually the prosecution did not make use of these confessions.[77] This case was another illustration of the pitfalls of criminal prosecution from the perspective of the Party–State. The fact that the remaining lawyer's case was heard several times without having been decided indicated hesitation and embarrassment on the part of the authorities,[78] and the case against Yang Zaixin was eventually dropped.

In sum, the use of Article 306 of the Criminal Law, much criticised, harmful and intimidating though it is, has also been fraught with difficulty for the

74 #85 2013-1. The attackers included women who had claimed a connection with the murder victim's family. *Ibid.* See also Human Rights In China, 'Defense lawyers in high-profile Beihai case beaten while police watch', 21 October 2011, at http://www.hrichina.org/en/content/5587, accessed 3 January 2014.

75 Lawyer Yang Zaixin was taken into 'residential surveillance' by the police, after having been held in pretrial detention for the maximum amount of time available to the authorities. '广西维权律师杨在新被监视居住后失踪 [Guangxi rights defence lawyer Yang Zaxin disappears after being put under residential surveillance]', 维权网/*Weiquanwang*, 17 March 2012, at http://wqw2010. blogspot.com/2012/03/blog-post_17.html, accessed 25 December 2013; Human Rights In China, 'Guangxi lawyer Yang Zaixin put under residential surveillance after nine months in detention', 22 March 2012, at http://www.hrichina.org/content/5936, accessed 25 December 2013. He was held in an apartment the authorities rented for this purpose and guarded by armoured police (#85 2013-1).

76 Jiang Qiming (江启明), '维权律师杨在新被中共软禁 家人生活困难 [Rights Lawyer Yang Zaixin house-arrested by the Party, family in difficulties]', *Dajiyuan* (大纪元) 18 May 2012, at http://www.epochtimes.com/gb/12/5/18/n3592191.htm%E7%BB%B4%E6%9D%83%E5% BE%8B%E5%B8%88%E6%9D%A8%E5%9C%A8%E6%96%B0%E8%A2%AB%E4%B8% AD%E5%85%B1%E8%BD%AF%E7%A6%81-%E5%AE%B6%E4%BA%BA%E7%94% 9F%E6%B4% BB%E5%9B%B0% E9%9A%BE, accessed 25 December 2013.

77 Author conversation (December 2011). Of the five co-defendants, one was released without charges whereas the other four's conviction was changed to a different crime (!), 'creating a social disturbance.' Despite not obtaining the full acquittal they deserved, this resulted in the four defendants immediate release from imprisonment. Chan Kai Yee, 'Criminal Defense Lawyers Rehabilitated in Beihai,' 10 February 2013 at http://tiananmenstremendousachievements.word press.com/2013/02/10/china-criminal-defense-lawyers-rehabilitated-in-beihai/.

78 Chen Yanhui (谌彦辉), '内地现律师组团打官司 [The phenomenon of lawyers' litigation teams emerges in Mainland]', 9 January 2012, at http://news.ifeng.com/shendu/fhzk/ detail_2012_01/09/11851698_0.shtml, accessed 25 December 2013. Wei Wenhao (韦文浩), '北海律师案息而未决 [Beihai lawyers: case resting, but not resolved]', Legal Weekend [法治周末], 28 December 2012, at http://news.sohu.com/20111228/n330507979.shtml, accessed 25 December 2013; Li Jinxing (李金星), '北海！警号 601153！警号020156！[Beihai! 601153 Police ID number! 020156 Police ID Number!]', Caijing Blog [财经网博客], 8 August 2011, at http://blog.caijing.com.cn/expert_article-151499-23239.shtml, accessed 25 December 2013.

authorities, not necessarily led to convictions,[79] and on occasion backfired.[80] Cases of a similarly 'embarrassing' nature had occurred already in the 1990s, for example in the case of lawyer Liu Zhengqing;[81] but the availability of mass online communication tools must make the potential embarrassment to the authorities an increasing concern.

Similar difficulties arise for the authorities if they rely on other criminal offences to prosecute (rights) lawyers. While rights lawyers and rights defenders have been charged with a variety of other crimes, three further criminal offences of special importance are 'obstructing public office',[82] 'creating a disturbance'[83] and 'inciting subversion' as well as 'subversion' until 2012;[84] from 2013, the authorities widely relied on the further offences of 'illegal assembly' and 'gathering a crowd in a public place to disrupt order'.[85] These criminal offences, in contrast to Article 306, are directly concerned with aspects of 'social stability preservation' and in the wide sense appropriate to describe the responsibility of the *guobao* police, with internal national security. 'Inciting subversion' and 'creating a disturbance', in particular, are frequently used in the context of criminal prosecutions for politically critical expression, and carry potentially high sentences. Persons who are suspected of such crimes tend to fall in the categories of

79 Fu Hualing, 'When lawyers are prosecuted: the struggle of a profession in transition', 2 *Journal of Comparative Law* (2007) 95–133.
80 In reaction to criticism, the Criminal Procedure Law (CPL) was changed in 2012 to reflect the view that it would be unfair to single out lawyers as particularly likely offenders. Its Article 42 now states that it is illegal 'for defence lawyers *or any other person*' to falsify or suppress evidence or induce others to do so. This does not remove the threat of prosecution under Article 306 of the Criminal Law. See also Chen Weidong (陈卫东), '刑诉法修改:权力与权利的博弈 [CPL revision: contest between power and rights]', Nanfang Renwu Zhoukan [南方人物周刊], 13 September 2011, at http://nf.nfdaily.cn/nfrwzk/content/2011-09/13/content_29780011. htm, accessed 25 December 2013.
81 'Review of selected Article 306 cases (5) – the case of Liu Zhengqing [刑法 306 条经典案例回放 (5)——湖南刘正清案]', at http://liusida.fyfz.cn/art/560557.htm, accessed 25 December 2013.
82 For example, rights advocate Ni Yulan (倪玉兰) was convicted of this offence in 2008. See He Yang (何杨), 应急避难场所 (Emergency shelter) (do you want to change to the same with note no. 96? – He Yang (何杨), *Emergency Shelter* (应急避难所), independent documentary, . . .), June 2010, at http://vimeo.com/12677411, accessed 25 December 2013; Paul Mooney, 'Shows of force', *South China Morning Post*, 25 October 2010, at http://www.scmp.com/article/728505/ shows-force, accessed 25 December 2013.
83 For example, Wang Lihong (王荔蕻) was convicted of this offence in 2011. See Ai Xiaoming (艾晓明), 王大姐 (*Auntie Wang*), 2011, independent documentary film on file with author; Charles Hutzler, 'Wang Lihong, Chinese online activist, sentenced to prison for staging protest', 9 September 2011, at http://www.huffingtonpost.com/2011/09/09/wang-lihong-prison_n_ 955226.html, accessed 25 December 2013. Ni Yulan (倪玉兰) was convicted of the same offence in July 2012. See BBC, 'China activist Ni Yulan's jail term reduced', 27 July 2012, at http://www.bbc.co.uk/news/world-asia-china-19009132, accessed 25 December 2013.
84 For a discussion of this crime, see Teng Biao (滕彪), 'The political meaning of the crime of "subverting state power"', in Jean-Philippe Béja, Fu Hualing and Eva Pils, *Liu Xiaobo, Charter 08 and Challenges of Political Reform in China*, Hong Kong University Press, Hong Kong: 2012. It discusses the fate of lawyer Gao Zhisheng (高智晟), convicted of 'inciting subversion' in 2006, among others.
85 Chinese Human Rights Defenders (CHRD), 'Individuals unlawfully detained in crackdown on peaceful assembly, association & expression', updated 23 December 2013, at http:// chrdnet.com/2013/07/individuals-detained-in-crackdown-on-assembly-and-association/, accessed 3 January 2014.

the already marginalised: petitioners, rights defenders, dissidents, rights lawyers, and so on. Their prosecution/persecution attracts much less criticism domestically; but it can be paid more attention internationally especially in cases of prominent dissidents such as the writer Liu Xiaobo, sentenced to 11 years for 'inciting subversion' in early 2010. The fact that crimes directly related to political action draw more attention was widely regarded as one of the reasons why the authorities chose to prosecute Xu Zhiyong, Guo Feixiong (Yang Maodong) and others for comparatively minor public order crimes in 2013.[86]

As mentioned above, any abuses, however 'ordinary', can become a source of recrimination, embarrassment, or even worse consequences, especially when the identity of the victim ensures a high degree of public attention. For example, during his period of criminal investigation detention, lawyer Gao Zhisheng was made to sit motionless for hours on end. The use of *zuo ban* is not unusual.[87] But with a high-profile detainee such as Gao Zhisheng, who later recanted his confession,[88] the facts about his treatment in investigation detention became publicly reported news. Rights defender Chen Guangcheng's experience of a flawed trial process was also widely reported in 2005 (even though at that time communication technology was more limited). Of course, when the degree of violence used against relatively well-known suspects, defendants or convicts is unusually high, this information is even more explosive. When rights defender and legal worker Guo Feixiong (Yang Maodong) reported about brutal torture suffered while serving a prison sentence, this was also widely reported,[89] as was the alleged torture of rights lawyer Wang Yonghang in pretrial detention in 2009.[90]

Describing his experience of torture while in formal detention, an interlocutor commented:

> I was arrested on [date] and I was nearly beaten to death . . . [The first time] they beat me because . . . I had refused to admit guilt. They had offered me

86 Beijing Municipal Procuracy No. 1, 'Indictment of Xu Zhiyong by Beijing Municipal Procuracy No. 1', 13 December 2013, translated by China Change, 21 December 2013, at http://chinachange.org/2013/12/21/indictment-of-xu-zhiyong-by-beijing-municipal-peoples-procuratorate-no-1-branch/, accessed 2 January 2014; Guangzhou Municipal Public Security Bureau, 'Police indictment opinion for Guo Feixiong and Sun Desheng', 10 December 2013, translated at Siweiluozi Blog, at http://www.siweiluozi.net/2013/12/translation-police-indictment-opinion. html, 26 December 2013, accessed 2 January 2014.
87 See http://blog.sina.com.cn/s/blog_54c8017f0100gfx5.html for a detailed description of what *zuo banr* (坐板儿) involves and for a domestic online dictionary entry mentioning the use of *zuo banr* http://zhidao.baidu.com/question/206073817.html?fr=qrl&cid=143&index=4, accessed 25 December 2013.
88 Gao Zhisheng, 'Gao Zhisheng solemnly denies all charges by Chinese authorities', *Epoch Times*, 8 September 2007, at http://en.epochtimes.com/news/7-9-8/59565.html, accessed 25 December 2013.
89 'Freed China dissident was tortured in custody, says human rights group', *Associated Press/Guardian*, 14 September 2011, at http://www.guardian.co.uk/world/2011/sep/14/freed-china-dissident-tortured, accessed 25 December 2013.
90 Bai Mei, 'Chinese human rights lawyer sentenced to seven years', *Epoch Times*, 2 December 2009, at http://www.theepochtimes.com/n2/china-news/chinese-human-rights-lawyer-sentenced-seven-years-25905.html, accessed 25 December 2013.

a deal – if I admitted guilt and said in court that democracy must develop under CCP leadership I would be let out and they would arrange for me to return to work . . . [*details omitted*]. I refused. They convicted me . . . even though they really had no evidence [*details omitted*]. Inside, the punishments I received were . . . oh, it was hundreds of hundreds of times of endurance. They interrogated me [over 150] times. They did not let me sleep for [over ten] days and nights. They pulled my hair out. And at last they electro-shocked me. . . . After what they did to me these methods became common and they treated some even worse. But until then, I was the first.

I don't want to speak about the details of my experience in prison. They knew anyway that I would not give up on democracy and freedom. So many people in history have been tortured for proselytising, burnt at the stakes, tortured to death, and yet no abandoned their faith. Just think if this can be done in China for the sake of democracy and freedom. How could they get us to accept the beliefs of totalitarianism by crushing our lives! One impor-tant way in which I resisted while inside was hunger-striking. At the climax of that resistance at one point I went on hunger strike for [many days]. My body weight fell [by about two fifths]. I was totally emaciated. Initially I had planned to carry out a [longer] hunger strike but then I was vomiting blood too badly, for several days on end; so I only struck for [a shorter period].[91]

Visitors who learned about the interlocutor's experience relayed it to international NGOs. His hunger strike and the preceding torture experience were reported internationally, triggering protests and appeals:

My hunger-strike was to express my political beliefs, my faith in democracy. It allowed me to make use of this spirit to use the legal authorities as though they were separate from the government whose accomplices they are in fact. This is a moral sort of force. My retaliation against them was not only for myself but also for those who struggle for democracy in the future; it has helped them a lot. Their situation may improve. The prison administration authorities of [the affected province] now all carefully respected the rules. Those policies of the Party and State [laughs] they can actually be turned into a moral force. They reduce some people's suffering.[92]

This rights defender's experience again illustrates the fact that even though the authorities can inflict extreme suffering in the ordinary, formal criminal process, they cannot entirely circumvent the public rules governing this process; and as the rights defender says, these rules express moral requirements bringing them directly in conflict with the pressures the security apparatus seeks to create, and is itself operating under.

91 #63 2012-1.
92 #63 2012-1.

Ni Yulan, after being released from prison, was able to provide a damning public account of her trial and allege horrific experiences in prison, to a widening domestic and international audience. Ni's plight was underlined by the fact that even after her release from prison, she and her husband were forced to camp out in a public park, since the police forbade anyone from renting accommodation to her.[93] She also became the main character in a documentary film published online in Chinese, and shown to an international audience in English.[94] Later, Ni and her husband Dong were forcibly removed to a guesthouse, where they stayed in conditions amounting to semi-confinement[95] for several months before being criminally detained, tried and convicted of 'creating a public disturbance'.[96]

In March 2012, after Bo Xilai's demotion, lawyer Li Zhuang reported that he, too, had been tortured during pretrial detention, when he was strapped to a metal 'tiger seat' chair and forced to sit motionless for three days and nights.[97] Ironically, the person who had ultimate responsibility for Lawyer Li Zhuang's torture, Bo Xilai, was later placed in informal *shuanggu*[98] detention, a measure generally imposed by the Party Discipline and Inspection Committee in cases in which the suspect is a Party official.[99]

In these cases, one obvious problem for the authorities is that responsibility can be clearly attributed to them as long as the person affected is in a stage of the formal criminal process. Critics had no difficulty in attributing violence inflicted on rights defenders to the authorities at that time holding them in various forms of 'lawful' detention, and so far as abuses could be documented, they triggered complaints and submissions to the relevant UN bodies.

Another problem is that the goals the Party–State needs to achieve, according to its own perception, by targeting rights lawyers as political enemies and 'inciting subversion' suspects, cannot be achieved by following the rules of criminal procedure. Cases in which public political expression is treated as crime, in particular, pose at least two special challenges to the authorities; first, *because* there is hardly ever any real issue concerning criminal evidence (in most cases, the forms of expression have been published in the name of the defendant or otherwise been publicly recorded), there is little opportunity for trying to extract information as such from the suspect or defendant. Second, the content on account of which

---

93 Author observation (June 2012).
94 He Yang (何杨), *Emergency Shelter* (应急避难所), independent documentary, 2010, at http://vimeo.com/12677411.
95 Author observation (July 2011–January 2012).
96 *Supra.*
97 Reuters, 'Lawyer tells of torture in a "tiger seat"', *South China Morning Post*, 30 March 2012. Li Zhuang reports being tied to a tiger chair for three days and three nights.
98 In Chinese characters, 双规.
99 Flora Sapio, *Sovereign Power and the Law in China*, Brill, Leiden and Boston, MA: 2010, Chapter 3. In conversation, a lawyer with insight into the working of the procuracy explained that in part this was due to the fact that people's procuracies were not allowed to use certain investigative techniques, including electronic surveillance, on Party officials. Therefore they would not be able to obtain information from them, the lawyer said. #69 2012-1.

dissidents, rights lawyers and other rights defenders nowadays are prosecuted for 'inciting subversion', etc. tends to be commonplace in the conditions of China's *de facto* widened opportunities for public expression and criticism of the government and the system.

Moreover the further effects of such trials are less controllable, as was seen notably in the case of dissident Liu Xiaobo. When Liu Xiaobo was sentenced to 11 years in prison, for instance, friends said that this had created 11 good reasons to award him the Nobel Peace Prize, which Liu Xiaobo duly received the following year. Far from stamping him as an outcast, and although it caused great personal suffering, his criminal conviction also raised Liu Xiaobo's status.

Lastly, the Party–State generally cannot achieve the educational goals it pursues or claims to pursue in dealing with cases of speech and thought related crimes. To be fully successful in its handling of a person deemed guilty of a crime of political dissidence or opposition, as certain rights lawyers targeted by 'inciting subversion' prosecutions clearly were, the Party–State must at least make an attempt at 'transforming' the thought of the person in question; or seek to neutralise the supposedly harmful effects that person may continue to have, even though they are punished for past 'crime'. Even though it can control the outcome of a criminal trial and send the targeted person to prison, it cannot reach this further goal in an ordinary criminal process in what has earlier been called the 'state of norms'. As discussed in the following section, the Party–State must therefore resort to the techniques of the 'state of measures' in such cases. A rights defender explained:

> There were two reasons for why I suffered torture in prison. Firstly, in the prison, I helped a Falun Gong practitioner to defend his rights. Second, they were hoping that upon getting out of prison I would be finished – that I would join my family, who had fled abroad.[100]

Yet as just discussed, by using torture in prison, the authorities again run the risk of public exposure and criticism.

As though they were conducting an experiment, having absorbed this lesson from its experiences of handling earlier cases such as that of Gao Zhisheng and Guo Feixiong, the authorities used a combination of 'pretrial' investigation techniques and the techniques of a 'forced disappearance' was used against rights lawyers in the context of the 2011 'Jasmine Crackdown':[101]

> It was not that they threatened him with interrogation, with being charged with crime, or with being imprisoned. It is no longer like that. No – perhaps

---

100 #63 2012-1.
101 Generally, on the jasmine crackdown, Donald C. Clarke, 'China's jasmine crackdown and the legal system', *Chinese Law Prof Blog*, 26 May 2011, at http://lawprofessors.typepad.com/china_law_prof_blog/2011/05/chinas-jasmine-crackdown-and-the-legal-system.html; and on how it affected lawyers. Committee to Support Chinese Lawyers (2011), 'Legal advocacy and the 2011 crackdown in China', at http://www.csclawyers.org/advocacy/, accessed 30 December 2013.

you will be just kept here, in this place, a place that no one even knows about. They will put a black hood over your head. And take you somewhere and torment you there. You won't even get a chance to go to court and get a trial.[102]

After the Jasmine Crackdown, the authorities went back to using the criminal process; but from 2013 they more often relied on public order crimes in doing so.

Enforced disappearance and torture

There can be no doubt, based on conversations with rights lawyers who have been subjected to 'forced disappearances' or *bei shizong*,[103] that the overwhelmingly important stated goal of uses of this measure is not the gathering of criminal evidence against them. Rather it is their 'conversion' (*bei zhuanhua*)[104] and the correction of their thoughts, especially their political views and attitudes toward the Party–State. There can be no doubt, because it is frequently stated to be the goal of the disappearance process by those carrying out disappearances, because of the clear attempts to get 'disappeared' persons to provide evidence of the successful 'correction' of their thoughts, and because victims interpret what is done to them as an attempt to convert or 'brainwash' (*xinao*)[105] them.

Yet rights lawyers who have been subjected to forced disappearances have not been converted, and against the background of detailed descriptions of what has been done to them, genuine conversion is an implausible goal. According to the view taken here, the purpose of forced disappearances and the treatment accompanying it may therefore be understood in analogy to the purported 'purpose' of torture in general. From the perspective of the person inflicting torture, torture's purpose is premised in a pretence of agency and freedom on the part of the torturer, for instance when a person is tortured in order to obtain 'information' from them.[106] Elaine Scarry has argued that torturers need to pretend, as it were, that their victims possess a degree of control over their thoughts and actions that is, in fact, impossible. They need to pretend, for instance, that the person tortured to obtain information is sufficiently in control to provide answers 'truthfully'. Yet in the case of torture, agency is destroyed by torture; under torture, truth loses meaning to the person who wants the torture to stop; and there is a certain sense in which the person themselves can feel that they have stopped being a person.[107] In the case of the forced disappearances detailed here, an added dimension of this process is that the 'disappeared' victim can be required very actively to

---

102 #9 2011-1.
103 In Chinese characters, 被失踪.
104 In Chinese characters, 被转化.
105 In Chinese characters, 洗脑.
106 Gisli H. Gudjohnsson *The Psychology of Interrogation and Confessions; A Handbook*, Wiley, Hoboken, NJ: 2003.
107 Elaine Scarry, *The Body in Pain: The Making and Unmaking of the World*, Oxford University Press, New York and Oxford: 1985.

collaborate in the pretence of free decision making. In view of this apparent logic of forced disappearance, it is suggested that some of the 'lighter' measures discussed above can also be understood as attempts to get their targets to collude in their own subjection.

According to the Declaration on the Protection of All Persons from Enforced Disappearance, an enforced disappearance occurs when 'persons are arrested, detained or abducted against their will or otherwise deprived of their liberty by officials of different branches or levels of government, or by organised groups or private individuals acting on behalf of, or with the support, direct or indirect, consent or acquiescence of the government, followed by a refusal to disclose the fate or whereabouts of the persons concerned or a refusal to acknowledge the deprivation of their liberty, which places such persons 'outside the protection of the law'.[108] In some political contexts, many enforced disappearances ended in assassination of the victim; this has so far not been the case in the disappearances discussed here. Rather, their victims have come back and been able – in some but not all cases – to speak of their experiences.

In the course of the forced disappearances that are reflected in the following narratives, a variety of forms of torture and inhuman and degrading treatment may be used. These include stress positions, for instance on the floor or in specially constructed chairs that allow one to strap a person to the armrests and legs of the chair ('tiger seat'), 'cold room' treatment, beatings with electric batons, in some instances on the detainee's genitals, denial of personal hygiene, denials of foods and sleep and sensory deprivation, as well as verbal abuses and threats. However, there are some publicly available accounts of the details of torture of lawyers during a forced disappearance, most notably among them that by Lawyer Gao Zhisheng, who has been repeatedly subjected to brutal torture and degradation, and after years during which he was largely disappeared, is currently serving a prison sentence.[109]

Assume that the person suffering a forced disappearance is a rights lawyer in his thirties or forties, with a spouse and child or children.[110] He has been engaging in the kinds of rights activism in and outside of institutional spaces such as courtrooms, the internet, and the streets, and has been subjected to the various measures discussed earlier for years. His family, too, have become used to suffering such measures. Prior to his forced disappearance, he has learned to expect it. When it happens, he is assaulted in the street; or asked to come out into the street 'for a chat' with the police; or called in to speak to the police in a police station; or

---

108 Declaration on the Protection of All Persons from Enforced Disappearance, proclaimed by the General Assembly in its resolution 47/133 of 18 December 1992, at http://www.un.org/documents/ga/res/47/a47r133.htm, accessed 25 December 2013.
109 Gao Zhisheng (高智晟) (2007–2), 'Dark night, dark hood, and kidnapping by dark mafia – my account of more than 50 days of torture in 2007', written in November 2007, translated from the Chinese by Human Rights in China, 8 February 2009, at http://blog.sina.com.tw/64777/article.php?pbgid=64777&entryid=595609&comopen=1&trackopen=1, accessed 26 December 2013.
110 The account in the following is amalgamated from narratives. I have discussed their forced appearances during the 'jasmine' crackdown in 2011 with 11 individuals, 10 of whom are rights lawyers.

dragged out of his own flat after the police have broken into it, or after they have obtained access on a pretext.[111] A black hood is placed over his head. He is placed in a car and taken to an undisclosed location:

> They pushed me down by the neck and [due to the black plastic bag] I was unable to tell where we were going. . . . They did not allow me to speak; and they scolded me when I tried, telling me things like, 'Be a bit clever!' and 'Show some quality' – what they mean by 'quality', in their view, that means just being compliant.[112]

At some time in the late evening or night, the hood is taken off, and two or more young men, police officers in their twenties, beat him, most likely by dealing him rapid slaps, possibly 'hundreds' of slaps, in the face. Perhaps they make him kneel in front of them, or try to. Perhaps they make him kneel naked. They may tell him, too, that 'you are not a human being':[113]

> At the time I felt no pain at all. It reminds me of once as a youngster when I was involved in a fight; while it happened I felt no pain at all but afterward I discovered that one finger was swollen and hurting a lot. After the beatings, I felt pain in lots of places all over my body.[114]

In more than one instance, the beatings took place on two consecutive evenings, and then stopped. In almost all instances, the black hood and some short-term use of violence, pain or humiliation such as indicated here comes at the very beginning of the 'disappearance'. It is followed by an opportunity to rest briefly in the lawyer's new environment, a simple hotel room, locked, with the blinds down, where the lawyer will be always in the company of two or more persons throughout his stay.

After a certain number of days (between two and seven), the disappeared person may be taken to a new location, and will be given a set of rules to govern his every minute from now on. For instance, he is allowed a certain number of hours of sleep. But it is part of the regimen that he may be deprived of those hours if police officers from the crime investigation team come to interrogate him:

> I observed that the rules governing me were like Chinese law – they never worked in your favour and could be broken at will! For instance during the first few days, shortly before midnight, they would begin interrogations, and these lasted until 4 or 5 am. That way I got barely any sleep at all.[115]

---

111 E.g. #101 2011-1; #104 2011-1; #105 2011-1; 107 2012–1; 108 2011–1.
112 #1112 2012-1.
113 As reported by Jiang Tianyong (江天勇). Ng Tze-wei, (2011–2), 'Making people vanish', 16 September 2011, at http://pjmooney.typepad.com/my-blog/2011/09/making-people-vanish.html#tp, accessed 26 December 2013.
114 #100 2011-1.
115 #100 2011-1.

Another part of the regimen, reminiscent of the *zuo ban*[116] procedure in police detention centres, is sitting motionless. Throughout the time of the disappearance, moreover, there are always two persons in the room with the lawyer; and they are not allowed to speak to him or to one another:

> First I had to sit facing the wall, in an upright seated position at a very short distance from the wall. The wall was white and I was not allowed to see anything or hear any human language. If I even just slumped a bit, one of the guards would immediately reprimand me, 'what's the matter', and get me to sit straight again. Later I had to sit on the ground with my legs stretched out, the soles of my feet against the wall; that was even more painful. Or they would made me sit on the ground with my knees drawn up, facing the wall. These extended periods of sitting motionless led to bedsores on my lower back; it was quite painful.[117]

Apart from the infliction of pain and sensory deprivation, interrogations are used to threaten people:

> I was told I was suspected of having committed 'incitement to subversion'. Of course I knew it might mean being sent to prison for ten years or longer.[118]
> They asked me three times about Gao Zhisheng, completely out of the blue. The first two times I didn't understand why they did this. The person just asked, 'do you know where Gao Zhisheng is?' I said, 'no – where is he? I don't know either.' But the third time I was asked that the person finally added, 'We can bury you alive,[119] too. The first two days some people will still be asking about you [but not afterward].' That was to threaten me. It did scare me. Not that I thought people would stop asking about me after two days; but I thought, if he dares say that perhaps they will keep me here forever! [One of them also] threatened me with what could happen to my wife and child. That made me *really* angry. When he threatened me like this, I snapped back, '*Your* wife and child might die in a car accident any day!' I was that angry and upset (. . .). What makes you anxious isn't the torture as such [but these kinds of threat].[120]

Indeed what appears to be most effective, from the perspective of the Party-State, is to convey a sense that nothing at all constrains the person in whose power one is:

116　In Chinese characters, 坐板.
117　#100 2011-1. Similar accounts of the situation in detention were provided in #101 2011-1; #108 2011-1; #106 2011-1; #112 2012-1. One of the accounts also described the use of air conditioning, in the middle of winter, and very scant clothing (cold-room torture). Another described the use of shackles for a prolonged period of several weeks.
118　#101 2011-1.
119　'To bury alive' or *huomai* (活埋) is slang for disappearing a person and does not necessarily imply assassination.
120　#100 2011-1.

You didn't know *anything* about what was happening outside . . . In my mind I felt that it might get *very* scary. They might even take me out somewhere and just shoot me dead. Or they might take me to a detention centre: that would have been better, because it would at least have meant that there was a procedure [they would have to follow]; this would not have been the worst.[121]

Through the infliction of physical and mental torture, the interrogations, and the sense of uncertainty described by some victims as 'the worst', the lawyer is gradually prepared for the process above referred to as 'conversion (*zhuanhua*)[122] or correction of his wrong political thought. Another human rights defender reported that he had simply become indifferent to any thoughts expressed in language; and only the most basic manual activities he was allowed to engage in retained meaning and the possibility of pleasure. Lawyer Gao Zhisheng, to date the Chinese lawyer treated worst by the authorities, similarly describes his experience as not only being told that he was not a human being but a beast,[123] but also as treating himself as a 'mere animal' in order to survive his ordeal.

The outward form conversion and correction must take is the writing of 'statements of repentance' (*huiguoshu*):[124]

I knew that no matter what I wrote first, I would definitely be required to rewrite my statement of repentance. At the time of the Cultural Revolution they called that 'making revolution in the depth of one's thoughts' [*sixiang shenchu nao geming*].[125] Initially I wrote that I had not done anything illegal, but perhaps erred in some of my methods. They said, you have not yet understood what your problem is. You must write this more deeply. You must understand that you have a problem with your understanding (*sixiang renshi*)[126] and views (*sixiang lichang*).[127] It was clear that you had to acknowledge that your thought, your political standpoint had been wrong.

While some individuals have expressed that due to the conditions during their disappearance, they became indifferent to ideas, there is no indication that anyone saw themselves as genuinely coming to believe what they professed to think after 'correction': 'Not only did they want to make you say *that* black was white. You also had to explain *why* black was white.'[128]

---

121 #101 2011-1.
122 In Chinese characters, 转化.
123 Compare to the report in Ng Tze-wei, (2011–2), 'Making people vanish', 16 September 2011, at http://pjmooney.typepad.com/my-blog/2011/09/making-people-vanish.html#tp, accessed 26 December 2013.
124 In Chinese characters, 悔过书.
125 In Chinese characters, 思想深处闹革命.
126 In Chinese characters, 思想认识.
127 In Chinese characters, 思想立场.
128 #100 2011-1.

In the last stage of the disappearance, just prior to his release, the lawyer has to write a number of promises in a 'statement of pledges' (*baozhengshu*):[129]

> They clearly needed the statement of pledges, but the statement of repentance was also important . . . They would tell me during the interrogation process that later I would not be allowed to do certain things [if I got out]. So, of course, because I wanted to get out, I would try to come up with some promises. The statement of pledges created psychological pressure. But different people think differently about this. Some people will dismiss it because they have written it under torture. But others feel that it is a deep moral humiliation . . . and there really are people who will look down on you for having written such a thing because it seems to show that your convictions were not strong enough. In Communist education, these kinds of letters were regarded as very, very important, and taken extremely seriously. If someone betrayed their political views after having been detained, it was a really serious matter.[130]

The promises made in the 'statement of pledges' vary from person to person but may include the 'pledge' not to handle sensitive cases, or not to handle any case without permission; not to meet with friends from the *weiquan*[131] circle; not to give interviews, especially not to the foreign media; and not to post political comments online, for instance, on blogs or microblogs: 'In addition, they demanded that I supply information on people in the circle but that I refused to do. That would have been dangerous and it would have made me their spy.'[132]

This method, on the one hand, aims to affect the person who is being interrogated, by making the detainee question their own resolve and integrity, and potentially also by destabilising the position of the detainee among his or her community of friends and allies. On the other hand, in its concrete application it reflects the way the Party–State functions as a bureaucratic organisation. The statements of pledges and of repentance must be obtained not only in order to achieve the psychological goals of coercive interrogation, but also, quite simply, to satisfy a bureaucratic requirement of relevance to the immediate interrogators and handlers of the detainee:

> So I thought of a way round this. I just wrote I would report 'on any criminal activities' I discovered in that circle; one has a duty to do that anyway as a Chinese citizen, according to law. The last day but one [before I was released] a high official appeared and I had to read out the thing into a camera with him there.[133]

---

129 In Chinese characters, 保证书.
130 #101 2011-1.
131 In Chinese characters, 维权.
132 *Ibid.*
133 *Ibid.*

Having given this 'promise' also allows for a semblance of liberty; but it appears from the above comments by a lawyer that this pretence is not for the benefit of the lawyer himself. Instead, it becomes apparent that both the statement of repentance and the statement of pledges are meant to create a pretence for the jailors and interrogators of the disappeared, or – so far as they entertain doubts, as we saw is possible – perhaps for certain higher ranking officials:

> It was a very, very complicated thing I feel that if they had wanted, if they had clearly wanted to brainwash me and to change my thinking, if they had really had that intention, then perhaps my thinking would have changed a little bit. But they could not possibly achieve that in [such a short time]. I think that sort of thing requires a year or so of psychological torture. The time was too short. They would not explicitly require me to change my thinking . . . However, I think that maybe at some level they did think that I had changed my thought. But my friends said that this was impossible; that they [the interrogators] just wanted to get me to produce those things in writings. They just needed to have me write those things . . . I wanted to leave. So of course I did not want to raise the fact I had been tortured with them. I must make them believe that my thought had changed. There was this one person who asked, 'What you wrote there, was that your real thinking or did you write it under pressure?' Of course I said, 'It was my real thinking.' These people did not necessarily know what exactly had been done to me. [And even if they did] they will not necessarily think of many of those things as 'torture'.[134]

How important the pretence at liberty and the possibility of truthfulness was illustrated not only by the dubious interrogator's question related above, but also by the fact that the interrogators sought technical reassurance of the 'truthfulness' of what they were told:

> They did not think that this was in any way false or that there was anything wrong about what they did. They thought that they were simply involved in criminal evidence gathering. Including those people who brought in the lie detector.[135]

Like torture, the use of statement of pledges and statements of repentance creates a pretence of agency that is wholly irrational, as well as humiliating, even though the degree of humiliation resulting from the writing of the statements may be experienced differently by different people.

Plainly, the uses of statements of repentance and pledges described above cannot be made sense of, if we try to understand it as part of a (however bizarre and idiosyncratic) process of criminal investigation. The lawyers were very

134 #101 2011-1.
135 *Ibid.*

clear about this; but also observed that 'thought correction' remained closely intertwined with a (pretence at a) regular criminal process:

> I don't think that they would usually make use of those kinds of statements of repentance in the ordinary criminal process. Maybe they used to – in the old days when there was 'counterrevolutionary crime', of course the statement of repentance could be criminal evidence. [But not today.] However, those officials will need the statement of repentance for internal use to give to their superiors [to demonstrate that they have achieved their mission]. Or perhaps they *might* use the statement of repentance in deciding about the sentence [of certain political criminals]. [Even though the statements I wrote could not be used,] the recordings of those interrogations I underwent are certainly evidence that could be used in court . . . They have everything prepared now [to prosecute me for 'inciting subversion']. They can come and get me any time.[136]

The effect of forced disappearances is not, apparently, the stated ostentatious goal of 'thought correction' or conversion (*zhuanhua*).[137] Neither is it that the lawyers will keep the 'pledges' they have made in their statement of pledges. The effects of forced disappearance became evident when, in mid-2011, persons who had been subjected to it gradually came back. They were returned home, most of them to the homes they had established in the larger cities where their families lived; in some cases the police chose to take them back to their original hometowns where they had family receiving them. They began to break their false 'pledges', so far as we know, the moment they were delivered back home for example by meeting their friends, because everybody recognises how important for mental recovery it is to be able to liaise and exchange experience. While one cannot exclude the possibility that the powers responsible for ordering 'forced disappearances', etc., verily believe that the ostentatious goals of 'thought correction' and 'pledges' are achieved through such processes, this seems somewhat implausible in the fact of all the evidence to the contrary considered above.

In those (apparently rare) cases in which forced disappearances include forcible psychiatric treatment, it seems even less plausible that the security apparatus might be seeking to effect a genuine 'change of mind' on the part of the detained rights defender. In the 2011 'Jasmine' crackdown, some three lawyers are believed to have been subjected to incarceration in psychiatric institutions:

> Only X has seen Y. He had apparently . . . started a hunger-strike [while in detention]. And then he was [taken to the psychiatric hospital and forcibly] given medication . . . So that is why he cannot remember the whole process. When he came out, it was said that he could not even recognize his friends.[138]

---

136 *Ibid.*
137 In Chinese characters, 转化.
138 #44 2011-1.

Y, who had been subjected to this treatment, appeared shaken by it, as well as reluctant to discuss it:

> I have no way of talking about it. I just want to go on working. I want to let past things be past. And I don't want to raise these issues again. I think it is important to move on. I know that in the west there are many healing methods for psychological trauma, but we here we can really only engage in self-guidance ... The most important thing is self-adjustment ... We are very grateful to international society. Without the force of international society we might not persist. But so far as I am concerned, I think that for China's development toward rule of law and democracy we must mainly rely on ourselves. Because if a person can't help themselves, and if they don't even want to help themselves, there is no hope for them.[139]

An attempt to understand forced disappearances and the abuses occurring in the context of disappearances must look beyond its superficial, stated goals. Beyond the obvious torture traumata resulting from the kinds of treatment discussed, its further effects can perhaps be described as a more diffuse, wider production of fear. While the Party–State is, at least in the eyes of rights lawyers, a master of the required techniques, the further consequences of fear are not so calculable. They can include habituation or becoming inured; recovery; and adaptation, for example, but also hatred, resentment, mental instability, the spread of fear to others such as family and friends. For example, shortly after his release, a lawyer wrote on Twitter:

> I think, maybe I have already gone mentally ill, my self-control and my sense of fear are often abnormal. I lost my life for a day. Now I am really afraid. I beseech you not to contact me, OK? I will now return to my hometown, firstly to be with my parents, and secondly to seek psychological counselling. I am not joking![140]

A few months later he added another tweet:

> One, two, three steps, courageously overcoming your fear, you enter the room. No smile, no coquetry; tiny you has become the most valiant defender. The clearest and truest look in your eyes, you scan this darkest and coldest of rooms – paper, pens, the table, Daddy, and the shoe-prints and bruises on Daddy's body. At only two, she has started understanding China![141]

---

139 #107 2012-1.
140 Li Xiongbing (黎雄兵), tweet of 19 May 2011, at https://twitter.com/#!/lixiongbing, accessed 26 December 2013.
141 Li Xiongbing (黎雄兵), tweet of 9 November 2011, at https://twitter.com/#!/lixiongbing, accessed 26 December 2013.

Another rights lawyer who had suffered particularly bad treatment during the Jasmine crackdown described how his family viewed him with anger and despair, as having failed to fulfil the promise of his earlier career, causing complex feelings of anger, and making him feel 'regret and sorrow'. When describing how his father reproached him for having abandoned a safe career and family life to 'fight the Communist Party', and how he tried to answer his father was the only time that he was overcome with emotion and could not go on speaking.[142]

As observed earlier,[143] the use of fear to 'persuade' suits a political morality of tutelage that rejects rights and liberties, and endorses 'thought reform' as an appropriate political task.[144] It stands in contrast to a political system whose coercive measures are thought to require justification as invasions of liberty; and it does not draw a principled distinction between persuasion and intimidation.[145] On this analysis, it is of no relevance to the Party–State if professions of repentance are false. There is no need for them to be truthful, precisely because from the illiberal perspective of this system, individual conscience or political belief is not valued.[146]

Precisely intelligible warnings or commands would be counter to the purposes of the Party–State. What is useful to it, rather, is the creation of a psychological state of uncertainty and pre-emptive caution. Even deciding to cross boundaries would require one to know where the boundaries are; and if they are unknown, one may only opt to cross imaginary boundaries all the time, because it is not clear what consequences any particular action may have: 'What an authoritarian society needs to achieve most is that you are so afraid that they don't even need to tell you what not to do – you just won't do it.'[147]

What also emerges from the above comments by interlocutors is that surveillance, torture, disappearances etc. serve important functions internally to the security apparatus, as formally defined tasks to be carried out following orders; and for those who administer the measures, form triumphs over substance. Pretence affects not only the administrator's view of the effect of measures (such as torture) carried out, but also his standing within the hierarchy; the procedure has been carried out not only by the book but also under the pretence that it has achieved something. Strict compliance with orders is after all the only thing that can protect those working within the security apparatus, who are in that sense also its victims; and jailors and jailed can become to some extent like each other. As Zeng Jinyan observes:

---

142 #105 2013-1.
143 In Chapter 3.
144 Robert Jay Lifton, *Thought Reform and the Psychiatry of Totalism: A Study of 'Brainwashing' in China*, Norton, New York: 1961.
145 As noted earlier in the case of Václav Havel's famous greengrocer instructed to display a Party slogan in his shop window, repression works by allowing people some semblance of freedom Václav Havel, *Moc Bezmocných* [*The Power of the Powerless*], Prague, 1978, published in translation by Jan Vladislav (ed.) *Living in Truth*, Faber & Faber, London and Boston, MA: 1986, pp. 36–122.
146 '#21-2011 uses the example of 'pointing to a deer and calling it a horse' (指鹿为马), discussed in Chapter 3.
147 #9 2011 2:01.

Through the process of interacting with the police for years we must learn to control and hide our feelings to avoid them grasping our weak points to make us psychologically break down.... Displays of emotional numbness and coldness, initially adopted as a form of political play-acting and falsehood just to stay safe in the totalitarian regime, eventually become internalized by ... many of those who resist totalitarian governments, through years in prison and under monitoring. If, living side by side with these plainclothes police and guards, neither side is to turn into devils, those who resist dictatorship require more intellectual and spiritual resources.[148]

'Persuasive' and 'caring' Party–State terror

Those who create fear often claim to be 'caring' – the creation of fear purports to be for the protection of its victims against the system the perpetrators operate within. In some rare cases the authorities reveal their strategies as deeply rooted in the approaches of the totalitarian Party–State under Mao. Thus in the summer of 2010, three prominent human rights lawyers were asked to have a 'chat' with the Justice Bureau, and given some 'caring' advice:

> [In a meeting in xx, the official] Y [used the phrase], *fenhua wajie, chengjie daji, jiaoyu wanjiu*[149] – 'split and disintegrate, discipline and strike, educate and rescue.' Twelve characters. At the time they wanted to see us, they were still regarding us as subjects to be 'rescued', I suppose. Their [real] meaning at the time was, 'the higher level has already made a decision about you. If you don't [change], we will use this strategy against you.' The purpose was to frighten us.[150]

The Party–State rules and mechanisms described in this and the preceding chapter rely in part on a form of 'self-enforcement' similar to self-censorship. We observed a psychological need to imagine that there is a line not to be crossed, apparently resulting from the desire for safety, the desire to imagine oneself on this side of the line the crossing of which leads to a feared sanction. Perhaps officials have a similar desire of imagining zones of toleration and repression. Maintaining this idea is at any rate a way of engaging people in the management of their own personal safety and thereby, up to a point, co-opting them. Caught up in the unhappy reasoning invited by the uncertainty of consequences, a rights lawyer once asked a disconcerting question, only weeks before his abduction by the authorities, toward the end of 2010:

> Do you think that *I* am a risk now? ... I used not to understand why Lawyer A was being subject to tighter surveillance [than I]. It seemed at the time that

---

148 Zeng Jinyan (曾金燕), draft (untitled) on file with author.
149 In Chinese characters, 分化瓦解, 惩戒打击, 教育挽救.
150 #23 2013-1.

the *guobao* of [location] were worse than those here. But now it looks as though I could not be free when they can be free. (. . .) Why is it that I am watched more severely now than they? I almost feel as though they had made a mistake about me! (. . .) That's right, there should be some equal treatment in this [laughs].[151]

As was seen earlier, the authorities also like to emphasise the imminence of sanctions e.g. by techniques such as telling someone that 'all the documents have been prepared [for indicting you for inciting subversion] and we can send you to prison any time now.'[152]

The system thus generates evidence of there being a red line every now and then; but it has no strong reasons for consistent application of sanctions. There are threats which are carried out or not often without apparent justification – the criminal prosecution of Liu Xiaobo but not of Zhang Zuhua and Jiang Qisheng, the three main co-authors of Charter 08 (with Zhang Zuhua perhaps being *the* main author) was a widely discussed example of this arbitrariness. The fact that retaliatory control measures are imposed for specific reasons does not mean just by itself that they are imposed in the implementation of a specific rule delineating a boundary not to be transgressed. There is a difference between the mistaken belief that the line demarcating rule obedience from transgression is just here, when in fact it is over there on a more reasonable interpretation; and the mistaken belief that there is any line or rule at all. In fact, the techniques of obscurity and caring terror there never was a red line, not even a 'moving' one. At best, as Teng Biao comments wryly, the level of repression at any given time can be determined by working 'backward' from the level of resistance:

From the perspective of society as a whole, exchanging safety for freedom will, I am afraid, ultimately result in attaining neither. From the perspective of the individual, if you cause the government a little less trouble your level of safety will rise by so and so many points. But the question is, to what level will you retreat? You retreat one step and feel that's still not enough, so you have to retreat another two steps, but after that you will still not feel safe and you will need to retreat further, all the way to when you have reached the bottom line and have to pretend to be deaf and mute, to look without seeing, and then only will you count it as safe. The problem is, assuming that everybody is moderate, i.e. 'rational, neutral and objective', pays attention to strategy, and does not provoke the authorities, will the government in this case not still be detaining people? If all retreat, the standard whereby people are detained will be a different one; if all engage in soft-spoken resistance, it will still be possible to single out one who speaks loudest amongst them. And if they can't find such a person, they will manufacture one.[153]

151 #9 2010-4.
152 Discussed in Chapter 6.
153 Teng Biao (滕彪), '一个反动分子的自由 [The freedom of a reactionary]', Taiwan Association

The image of the red line becomes not only meaningless but also misleading. By directing our minds to engage with the forever vexing question of what supposedly hidden rules[154] may govern the imposition of sanctions we are directed to accept at some level that certain conduct is wrong, if not by the standards we embrace, then at least by the standards of the repressive system. In contrast to even a legal system that embraces clarity about the source of coercion and an accompanying efficiency,[155] this control system thus thrives on techniques of obscurity resulting in uncertainty; it is a system in which arbitrariness is in and of itself a powerful tool.

Fu Hualing has used the expressions 'extra-legal' and 'extra-extra-legal' to characterise certain particularly dark areas of obscurity and fear in the Chinese legal system must be treated with caution. The image of the 'extra-extra-legal' very well captures the idea of certain Party–State practices being particularly harsh violations of the law. The two expressions can be used to describe control techniques deployed in a variety of settings such as Re-education Through Labour ('RTL'), on the one hand, and 'black jails' and forced disappearances, on the other. This language reflects a sense that some measures such as RTL are based in sets of rules that, while they are not 'legislation' in accordance with the 2000 Law on Legislation, and while violating higher legal norms, still indicate a degree of regulation of State conduct, whereas others seem to be much more ad hoc and not based in rules – like outer circles, they seem even further removed from the central idea of law. It is useful if law is thought of as rules governing State officials. But it can also be taken to suggest that there are inner or central realms within which the Party–State operates legally and within which citizens are free from fear. This would be wrong, because obscurity and fear reach far into the realm of voluntary personal decision free from externally visible legal sanctions.

In fact, State uses of criminalisation of what is termed 'subversion' and 'inciting subversion' show why they will in current judicial practice not involve a good faith application of rules or respect for legal values.[156] To the extent that arbitrariness and irrationality pervade 'the law' as it might be understood on a positivistic or social science reading (law as social fact), rule of law is therefore undermined throughout, as Fraenkel also argued;[157] and there is no line of demarcation between zones of legality and extra-legality or extra-extra-legality. The fearful state of having no legal rules is of course one of the moral arguments for legal rules, or for certainty as a virtue of law, as jurists across a spectrum of theoretical positions have recognised. So corroded is the structure of 'law' and

for China Human Rights (台湾关怀中国人权联盟), 中国生死书 [*China, the Book of Living and Dying*], Mufeng Publishing Company, Taipei: 2013, pp.178–185 ('The freedom of a reactionary').

154 The concept of hidden rules was widely discussed after Wu Si's publication of a book by that title. Wu Si (吴思), 潜规则 [*Hidden Rules*], 2005, at http://zhidao.baidu.com/question/91876798.html, accessed 26 December 2013. This concept is also addressed in Chapter 3.

155 H.L.A. Hart, *The Concept of Law*, Oxford University Press, Oxford: 1961.

156 Teng Biao, *supra*.

157 Fraenkel, *supra*.

'regulation' without principles that the Party–State can always say that those who skate on thin ice cannot complain if they fall in.

The 'dual state' logic of Party–State control

In the face of the 2011 'Jasmine Crackdown' some rights lawyers characterised these developments as a turn against rule of law or *qu fazhi hua*.[158] Other observers – also including rights defenders suffering repression – have viewed the repressive activities of that apparatus not so much as an aberration from a normative model based in law, as a sign of a promising, if gradual, transformation of the system that will involve the subjugation of the security apparatus to the rule of law:

> Last year they had already planned to annihilate us. But then in the course of the internal political struggles within the party, the slightly more enlightened faction was able to 'retire' the faction that would have supported [our] bodily annihilation. But we were in very great danger.[159]

The latter group may draw on the fact that despite its cruelty in repressing rights lawyers and rights defenders, there have not been many cases of deaths associated with forced disappearances of rights defender. A rights defender commented on this observing that this was a way in which the CCP today was different from the CCP of the era of the Cultural Revolution:

> The assassinations in South America were due to their systems of auto-cratic military rule. Those governments tend to be conservative in nature and rather tolerant toward religion but very cruel toward political opposition. The CCP went through an experience like South American military rule during the period of the Cultural Revolution.[160] But in the post-Cultural Revolution era it displays some of the traits of civil rule, and does not engage directly in assassinations. This is how we can distinguish between totalitarianism and post-totalitarianism.
>
> [The system now] still has a core of murderous violence, displayed, for example, toward ethnic minorities, toward the underclass, toward mass resistance, they are very tough. But . . . it is partly rational. It respects some rules. For example it would not impose the death penalty on a member of the Politburo.[161]

---

158 In Chinese characters, 去法治化. #23 2011-3. See also Carl Minzner, 'China's turn against law', 59 *American Journal of Comparative Law* 935.

159 #63 2012-1.

160 For a collection of video reports on forced disappearances in Argentina, for example, see 'Desaparecidos', at http://www.desaparecidos.org/arg/victimas/eng.html, accessed 26 December 2013; website of the European Center for Constitutional and Human Rights, at http://www.ecchr.de/argentina.370.html, accessed 26 December 2013. See also Brian Finucane, 'Enforced disappearance as a crime under international law: a neglected origin in the laws of war', 35 *Yale Journal of International Law* (2010) 171, at http://ssrn.com/abstract=1427062.

161 #63 2012-1 (2).

Against the background of such considerations, the death by hanging of rights defender Li Wangyang shortly after his release from prison under suspicious circumstances triggered an intense reaction, when the authorities insisted that Li Wangyang had hanged himself.[162] Rights defenders and rights lawyers were especially vocal in calling for independent investigations:[163]

> We must prevent the Li Wangyang incident from becoming part of a 'hidden rule' that leads to the bodily annihilation of rights defenders. Not because rights defenders should have special rights – it is just that they are by virtue of who they are at great risk.

The arsenal of measures at the disposal of the security apparatus discussed in this chapter, and the fact that it uses these measures while at the same time acting in various roles of 'law enforcement', suggest that there is an increasingly evident dualism – that there may be concurrent trends, concurrent growth of the normative *and* the prerogative State in China:

> At the time of the Jasmine Crackdown I felt they were improvising and they may have been afraid of an immediate collapse of the system. So my sense is that the Jasmine Crackdown was an unusual example. The 2013 crackdown is undoubtedly more ferocious.[164]

But its advantage was to give rights defenders a platform to defend themselves, the interlocutor added:

> The logic of this is that if they use black prisons and abductions to control rights defenders the costs they incur is even higher because the real cost for them is not in money but in terms of moral costs. The cost they face is that more people will *weiguan*[165] and show concern and that internationally there will be heightened concern as well. In addition they believe that using the judicial process they can control the situation better.[166]

On the one hand, State laws increasingly make reference to rights. This gradual change can be seen in Article 2 of the 2012 Criminal Procedure Law (CPL), for

---

162 Teddy Ng, 'The agony of Li Wangyang', *South China Morning Post*, 13 July 2012.
163 Two petitions were launched. See 'Support group proposing an investigation into Li Wangyang's 'Suicide' established [推进李旺阳先生"自杀"事件真相调查的法律和公民后援团成立], 30 June 2012, at http://www.liwangyang.org/2012/06/blog-post_30.html, accessed 26 December 2013; 'Ten lawyers send letter questioning severe illegalities in police report regarding the Li Wangyang Incident [十律师就李旺阳事件致函人大 质疑警方处置过程严重违法], Radio Free Asia (Mandarin Desk), 23 July 2012, at http://www.rfa.org/mandarin/yataibaodao/li-07232012093756.html, accessed 26 December 2013. Teddy Ng, 'Call for fresh Li inquiry', *South China Morning Post*, 23 July 2012.
164 #2 2013-7 1:00.
165 In Chinese characters, 围观.
166 #88 2013-2 47.

instance,[167] which states that the Criminal Procedure Law protects human rights and other rights. On the other hand, the Party–State remains committed to policing thoughts and educating those whose political ideas, in particular, are deemed incorrect; and it needs to use the methods of the 'state of measures' to pursue this goal. Because anyone is capable of falling into political error, thought policing targets not only the victims of persecution, but potentially also its perpetrators and, indeed, the whole of society.

It follows that resistance begins by understanding that an effective way of frightening citizens, and of drawing them in, is by holding out the elusive possibility of being 'safe'. It requires not only a rejection of the norms of the State but also the conscious and active rejection of the purported boundaries of safety, the lines of transgression the Party–State wants its stability maintenance targets to imagine but also keeps hidden from them. In that sense, rights lawyers can make the 'red line' of transgression, the line that separates them from places of danger disappear in their minds, albeit only at the cost of knowing that they are never safe:

> [T]he degree of government tolerance is basically determined by the average level of those already imprisoned. This is where this kind of system is mysterious and paradoxical; and it is what defines the fate of democrats and human rights defenders. Only those who love freedom will lose it; only those who lose it are able to struggle for it. Those who recognize this have actually nowhere to retreat to.[168]

Bibliography

International law instruments

Declaration on the Protection of All Persons from Enforced Disappearance, proclaimed by the General Assembly in its resolution 47/133 of 18 December 1992, at http://www.un.org/documents/ga/res/47/a47r133.htm.

NPC laws

PRC Criminal Law [中华人民共和国刑法], passed on 1 July 1979, promulgated on 6 July 1979, and effective as of 1 January 1980, last revised on 25 February 2011, http://www.moj.gov.cn/Prison_work/content/2013-05/07/content_4436670.htm?node=43130. For an English translation, see http://www.cecc.gov/resources/legal-provisions/criminal-law-of-the-peoples-republic-of-china.

PRC Criminal Procedure Law [中华人民共和国刑事诉讼法], passed on 1 July 1979, promulgated on 7 July 1979, effective as of 1 January 1980, last revised on 14 March

---

167 CPL (2012) passed on 14 March 2012 to come into effect on 1 January 2013, see 中华人民共和国刑事诉讼法 [PRC Criminal Procedure Law], at http://www.law-lib.com/law/law_view.asp?id=378480, accessed 26 December 2013.

168 Teng Biao (滕彪), 'The freedom of a reactionary', *supra*.

2012, at http://www.law-lib.com/law/law_view.asp?id=378480, accessed 4 January 2014.

Administrative and judicial decisions

Beijing Municipal Procuracy No. 1, 'Indictment of Xu Zhiyong by Beijing Municipal Procuracy No. 1', 13 December 2013, translated by China Change, 21 December 2013, at http://chinachange.org/2013/12/21/indictment-of-xu-zhiyong-by-beijing-municipal-peoples-procuratorate-no-1-branch/, accessed 2 January 2014.

Guangzhou Municipal Public Security Bureau, 'Police Indictment Opinion for Guo Feixiong and Sun Desheng', 10 December 2013, translated at Siweiluozi Blog, at http://www.siweiluozi.net/2013/12/translation-police-indictment-opinion.html, 26 December 2013, accessed 2 January 2014.

Books and articles

Anonymous Contributor, Carter, Liz, Henochowitz, Anne and Xiao, Qiang, *The Grass-Mud-Horse Lexicon*, Kindle Books: 2013.

Associated Press/The Guardian, 'Freed China dissident was tortured in custody, says human rights group', 14 September 2011, at http://www.guardian.co.uk/world/2011/sep/14/freed-china-dissident-tortured.

Bai, Mei, 'Chinese human rights lawyer sentenced to seven tears', *Epoch Times*, 2 December 2009, at http://www.theepochtimes.com/n2/china-news/chinese-human-rights-lawyer-sentenced-seven-years-25905.html.

BBC, 'China activist Ni Yulan's jail term reduced', 27 July 2012, at http://www.bbc.co.uk/news/world-asia-china-19009132.

Chen Kai Yee, 'Criminal Defense Lawyers Rehabilitated in Beihai,' 10 February 2013 at http://tiananmenstremendousachievements.wordpress.com/2013/02/10/china-criminal-defense-lawyers-rehabilitated-in-beihai/.

Chen Weidong (陈卫东), '刑诉法修改:权力与权利的博弈 [CPL Revision: contest between power and rights]', Nanfang Renwu Zhoukan [南方人物周刊], 13 September 2011, at http://nf.nfdaily.cn/nfrwzk/content/2011-09/13/content_29780011.htm.

Chen, Yanhui (谌彦辉), '内地现律师组团打官司 [The phenomenon of lawyers' litigation teams emerges in Mainland]', 9 January 2012, at http://news.ifeng.com/shendu/fhzk/detail_2012_01/09/11851698_0.shtml.

China Aid, 'Lawyer who had taken on legal representation in "My Father is Li Gang" case aggressively chased by unidentified individuals in middle of night' (代理过 "我爸是李刚"案的张凯律师, 半夜突遭不明身份多人追杀)', 14 December 2010, at http://www.chinaaid.net/2010/12/blog-post_14.html.

China Digital Times, 'New social management grids to preserve stability', 24 January 2011, at http://chinadigitaltimes.net/2011/02/new-social-management-grids-to-preserve-stability/.

Chinese Human Rights Defenders (CHRD), 'Individuals unlawfully detained in crackdown on peaceful assembly, association & expression', updated 23 December 2013, at http://chrdnet.com/2013/07/individuals-detained-in-crackdown-on-assembly-and-association/.

Clarke, Donald C., 'China's jasmine crackdown and the legal system', Chinese Law Prof Blog, 26 May 2011, at http://lawprofessors.typepad.com/china_law_prof_blog/2011/05/chinas-jasmine-crackdown-and-the-legal-system.html.

Committee to Support Chinese Lawyers, 'Legal advocacy and the 2011 crackdown in China', 2011, at http://www.csclawyer s.org/advo cacy/, accessed 30 December 2013.

Deng, Yanhua and O'Brien, Kevin, 'Relational repression in China: using social ties to demobilise protesters', 215 *China Quarterly* (2013) 533–552.

Finucane, Brian, 'Enforced disappearance as a crime under international law: a neglected origin in the laws of war', 35 *Yale Journal of International Law* (2010) 171, at http://ssrn.com/abstract=1427062.

Fraenkel, Ernst, *The Dual State. A Contribution to the Theory of Dictatorship*, translated by E.A. Shils, Oxford University Press, New York: 1941.

Fu, Hualing, 'When lawyers are prosecuted: the struggle of a profession in transition', 2 *Journal of Comparative Law* (2007) 95–133.

Fuller, Lon, *The Morality of Law*, Yale University Press, New Haven, CT: 1969.

Gao, Zhisheng (高智晟), 'Dark night, dark hood, and kidnapping by dark mafia – my account of more than 50 days of torture in 2007', written in November 2007, translated from the Chinese by Human Rights in China, 8 February 2009, at http://blog.sina.com.tw/64777/article.php?pbgid=64777&entryid=595609&comopen=1&trackopen=1.

Gao, Zhisheng, 'Gao Zhisheng solemnly denies all charges by Chinese authorities', *Epoch Times*, 8 September 2007, at http://en.epochtimes.com/news/7-9-8/59565.html.

Gudjohnsson, Gisli H., *The Psychology of Interrogation and Confessions; A Handbook*, Wiley, Hoboken, NJ: 2003.

Havel, Václav, *Moc Bezmocných* [*The Power of the Powerless*], Prague, 1978, published in translation by Jan Vladislav (ed.) *Living in Truth*, Faber & Faber, London and Boston: 1986.

Human Rights In China, 'Guangxi Lawyer Yang Zaixin put under residential surveillance after nine months in detention', 22 March 2012, at http://www.hrichina.org/content/5936.

Human Rights Watch, 'Defense lawyers in high-profile Beihai case beaten while police watch', 21 October 2011, at http://www.hrichina.org/en/content/5587.

Hutzler, Charles, 'Wang Lihong, Chinese online activist, sentenced to prison for staging protest', 9 September 2011, at http://www.huffingtonpost.com/2011/09/09/wang-lihong-prison_n_955226.html.

Jiang, Qiming (江启明), '维权律师杨在新被中共软禁 家人生活困难 [Rights Lawyer Yang Zaixin house-arrested by the Party, family in difficulties]', *Dajiyuan* (大纪元) 18 May 2012, at http://www.epochtimes.com/gb/12/5/18/n3592191.htm% E7% BB%B4%E6%9D%83%E5%BE%8B%E5%B8%88%E6%9D%A8%E5%9C%A8% E6%96%B0%E8%A2%AB%E4%B8%AD%E5%85%B1%E8%BD%AF% E7%A6%81-%E5%AE%B6%E4%BA%BA%E7%94%9F%E6%B4%BB%E5% 9B%B0%E9%9A%BE.

Lan, Rongjie, 'Killing the lawyer as the last resort: the Li Zhuang case and its effects on criminal defence in China', in Mike McConville and Eva Pils (eds.), *Criminal Justice in China: Comparative Perspectives*, Edward Elgar Publishing, Cheltenham: 2013.

Li, Jie (李杰), quoted in Liu Junguo, Xiao Da, Wang Gang, Qing Mu, Yang Ming, Ji Shuangcheng, Yang Jingjie, Wang Xi and Liu Zhi (刘军国, 萧达, 王刚, 青木, 杨明, 纪双城, 杨静婕, 汪析, 柳直), '世界解读三中全会公报 感叹中国改革决心 [The world is analyzing the Third Plenary Meeting report, sighing over China's commitment to reform]', *Global Times* (环球时报), 13 November 2013, at http://world.huanqiu.com/depth_report/2013-11/4558902_2.html.

Li, Jinxing (李金星), '北海! 警号 601153! 警号 020156 ! [Beihai! 601153 Police ID number! 020156 Police ID Number!]', Caijing Blog (财经网博客), 8 August 2011, at http://blog.caijing.com.cn/expert_article-151499-23239.shtml.

Liu, Sida, Liang, Lily and Halliday, Terence C., 'The trial of Li Zhuang: Chinese lawyers' collective action against populism', 1 *Asian Journal of Law and Society* (2014), at http://ssrn.com/abstract=23332 58, accessed 1 January 2014.

Lynch, Elizabeth, 'China's rule of law mirage: the regression of the legal profession since the adoption of the 2007 Lawyers Law', 42 *Georgetown University International Law Review* (2010) 535.

Mao, Lixin (毛立新), '律师伪证罪的追诉程序探析 [Analysis of the handling of crimes of falsification of evidence by lawyers]', 30 August 2011, at http://blog.sina.com.cn/s/blog_4e7afe890102dssf.html.

Mao, Zedong, 'Where do correct ideas come from?' (1963), at http://www.marxists.org/reference/archive/mao/selected-works/volume-9/mswv9_01.htm.

Minzner, Carl, 'China's turn against law', 59 *American Journal of Comparative Law* 935.

Mooney, Paul, 'Shows of force', *South China Morning Post*, 25 October 2010, at http://www.scmp.com/article/728505/shows-force.

Nanfengchuang (南风窗), '"维稳办"走上前台 ["Stability preservation" offices come to the fore]', 14 April 2009, at http://www.nfcmag.com/articles/1463/page/2.

Ng, Teddy, 'The agony of Li Wangyang', *South China Morning Post*, 13 July 2012.

Ng, Tze-wei, 'Making people vanish', 16 September 2011, at http://pjmooney.typepad.com/my-blog/2011/09/making-people-vanish.html#tp.

Ng, Tze-wei, 'Until clause goes, defence lawyers are just decoration', *South China Morning Post*, 7 July 2011, at http://www.scmp.com/article/972741/until-clause-goes-defence-lawyers-are-just-decoration.

Perlez, Jane, 'New Chinese panel said to oversee domestic security and foreign policy', *New York Times*, 13 November 2013, at http://www.nytimes.com/2013/11/14/world/asia/national-security-committee-china.html?_r=0&pagewanted=all.

Radio Free Asia (Mandarin Desk), 'Ten lawyers send letter questioning severe illegalities in police report regarding the Li Wangyang Incident [十律师就李旺阳事件致函人大质疑警方处置过程严重违法]', 23 July 2012, at http://www.rfa.org/mandarin/yataibaodao/li-07232012093756.html.

Ran, Yanfei, 'When Chinese criminal defense lawyers become the criminals', (32) *Fordham International Law Journal* (2009) 986, at http://ir.lawnet.fordham.edu/cgi/viewcontent.cgi?article=2152&context=ilj.

Reuters, 'Lawyer tells of torture in a "tiger seat"', *South China Morning Post*, 30 March 2012.

'Review of selected Article 306 cases (5) – the case of Liu Zhengqing [刑法 306 条经典案例回放(5) – 湖南刘正清案]', at http://liusida.fyfz.cn/art/560557.htm.

Sapio, Flora, *Sovereign Power and the Law in China*, Brill, Leiden and Boston, MA: 2010, Chapter 3.

Scarry, Elaine, *The Body in Pain: The Making and Unmaking of the World*, Oxford University Press, New York and Oxford: 1985.

Sound of Hope, 'Lawyer Liu Shihui attacked by Guangzhou *guobao*, suffers bone fracture' [刘士辉律师遭广州国保暴打骨折]', 20 February 2011, at http://soundofhope.org/programs/162/181866-1.asp.

Teng, Biao (滕彪), '一个反动分子的自由 [The freedom of a reactionary]', Taiwan Association for China Human Rights (台湾关怀中国人权联盟), 中国生死书 [*China, the Book of Living and Dying*], Mufeng Publishing Company, Taipei: 2013.

Teng, Biao (滕彪), 'The political meaning of the crime of "subverting state power"', in Jean-Philippe Béja, Fu Hualing and Eva Pils, *Liu Xiaobo, Charter 08 and Challenges of Political Reform in China*, Hong Kong University Press, Hong Kong: 2012.

Thompson, Tyler, 'Reviving the Cultural Revolution – China's social management campaign targets "radical thought"', 1 April 2011, at http://chinaelectionsblog.net/?tag=social-management.

Tian, Xi (田溪), '江天勇律师被海淀分局国保殴打 [Lawyer Jiang Tianyong beaten by Haidian branch police office guobao officers]', *Sound of Hope*, 16 February 2011, at http://www.soundofhope.org/node/69493/print.

Wei, Wenhao (韦文浩), '北海律师案息而未决 [Beihai lawyers: case resting, but not resolved]', Legal Weekend [法治周末], 28 December 2012, at http://news.sohu.com/20111228/n330507979.shtml.

Weiquanwang/维权网, '广西维权律师杨在新被监视居住后失踪 [Guangxi rights defence lawyer Yang Zaxin disappears after being put under residential surveillance]', 17 March 2012, at http://wqw2010.blogspot.com/2012/03/blog-post_17.html.

Xu, Kai (徐凯), '李庄案第三季前传 [Prequel to Third Phase of the Case of Li Zhuang]', Caijing Net [财经网], 14 December 2011, at http://blog.caijing.com.cn/expert_article-151567-27454.shtml.

Zhao, Yanhong (赵艳红), '"北海律师伪证案"追踪: 维权律师团成员称遭围攻 警方回应 [Follow-up on Beihai Lawyers Case: Rights defence lawyers claims they were besieged and attacked, police responds]', People's net (人民网), 19 July 2011, at http://legal.people.com.cn/GB/15195351.html.

Zhou, Benshun (周本顺), '走中国特色社会管理创新之路 [The path to innovation of social management with Chinese characteristics]', *Seeking Truth* (求是), 16 May 2011, at http://www.qstheory.cn/zxdk/2011/201010/201105/t20110513_80501.htm. For a translation, see Flora Sapio *Forgotten Archipelagos* blog, entry of 6 July 2001, at http://florasapio.blogspot.hk/2011/06/belated-translation-zhou-benshun-road.html.

Websites, blog and microblog entries

A collection of video reports on forced disappearances in Argentina, see 'Desaparecidos' website at http://www.desaparecidos.org/arg/victimas/eng.html.

A detailed description of *zuo banr* (坐板儿), at http://blog.sina.com.cn/s/blog_54c8017f0100gfx5.html.

A domestic online dictionary entry mentioning the use of *zuo banr* (坐板儿), at http://zhidao.baidu.com/question/206073817.html?fr=qrl&cid=143&index=4.

Bridgeduan (blogger pseudonym) (2011), (喝茶谈话守则普及: 自己的事不记得, 别人的事不清楚, 特定事件不了解, 没看法), 17 April 2011, available as retweet at https://twitter.com/#!/sanzuwu/statuses/59823408686448642.

China Change, 'Indictment of Xu Zhiyong by Beijing Municipal Procuracy No. 1', http://chinachange.org/2013/12/21/indictment-of-xu-zhiyong-by-beijing-municipal-peoples-procuratorate-no-1-branch/, 21 December 2013, accessed 2 January 2014.

Li, Xiongbing (黎雄兵), tweet of 9 November 2011, at https://twitter.com/#!/lixiongbing.

Li, Xiongbing (黎雄兵), tweet of 19 May 2011, at https://twitter.com/#!/lixiongbing.

Lifton, Robert Jay, *Thought Reform and the Psychiatry of Totalism: A Study of 'Brainwashing' in China*, Norton, New York: 1961.

Siweiluozi Blog, 'Translation: police indictment opinion for Guo Feixiong and Sun Desheng', 26 December 2013, at http://www.siweiluozi.net/, accessed 2 January 2014.

'Support group proposing an investigation into Li Wangyang's "suicide" established [推进李旺阳先生"自杀"事件真相调查的法律和公民后援团成立], 30 June 2012, at http://www.liwangyang.org/2012/06/blog-post_30.html.

Twitterer named 'bridgeduan', 17 April 2011, at http://twitter.com/#!/bridgeduan 110417.

Website of the European Center for Constitutional and Human Rights, at http://www.ecchr.de/argentina.370.html.

Wu, Si (吴思), 潜规则 [Hidden Rules], 2005, at http://zhidao.baidu.com/question/91876798.html.

Documentary and multimedia sources

Ai, Xiaoming (艾晓明), 王大姐 [*Auntie Wang*], 2011, independent documentary film, on file with author.

He, Yang (何杨), 应急避难所 [*Emergency Shelter*], independent documentary, 2010, at http://vimeo.com/12677411.

He, Yang (何杨), 吊照门 [*Disbarment*], documentary film, June 2010, at http://vimeo.com/12938865.

NDTV, '专访耿格 (二): 迫害中像狗　来美挺胸做人 [Interview with Geng Ge (2) – Being like a dog under repression, holding her head up like a person after coming to the U.S.]', posted 20 July 2012, at http://www.youtube.com/watch?v=xc-DLHS5fTc&feature=related.

DraftsZeng Jinyan (曾金燕), draft (untitled) on file with author.

7   Resistance and wider legal and political advocacy

Reflecting on his experience of over 10 years, a human rights lawyer commented in 2013:

> As long as there is no judicial independence, whatever you do in the court-room in those cases of repression really just amounts to helping them act out a piece of theatre. They don't care. You have to take the action from inside the courtroom to outside, and let the Great Public Jury [the Court of Public Opinion] decide. That's what they fear now: all the constraints [they impose] are in this area. The lawyers they really detest are the ones who make cases public, who speak to the public media, and so on.[1]

This comment encapsulates the Chinese human rights movement's shift to wider legal and political advocacy outside the judicial process. This shift begins with acts of resistance in the courtroom, and remains dependent on the court-room as an ideational platform: that lawyers' out-of-courtroom advocacy has been informed by how lawyers act within their institutionally defined (and con-fined) roles. They take 'the action inside' the courtroom – their arguments and evidence, their efforts to participate in a judicial process ideally directed at a just decision – beyond the courtroom into the streets and to the internet. This com-bined experience allows rights lawyers to overcome the reluctant complicity exacted from them in the ordinary legal process. Over the past decade, human rights lawyers have articulated a political identity as citizens capable of autono-mous association and solidarity, on terms of a political theory the current Party–State does not and could not accept. Citizenship has, in turn, enhanced human rights lawyers' professional identity as lawyers. Their resistance and wider advo-cacy remain at this point a pre-democratic, pre-transition engagement with politi-cal liberties and other rights; but in exercising these liberties, lawyer–citizens also already take power.

1 #23 2013-1.

The logic of resistance to Party–State control

Resistance to Party–State control requires not only insistence on legal rights and principles, but also active advocacy to overcome the psychology of obscurity, uncertainty and fear discussed at the end of the last chapter. In this process, choices such as the decision for or against joining the Party, for or against expressing criticism of the system, and joining or quitting an independent association of lawyers can represent decisions to support control or to reject it. The decision of a moment can, due to its heightened political significance as a moment of resistance or subordination, determine someone's entire career (if this word can be used here) as a rights lawyer. Acts of resistance, once performed, can be recorded not only by the Security apparatus, but also be important to the memory of and self-understanding of individual lawyers themselves. In this context, the focus of resistance has changed in subtle but important ways.

In the 'Sun Zhigang Incident', at the beginning of the contemporary Chinese human rights movement, the rejection of formally enacted 'legal' rules as *e fa*,[2] 'bad' or 'evil' – and unconstitutional – laws was of central importance. For in the aftermath of Sun Zhigang's untimely death in police detention, it was the State Council Measures for Custody and Repatriation of Vagrants whose constitutionality was challenged by three young scholars including *Gongmeng* founders Teng Biao and Xu Zhiyong. The fact that 'bad law' had been challenged set a precedent for legal human rights advocacy. Calls for abolition of similar unconstitutional detention systems have not subsided since then; and in November and December 2013, the Party's Third Plenary and – later – NPC Standing Committee decisions announcing that the Re-education Through Labour System would be abolished indicated that similar success was still possible.[3] From the experience of the 'Sun Zhigang Incident' it also followed, however, that what could be achieved by the revoking of one or another regulation – and the enactment of one or another law or regulation to replace it – was limited, as Teng Biao showed when examining the new 'aid' centres that replaced the old 'custody and repatriation' ones and finding their practices still similarly restrictive and coercive.[4]

Rights advocates have also recognised and protested against legal rules limiting expression and association, and rules that make professions of Party loyalty or political conviction a prerequisite, for example, of admission to the legal profession, as discussed in Chapter 5. The right to assembly and association is limited, for the legal profession and beyond, as discussed in Chapter 3. It is in consequence of such restrictions that certain organisations including Open Constitution Initiative

---

2 In Chinese characters, 恶法.
3 Discussed in Chapter 3.
4 Teng Biao, 'The Sun Zhigang Incident and the future of constitutionalism: does the Chinese Constitution have a future?', CRJ Occasional Paper, 30 December 2013, at http://www.law.cuhk.edu.hk/research/crj/download/papers/2013-tb-szg-constitutionalism.pdf, accessed 30 December 2013; and 'Nine years on: the "Sun Zhigang Incident" and the future of constitutionalism in China', public lecture, 19 November 2012 at the Chinese University of Hong Kong.

(Gongmeng),[5] Transition Institute[6] and China Against Death Penalty[7] are either registered as commercial not-for-profit enterprises, or not registered at all, placing them in a grey zone between toleration and persecution and at risk of being charged with tax violations, for instance, as Gongmeng was in 2009.[8]

There are good constitutional and human rights arguments against legal rules attempting to govern thought, expression and association. Rights lawyers have pointed out that they violate core rights safeguarded in the Constitution and international human rights treaties, in various petitions for abolition and scholarly criticisms of, for example, the provisions criminalising 'subversion' and 'inciting subversion' document.[9] Their criticism has also addressed the arbitrariness with which subversion laws and similar laws are applied, because it would be impossible to police everybody's expressed thoughts in the way a successful totalitarian system would require.[10]

Rights lawyers regard neither such restrictions nor rules requiring them to profess certain political convictions as legitimate. Some insist that certain of these rules can affect only their external behaviour, and describe any decisions to abide by them as merely strategic. A lawyer used the examples of officially required 'thought reports' and of the oath of loyalty to the Party to illustrate this view:

> I think that the vast majority of lawyers, if they are required to write some-thing about 'loyalty to the CCP' [to pass their annual assessment exercise] won't even care ... It is rather like the lawyer's oath demanded of new lawyers [as a prerequisite of entering the profession]. I feel that this has no brainwashing function at all ... You have to pay attention to the con-sequences [of insubordination]. Assume that if you don't write a 'thought report' you will not pass the annual re-assessment and can't be a lawyer. Then that is just like a law, a bad law.[11]

In other words, the oath extorted in exchange for the obviously valuable goal of practising law can be seen as just another empty 'procedure', a 'bad law' that – like the requirement for statements of repentance as a precondition of release – can be and should be discounted, inviting only ridicule and scarcely worth resisting. If lawyers are so alienated from requirements of this kind that

---

5 In Chinese characters, 公盟.
6 传知行经济研究所 [Transition Institute], http://www.zhuanxing.cn/, accessed 27 December 2013.
7 北京兴善研究所 [China Against Death Penalty], http://www.cadpnet.org/en/, accessed 27 December 2013.
8 Evan Osnos, 'Where is Xu Zhiyong?', *New Yorker*, 31 July 2009, at http://lawprofessors.typepad.com/china_law_prof_blog/2009/07/where-is-xu-zhiyong-evan-osnos-in-the-new-yorker.html, accessed 26 December 2013. #76 2012-1; #29 2011-1.
9 Teng Biao, 'The political meaning of the crime of "subverting State power"', in Jean-Philippe Béja, Fu Hualing and Eva Pils, *Liu Xiaobo and Challenges of Constitutional Reform in China*, Hong Kong University Press, Hong Kong: 2012.
10 Teng Biao, *ibid.*
11 #2 2013-1 27:50.

neither obedience nor transgression really matters any longer, their indifference could result in total apathy, but it could also make the neo-totalitarian system vulnerable: evidently, in any case, the legal forms the system adopts are not suited to its goal of ensuring 'correct' political thought among the people it governs, especially those who, like lawyers, are expected to support 'the system'. Contrasting his example with that of Havel's greengrocer, the lawyer commenting on the meaninglessness of the oath of Party loyalty went on to observe:

> If there is no clearly prescribed consequence [of a decision not to participate] then if someone participates nevertheless we can express moral criticism. (. . .) E.g. the law does not require you to join the Party but joining it will give you many advantages. Now if, based on my conscience, I do not join the Party, this is not like civil disobedience, because there was no legal duty to join in the first place.[12]

If, by the same token, you *do* join the Party, you do this voluntarily and hence express commitment to the wider system and its goals; however reluctant, hesitant or cynical your participation, it is a participation based on your own, personal decision to submit to the system (and in that sense the very opposite of exercising the intellectual, expressive and associative freedoms the law recognises), a decision that requires a stronger justification to yourself. Compliance in order to secure professional advantages or avoid uncertain adverse consequences of oncompliance can all the more easily become blameworthy complicity.

Resistance in this situation requires a more fundamental opposition to the system than resistance to individual rules whose vagueness chills and intimidates,[13] in the context of an overall respectable legal system. It is also, as the lawyer just above states, 'not like civil disobedience', understood as a public and non-violent breach of law undertaken conscientiously with the aim of bringing about a change in the laws or policies that will render them more consonant with the legal system's inherent principles.[14] In many (although not all) contexts, rights defenders in China do not have the basic trust in and respect for the existing system that civil disobedience would require. Neither do they expect any more that the system could improve significantly in response to their conscientious efforts; nor do they deem certain existing bad laws worth targeting with criticism. Their resistance therefore cannot primarily tackle bad laws; rather, it must tackle the Party–State's

---

12 #2 2013-2. 'If there is no clear consequence in law then you have a moral duty . . . then it is a moral issue, it becomes a problem like in Havel, who [writes about the duty to] live in truth.' *Ibid.* Cp. Václav Havel, *Moc Bezmocných* [*Living in Truth*], Prague, 1978, translated into English as *The Power of the Powerless* and published in Jan Vladislav (ed.) *Living in Truth*, Faber & Faber, London and Boston, MA: 1986, pp. 36–122.

13 Cp. Frederick Schauer, 'Fear, risk, and the First Amendment: unraveling the "chilling effect"', 58 *Boston University Law Review* (1978) 685.

14 John Rawls, *A Theory of Justice*, Harvard University Press, Cambridge, MA: 1971; Ronald Dworkin, *Taking Rights Seriously*, Duckworth, London: 1977.

anti-legal strategies and measures. Resistance on these terms requires a non-authoritarian, non-positivistic and moral conception of law;[15] and some rights lawyers reject claims about 'staying within the law' as meaningless in the context of a Party–State that routinely ignores law. A lawyer commented:

> There used to be this view that lawyers must 'stay within the law' and so on ... This had become something of a widely accepted truth ... But it really was just a manifestation of the high pressure we were under.[16]

As lawyers reflect on the inadequacies of the once widely accepted wisdom of staying out of politics, they also discuss the meaning of political advocacy.[17] Another lawyer said:

> [At seminars with other lawyers], I sometimes analyse this phrase that [some older generation lawyers] cite like gospel truth: 'turn political problems into legal problems, legal problems into expert problems, expert problems into technical problems.'[18] ... I say to them that in China, 'politics' means something entirely different from what it means in normal countries. In a normal country, there is a public system; one where the people can participate [in politics] through various mechanisms; whereas in China, there is only a political game played by a minority of people in power. The vast majority of lawyers are not able to participate in these politics at all. How then can you say that we should 'turn political problems into legal ones!'[19]

As they stop shunning political advocacy as taboo, however, they also recognise that political action would require a far greater number of people than rights lawyer groups command at this point, which might require 'lowering the threshold' for 'ordinary people' to engage in resistance.[20]

In sum, rights advocacy began over a decade ago on the principle of acting as if the pretended rules of the written public laws purporting to protect liberties were meant for real. Now, it increasingly means refusal to continue accepting

---

15 If contrary to positivistic belief, *rules* are not capable of demarcating areas of licence or prohibition independent of moral values, the same argument weakens the authority of mere commands and merely imaginary lines of transgression.

16 # 23 2013-1.

17 For a discussion of the debate around 2006 see Eva Pils, 'Rights activism in China: the case of Lawyer Gao Zhisheng, *Building Constitutionalism in China* (2009) 243–260, Stephanie Balme and Michael C. Dowdle (eds.), Basingstoke, Palgrave: 2009, at http://ssrn.com/abstract=1563926.

18 Often Lawyer Mo Shaoping (莫少平) is quoted as upholding the first three of these transformations in '持守心底法治、民主、宪政信念而风雨前行 [Marching on through the storm, holding fast to my belief in rule of law, democracy and constitutional government]', *Weiquanwang*, 10 September 2008, at http://www.weiquanwang.org/?p=10527.

19 #25 2012-5.

20 Xiao Shu, comments delivered at 'The Constitution, the media and the Chinese rights defence movement: ten years after the death of Sun Zhigang', public seminar at the Centre for Rights and Justice, Faculty of Law, the Chinese University of Hong Kong, 13 April 2013.

the paradox of putative, hidden, secret 'rules' engendering fear and self-limiting calculation. Given the system's technique of drawing targets in by engaging them in calculations of risk, the most immediately obvious way of challenging and overcoming control is through public exposure of the practices the authorities engage in to create fear. Human rights lawyers today adopt a variety of strategies, including not only calls to revoke or ignore unconstitutional legal rules and insistence that the authorities follow those rules that are in keeping with the reform era's spirit, but also a new creativity in engaging with the idea of law. Most importantly, they make more active use of the liberties the system denies them.

Advocacy of and through openness and democratic expression rights

Rights lawyers' testimonies overwhelmingly suggest that exercising the classic liberal rights to freedom of thought and conscience, expression, and association can be a way of overcoming fear of the system. An oppositional internal attitude, expression of criticism of a State law or policy, or organisation of protest actions have normative and political significance beyond rejecting the binding nature of certain Party–State restrictions on speech and association; and the initial threshold is low. The signs of rights lawyers' resistance through expression and advocacy of openness are ubiquitous; several of them have already been observed in passing in earlier chapters. Examples of expression-related advocacy also remind us that lawyers in many ways depend on others to spread their message. For example, the 2003 Sun Zhigang Incident would not have had the impact it did had it not been for reports in the officially tolerated print media – at that time the most liberal media outlets available, and already accessible via the internet;[21] and its effects might have been more transient had it not been for the subsequent foundation of *Gongmeng* or Open Constitution Initiative. What can be observed from a few further examples analysed in this and the following section is that expressive and associative advocacy strategies are consciously connected to wider political advocacy – an exercise of democratic rights – and that the principle of information openness is accentuated by the phenomenon of an internet society that could be described as simultaneously open and prying. There is a move from online to (back) offline, evidenced in the *weiguan*[22] (surround and watch) actions, the flash mobs and similar forms of visual advocacy, that would be meaningless were it not for the possibility of reporting offline actions online.

21 Keith Hand, *ibid.*
22 In Chinese characters, 围观.

Case advocacy from and beyond the courtroom

Resistance within the range of activities understood as professional rights advocacy often exposes official obstruction of the judicial process. It ranges from the refusal to stop presenting one's defence statement in court – as e.g. in Liu Wei's and Tang Jitian's case in Luzhou – to the online publication of litigation materials, as in the well-known real-time tweeting of an ongoing court hearing in the famous case of Guiyang and other cases.[23] It can take the form, for instance, of demanding that an apparently illegal instruction be issued in writing:[24]

> Before the [x] case the Justice Bureau spoke to me and A, and said, 'This case has already attracted international attention. We hope that you will not take on the representation in 2nd instance.' We said, 'Can you give us that in writing?' Well, of course they were not going to do that.[25]

It can also mean lawyers silently holding up a sign demanding access to case files outside a court building, as in the 2012 case of Lawyers Li Jinxing and Shi Qing (a pen name). They had travelled to a small provincial city to see their client, many months after the trial hearing, which had not yet resulted in a verdict. The client had reportedly been tortured during investigation and his original defence lawyers had been told that they must not mention the issue of torture at the first-instance trial, and must present their defence statements in a stipulated number of minutes. The trial, involving 77 defendants, had concluded after a mere nine days. Defendant Yuan Chengjia had remained in detention since its conclusion on 18 October 2012 and by April 2013, he was therefore under 'excessive detention' (cp. Article 96 CPL), amounting to false imprisonment (cp. Article 238 CL). The court refused twice to recognise the lawyers as defence lawyers, saying that lawyers could not be newly appointed between the trial hearing and the passing of the verdict.[26] Having argued at length without any success, the two lawyers resolved to stage a protest. A photo posted online depicts them, sober in their business suits and with their attaché cases, standing in front of the heavy steel gates of the court behind which rises the usual imposing court building, looking serious and holding up a sign that reads: 'CRIMINAL DEFENCE LAWYERS DEMAND ACCESS TO FILES':

---

23 For instance in the case of the woman petitioner Zhou Li: '周莉案两次庭审回顾: 辩方有理有据 [Zhou Li's 1st- and 2nd-instance trials revisited: a reasonable and well-founded defence]', Boxun (博讯), 24 April 2010, at http://www.peacehall.com/news/gb/china/2010/04/201004241238.shtml, accessed 27 December 2013.

24 Discussed in Chapter 5.

25 #4 2012-1.

26 Lawyer Shi Qing (石青律师) [pen name], '营口中院非法剥夺律师阅卷权 [The Intermediate Court of Yingkou illegally refuses lawyers access to files]', 20 April 2013, at http://news.boxun.com/news/gb/china/2013/04/201304040209.shtml, accessed 27 December 2013.

At one point, a person who looked like a senior official (*lingdao*)[27] drove up to the court in his car. He rolled down the car window and asked, 'Which case is this about?' We said, 'About the case of Yuan Chengjia, handled by [Judge] Zhang Qiang.' When he heard that, his look became as strange as that of the Procuracy and Court officials in the week before, when they realised this was a case handled by a 'special case handling group'. He rolled the car window shut and drove inside the court compound without making any reply.[28]

Because official intransigence characterises the routine of protest, rights lawyers at some point express their views, concerns, and criticism not so much in order to persuade the authorities to follow the law, as to create a public setting that will allow for the Party–State to be criticised even if such criticism does not bear any immediate results. A lawyer commented as follows on the purpose of expressive advocacy inside the courtroom in the 'Beihai Lawyers Case':

> The lawyers directly engaged in criminal defence in these cases in order to resist official attempts to conduct closed adjudication (*sifa fengbi*).[29] For example in the 'Beihai Lawyers case', . . . the local government departments or power-holders officials will take measures to ensure that the media cannot get involved or reporters cannot attend trial, and in this situation lawyers become a source of information. Then the lawyers can report directly about the case through micro-blogs and such media. Society will support them in doing so.[30]

Lawyers expressively resisting control by the justice bureaucracies 'talk back' ostensibly to the authorities; but in doing so they have wider political purposes and address a wider public audience. They do not necessarily expect that the authorities will listen; rather they would see official responsiveness as a secondary bonus:

> In these typical cases, lawyers resisting together achieve that first, they raise legal consciousness and promote the idea of rule of law [in the general population]. Secondly, through lawyers' resistance the so called system-internal forces of public power are also prompted to gain a better understanding of problems that exist in their own work and that up to a point may help to prevent . . . it may help to encourage them to respect the law more in future.[31]

27 In Chinese characters, 领导.
28 Lawyer Shi Qing, *ibid.*
29 In Chinese characters, 司法封闭.
30 #74 2013-1. See also Zhang Xueran, 'China's all-star legal team pleads for defendants' rights on social media', Tea Leaf Nation, 25 July 2012, at http://tealeafnation.com/2012/07/bilingual-brew-chinas-all-star-legal-team-pleads-for-defendants-rights-on-social-media, accessed 27 December 2013.
31 #74 2013-1.

There is a vibrant debate among rights lawyers as to whom certain cases of rights defence 'belong to', with some arguing that in cases of dissidence and freedom of conscience, the cases themselves are public, and defence strategies ought to be shared with other rights lawyers via restricted social media groups such as *Weixin*.[32]

In the age of the social media, expressive resistance to the methods of the security apparatus has also included public exposure of vicious pranks and other forms of harassment by the security apparatus. The social media have enabled rights lawyers to shame their persecutors through such exposures:

> For example if you want to glue up Lawyer Y's door lock,[33] some four or five years ago, if you glued it up, at that time, only a few people would hear about this. But today, let's say you have a police officer whose daily job is to glue up Y's door lock – well, people [will learn about this and] will think, 'how mean!' [*xia zuo*].[34,35]

Despite the pain they can produce, such disclosures can be experienced as liberating and empowering. Human rights lawyer Li Tiantian disclosed that the authorities had taken secret film footage of her meetings with different men in hotels, by discussing the matter on Twitter after her release from secret detention;[36] and as observed earlier in Chapter 6, other lawyers also came forward and disclosed their experiences through the press (e.g. Jiang Tianyong)[37] and through social media (e.g. Liu Shihui and Liu Xiaoyuan).[38] Commenting on the ordeal of being disappeared and tortured, and of having his newlywed foreign wife expelled from China (she was told her husband had committed crimes), Liu Shihui wrote on his Twitter account:

> I don't want to become a Yang Jia,[39] so I'm speaking out. If the security police get upset about this, I'd ask them to think it over – what would you be thinking if it happened to you? . . . I feel better to talk about this a little.

---

32 #25 2013-5 and observation (December 2013).
33 One prank frequently used against a particular lawyer took the form of locking them out of the flat on multiple occasions, by using a fast-acting glue to block the door lock. Another was to use his spouse's private mobile phone (controlled by the police) to advertise the flat at a low price for sale. See Chapter 6.
34 In Chinese characters, 下作.
35 #23 20130-1.
36 Translated at Siweiluozi Blog, 'The fable of the hornet and the bird', May 2011, at http://www.siweiluozi.net/2011/05/li-tiantian-fable-of-hornet-bird-and.html (Chinese and English versions available from this blog), accessed 27 December 2013.
37 Ng, Tze-wei (2011–2), 'Making people vanish', 16 September 2011, at http://pjmooney.typepad.com/my-blog/2011/09/making-people-vanish.html#tp, accessed 27 December 2013.
38 Lawyer Liu Shihui, 'I've only begun to scratch the surface', translated at Siweiluozi Blog, 22 August 2011, at http://www.siweiluozi.net/2011/08/ive-only-begun-to-scratch-surface-liu.html, accessed 27 December 2013 (with link to original text), at http://www.boxun.com/news/gb/china/2012/04/201204150020.shtml, accessed 27 December 2013.
39 See Chapter 3 on Yang Jia.

Otherwise, I'd explode! – Some Twitter followers say that I'm revealing everything. On the contrary – I've only begun to scratch the surface! I'll stop here for now.[40]

Anonymity can – up to a point – protect those who make direct and potentially consequential accusations against individuals within the security apparatus. Thus, the anonymous owner of a Twitter account called 'evilsfiles' has circulated the names of well-known officers within the *guobao* police and other government departments, specifying allegations of unlawful repression against them, as for example against 'Sun Di, Head of the Division for Internal National Security of the Beijing Municipal Public Security Bureau', whom 'evilsfiles' holds responsible for inhumane treatment of several rights defenders, including lawyer Gao Zhisheng.[41]

Protesting retaliation against advocates

Protest against official retaliation can play a similar role. In another example, in March 2013, after having vocally represented a client in a Falun Gong case at trial, Lawyer Wang Quanzhang failed to emerge from the court building at the end of the trial. After a while it transpired that the court had 'judicially detained' (*sifa juliu*)[42] him to discipline him. Within a day or two, lawyers including Liu Weiguo, flocked to the town in which he had been detained and started a campaign for his release.[43] Their campaign involved a public signature campaign and the posting of pictures of protesters, including a number of rights lawyers, outside the Jixi City court building inside which Wang had been detained. Concurrently, citizens in seven different cities organised 'citizen broadcasts' posted online, calling for his release (circulated via Weibo and other media).[44] Similarly, Lawyer Tang Jitian's 'administrative detention' after an altercation with the feared and obscure '610 Office' resulted in another flock of rights defenders converging on the city of Jixi, in which Tang was held.[45]

Expressive advocacy of this kind also includes the 'surround-and-watch' (*weiguan*) protests,[46] online appeals, and other efforts lawyers have engaged in on behalf of other lawyers and rights defenders against ongoing criminal

40 *Ibid.*
41 罪恶档案 @evilsfiles at https://twitter.com/evilsfiles, accessed 20 August 2012. The evilsfiles account appears to have been suspended as of December 2013.
42 In Chinese characters, 司法拘留.
43 Anonymous, 23省市139名律师共同呼吁保障王全璋律师权益 [139 Lawyers from 23 provinces call for the protection of lawyer Wang Quanzhang's rights], signed by 139 lawyers, at http://wq9884.zfwlxt.com/SKZX/20130406/960.html, accessed 27 December 2013.
44 '公民播报：声援遭拘禁的维权律师 [Citizen broadcast: Supporting falsely imprisoned rights lawyers]' at http://www.youtube.com/watch?v=wMGTieMPF-U, accessed 27 December 2013.
45 Patrick Boehler, 'Rights lawyer Tang Jitian detained over Falun Gong case', *South China Morning Post*, 21 October 2013, at http://www.scmp.com/news/china-insider/article/1336488/rights-lawyer-tang-jitian-detained-over-falun-gong-case, accessed 27 December 2013.
46 In Chinese characters, 维权.

investigation and prosecution, as, for example, in the cases of Hu Jia,[47] Wang Lihong,[48] Wu Huaying,[49] Ding Jiaxi, Xu Zhiyong and other activists detained in 2013;[50] or their non-criminal detention, as in the already mentioned cases of Wang Quanzhang[51] and Tang Jitian.[52] Citizens have used *weiguan* protests for some time to draw attention to particular issues; and since the emergence of citizen documentaries, they have used images of protest to spread their messages further.

The authorities, insofar as they react at all to protests of this kind, are rarely able to react in ways the protesters deem satisfactory. In many cases, including that of Ding Jiaxi's, Xu Zhiyong's, Guo Feixiong's and others' detentions,[53] protest triggered no or only retaliatory measures;[54] thus after release of a video message by Xu Zhiyong from his place of detention lawyers were denied any further access to Xu.

When the authorities do react, it can be difficult for them to avoid appearing baffled or embarrassed. For example, when the Jingjiang court released Lawyer Wang Quanzhang two days early, it said that his detention had 'already achieved its intended corrective effect';[55] yet emerging from detention, Wang was welcomed by a group of triumphant supporters who felt certain that his release was due to their protest;[56] and quite 'incorrigibly', Wang himself immediately announced that he would complain against the court that had detained him.[57]

47 For example, Teng Biao wrote several open letters after the detention of rights defender Hu Jia, including Teng Biao (滕彪), '关于《奥运前的中国真相》一文的说明—声援胡佳之一 [Explanation about the essay "The real China before the Olympics" – first statement in support of Hu Jia]', Boxun (博讯), 17 January 2008, at http://www.peacehall.com/news/gb/pubvp/2008/01/200801170208.shtml.
48 Rights lawyers and other rights defenders gathered outside the court building where she was tried.
49 See Chapter 4.
50 CHRD, 'Individuals unlawfully detained in crackdown on peaceful assembly, association & expression', 23 December 2013, at http://chrdnet.com/2013/07/individuals-detained-in-crackdown-on-assembly-and-association/, accessed 28 December 2013.
51 Comments by Lawyer Liu Weiguo at public seminar 'The Constitution, the media and the Chinese Rights Defence Movenment', 13 April 2013 at the Chinese University of Hong Kong.
52 Patrick Boehler, 'Rights lawyer Tang Jitian detained over Falun Gong case', *South China Morning Post*, 21 October 2013, at http://www.scmp.com/news/china-insider/article/1336488/rights-lawyer-tang-jitian-detained-over-falun-gong-case, accessed 27 December 2013.
53 For example, 'Chinese human rights lawyers: appeal to safeguard human rights and realise constitutional government', 4 December 2013, at http://www.siweiluozi.net/, accessed 10 December 2013.
54 See e.g. Michael Bristow, 'China rights activist Wang Lihong jailed', BBC, 9 September 2011, at http://www.bbc.co.uk/news/world-asia-pacific-14850435, accessed 27 December 2013. On Wang Lihong, see also Chapter 4.
55 Jingjiang City Judiciary website (靖江市法院网), '关于提前解除拘留王全璋律师的公告 [Notice on early releasing Lawyer Wang Quanzhang from Detention]', 6 April 2013, at http://jjsfy.chinacourt.org/public/detail.php?id=1689, accessed 27 December 2013.
56 '围观彰显力量: 维权律师王全璋提前获释后发声 [The power of surrounding observation: comments on Wang Quanzhang's early release from detention]', Boxun (博讯), 6 April 2013, at http://www.peacehall.com/news/gb/china/2013/04/201304061555.shtml, accessed 27 December 2013.
57 *Southern Metropolis Daily* (南方都市报), '律师王全璋被江苏靖江法院拘留后提前释放拟提出复议 [Lawyer Wang Quanzhang, detained by Jingjiang court, considers seeking administrative

His subsequent applications for reconsideration and litigation under the State Compensation Law were unsuccessful,[58] but this did not stop him. A self-edited dossier documents the entire case of Lawyer Wang Quanzhang's detention. It contains, among other things, a diary-style account of Lawyer Wang's detention; a list of 278 lawyers who signed the online signature campaign (of these, 90 were based in Beijing, 45 in Guangdong and 16 in Shanghai); a list of phone text messages sent when he was detained; a list of actions taken individually by his former university teachers, colleagues at his law firm; a former black prison inmate ('who had received a death threat') and a lawyer who, the dossier states, had told the Jingjiang Court that 'making a lawyer disappear for eight hours without any reason whatsoever is a form of fascist terror'.[59] It also contains a detailed refutation of the court's account of Wang's alleged disruption of the trial process, provided to the media in the wake of his release,[60] a list of alleged illegalities including torture in the criminal process against the defendant[61] and a table entitled 'Indicators of China's rule of law development – assessment of judges by public defenders'. Mock modelled on the official 'annual assessment' forms the system commonly uses for its own purposes, this table specifies assessment criteria such as 'Has the lawyer received timely notice of the date and time of the trial hearing?' and 'Was the defendant forced to wear shackles and prison clothes?', and provides a Gmail (i.e. clearly not an official email) address to which the completed form can be sent.[62]

Lawyers sometimes engage experimentally with liberal legal principles, even choosing forms of resistance that go beyond challenging illegitimate legal rules, or insisting that legitimate rules be followed. For example, some lawyers began to engage in a practice of reporting officials to the people's procuracy for 'crimes' not contained in the Criminal Law. CHRD reports on the criminal defence lawyer for three evictees who stood trial for 'obstructing public office' after resisting a forced eviction, reporting a judge for 'undermining implementation of the law'.[63] In another case, a rights lawyer comments:

> Lawyer A and I reported [certain police] officials for three crimes: the crime of abuse of power, the crime of false imprisonment . . . and the crime of

reconsideration after early release]', 7 April 2013, at http://www.scxsls.com/a/20130407/89818. html, accessed 27 December 2013.

58 Wang Quanzhang (王全璋), '一个苹果引发的司法公案 [A public administration of justice case triggered by Apple devices]', April 2013, copy on file with author, p. 143 ff, quoted with author's permission.

59 *Ibid.*, at pp. 109–116.

60 *Ibid.*, at p. 93.

61 *Ibid.*, at pp 139 ff.

62 *Ibid.*, at pp. 159–162.

63 CHRD, '陈建刚律师控告法官庭审中破坏法律实施 [Lawyer Chen Jiangang reports judge for crime of undermining implementation of the law]', 6 November 2013, at http://wqw2010. blogspot.hk/2013/11/blog-post_1638.html, accessed 27 December 2013. The account includes the letter sent to the people's procuracy. It charges the judge with 'undermining the implementation of the law', 'violating the defendant's and defence lawyer's right to criminal defence', and 'making a judicial decision bending the law.'

'using official power to undermine the implementation of the national law'.[64] Actually, this 'crime' is one that I just came up with. In China, there is actually only a crime of 'abusing an evil sect to undermine the implementation of the national law'.[65] (. . .) But, if you use public power to undermine the implementation of the national law, that is the worst sort of crime![66]

Like the form for lawyers' assessment of judges, we see the lawyer here no longer pretending that the system was meant for real, even though it is only strategically enacted by the authorities. Rather, this lawyer is creating a political-legal fiction of his own. This fiction is independent from the State; and, of course, lawyers do not expect any prosecutions following such charges, but they mockingly, insistently, use the language of enacted laws to make their point. The lawyer here does not deny the force of the principle of *nullum crimen, nulla poena sine praevia lege poenali*, in a legitimate legal system but he implicitly declines to recognise the existing system of legislation as legitimate.

Lawyers' accusations and recriminations in these contexts primarily address a public audience;[67] they are generally no longer addressed to the authorities; and as they find new audiences, lawyers practise differentiating their messages. However, despite their opposition to the system and incidental anger against individual officials,[68] rights lawyers generally appear to believe that a confrontation with those who represent the Party–State on terms of sustained enmity or hatred is against their purposes, as well as their principles.

Articulating principles and strategies of political action

Especially those rights lawyers, whose personal biographies included time working as a public official, could come up with accounts reflecting, if not sympathy, at least a degree of empathetic understanding of the officials' motivation, as well as of the role of 'internal terror' in controlling them:

> Officials are mostly motivated by self-interest. If there is a change in the system [*gezhi*],[69] will their interests be protected and will they continue to enjoy recognition? But when it comes to ideals [*linian*],[70] I think that both inside and outside the system, there are now more and more people who have a clear understanding of the problems. Perhaps they are on the rise even faster than we are aware (. . .) At some point, I think that some

64 In Chinese characters, 利用职权破坏国家法律实施罪.
65 In Chinese characters, 利用邪教组织破坏国家法律实施罪, Article 300 PRC Criminal Law. The underlying criminal case was not one involving this crime.
66 #88 2013-2.
67 It should be noted that Twitter can only be accessed outside the GFW and similar *Weibo* posts are liable to be deleted.
68 #88 2013-2.
69 In Chinese characters, 革职.
70 In Chinese characters, 理念.

individuals within the system may choose to oppose it [*zhandui*].[71] But for the moment, I think it remains hard to imagine this to happen, especially at the higher levels. They continue to think they can keep things under control and maintain the stability of this autocratic system. (. . .) To some extent, [stability maintenance] actually also serves the purpose of letting other officials see that if you do something for the organisation [the Party], the organisation will let you benefit.[72]

Contexts in which rights lawyers have defended violence outright have been restricted to two kinds: to professional contexts in which self-defence and necessity were at issue (Deng Yujiao, Chen Kegui), on the one hand,[73] and to discussions of the theoretical limits of justifiable political resistance, on the other. For example, a rights lawyer provided the following qualified defence of actual perpetrators of violence:

I am against violence for three main reasons, namely: it harms the innocent, it denies the legal rights of the guilty, and experience shows that ultimately it always hits those who advocated or condoned it. But, in the cases of the Yang Jia police killing [and similar cases], I think that these are entirely understandable [*wanquan keyi lijie*][74] on the part of people who, first, are desperate and angry and, second, have no one specific to direct their anger against, because they're up against the whole system. . . . What gains admiration [among the people] is more the spirit of resistance than that of violence, and that is because Chinese people have been *too* much prepared to put up with things [*renshou*];[75] because their current situation is therefore well-deserved [*huogai*].[76]

Another lawyer among the ones contacted for the purpose of this study expressed great scepticism about the possibility of nonviolent resistance working to achieve political change in China. He thought that 'great bloodshed' might occur in China as a result of mounting political tension:

71 In Chinese characters, 站队.
72 # 114 2013-1(3)
73 See Deng Yujiao case at 'Chinese waitress freed after stabbing official to death during sex assault', *The Telegraph*, 16 June 2009, at http://www.telegraph.co.uk/news/worldnews/asia/china/5549081/Chinese-waitress-freed-after-stabbing-official-to-death-during-sex-assault.html, accessed 27 December 2013; Chen Kegui case, see 'China: Chen Kegui's Case Tests Rule of Law', Human Rights Watch, 15 October 2012, at http://www.hrw.org/news/2012/10/15/china-chen-kegui-s-case-tests-rule-law, accessed 27 December 2013; 'Chen Guangcheng: nephew Chen Kegui sentenced', BBC, 30 November 2012, at http://www.bbc.co.uk/news/world-asia-china-20551967, accessed 27 December 2013.
74 In Chinese characters, 完全可以理解.
75 In Chinese characters, 忍受.
76 In Chinese characters, 活该. #9 2010-2.

I recall the Soviet troops dispatched to Moscow before the dissolution of the Soviet Union were explicitly told they must not shoot at ordinary people. Whereas during June Fourth – at that time the troops dispatched to Beijing were explicitly told they could shoot at people. And how quickly they dispatched the troops! And if someone at the time would not shoot at the people they were later given criminal punishment. (. . .) Some people now are optimistic, they think that bloodshed like on June Fourth cannot happen again; but no one can beat the troops . . . It is quite true [that civil society and the internet are on the rise but] what they are expanding is only the power of speaking! There is a saying in China, 'faced with soldiers, a scholar may be in the right, but still unable to make himself understood.'[77] And Deng Xiaoping at the time, in 1989, had said so clearly, 'if there are three million students, I will have three million troops.[78]

He did not at this point advocate violent resistance or indeed give any indication of wishing to organise resistance; but he clearly thought violent resistance might occur. In the same vein, another rights lawyer commented that whether there would at some point be violent resistance in China would be a question 'to be decided by the Chinese people'.[79] He added:

If America had not resisted, would Britain have given it independence of its own accord? If England in its 'Glorious Revolution' had not chopped off the head of [the king], would there have been a sharing of power? . . . The South African, Taiwanese, Korean, and Indian examples just don't work here – I'll be direct; I have [on different platforms] said so and I don't fear the *guobao* when I say so now – the Chinese Communist Party are really especially evil, they are worse than any other country's Communist Party or ancient tyranny in Europe or China. If you as an individual make a choice and go for non-violence, there is nothing to criticise about it. If you want to practice non-violence, fine. But, violence against a government, against officials who have perpetrated crimes and will neither change nor desist, is justified in accordance with principles of natural justice. There is a natural right to resist tyranny [*baozheng*][80] (. . .) So, I think one must not speak in absolutes . . . Of course, some argue (using rude language, too) that non-violence can't possibly succeed – but this is not a foregone conclusion, it is something that reality will decide. It is something the people will decide. Conversely, advocates of non-violence should not confuse different concepts and argue that violence [*baoli*][81] will 'necessarily' result in [another] tyrannical government [*baozheng*]. In logic, that does not follow [either]. You have to differentiate.[82]

77 In Chinese characters, 秀才遇到兵, 有理讲不清.
78 #21 2010-3.
79 #113 2013-1.
80 In Chinese characters, 暴政.
81 In Chinese characters, 暴力.
82 *Ibid.*

Teng Biao wrote in June 2013:

> As disgruntled and inexperienced members of the [New] Five Black
> Categories[83] or [other] Bad Elements join them incessantly, popular forces
> will at some point have become numerous like sand, they will petition, go
> online, go into the streets, go to court, they will lose the more the more they
> fight, and fight the more the more they lose, and be almost ready to 'go into
> the Liang Mountains' [i.e. become rebels engaging in guerilla warfare].[84]

This can be read as a mere recognition of the abstract fact that liberal political
theory does not reject violent resistance in all circumstances. Or it can be read as
hinting that violent resistance and self-sacrifice are impending.

There is no visible disagreement, however, about the fact that the democratic
transition rights lawyers aim at hinges on, not the actions of a (in the orthodox
language which rights lawyers must repudiate, heroic, reactionary and counter-
revolutionary) few but, rather, on wider support from society. As another rights
lawyer put it, using the image of bringing down a wall, not everybody will be at
the frontline of those who rush to the wall and begin knocking it down:

> If you have courage, you can participate directly in this work, pushing,
> digging, shoving bricks and so on. But even a person who has no courage at
> all, who only dares to walk up to the wall when nobody is looking and pee on
> it – I say, you're great, too! We shouldn't keep comparing and competing to
> see who is prominent and who isn't. At the ultimate moment, everybody will
> have a role to play.[85]

In sum, advocacy and resistance through expression are of central importance to
the turn from legal to political advocacy. As lawyers communicate their experiences of everyday difficulties in the legal process, they begin to experience and
practise solidarity in confronting the authorities. While expressive resistance has
helped rights lawyers identify as opponents of the system, its content has largely
remained defined (and limited) by the liberal principles rights lawyers assert
actively in protesting against the Party–State. Even those lawyers who do articulate the idea of resistance against tyrannical government as a natural right argue

---

83 In 2012, an editorial in the overseas edition of *People's Daily* discussed groups in society that
    were potentially hostile to the Party–State; since then mockingly referred to as the 'New Five
    Black Categories (*xin hei wu lei* 新黑五类). See China Digital Times, 'Word of the week: new
    five black categories', 8 August 2012, at http://chinadigitaltimes.net/2012/08/word-of-the-week-
    the-new-five-black-categories/, accessed 30 December 2013. 'Five elements' or 'Five categories
    of black elements' (*hei wu lei*) included landlords, rich peasants, counter-revolutionaries, bad
    elements, and rightists. Gucheng Li, *A Glossary of Political Terms of the People's Republic of China*, Hong
    Kong: Chinese University Press: 1995, at p. 150.
84 Teng Biao (滕彪), '一个反动分子的自由 [The freedom of a reactionary]', Taiwan Association
    for China Human Rights (台湾关怀中国人权联盟), 中国生死书 [*China, the Book of Living and
    Dying*], Mufeng Publishing Company, Taipei: 2013, pp. 178–185.
85 #25 2013-1 43:00.

from a standpoint of impersonal principle, rather than enmity toward officials as a group, and warn against lightly giving up on nonviolence. Some rights lawyers believe that, following these principles, officials of the current system must be given a realistic option of also regarding themselves as citizens. Not only must the traditional juxtaposition of *min* and *guan*,[86] the people and the officials, be overcome, but also must the opponents of the current system avoid the trap of the more dangerous, in it its origins totalitarian enemy–friend juxtaposition which the post-totalitarian Party–State keeps echoing and invoking.[87]

Advocacy and resistance through association

When in 2003 the group Gongmeng, short for *Gongmin Lianmeng*,[88] 'Civic Alliance' or 'Citizen Alliance',[89] was founded as a constitutional rights advocacy group, civil society groups involved in rights advocacy had to be either visible with some state recognition, as *Gongmeng* opted to be – having failed to obtain NGO registration it was nevertheless founded as a research unit that was part of a company registered with the Commercial Register. Or they must be invisible and underground, which would have been risky, or visible and oppositional, which would have been suicidal, as rights lawyers well understood. Drawing on past examples of failed attempts openly to found a political party, one lawyer commented:

> Just think, whether we talk about the Chinese Democratic Party of 1998,[90] or the Chinese Social Democratic Party of 1992,[91] everybody has by now thought it through; or perhaps as a result of recent developments, we are now even clearer than before: the risks associated with this kind of organisation are extremely high. Consider that Hu Shigen,[92] for example, was sentenced to 20 years. And Qin Yongmin [to 11 years].[93] Their prison sentences were just too long. If everybody now got only two years for founding

---

86 In Chinese characters, 民 and 官.
87 Mirrorbooks (明镜), '"明镜"月刊独家全文刊发中共9号文件 ["Mirrorbooks Monthly" exclusive full text of CCP Document No. 9]', 20 August 2013, at http://www.molihua.org/2013/08/9_7925.html, accessed 28 December 2013; ChinaFile, 'Document No. 9', at http://www.chinafile.com/document-9-chinafile-translation, accessed 30 December 2013 (with further links). See also Liu Jie, 'A biased view of China', *China Daily*, 30 January 2012, at http://www.chinadaily.com.cn/cndy/2012-01/30/content_14502312.htm.
88 In Chinese characters, 公民联盟.
89 #2 2013-3 (no audio recording).
90 See the Chinese Democratic Party [中国民主党], at http://www.hqcdp.org/ (Chinese) and http://www.hqcdp.org/english/(English), accessed 28 December 2013.
91 See the Chinese Social Democratic Party [中国社会民主党], at http://www.csdparty.org/index.html, accessed 28 December 2013.
92 Human Rights in China, 'Prisoner profile: Hu Shigen', at http://www.hrichina.org/sites/default/files/PDFs/CRF.4.2004/PrisonerProfile4.2004.pdf, accessed 28 December 2013.
93 Human Rights in China, 'Democracy activist Qin Yongmin released from prison after 12-year sentence', HRIC, 29 November 2010, at http://www.hrichina.org/en/content/4879, accessed 28 December 2013.

a political party – then there'd be a whole bunch of people in Guangdong, Beijing, and other places who would dare to found a party![94]

As a rights lawyer connected to Gongmeng explained, moreover, it would have been too 'sensitive' to use Gongmeng's longer appellation openly – Gongmeng, by contrast, was less obvious and hence thought to be less harmful.[95] The option of registration that Gongmeng made use of in 2003 therefore reflected what Béja has characterised as a strategic shift after 1989: a decision by the authorities especially in the wake of the 1995 World Women's Forum in Beijing to allow the creation of controlled civil society organisations, but not of political groups.[96] Other choices made at the time were dictated by the means of communication available. As another lawyer observed:

[In 2005] you couldn't even send any group emails yet! From around 2006 or 2007, if you had some matter to discuss you could use a group email. But only some social elites could communicate [in this way].[97]

Ten years later, in April 2013, the group rushing to Jixi City to support detained lawyer Wang Quanzhang, for example, could not have formed without using online communication. In these 10 years, expression outside of institutionally tolerated channels has allowed human rights defenders to create associative structures, through social media, the wider internet, collectively organised appeals, signature campaigns, etc. Towards the end of this 10-year period, communication technology such as *Weixin* ('WeChat') allowed rights lawyers to decide to put out a joint appeal, negotiate the draft text of the appeal, and publish the finalised appeal with over 80 lawyers' signatures in just over six hours.[98] At the time of this writing, such groups include lawyers from major and some medium sized cities across the nation. The tone adopted in their chats is one of familiarity and friendship, with topics of discussion ranging from political jokes to the discussion of cases and expressions of personal sympathy or support (such as, 'You not dead yet, [name]? Got out alright?', to a lawyer who was recently house-arrested): 'I think that lawyers are huddling together like people in cold winter. In doing this a lawyer can maximise their own voice while at the same time reducing their own risk.'[99]

---

94 #2 2013-7.
95 *Ibid.*, also #2 2013-3.
96 Jean-Philippe Béja, *À la recherche d'une ombre chinoise: le movement pour la démocratie en Chine* [*In search of a Chinese shadow: the movement for democracy in China*], Editions du Seuil, Paris: 2004, Chapter 11; Jean-Philippe Béja, 'Civil society against democracy', a paper delivered at Workshop on New Developments in Chinese Civil Society held at Hong Kong University on 30–31 October 2013, on file with author.
97 #23 2013-2.
98 A human rights lawyer *Weixin* group accomplished this on one occasion, which I observed in November 2013.
99 #14 2013-1.

Case-focused teams

Initial formations of 'lawyer teams' (*lüshituan*)[100] in rights cases could be observed as early as 2005 in cases such as that of Cai Zhuohua,[101] of the Three Classes of Servants House-church,[102] and of Falun Gong defendant Wang Bo and her parents.[103] One lawyer attributed the rule that only two criminal defence lawyers are allowed per defendant to the role rights lawyers had played as a team in the 2008 case of Yang Jia, the young petitioner turned folk hero who was convicted of murdering six police officers;[104] another mentioned the joint open letter by 18 rights lawyers who declared themselves willing to provide criminal defence to Tibetans detained in the context of the March 2008 unrest in Tibet.[105] In the early years of lawyer teams, their purpose was largely limited to the handling of the specific case at hand:

> Initially, lawyers forming teams to defend rights concerned themselves with the cases they were handling as such. Also, if they had from the start taken on so-called sensitive cases, they would have been stopped immediately. (. . .) But, the moment they had started [creating these teams], they began to discover systemic problems and problems of corruption concerning individual officials as well as administrative interference in the judicial process, and all of this got exposed and reported. If you look at this practice from a war-craft viewpoint, it was an easy thing to do, but very explosive.[106]

As a widely recognised phenomenon, 'legal teams' or *lüshituan* – not a technical legal term, but initially used for criminal cases with many defendants among whom, one lawyer explained, there was no conflict of interest,[107] did not emerge until the 2011 Beihai Lawyers Case and subsequent, similar

---

100 In Chinese characters, 律师团.
101 'Pastor Cai Zhuohua', Prisoner alert at http://www.prisoneralert.com/pprofiles/vp_prisoner_152_profile.html, accessed 28 December 2013.
102 Joseph Kahn, 'China executes at least 12 members of a secret Christian sect', *New York Times*, 30 November 2006, at http://www.nytimes.com/2006/11/30/world/asia/30china.html, accessed 2 January 2014.
103 Discussed in Chapter 3.
104 #4 2013-1; Eva Pils, 'Yang Jia and China's unpopular criminal justice system', 1 *China Rights Forum* (2009) 59–66. See also Chapter 3.
105 '我们愿意为被捕藏民提供法律帮助 [We are willing to provide legal aid to arrested Tibetans]', Boxun [博讯], 2 April 2008, at http://www.peacehall.com/news/gb/china/2008/04/200804022305.shtml, accessed 28 December 2013.
106 #6 2013-1.
107 #74 2013-1.

cases.[108] In these more recent cases, as lawyers were naturally driven to collaborate:

> This created the impression on the outside that there was a team that was engaging in resistance to the prosecution authority (. . .) This drew a high degree of attention, and [as a result] many more people followed and participated in these cases on the internet.[109]

As rights lawyers close to these developments assert, moreover, legal teams that formed with the help of social media could benefit from information about and comments on some egregious cases of lawyers' persecution disseminated earlier via the social media. While information about the worst cases in the context of the 2011 jasmine crackdown described in Chapter 6 had travelled slowly, impeded by intensive online censorship, the case of Lawyer Li Zhuang was widely discussed on the domestic internet, for example. Later, Lawyer Yang Zaixin, the lawyer most centrally targeted in the Beihai Lawyers Case, decided to task colleagues with seeking help from Lawyer Yang Jinzhu and Chen Youxi in the event of his detention, because he was impressed with their online postings on the case of Lawyer Li Zhuang. The Li Zhuang case, in turn, had been used both by the authorities and by rights lawyers to advance their arguments and causes.[110] Echoing this analysis, another lawyer added some further factors that in his view played a role in the emergence of the 'legal team':

> Second, legal teams emerge in cases with many defendants, such as cases with a mafia element. Third, since there are so many cases of injustice legal teams can be concerned about, and since the injustice is so extreme, there is a basis for popular concern. Fourth, the media clearly pay a lot of attention. We felt at some point that we became a real focus of the domestic media. At the time perhaps the Propaganda Department simply had not got round to suppressing the discussion yet (. . .) Also, we had so much popular support for example in the Beihai Lawyers case, lots of small-amount donations, including from retired workers, sums of a few hundred Yuan and so on. Fifth, without the internet, no legal teams would have emerged – no one would ever have learned about Teng Biao or Gao Zhisheng and what they had done. Sixth, I think that the emergence of the lawyer team has really broken

---

108 Zhang Qing (张倩), '律师团现象：从组团自救到组团公益援助 [The phenomenon of "legal teams": from getting organised for the purpose of self-rescue to organising to provide pro bono legal aid]', *Caijing Magazine*, 3 January 2012. See also Chapter 4 and Zhang Xueran, 'China's all-star legal team pleads for defendants' rights on social media', Tea Leaf Nation, 25 July 2012, at http://tealeafnation.com/2012/07/bilingual-brew-chinas-all-star-legal-team-pleads-for-defendants-rights-on-social-media, accessed 28 December 2013; Teng Biao, 'Rights defence, microblogs, and the surrounding gaze: the Rights Defence Movement online and offline', in *Locating Civil Society: Communities Defending Basic Liberties*, Special Issue of *China Perspectives* 2012/3.

109 #74 2013-1.

110 #85 2013-1 and #73 2012-1. The case of Lawyer Li Zhuang is discussed in Chapter 6.

through the barriers separating poor from rich and sensitive from non-sensitive lawyers. Formerly one had the feeling that rights defence lawyers were mostly poor lawyers and that the more they defended rights, the poorer they got. But now, many wealthy lawyers who have been very successful have also begun to participate in these cases.[111]

The function of loose online association amongst lawyers in overcoming the control logic discussed above is obvious. It is through association that lawyers overcome the 'boundaries of sensitivity' created through fear:

> This changes [our] consciousness; there is increasingly a feeling that there isn't any difference between 'sensitive' and 'non-sensitive' cases. (. . .) This includes myself. I used to admire Teng Biao very greatly but I did not dare to do what he did. I thought it was too scary; so I focused on making money. After a while, making money didn't make me happy any longer.[112]

Loose association, moreover, allows lawyers to connect across great regional distances, and to form larger groups.[113] Perhaps because these independent and very loose associations come to oppose the institutions and associations of the Party–State at such a deep level, they are often explained as a reaction to a sense that official institutions are not working – that organisations officially supposed to represent lawyers' interests are 'failing' them.[114] Some lawyers directly blamed lawyers' associations' complicity in persecuting lawyers for their creation:

> I am Lawyer Y from Z, but no longer have a lawyer's licence. I participated in [a well-known rights defence case] but actually, the moment I had announced that I was willing to participate, without having yet done anything, I lost my lawyers' licence. So I didn't even get round to actually engaging in rights defence, or to working on other cases. My view on legal teams is that their creation is a way of expressing exasperation with the Lawyers' Associations.[115]

Another rights lawyer attributed their emergence to what he saw as the failure of lawyers' associations to serve the purpose of protecting them while doing their job:

---

111 #73 2012-1. #88 2013-2 supports this analysis by arguing that lawyers belonging to *sikepai/* 死磕派, that is, a category of lawyers who argue vehemently and uncompromisingly, but do not take on politically sensitive cases, have most recently begun to join ranks with human rights lawyers.
112 #73 2013-1.
113 *Ibid.*
114 #732013-1. Note that occasionally, lawyers' associations have acted on behalf of lawyers, e.g. in the case of Lawyer Liu Yao in 2009. Tom Mitchell, 'Chinese Court upholds lawyer's conviction', *Financial Times*, 23 December 2008, at http://www.ft.com/cms/s/0/85ac3c40-d01a-11dd-ae00-000077b07658.html#axzz2pEMk9FA9, accessed 2 January 2014.
115 #70 2013-1; similarly, #30 2013-1: #67 2013-1 (no audio-recording).

Lawyers' teams emerged because the judicial authorities didn't act in accord-ance with the law and do not respect the law. If lawyers could engage in regular legal practice, then the judicial authorities would not have triggered resistance from the lawyers. The lawyers resist, because very commonly there is no justice in the judicial process. Lawyers feel that if each one of them just relies on themselves, they are too weak. So they get together and unite – spontaneously, without there being an organisation.[116]

This lawyer's comment must be seen in the context of a system that controls associa-tions severely. He emphasizes the spontaneity of the legal teams' formation and the failure of official associations, almost as though he were offering this consideration in mitigation. However, the pattern of developments since the emergence of the social media and since information about the jasmine crackdown started transpir-ing among professional lawyers does not fully bear out the assertion that associative structures among lawyers have emerged in a spontaneous way:

I have participated in lawyer teams myself. The earliest in my case was at the time of participating in the local People's Congress elections [as an independent candidate], at the time three lawyers including myself formed a 'team to investigate the People's Congress elections'. Of course, the moment we had created that team, the authorities got very nervous and said this was simply going too far. They said we couldn't do this and must dissolve [the team].[117]

Where they were not immediately suppressed, groups could rapidly develop beyond a 'spontaneous' level, acquiring memberships, rudimentary financial structures and, in some cases, names.

Groups focusing on causes

In addition to associative structures in the form of case-specific legal teams, lawyers have increasingly established rights-specific or issue-specific lawyer concern groups, including for example, the group China Against Death Penalty founded by Teng Biao, a group working on wrongful death sentences along the lines of an 'Innocence' project,[118] and groups without names that work on issues such as torture, forced abortion and forensic evidence. Groups of this kind may take on the structure of a (possibly unregistered) NGO; and they work in a sustained way, on an open number of cases, and adopting techniques and strate-gies no longer limited to case-based rights advocacy. Their activities include the holding of workshops for training and discussion, the production of reports, and the use of independent citizen documentary film to disseminate their messages.

---

116 #71 2013-1.
117 #71 2013-1. Similarly, #72 2013.
118 Introductory materials (2013) on file with author.

As they take on more consolidated structures and move beyond the exclusive focus on handling cases, lawyers involved in such groups begin to see themselves as part of a wider, greater cause:

> I think it is important to be aware of the fact that the domestic human rights defence movement is just part of a much larger movement.[119]

Far from integrating them further with officially supported structures, coordinated professional rights advocacy and an expanded repertoire of advocacy strategies deepen the rift between rights lawyers and the official organisation purporting to represent them, while at the same time attracting professionally licensed lawyers previously wary of forming such dangerous associations. The experience of joining in such discussions is psychologically liberating and at times – during meetings, joint actions, and even in online discussions – exhilarating. From late 2012 onward, as it became easier to join the loose associations formed in particular through the social media, the numbers of lawyers willing to joining groups explicitly referring to themselves as human rights lawyers and public interest lawyers, to discuss cases and issues of a highly sensitive nature in very open ways, to document their offline actions in real time,[120] to welcome new members and offer moral support to each other, rose rapidly from a few dozen known 'rights lawyers' around 2010 to an estimated over 200 rights lawyers at the end of 2013.[121]

With more support from comparatively established and economically more secure individuals able to support themselves and others on the basis of their own earnings or wealth accumulated before they joined the movement, human rights lawyers' professional legal representation can become more independent, also at a financial level. Foreign nongovernmental organisations had in some cases provided direct legal aid payments to the clients of human rights lawyers; but with more individuals joining relevant domestic groups, new groups with a focus on professional legal aid are being discussed, even as transnational civil society remains relatively hesitant about supporting domestic advocacy groups.[122] As the more permanent, visible and structured rights advocacy have increasingly come under pressure to abandon foreign funding due to new restrictions,[123] domestic donors including businesspeople have stepped in to provide support. As a consequence, it seems that human rights lawyers' advocacy has become more

---

119 #73 2013-1.
120 For example, rights lawyers can use social media such as *Weixin* to send pictures and audio-recordings of their interaction with the authorities in various scenarios directly to their *Weixin* groups (observation, November 2013).
121 This estimate is based on observation through participation in online groups and offline meetings.
122 Thomas E. Kellogg, 'Western funding for rule of law initiatives in China: the importance of a civil society-based approach', *Locating Civil Society: Communities Defending Basic Liberties*, Special Issue of *China Perspectives* (2012) vol. 3, September.
123 Kellogg, *ibid.*

integrated with domestic civil society, more reliant on it, but perhaps also more significant within it.

Gradually, in this process, the authorities lose the power to define what professional lawyering means, even though they do, importantly, retain the power to control the legal profession bureaucratically, and to persecute individuals through the security apparatus. Rights lawyers' status *qua* professionally licensed lawyers remains precarious, even though the discussion here has shown that lawyers engage in alternative discourses and associations to overcome these Party–State constraints. While licensed, they operate under the control of the justice bureaucracies, and as rights lawyers they are subject to marginalisation and persecution. This loss of status and identity is feared and remains difficult to live with but, once it has occurred, it can also be liberating. Persecution can devastate, but the ability to discuss it with others can transform it into a shared reason for continued advocacy. Stripped of their professional status as lawyers, and victimised by methods they know from the experience of their clients, rights lawyers can hold on to their constitutional and political status as citizens; and even while they retain their professional status, some rights lawyers have begun to use a more explicitly political interpretation of who they are by describing themselves as 'citizens', *gongmin*.[124]

Novel forms of civic activism: the New Citizen Movement and its repression

A political conception of citizenship

The concept of 'citizen' or *gongmin*, the scholar, advocate and *New Citizen Movement* co-initiator Xu Zhiyong explained at a 'citizen meal' in late 2012:

> [H]as a very rich meaning, reflecting what sort of system the State should have, what the relationship between State and its citizens should be, and [the idea of] civil society as an independent and free entity, etc. All these ideas are contained in the one word 'citizen' . . . and 'citizen' is an idea that is broader even than democracy, rule of law and such ideas, it serves better than those to capture our ideals. It also captures our methods, our peaceful, rational, and constructive, positive approach, that is [the approach of] citizens.[125]

Xu's comments reflect the modern history of Chinese engagement with the political idea of citizenship, and the word 'citizen' evokes an even older philosophical tradition. At its most basic, the concept of *gong* (公) means 'public', and it also carries connotations of 'open' and 'just'. It figures in a number of different combinations in the Chinese language: citizens, *gongmin*, are 'public persons'; and

---

124 In Chinese characters, 公民.
125 Xu Zhiyong, transcript of comments at a civic meal meeting on Christmas Eve 2012, 公民专刊第8期 p. 78.

words to express the ideas of justice and fairness show their connection to a conception of the public (*gongping, gongzheng, gongyi, gongdao*).[126] The notion of a public realm and of civic obligation connects these ideas to the distant classical past, for example through the old dictum *tian xia wei gong*, 'all under heaven is public';[127] but most centrally, it is part of the tradition of Chinese liberalism, now over 100 years old. As Merle Goldman has pointed out, the modern use of *gongmin* goes back to the scholar–reformers in the declining years of the Chinese empire, in particular Kang Youwei and Liang Qichao.[128] Others have drawn a line from these later imperial scholars to the liberal scholars of the republican period, notably Sun Yat-Sen, and to scholar–activists of contemporary China, such as Liu Xiaobo.

A feature of Sun Yat-sens' liberalism is that it is infused with a particularly strong idea of civic responsibility and conscientious republican duty. Its tone and spirit resembles that of the European and American 18th and 19th century more than it does the 20th-century liberalism of Rawls and his contemporaries. Its conception of citizenship, of the relationship between the individual and the institutions of the State, is as active and spirited as that of the *citoyen* of the philosophers of the French Revolution and of the citizen of the American founding fathers. Sun Yat-sen's enthusiasm and confidence were reflected in his belief that procedures such as the 'Roberts' Rules' could not only structure civic deliberation but also educate and transform those who used them.

Contemporary liberals, in addition to drawing on Sun Yat-sen and the tradition he stands in, also make references to Havel and Michnik as well as to certain aspects of Hayek's philosophy and sometimes to Hannah Arendt. Their need for wit and satire in order to cope with everyday absurdities reminds one of the mood in eastern European countries in the 1980s. For example, Chen Yongmiao as a representative of a 'republican constitutionalist' school of thought advocating a return to the republican, Sun Yat-sen-inspired era, not only draws explicitly on Sun's 'Three Principles of the People', but also uses the notion of 'as if' attributed to Michnik.[129] A rights lawyer explained that Sun Yat-sen made for a good reference point because he is popularly known and officially not repudiated, as philosophers representing foreign enemy forces such as

---

126 In Chinese characters, 公民 and 公平, 公正, 公义, 公道.
127 '大道之行也, 天下为公' translates as 'When the Way is practiced, the world is for the public' or 'the world is just'. 小戴礼记 [*The Classic of Rites*], Warring States Era (475 BC–221 BC). Sun Zhongshan used this phrase to promote his political ideas.
128 Kang and Liang drew on western sources and who used the expressions *gongmin* (public person) and *guomin* (person of the nation) interchangeably. Goldman characterises Kang Youwei's definition of citizenship as essentially tied to a right to political participation, combined with civic responsibility for one's country. Merle Goldman, *From Comrade to Citizen*, Harvard University Press, Cambridge, MA, and London: 2005, at p. 11.
129 Chen Yongmiao (陈永苗), '大陆沦陷区的"民国党人"' [The "pepublicans" on the occupied territory of the mainland]', 8 June 2012, at http://www.peacehall.com/news/gb/pubvp/2012/06/201206082208.shtml, accessed 28 December 2013. Jonathan Shell, 'Introduction' in Adam Michnik, *Letters from Prison and other Essays*, translated by Maya Latynski, University of California Press, Berkeley, Los Angeles and London: 1985, at pp. xxx ff. on uses of the 'as if' technique.

the United States surely would be.[130] Everyday jokes such as rights lawyers will exchange in their daily conversation often come (or purport to come) from Poland, the former Czechoslovakia and other eastern European countries.[131]

The liberal conception of *gongmin*, the 'public person' (Goldman), is thus as rich and demanding as Xu Zhiyong asserts. It reflects a public–private divide that Chinese liberals use when emphasising the importance of protecting private rights against public power (*siquanli* and *gongquanli*).[132] It also indicates the individual's participation in the public realm as *gongmin*, a public person, as an aspect of democracy dependent on the conceptual distinction between public and private, and connects seamlessly to the idea of civic virtue – the term *gongyi* could be translated as 'public justice' but also as 'civic obligation', or interpreted more broadly as the demands justice places on each person, the duty we have toward all and everyone. In this interpretation, citizenship can be understood as connected to civic-mindedness as a personal virtue, reminiscent of the western Aristotelian or Confucian Chinese tradition.[133]

Human rights lawyers have exploited the fact that some of these ideas, very notably that of the citizen, have become part of the fabric of the existing legal–political system and of official discourse at domestic and international levels. The current (1982) PRC Constitution has been built around the concept of *gongmin*, as were its three predecessors. Constitutional rights according to the PRC Constitution, for example, are held by 'PRC citizens', and the 'civil rights' stipulated in the International Covenant on Civil and Political Rights (ICCPR) and in the Universal Declaration of Human Rights (UNDHR) are also 'citizens' rights' in China (*gongmin quanli*). It was also seen that in many situations, lawyers fight for trials to be more genuinely public and open; and these efforts in many ways connect seamlessly to the wider activism relying on the status of lawyers as citizens. The move from inside to outside the courtroom discussed earlier is dependent on the presence of and even on collaboration from other citizens; it 'works' when people understand and affirm their identity as citizens with rights and responsibilities.

In popularising and interpreting the concept *gongmin*, lawyers have challenged the limited, officially tolerated discourse. Expressions such as 'citizens' society'

---

130 #2 2013-3.

131 For example, a lawyer used social media to pass on the joke: 'Under Communist Party rule in Poland, intellectuals had the following, well-known five precepts: 1. Don't think. 2. If you think, don't speak. 3. If you speak, don't write. 4. If you write, don't sign. 5. If you sign, don't be surprised. For circulation.' Another, non-Christian lawyer immediately commented, 'But at least they had a relatively independent Church!' (Observation, November 2013.) Wikipedia attributes this joke to Russia at http://en.wikipedia.org/wiki/Russian_political_jokes, accessed 28 December 2013.

132 In Chinese characters, 私权利 and 公权力. In this usage, both *gong*/公 and *si*/私, the public and the private, have normative meanings. He Weifang (贺卫方), '刑诉法大修：最后的博弈 [The great revision of the Criminal Procedure Law: the last contest]', 13 March 2012, at http://heweifang.blog.caixin.com/archives/38257, accessed 28 December 2013; Jiang Ping (江平) interview '私权神圣公权力行使需受限 [Private power is sacred, public power requires to be restricted]', 14 October 2011, at http://www.china-review.com/lishipindaoa.asp?id=29139&parapage=1, accessed 28 December 2013.

133 David Wiggins, 'Neo-Aristotelian reflections on justice', 113 *Mind* (2004) 477.

(i.e. civil society), 'citizen consciousness', 'citizen (civic) journalist', 'civic forum',[134] 'citizen meal',[135] 'citizen rights defence',[136] 'civic pledge' and 'citizen broadcast'[137] illustrate that the concept of the citizen has become intimately connected with the rise of civil society and of the *weiquan* movement since the early 2000s. These uses of *gongmin* have inspired an alternative conception of personal identity to the view promoted by the existing political system, as the term more commonly employed by the Party is *renmin*,[138] a plural word for 'people'.

As in France under the *ancien régime*, the equalising and democratising idea of the citizen itself becomes a challenge to established authorities.[139] It not only opposes the Leninist characterisation of ordinary people as those who are to be led by the Party; it also cuts through distinctions the Party–State must draw on in attempts to justify its treatment of some people as enemies of the people. As *gongmin*, lawyers, legal advocates without professional licences, petitioners, journalists, people from all walks of life and with diverse backgrounds can give support to the liberal communities promoting civil society; and no one is conceptually excluded.[140] It is therefore not surprising that the expression 'civil society' was officially rejected and reportedly banned by the authorities from about 2009 onward;[141] and that it is now, along with 'human rights' and 'universal values' understood to be part of the discourses rejected officially in the 2013 (Party) 'Document no. 9'.[142] But crucially, the concept of the citizen as such is so entrenched in official language that it could not easily be censored or suppressed.

The emergence of the 'New Citizen Movement' and related initiatives

Seen against this background, the authorities' handling of the group Gongmeng or Open Constitution Initiative illustrates the dispersal of a relatively small organisation that was well defined by its registration, legal structure, office location,

---

134 The founders of Transition Institute launched 'civic forum', a combination of biweekly seminars and a publication based on these seminars, in 2003; it was later run by Transition Institute. It was always under pressure and in the context of the 2011 jasmine crackdown it was stopped altogether. #76 2013-1.
135 '京沪等地同城聚餐讨论"宪政梦" 北京公民促高官公开财产被拘 [Same-city dinners discuss "Dream of constitutionalism," Beijing citizens requesting asset disclosure by high officials detained]', RFA, 1 April 2013, at http://www.rfa.org/mandarin/yataibaodao/renquanfazhi/jh-04012013105407.html, accessed 28 December 2013.
136 '著名维权人士许志永发布《公民维权手册》 [Well-known human rights defender Xu Zhiyong publishes "Citizen rights defence manual"]', Boxun (博讯), 18 April 2013, at http://boxun.com/news/gb/china/2010/04/201004182312.shtml, accessed 28 December 2013; copy available at http://www.scribd.com/doc/17479805/%E5%85%AC%E6%B0%91%E7%BB%B4%E6%9D%83%E6%89%8B%E5%86%8C, accessed 28 December 2013.
137 '视频: 2013公民播报首版 [First edition of 2013 citizen broadcast]', undated, around Chinese New Year 2013, http://www.youtube.com/watch?v=ND9I0HPi-ZU, accessed 28 December 2013. Further links provided at this link.
138 In Chinese characters, 人民.
139 Simon Shama, *Citizens. A Chronicle of the French Revolution*, Penguin Books, London: 1989.
140 Pils, *ibid*.
141 Pils, *ibid*.
142 ChinaFile, 'Document 9: a ChinaFile translation', 8 November 2013, at http://www.chinafile.com/document-9-chinafile-translation, accessed 28 December 2013.

accounts and other documentation, into a looser association of citizens, as a consequence of Party–State persecution. Founded, as mentioned earlier, in 2003 by two of the 'three doctors' of law who had submitted a call to abolish the Custody and Repatriation system to the NPCSC,[143] it developed successfully until 2009. It rose to some prominence and international attention through its work on rights defence cases including the petitioning system, extra-legal detention and black jails, forced evictions, Tibetans' human rights, second-generation migrant workers' rights and their children's equal right to education. In 2009 it was closed down by the Civil Affairs Bureau as an 'illegal social organisation', and its head Xu Zhiyong and a co-worker were accused of tax evasion (they were later released and charges were eventually dropped).[144] However, the company that had been registered to give *Gongmeng* a legal existence continued to be registered as such; and the group continued to operate, albeit no longer with foreign funding.[145]

In the years after *Gongmeng* had come under attack, its members and supporters began to refer to it as *Gongmin* or 'Citizens', a name that simply went back to the original appellation 'Citizens' Alliance (*gongmin lianmeng*)',[146] initially deemed too sensitive to be used openly.[147] In the following, Xu Zhiyong and others belonging to the organisation proceeded to lay greater emphasis on the connection between their activism and a wider political conception of citizenship. In June 2010 several lawyers and human rights defenders including Xu Zhiyong published a call for citizens to sign pledges titled 'Citizen's Pledge'. The Pledge articulates values and standards to be pursued specifically by members of different professions, including officials in the legal system, and lawyers. Its phrase 'a modern nation by the people, for the people, and of the people', refers both (it seems) to Lincoln and (more directly) to Sun Yat-sen. To the general pledge:

1. My conduct will be rooted in conscientiousness, understanding, respect, and caring concern for my fellow human beings;
2. I will respect the Constitution and the laws and defend their correct implementation;
3. In my life, I will, relying on legal means and altruism, defend justice and righteousness in society.[148]

---

143 Discussed in Chapter 2.
144 Karla Simon discusses the closure and their based in 'Measures for banning illegal nongovernmental organisations', in *The Regulation of Civil Society Organisations in China*, 2011, available online.
145 #2 2009-1 (no audio-recording).
146 In Chinese characters, 公民联盟. Teng Biao (滕彪), '公盟不死 [Gongmeng is not dead]', 17 January 2009, at http://blog.qq.com/qzone/622007804/1248271496.htm, accessed 28 December 2013; 公民在行动 [Citizens are being active], *Citizen Monthly* (公民月刊), January 2009.
147 As discussed earlier on in this chapter.
148 '许志永、滕彪等人发起《公民承诺》签署 [Xu Zhiyong, Teng Biao initiate "Citizen's Pledge" signature campaign]', Boxun (博讯), 19 June 2010, at http://boxun.com/news/gb/china/2010/06/201006191908.shtml, accessed 28 December 2013. See also Custer (trans.), 'The Citizen's Pledge', 20 June 2010, at http://chinageeks.org/2010/06/xu-zhiyong-et-al-the-chinese-citizens-pledge/, accessed 28 December 2013. The website at which one can sign up is at http://survey.activepower.net/service/survey/survey.asp?survey_id=58235, accessed 28 December 2013.

It adds special pledges according to the signatory's work responsibilities as judges, prosecutors, police officers, People's Congress representatives, lawyers, workers, farmers, and so on. For example:

> 4. In my station at work I will follow the following minimum moral standards:
> . . . . As a lawyer, I will be true to the law and not bribe judges.
> . . . . As a citizen in any position, I will keep the public apart from the private, I will not be corrupt, and I will not seek special powers.[149]

The 2010 email action provided the initiators with a database of the names of those who signed, which they could then contact to initiate further activities. On this basis (and presumably making use of their many contacts with clients and fellow rights defenders), in the course of meetings beginning in May 2012,[150] Xu and others initiated the New Citizen Movement or *Xin Gongmin Yundong*.[151] It uses as its logo a distinctive calligraphy of the two characters for *gongmin* by Sun Yat-sen, usually displayed in white or silver on blue.[152] It thus openly claims a connection with efforts to change China's political system that were made prior to the Party's regime, even though the Party also claims them to be part of its own history. Adherence to Sun Yat-sen's ideas runs through much of the activism associated with ideas of citizenship: from the use of his calligraphy to references to his 'Three Principles of the People'[153] and enthusiasm for techniques he advocated to infuse a more democratic spirit, such as the use of 'Roberts' Rules' at seminars held by rights lawyers.[154] The wider motto of the New Citizen Movement, 'freedom, justice, love'[155] indicates its intention to include and accommodate everybody. It is noteworthy that the Citizen Pledge does not envisage the possibility of (in most contexts of civil disobedience, nonviolent) breaches of the law; rather, it insists on 'correctly implementing' the Constitution and laws. This may be read as an indirect reference to the authorities' own failure to adhere to law, especially to respect constitutional rights guarantees.

149 *Ibid.*
150 The initial meeting was organised in a discreet manner but nevertheless interrupted by the police, which in later months focused on those who had participated in the initial meeting, even though some of them may have participated for random reasons.
151 In Chinese characters, 新公民运动.
152 The Gongmin logo is used by a number of lawyers including some well-known rights lawyers for their Twitter and/or *Weibo* accounts. Rights lawyers Liang Xiaojun, Liu Weiguo, Xu Zhiyong, for example, use this logo. Lawyers Fu Yonggang, Fan Biaowen, Cheng Bin, Yan Wangli, Liu Jinbin also use it. Rights lawyers Wang Chuxiang (Wang Cheng), Liu Weiguo, Liang Xiaojun, Xu Zhiyong, Wu Zhenqi, Liu Xiaoyuan and Xu Zhiyong describe themselves as 'citizens' in their Twitter self-introductions. Several lawyers also use the logo for their (not entirely public) *Weixin* accounts; some of these in the form of a picture of themselves wearing a T-Shirt with the logo. Xu Zhiyong tweet of 27 May 2012, 'Advocating the use of the "citizen" image, the joint promotion of a new civil society!', at https://twitter.com/zhiyongxu/status/206444691267391488, accessed 28 December 2013.
153 E.g. #85 2013-1.
154 Observation.
155 In Chinese characters, 自由, 公义, 爱.

In the summer of 2012, some of those who had signed the 'citizen pledges' became organisers of the New Citizens Movement, reaching out to others and participating actively in the movement's 'low-threshold' activities. Such actions, rather like forms of organising without organisation described by Clay Shirky,[156] initially intended simply to allow people to gather 'for a meal', to 'discuss current issues', as a way of coordinating among like-minded rights defenders that had been tried on other occasions. Amongst these is the already mentioned 'citizen meal'.[157] It was a form of action borne from the desire to make participation 'low threshold', so as to meet a challenge identified by Xiao Shu and others: on the one hand, the initiators thought, a much greater number of people must overcome fear of the system and, on the other hand, new movements must avoid the fate of past movements and parties that either faced almost immediate extinction, or had to remain in isolation from a wider Chinese public in order to stay underground, just because they were regarded as secretly plotting the overthrow of the regime:

> 'Civic meals' [is an activity with] a very low threshold that is very simple. Everybody comes together under a shared identity to join in a meal and to discuss some common issues together. In a traditional sense, China has always had its many separate hills [territories, spheres of control] and so on; but now, whether or not you agree with others, you are all citizens. You recognize, first, that you are a citizen and you recognize, second, democratic principles: so we are all sitting here together, sharing a common platform that does not belong to any particular person, that does not belong to a particular 'fiefdom' but, rather, is a common one that belongs to all of us and that is a union of free citizens. On this platform citizens decide through democratic principles what they will do. This is why we emphasize that citizens in all locations shall develop spontaneously, that they control their own stories and that people in each location do their own thing and have their own local topics, so that Guangzhou and Chengdu have their different local topics. But they are all citizens, and they mutually recognize their status, as 'citizens'.[158]

Coming together for a meal has long been a technique people have used to meet in settings the authorities find comparatively hard to control. While the security apparatus can, of course, disrupt such meetings and detain its partici-

---

156 Clay Shirky, *Here Comes Everybody: The Power of Organising Without Organisations*, Penguin, London: 2008. Shirky argues that certain uses of the internet allow for mass amateurisation of certain kinds of action, such as journalistic reporting, and that they challenge traditional ideas of how political power is organised in (sovereign) states with governments and related structures. Cp. also Teng Biao 'Rights defence, microblogs, and the surrounding gaze: the Rights Defence Movement online and offline', in *Locating Civil Society: Communities Defending Basic Liberties*, Special Issue of *China Perspectives* 2012/3.
157 In Chinese characters, 公民聚餐.
158 Xu, Zhiyong, '谁把"自由, 公义, 爱"当成敌人, 一定是中华民族的敌人! [Who turns "freedom, justice, love" into an enemy is clearly an enemy of the Chinese nation!]', Special Issue (8) *Citizen* (公民专刊) 76 ff.

pants, such highly visible measures are rare; they would generate opportunities for public records the authorities may want to avoid.[159] Meals, therefore, while far from perfectly safe, often represent a viable setting for civic activism of the 'low-threshold' kind envisaged by Xiao Shu (cited earlier in this chapter). The setup for these citizen meals varied from place to place,[160] and apart from core organisers, participants varied from one meal to another. At one point in 2013, citizen meals were held simultaneously in some 30 cities across China; and participants may have numbered in the hundreds or thousands, according to a rights lawyer.[161]

One such citizen meal, for example, organised in late May 2012, included about a dozen members, and addressed China's political situation in a very broad manner, while also addressing ways of resuscitating the public memory of June Fourth. Its organisation was clandestine. Another, in a different city and some weeks later, seemed more open; it included some 20 or 30 participants including several rights lawyers and well-known online activists, as well as one or two persons who had seen an online announcement and just come along out of curiosity, they said. Discussion ranged across a variety of topics; and the meeting took place in an open space. A third citizen meal, in early 2013, was again organised in clandestine fashion; it involved several rights lawyers as well as other citizens, and its topic was the creation of a concern group to work on a distinct rights issue through a variety of forms of advocacy.[162]

Further initiatives included street gatherings of people calling for financial disclosure by officials, in the context of an official anti-corruption campaign under China's new leadership. While in the official campaign, the authorities decide who is to be investigated through official channels, the New Citizen Movement protesters insisted on their right to demand financial transparency as citizens, and thereby indirectly also made the point that to be effective, anti-corruption measures must eliminate the politically motivated selection of its targets. The financial disclosure appeals garnered support from citizens in different cities, as a privately circulated 'Citizen Monthly' illustrates by pictures of citizens demonstrating with banners taken in well-known public spots, with many banners displaying the now familiar calligraphy by Sun Yat-sen (in white on red).[163]

159 As the example of police disruption of celebratory dinner meetings after the announcement of the 2010 Nobel Peace Prize for Liu Xiaobo and disruption in the case activists congregating in Fuzhou (where the authorities instructed restaurants to refuse serving activists) illustrated. E.g. Cao Guoxing (曹国星), '何杨疑因保存乐清案中钱成宇被刑讯证据被捕 [He Yang detained, possibly for having kept evidence of torture in the Leqing (criminal) case]', 21 March 2011, at http://tw.aboluowang.com/news/2011/0322/199378.html, accessed 28 December 2013; He Yang (何杨), 赫索格的日子 [*Herzog's Days*], independent documentary film, Beijing, 2010, at http://www.youtube.com/watch?v=BSi2CCiTeDI, accessed 5 January 2014.
160 An announcement made via an online chat forum stipulated a meeting point, provided a rough schedule and described as the topic 'deeply studying the Constitution and other laws, connecting theory and practice, discussing "ruling the country in accordance with law" and "my Chinese Dream".' Shared online, March 2013. On file with author.
161 #2 2013-7.
162 Observation (2012, 2013).
163 Copy on file with author.

While the New Citizen Movement was unfolding, initiated by people in the north of China, citizen actions in the south took actions that seemed to have more straightforwardly political agendas. The rights activist and scholar Guo Feixiong (Yang Maodong), released from a prison sentence in the summer of 2012, was among the figures at the centre of demonstrations for constitutionalism that followed an especially crude instance of Party–State interference with a major relatively liberal newspaper, *Southern Weekend*. The Southern Weekend Incident saw certain individuals stage demonstrations upholding banners demanding 'constitutionalism', 'human rights' and 'freedom'.[164]

Rights lawyers and other sympathisers kept critically discussing these various actions and strategies. There appeared to be agreement that 'leaderless-ness' was strategically desirable and endorsed by persons at the centre of such initiatives; but rights lawyers generally also recognised the inevitable importance of certain central figures. One rights lawyer commented:

> Guo Feixiong always said [to his supporters], 'When I am no longer in Guangzhou, you must continue just the same as when I was still here. If you do that, I will be safe. If you do things differently once I am no longer here, they will think that I am important, and then they will definitely "fix" me.'

> But, so far as I am concerned, it is very difficult for me to live up to that, because I think I just don't have that experience and ability.[165]

He added that while it was impossible not to be affected by the detention of central figures:

> The sort of organisation they [the authorities] imagine is the sort that is mafia-like, that has procedures and structures; whereas our kind of organisation now has a 'flat' structure, like in the west. That's different.[166]

Xu also said that not everybody had fully grasped how much the New Citizen movement differed from older attempts to 'subvert' the existing political power:

> We emphasise a constructive approach and emphasise 'freedom, justice, love'; these are our credos. The most ideal form of change [*biange*][167] in China would be a Constitution-drafting process through negotiation between forces inside and outside the system; our mission is to end authoritarian rule through

---

164 Cp. David Bandurski, 'Inside the Southern Weekly Incident', *China Media Project*, 7 January 2013, at http://cmp.hku.hk/2013/01/07/30402/, accessed 5 January 2014.

165 #88 see also Xu Zhiyong's public comments at April 2013 seminar, *supra*.

166 #88 2013-2. Also: 'We don't fear spies, because our principle has from the very beginning has been openness.' #2 2013-7.

167 In Chinese characters, 变革.

constructive methods and we will maintain a benevolent attitude toward any individual. If one day such peaceable citizens as we no longer have room to operate in, violence will occur, that will be a national misfortune. (. . .) It is important that [others] do not disturb or destroy what others are doing, that no one impose their own violent revolutionary ideas and standards on a community of citizens that is only just budding inside China, thus pushing them into a situation of danger.[168]

Sympathetic critics expressed scepticism about this purportedly non-provocative stance, advocating a more direct approach:

The New Citizen Movement mostly raises issues like equal education rights and financial disclosure: this does not touch so much on the system and is still more moderate. Whereas actions here in the streets in the South address more directly the central problems of the system, for example, by requesting that the State ratify the ICCPR.[169] And, many of the slogans here are about democracy and constitutionalism and so on. They are more direct. Of course in the South, we also made some specific requests such as financial disclosure.[170]

You should stop only reacting to what the Communist Party does. If you copy them by public calls against corruption when they have just started their own corruption campaign, don't think they're that stupid – as long as you make political demands of any kind, they will assume that you want a share of their power. They won't let you off, just because the slogans you shouted were identical with their own.[171]

At the same time, the intended leaderless-ness of the movement meant that actions citizens in some places took unforeseen initiatives. A rights lawyer close to these developments commented that:

There was a sense – I felt there was some loss of control; because the people who participated all had their own preferences, and they were getting so enthusiastic . . . also with those civic meals; X [a co-initiator] actually said he didn't know about these [beforehand].[172]

Xu Zhiyong, '公民 许志永: 关于月末公民同城聚餐和"小圈子"区别的说明 [Citizen Xu Zhiyong: explanation concerning the difference between end-of-month same-city citizen dinners and "small circles"]', 6 May 2013, at http://www.canyu.org/n72755c6.aspx, accessed 28 December 2013.
169 Yang Ming (杨明), '公民权利无保障 连署促批准人权公约 [Civil rights lack protection, urging the ratification of the ICCPR]', 3 May 2013 at http://www.voachinese.com/content/china-human-right-20130305/1615327.html, accessed 28 December 2013.
170 #88 2013-1.
171 #25 2013-2.
172 #19 2013-1.

The clampdown on the New Citizen Movement, the Southern Street Movement, etc.

From March 2013, the authorities clamped down. Lawyers Ding Jiaxi, Xu Zhiyong, Zhao Changqing, Song Ze, and entrepreneur Wang Gongquan and many others connected (by the authorities) to the New Citizen Movement were detained on various charges including 'creating a social disturbance', illegal assembly and 'gathering a crowd to disrupt order in a public place'.[173] Some others, the authorities detained temporarily before releasing them again.[174] In the south, Guo Feixiong was detained in the month after Xu Zhiyong's detention.[175] A clampdown had been anticipated, and some, such as Xu Zhiyong, had made it clear that they were prepared to go to prison; Xu was able to release a short video-clip from police detention.[176] Even so, a rights lawyer commented that as a result of the extraordinary pressure faced by groups who sought to persist in holding citizen meal meetings and engaging in other actions, the movement had to some extent 'gone underground':

> There were some thirty cities; and a few thousand persons in total were rather active in participating in citizen meals and so on. But it is impossible to come up with precise statistics. Because in some cities, there will be events and activities held spontaneously. They might use some New Citizen Movement tags; but there will also be various spontaneous actions; and what with the on-going repression now, some activities now may be more low-profile; but they nevertheless continue. There is simply no way that civil society in China could be shut down ... In any case, the number of persons detained this time because they made use of their right to free speech is more than ten times the number affected in [the Jasmine Crackdown of] 2011.[177]

---

173 China Human Rights Defenders (CHRD), 'Individuals unlawfully detained in crackdown on peaceful assembly, association & expression', 23 December 2013, at http://chrdnet. com/2013/07/individuals-detained-in-crackdown-on-assembly-and-association/, accessed 28 December 2013. See also Beijing Municipal Procuracy No. 1, 'Indictment of Xu Zhiyong by Beijing Municipal Procuracy No. 1', 13 December 2013, translated by China Change, 21 December 2013, at http://chinachange.org/2013/12/21/indictment-of-xu-zhiyong-by-beijing-municipal-peoples-procuratorate-no-1-branch/, accessed 2 January 2014.
174 This included Xiao Shu and Lawyer Wang Cheng (Wang Chuxiang).
175 Guangzhou Municipal Public Security Bureau, 'Police indictment opinion for Guo Feixiong and Sun Desheng', 10 December 2013, translated at Siweiluozi Blog, at http://www. siweiluozi.net/2013/12/translation-police-indictment-opinion.html, 26 December 2013, accessed 2 January 2014.
176 In the video-clip, Xu Zhiyong says, among other things, that his only crimes were 'calling on everyone to be a citizen, a forthright citizen who exercises their civil rights guaranteed under the Constitution and fulfils a citizen's civic duty, advocating for equal rights to education . . . and asset disclosure by public officials'. Josh Chin, 'Prominent rights advocate Xu Zhiyong releases jail video', 8 August 2013n at *China Real Time Report* blog (Washington Post), http://blogs.wsj. com/chinarealtime/2013/08/08/prominent-chinese-activist-releases-jail-video/?mg=blogs-wsj&url=http%253A%252F%252F blogs.wsj.com% 252Fchinarealtime%252F2013%252F08% 252F08%252Fprominent-chinese-activist-releases-jail-video, accessed 28 December 2013.
177 #2 2013-7 1:30.

Despite all efforts to overcome the logic of Party–State control, and to devise strategies that do not expose human rights defenders to the risk of annihilation, the expansive goals of the New Citizen Movement are in some conflict with their hope of allowing for low-risk participation:[178] 'If they make the connection with the New Citizens Movement clearer, they become more significant, and more media will report on them. But at the same time, that also puts them more at risk.'[179]

But due to the new techniques it has used, a disappearance from view, and even the detention of and prison terms for some leading figures, no longer means the sort of absolute extinction it might have meant before. So far as rights lawyers are concerned there is little doubt that the New Citizen Movement and similar initiatives are factors in rights lawyers' rapid rise in numbers. Rights lawyers who have recently joined human rights lawyer circles mention that their participation began with taking part in some 'citizen meals', for example:

> I had not had any interaction with the Justice Bureau or the *guobao* police yet at that time; I had only heard about those things. But I heard about them when I took part in some citizen meals and that way, I gradually freed myself from fear. I met people like [a well-known dissident] and so on; and then I took on some rather sensitive cases, and eventually also a Falun Gong case.[180]

And there is a sense that, with fluid, complex, yet 'flat' networks established via the internet, connections might be revitalised again at any moment:

> The crucial thing now is, there are many of us. When there are many people, you have less fear (. . .) Now that they have gradually established human rights lawyer groups and so on (. . .) We have learned to react quickly. When something happens to a lawyer, everybody else will come out and speak up for them. So, really, lawyers have opened up a space for themselves. It is like with freedom of speech. China has never really had any freedom of speech, and yet there has been steady sense of improvement in this area, simply because more and more people have dared to speak up.[181]

The goal of inclusive transformation

Arendt has argued that the human capacity to make a new beginning is a principle that counteracts the principle of terror she describes as characteristic of totalitarian dictatorship.[182] Society under the current post-totalitarian system

178 #2 2013-3.
179 #2 2013-3.
180 #92 2013-2.
181 #88 2013-2.
182 To quote Anthony Court, 'Insofar as totalitarianism has not completely eliminated all forms of spontaneous human action, freedom, or the inherent human capacity to "make a new beginning",

in China is much less restricted and in that sense freer. Advocates using their freedoms can counteract the fear that post-totalitarian government in China, according to the analysis presented here, continues to rely on. Their active exercises of basic expressive and associative freedoms are in fact the most effective way of counteracting fear, to judge by how human rights lawyers experience their initiation to such political actions. Confronted with extra-legal measures, a rising number of lawyers have abandoned their earlier concerns about staying 'within the law;' they have largely realised that there is no such thing as depoliticised rights advocacy, even though there continues to be disagreement about the issue of politicisation.[183] Following this insight, they have drawn the lesson that resistance grows stronger if it can overcome the schisms and rivalries characteristic of social movements. Phenomena such as the lawyers' team built around individual cases and the 'New Citizen Movement' must be understood in this light. These forms of advocacy seek to avoid directly addressing the shift of political power they ultimately hope will occur.[184] Not to plan the end of the current system can be seen as part of a strategy to avoid persecution; it is also a vital aspect of rights lawyers' goal of an inclusive transformation of Chinese society.

Bibliography

NPC laws

PRC Criminal Law [中华人民共和国刑法], passed on 1 July 1979, promulgated on 6 July 1979, and effective as of 1 January 1980, last revised on 25 February 2011, at http://www.moj.gov.cn/Prison_work/content/2013-05/07/content_4436670. htm? node=43130. For an English translation, see http://www.cecc.gov/resources/ legal-provisions/criminal-law-of-the-peoples-republic-of-china.

Administrative and judicial decisions

Beijing Municipal Procuracy No. 1, 'Indictment of Xu Zhiyong by Beijing Municipal Procuracy No. 1', 13 December 2013, translated by China Change, 21 December 2013, http://chinachange.org/2013/12/21/indictment-of-xu-zhiyong-by-beijing-municipal-peoples-procuratorate-no-1-branch/, accessed 2 January 2014.

Guangzhou Municipal Public Security Bureau, 'Police Indictment Opinion for Guo Feixiong and Sun Desheng', 10 December 2013, translated at Siweiluozi Blog, at http://www.siweiluozi.net/2013/12/translation-police-indictment-opinion.html, 26 December 2013, accessed 2 January 2014.

---

exists as an ever-present potential within society.' Anthony Court, *Hannah Arendt's Theory of Totalitarianism – Part 2*, 23 May 2012, at http://rozenbergquarterly.com/?p=3115, accessed 28 December 2013.

183 Zhao Sile (赵思乐), '郭玉闪：抱着绝望姿态做专业的维权 [Guo Yushan: Engaging in professional rights defence in an attitude of despair];' Kuang Da (旷达), '滕彪:一个单纯的反对者 [Teng Biao – a pure opponent], both in 34 iSun Magazine (阳光时务周刊), 6 December 2012.

184 Xiao Shu (笑蜀), '以负责任的社会运动倒逼中国转型 —— 我的人权联署自白书', 31 March 2013, at http://blog.sina.com.cn/s/blog_6314a9890102e0i7.html, accessed 28 December 2013.

Jingjiang City Judiciary Website (靖江市法院网), '关于提前解除拘留王全璋律师的公 d 告 [Notice on early releasing Lawyer Wang Quanzhang from Detention]', 6 April 2013 at http://jjsfy.chinacourt.org/public/detail.php?id=1689, accessed 27 December 2013.

Books and articles

Anonymous, 23 '省市139名律师共同呼吁保障王全璋律师权益' [139 Lawyers from 23 provinces call for the protection of lawyer Wang Quanzhang's rights], signed by 139 lawyers, at http://wq9884.zfwlxt.com/SKZX/20130406/960.html, accessed 27 December 2013.

BBC, 'Chen Guangcheng: nephew Chen Kegui sentenced', 30 November 2012, at http://www.bbc.co.uk/news/world-asia-china-20551967, accessed 27 December 2013.

Béja, Jean-Philippe, 'Civil society against democracy', a paper delivered at Workshop on New Developments in Chinese Civil Society held at Hong Kong University on 30–31 October 2013, on file with author.

Béja, Jean-Philippe, *À la recherche d'une ombre chinoise: le movement pour la démocratie en Chine* [*In search of a Chinese shadow: the movement for democracy in China*], Editions du Seuil, Paris: 2004, Chapter 11.

Boehler, Patrick, 'Rights lawyer Tang Jitian detained over Falun Gong case', *South China Morning Post*, 21 October 2013, at http://www.scmp.com/news/china-insider/article/1336488/rights-lawyer-tang-jitian-detained-over-falun-gong-case, accessed 27 December 2013.

Boxun (博讯), '周莉案两次庭审回顾：辩方有理有据 [Zhou Li's 1st and 2nd instance trials revisited: a reasonable and well-founded defence]', 24 April 2010, at http://www.peacehall.com/news/gb/china/2010/04/201004241238.shtml.

Boxun (博讯), '围观彰显力量: 维权律师王全璋提前获释后发声 [The power of sur-rounding observation: comments on Wang Quanzhang's early release from detention]', 6 April 2013, at http://www.peacehall.com/news/gb/china/2013/04/201304061555.shtml, accessed 27 December 2013.

Boxun (博讯), '著名维权人士许志永发布《公民维权手册》[Well-known human rights defender Xu Zhiyong publishes 'Citizen rights defence manual]', 18 April 2013, at http://boxun.com/news/gb/china/2010/04/201004182312.shtml, accessed 28 December 2013; copy available http://www.scribd.com/doc/17479805/%E5%85%AC%E6%B0%91%E7%BB%B4%E6%9D%83%E6%89%8B%E5%86%8C, accessed 28December 2013.

Boxun (博讯), '许志永、滕彪等人发起《公民承诺》签署 [Xu Zhiyong, Teng Biao initiate "Citizen's Pledge" signature campaign]', 19 June 2010, at http://boxun.com/news/gb/china/2010/06/201006191908.shtml, accessed 28 December 2013.

Boxun (博讯), '我们愿意为被捕藏民提供法律帮助 [We are willing to provide legal aid to arrested Tibetans]', 2 April 2008, at http://www.peacehall.com/news/gb/china/2008/04/200804022305.shtml, accessed 28 December 2013.

Bristow, Michael, 'China rights activist Wang Lihong jailed', BBC, 9 September 2011, at http://www.bbc.co.uk/news/world-asia-pacific-14850435, accessed 27 December 2013.

Cao, Guoxing (曹国星), '何杨疑因保存乐清案中钱成宇被刑讯证据被捕 [He Yang detained, possibly for having kept evidence of torture in the Leqing (criminal) case]', 21 March 2011, at http://www.chinese.rfi.fr/%E4%B8%AD%E5%9B%BD/20110321-%E4%BD%95%E6%9D%A8%E7%96%91%E5%9B%A0%E4%BF%9D%E5%AD%98%E4%B9%90%E6%B8%85%E6%A1%88%E4%B8%AD%E9%

92%B1%E6%88%90%E5%AE%87%E8%A2%AB%E5%88%91%E8%AE%
AF%E8%AF%81%E6%8D%AE%E8%A2%AB%E6%8D%95, accessed
28 December 2013.

Chen, Yongmiao (陈永苗), '大陆沦陷区的"民国党人" [The "Republicans" on the
occupied territory of the mainland]', 8 June 2012, at http://www.peacehall.com/
news/gb/pubvp/2012/06/201206082208.shtml, accessed 28 December 2013.

Chin, Josh, 'Prominent rights advocate Xu Zhiyong releases jail video', *China Real Time
Report* blog (*Washington Post*), 8 August 2013, athttp://blogs.wsj.com/chinarealtime/
2013/08/08/prominent-chinese-activist-releases-jail-video/?mg=blogs-wsj&url=http%
253A%252F%252Fblogs.wsj.com%252Fchinarealtime%252F2013%252F08%252
F08%252Fprominent-chinese-activist-releases-jail-video, accessed 28 December 2013.

China Digital Times, 'Word of the week: new five black categories', 8 August 2012, at http://
chinadigitaltimes.net/2012/08/word-of-the-week-the-new-five-black-categories/,
accessed 30 December 2013.

China Digital Times, 'Xu Zhiyong: on the New Citizens' Movement', at http://
chinadigitaltimes.net/2013/05/xu-zhiyong-on-the-new-citizens-movement/, accessed
28 December 2013.

Chinese Human Rights Defenders (CHRD), 'Individuals unlawfully detained in crackdown on peaceful assembly, association & expression', updated 23 December 2013,
at http://chrdnet.com/2013/07/individuals-detained-in-crackdown-on-assembly-
and-association/, accessed 28 December 2013.

Chinese Human Rights Defenders (CHRD), '陈建刚律师控告法官庭审中破坏法律实
施 [Lawyer Chen Jiang reports judge for crime of undermining implementation of the
law]', 6 November 2013, at http://wqw2010.blogspot.hk/2013/11/blog-post_1638.
html, accessed 27 December 2013.

Citizen Monthly (公民月刊), '公民在行动 [Citizens are being active]', January 2009.

Classic of Rites [小戴礼记], Warring States Period (475 BC–221 BC).

Court, Anthony, 'Hannah Arendt's theory of totalitarianism – Part 2', 23 May 2012, at
http://rozenbergquarterly.com/?p=3115, accessed 28 December 2013.

Custer, C. (trans), 'The Citizen's Pledge', 20 June 2010, at http://chinageeks.org/2010/06/
xu-zhiyong-et-al-the-chinese-citizens-pledge/, accessed 28 December 2013.

Dworkin, Ronald, *Taking Rights Seriously*, Duckworth, London: 1977.

Fuller, Lon, 'The forms and limits of adjudication' (1978), Chapter 1 in Freeman, Michael
(ed.), *Alternative Dispute Resolution*, New York University Press, New York: 1995.

Goldman, Merle, *From Comrade to Citizen: The Struggle for Political Rights in China*, Harvard
University Press, Cambridge, MA, and London: 2005.

Havel, Václav, *Moc Bezmocných* [*The Power of the Powerless*], Prague, 1978, published in
translation by Jan Vladislav (ed.), *Living in Truth*, Faber & Faber, London and Boston,
MA: 1986.

He, Weifang (贺卫方), '刑诉法大修：最后的博弈 [The great revision of the Criminal
Procedure Law: the last contest]', 13 March 2012, at http://heweifang.blog.caixin.com/
archives/38257, accessed 28 December 2013; http://chinadigitaltimes.net/2013/05/
xu-zhiyong-on-the-new-citizens-movement/, accessed 28 December 2013.

Human Rights in China, 'Democracy activist Qin Yongmin released from prison after
12-year sentence', 29 November 2010, at http://www.hrichina.org/en/content/4879,
accessed 28 December 2013.

Human Rights Watch, 'China: Chen Kegui's Case tests rule of law', 15 October 2012,
at http://www.hrw.org/news/2012/10/15/china-chen-kegui-s-case-tests-rule-law,
accessed 27 December 2013.

Jiang, Ping (江平), interview '私权神圣公权力行使需受限 [Private power is sacred, public power requires to be restricted]', 14 October 2011, at http://www.china-review.com/lishipindaoa.asp?id=29139&parapage=1, accessed 28 December 2013.

Kahn, Joseph, 'China executes at least 12 members of a secret Christian sect', *New York Times*, 30 November 2006, at http://www.nytimes.com/2006/11/30/world/asia/30china.html, accessed 2 January 2014.

Kellogg, Thomas E., 'Western funding for rule of law initiatives in China: the importance of a civil society based approach', in *Locating Civil Society: Communities Defending Basic Liberties*, Special Issue of *China Perspectives* 2012/3.

Kuang, Da (旷达), '滕彪:一个单纯的反对者 [Teng Biao – a pure opponent]', 34 iSun Magazine (阳光时务周刊), 6 December 2012.

Lawyer Shi Qing (石青律师) [pen name], '营口中院非法剥夺律师阅卷权 [The Intermediate Court of Yingkou illegally refuses lawyers access to files]', 20 April 2013, at http://news.boxun.com/news/gb/china/2013/04/201304040209.shtml.

Li, Gucheng, *A Glossary of Political Terms of the People's Republic of China*, Chinese University Press, Hong Kong: 1995.

Liu, Jie, 'A biased view of China', *China Daily*, 30 January 2012, http://www.chinadaily.com.cn/cndy/2012-01/30/content_14502312.htm, accessed 4 January 2014.

Liu, Shihui, 'I've only begun to scratch the surface', translated at Siweiluozi Blog, 22 August 2011, at http://www.siweiluozi.net/2011/08/ive-only-begun-to-scratch-surface-liu.html, accessed 27 December 2013 (with link to original text) at http://www.boxun.com/news/gb/china/2012/04/201204150020.shtml, accessed 27 December 2013.

Luban, David, 'Settlements and the erosion of the public realm', 83 *Georgetown Law Journal* (1995) 2619.

Mirrorbooks (明镜), '《明镜月刊》独家全文刊发中共9号文件 ["Mirrorbooks Monthly" exclusive, full text of CCP Document No. 9]', 20 August 2013, at http://www.molihua.org/2013/08/9_7925.html, accessed 28 December 2013.

Mitchell, Tom, 'Chinese court upholds lawyer's conviction', *Financial Times*, 23 December 2008, at http://www.ft.com/cms/s/0/85ac3c40-d01a-11dd-ae00-000077b07658.html#axzz2pEMk9FA9, accessed 2 January 2014.

Mo, Shaoping (莫少平), '持守心底法治、民主、宪政信念而风雨前行 [Marching on through the storm, holding fast to my belief in rule of law, democracy and constitutional government]', *Weiquanwang*, 10 September 2008, at http://www.weiquanwang.org/?p=10527.

Ng, Tze-wei (2011–2), 'Making people vanish', 16 September 2011, at http://pjmooney.typepad.com/my-blog/2011/09/making-people-vanish.html#tp.

Osnos, Evan 'Where is Xu Zhiyong?', *New Yorker*, 31 July 2009, at http://lawprofessors.typepad.com/china_law_prof_blog/2009/07/where-is-xu-zhiyong-evan-osnos-in-the-new-yorker.html, accessed 26 December 2013.

Pils, Eva, 'Yang Jia and China's Unpopular Criminal Justice System', 1 *China Rights Forum* (2009) 59–66.

Pils, Eva, 'Rights activism in China: the case of Lawyer Gao Zhisheng', in Stephanie Balme and Michael C. Dowdle (eds.), *Building Constitutionalism in China*, Palgrave, New York: 2009, pp. 243–260, at http://ssrn.com/abstract=1563926.

Radio Free Asia (Mandarin Desk), '京沪等地同城聚餐讨论"宪政梦" 北京公民促高官公开财产被拘 [Same-city dinners discuss "dream of constitutionalism," Beijing citizens requesting asset disclosure by high officials detained]', 1 April 2013, at http://www.rfa.org/mandarin/yataibaodao/renquanfazhi/jh-04012013105407.html, accessed 28 December 2013.

Rawls, John, *A Theory of Justice,* Harvard University Press, Cambridge, MA: 1971.

Schauer, Frederick, 'Fear, risk, and the First Amendment: unravelling the "chilling effect"', 58 *Boston University Law Review* (1978) 685.

Shama, Simon, *Citizens. A Chronicle of the French Revolution,* Penguin Books, London: 1989.

Shell, Jonathan, 'Introduction' in Adam Michnik, *Letters from Prison and other Essays,* translated by Maya Latynski, University of California Press, Berkeley, Los Angeles, London: 1985.

Shirky, Clay, *Here Comes Everybody: The Power of Organising Without Organisations,* Penguin, London: 2008.

Simon, Karla, 'The regulation of civil society organisations in China', 9 *International Journal of Civil Society Law* 1 (2011) 55–84; CUA Columbus School of Law Legal Studies Research Paper No. 2011–5, at http://papers.ssrn.com/sol3/papers.cfm?abstract_id=1781075.

Siweiluozi Blog, 'The fable of the hornet and the bird', May 2011, at http://www.siweiluozi.net/2011/05/li-tiantian-fable-of-hornet-bird-and.html (Chinese and English versions available from this blog), accessed 27 December 2013.

Siweiluozi Blog, 'Chinese human rights lawyers: appeal to safeguard human rights and realise constitutional government', 4 December 2013, at http://www.siweiluozi.net/, accessed 10 December 2013.

Southern Metropolis Daily (南方都市报), '律师王全璋被江苏靖江法院拘留后提前释放拟提出复议 [Lawyer Wangquanzhang, detained by Jingjiang court, considers seeking administrative reconsideration after early release]', 7 April 2013, at http://www.scxsls.com/a/20130407/89818.html, accessed 27 December 2013.

Sun, Liping (孙立平), '中国有没有公民社会 [Does China have a civil society]', 18 August 2009, at http://sun-liping.i.sohu.com/blog/view/129843127.htm, accessed 28 December 2013.

Telegraph, 'Chinese waitress freed after stabbing official to death during sex assault', 16 June 2009, at http://www.telegraph.co.uk/news/worldnews/asia/china/5549081/Chinese-waitress-freed-after-stabbing-official-to-death-during-sex-assault.html, accessed 27 December 2013.

Teng, Biao (滕彪), '一个反动分子的自由 [The freedom of a reactionary]', Taiwan Association for China Human Rights (台湾关怀中国人权联盟), 中国生死书 [*China, the Book of Living and Dying*], Mufeng Publishing Company, Taipei: 2013.

Teng, Biao (滕彪), '关于《奥运前的中国真相》一文的说明—声援胡佳之一 [Explanation about the essay "The real China before the Olympics" – first statement in support of Hu Jia]', Boxun (博讯), 17 January 2008, at http://www.peacehall.com/news/gb/pubvp/2008/01/200801170208.shtml.

Teng, Biao (滕彪), '公盟不死 [Gongmeng is not dead]', 17 January 2009, at http://blog.qq.com/qzone/622007804/1248271496.htm, accessed 28 December 2013.

Teng, Biao, 'Rights defence, microblogs, and the surrounding gaze: the rights defence movement online and offline', in *Locating Civil Society: Communities Defending Basic Liberties,* Special Issue of *China Perspectives* 2012/3.

Teng, Biao, 'The political meaning of the crime of "subverting State power"', in Jean-Philippe Béja, Fu Hualing and Eva Pils, *Liu Xiaobo and Challenges of Constitutional Reform in China,* Hong Kong University Press, Hong Kong: 2012.

Teng, Biao, 'The Sun Zhigang Incident and the future of constitutionalism: does the Chinese Constitution have a future?', CRJ Occasional Paper, 30 December 2013, at http://www.law.cuhk.edu.hk/research/crj/download/papers/2013-tb-szg-constitutionalism.pdf (accessed 30 December 2013).

Wang, Quanzhang (王全璋), '一个苹果引发的司法公案 [A public administration of justice case triggered by Apple devices]', April 2013, copy on file with author.

Wiggins, David, 'Neo-Aristotelian reflections on justice', 113 *Mind* (2004) 477.

Xiao Shu (笑蜀), '以负责任的社会运动倒逼中国转型 —— 我的人权联署自白', 31 March 2013, at http://blog.sina.com.cn/s/blog_6314a9890102e0i7.html, accessed 28 December 2013.

Xu, Zhiyong (许志永), '谁把"自由,公义, 爱"当成敌人, 一定是中华民族的敌人! [Who turns "freedom, justice, love" into an enemy is clearly an enemy of the Chinese nation!]', Special Issue (8) of *Citizen* (公民专刊) 76 ff.

Xu Zhiyong (许志永), '公民许志永: 关于月末公民同城聚餐和"小圈子"区别的说明 [Citizen Xu Zhiyong: Explanation concerning the difference between end-of-month same-city citizen dinners and "small circles"]', 6 May 2013, at http://www.canyu.org/n72755c6.aspx, accessed 28 December 2013.

Yang, Ming (杨明), '公民权利无保障连署促批准人权公约 [Civil rights lack protection, urging the ratification of the ICCPR]', 3 May 2013, at http://www.voachinese.com/content/china-human-right-20130305/1615327.html, accessed 28 December 2013.

Zhang, Qing (张倩), '律师团现象: 从组团自救到组团公益援助 [The phenomenon of "legal teams": from getting organised for the purpose of self-rescue to organising to provide pro bono legal aid]', *Caijing Magazine*, 3 January 2012.

Zhang, Xueran, 'China's all-star legal team pleads for defendants' rights on social media', Tea Leaf Nation, 25 July 2012, at http://tealeafnation.com/2012/07/bilingual-brew-chinas-all-star-legal-team-pleads-for-defendants-rights-on-social-media, accessed 28 December 2013.

Zhao, Sile (赵思乐), '郭玉闪: 抱着绝望姿态做专业的维权 [Guo Yushan: engaging in professional rights defence in an attitude of despair]', 34 iSun Magazine (阳光时务周刊), 6 December 2012.

Websites, blog and microblog entries

China Against Death Penalty [北京兴善研究所], http://www.cadpnet.org/en/.

ChinaFile, 'Document No. 9', at http://www.chinafile.com/document-9-chinafile-translation, accessed 30 December 2013.

Chinese Democratic Party [中国民主党] at http://www.hqcdp.org/ (Chinese) and http://www.hqcdp.org/english/ (English), accessed 28 December 2013.

Chinese Social Democratic Party [中国社会民主党] at http://www.csdparty.org/index.html, accessed 28 December 2013.

'Citizen's Pledge', at http://survey.activepower.net/service/survey/survey.asp?survey_id=58235, accessed 28 December 2013.

David Bandurski, 'Inside the Southern Weekly Incident', *China Media Project*, 7 January 2013, at http://cmp.hku.hk/2013/01/07/30402/, accessed 5 January 2014.

Evilsfiles [罪恶档案@evilsfiles], https://twitter.com/evilsfiles.

Human Rights in China, 'Prisoner profile: Hu Shigen', at http://www.hrichina.org/sites/default/files/PDFs/CRF.4.2004/PrisonerProfile4.2004.pdf, accessed 28 December 2013.

Prisoner Alert, 'Pastor Cai Zhuohua', at http://www.prisoneralert.com/pprofiles/vp_prisoner_152_profile.html, accessed 28 December 2013.

Russian political jokes, at http://en.wikipedia.org/wiki/Russian_political_jokes, accessed 28 December 2013.

Transition Institute [传知行经济研究所], http://www.zhuanxing.cn/.
Xu Zhiyong tweet of 27 May 2012, 'Advocating the use of the "citizen" image, the joint promotion of a new civil society!' at https://twitter.com/zhiyongxu/status/206444691267391488, accessed 28 December 2013.

Documentary and multimedia sources

He, Yang (何杨), 赫索格的日子 [*Herzog's Days*], independent documentary film, Beijing (2010).
'公民播报: 声援遭拘禁的维权律师 [Citizen broadcast: supporting falsely imprisoned rights lawyers]', at http://www.youtube.com/watch?v=wMGTieMPF-U, accessed 27 December 2013; also available at http://www.peacehall.com/news/gb/china/2013/04/201304051459.shtml, accessed 27 December 2013.
'视频: 2013公民播报首版 [First edition of 2013 citizen broadcast]', undated, around Chinese New Year 2013, http://www.youtube.com/watch?v=ND9I0HPi-ZU, accessed 28 December 2013.

Presentations and recorded speeches

Liu, Weiguo (刘卫国), comments delivered at public seminar 'The Constitution, the media and the Chinese Rights Defence Movement', 13 April 2013 at the Chinese University of Hong Kong.
Teng, Biao, 'Nine years on: the "Sun Zhigang Incident" and the future of Constitutionalism in China', public lecture, 19 November 2012 at the Chinese University of Hong Kong.
Xiao Shu, comments delivered at 'The Constitution, the media and the Chinese Rights Defence Movement: ten years after the death of Sun Zhigang', public seminar at the Centre for Rights and Justice, Faculty of Law, the Chinese University of Hong Kong, 13 April 2013.

8 Stability, reform and rights advocacy

Our goal now, I think, is mostly to break through the [barriers of] fear. . . . Only a very few people believe that there is a clear goal to move toward. Even if you have one, you might well have got it wrong. The fact is, in our current situation, it is simply impossible to predict what the situation will be like, say, three years from now. The only thing we can do is go ahead, go ahead together.[1]

(March 2013)

Rights lawyers are generally wary of predicting the future, beyond sometimes commenting on the unequal distribution of power between the authorities and the human rights movement. As one of the rights lawyers remarked, it would take little effort on the part of the government to lock them all up.[2] And, while members of the New Citizen Movement might counter that 'you can't nick all citizens', the account here has shown that professional lawyers have a specific role to play in the struggle for rights, and in any case, the crucial question of who will commit to 'being a citizen' (*zuo gongmin*)[3] on this and similar initiatives' exacting moral standards remains open.

These cautions notwithstanding, it is safe to say that rights defence lawyers have grown in numbers and that their advocacy is drawing increasing attention in Chinese society today. Each of the individual lawyers whose comments contributed to this book is connected to colleagues, clients, and a wider public in a variety of ways. Most importantly, they are connected to many others in Chinese society through their experiences and hopes for a less repressive system able to handle citizen grievances better. As noted earlier, the Party–State itself has not without some accuracy identified '"rights defence lawyers", underground religion, dissidents, internet leaders and disadvantaged social groups' as civil society forces challenging its own system and political power.[4] The fact that rights

---

1 # 23 2013-1.
2 #22 2011-1.
3 In Chinese characters, 做公民.
4 'Through the use of "rights lawyers", underground religion, dissidents, internet leaders and disadvantaged social groups as the core forces, they [the United States, western countries] will push for a "bottom-up" approach to Chinese governance from the grassroots to lay a foundation

advocacy is both increasingly entrenched and systematically repressed invite a critical revision of how we think about rights lawyers and wider rights advocacy.

Implications for stability discourse and rights lawyer categorisations

Against the background of the Party–State-driven stability preservation campaigns, and taking the repression of lawyers it leads to into account, the radical–moderate distinction used to categorise (rights) lawyers as well as various auxiliary grids, rankings and taxonomies deserve to be reconsidered. They have limited use, but do not justify marginalisation of lawyers deemed 'radical'.

First, as Chapters 3 and 4 have argued, rights lawyers differ from other lawyers on many occasions merely by insisting forcefully that the law and its central principles be respected. Thus, for example, when criminal defence lawyers insist on access to their clients in accordance with law, or on initiation of a procedure to examine torture allegations in accordance with the 2010 joint rules or (later) the 2012 CPL; or when they enter a plea of not guilty despite explicit official instructions not to do so, or when they take measures to remedy violations of the rules and principles a fairer system would require – e.g. by using social media and other means to open up trials that purport to be public, but are *de facto* closed – they do this in service of, not in opposition to, officially acknowledged legal principles and rules. What they contest on such occasions are rules of the system sometimes called 'covert' or 'hidden', and expectations communicated to them by officials who at times explicitly reject the laws of the State. When they take on so-called sensitive cases, they merely choose not to reject certain clients because of who they are, what group they belong to, or what kind of complaint they have. Theirs is a choice 'not to reject' because it is a choice opposing instructions from the authorities not to take on such cases, instructions that are often clear and explicit. These instructions, as observed in Chapters 4 and 5, are usually only part of the law on the thinnest possible conception of law, a conception that not even legal formalism would appear to support – they are merely measures of the Party–State exercising its prerogative to use power without justification.[5]

The official bafflement and occasional unease that was described by several rights lawyers in passages quoted in preceding chapters (for example, Chapter 5 describing a meeting a rights lawyer has with various officials seeking to 'persuade' him to abandon a group of clients) – awkwardness and silences sometimes captured on camera or voice-recorder – is merely reflective of the fact that there is no legal argument for the maintenance of taboo zones in a system whose written

---

for changing China.' People's Daily, '中国真正的挑战是未来 5–10 年 [China's real challenges lie in the 5 to 10 years ahead]', 1 July 2012, at http://ccnews.people.com.cn/n/2012/0731/c141677-18636091.html, accessed 30 December 2013; translation by Harold Scott, at http://chinadigitaltimes.net/2012/08/peoples-daily-chinas-real-challenge-is-the-next-5-10-years/, accessed 30 December 2013.

5 Ernst Fraenkel, *The Dual State. A Contribution to the Theory of Dictatorship*, translated by E.A. Shils, Oxford University Press, New York: 1941.

Constitution claims that 'all persons are equal before the law' (Article 33). It is therefore not surprising if many in the legal field (including some officials, as seen when officials occasionally congratulated a lawyer on his performance) are in spirit supportive of what rights lawyers do – that they are in that sense no less 'radical' than these lawyers and that increasing numbers of lawyers are willing to join rights lawyer group chats and actions. To characterise lawyers making the kinds of choice described above as 'radical' is bizarre; it is at best a way of suggesting that following the law in certain situations and cases would be a radical departure from established Party–State practice.

Second, the extrajudicial advocacy strategies rights lawyers choose are directly connected to the principles of political action rights lawyers identify as necessary in the conditions of the post-totalitarian system they have to deal with. Their own confrontations with and personal experiences of Party–State violence notwithstanding, these strategies have so far on all occasions we know of been strictly nonviolent, consisting on most occasions in verbal advocacy, and sometimes in sit-ins or 'surround-and-watch' actions, and very occasionally in peaceful hunger strikes.[6] As noted in Chapter 7, rights lawyers have in public and private statements consistently refrained from advocating any violent acts of resistance. While some of them consider violent resistance to tyranny sometimes eligible, pointing to the classical, rights-centred political theories that support this view, none has expressed the view that there should be violent resistance to the Chinese Party–State in current conditions. They have defended some people engaging in violence against officials in cases of (alleged) self-defence or mental illness; but in those cases, rights lawyers have expressed their 'understanding' rather than their approbation or support. Their predictions and premonitions of violent clashes between citizens and the government are couched in terms of perhaps unavoidable own sacrifice, not in terms of aggression, since clearly, some rights lawyers expect the State to use more violence in the coming years as, from their perspective, it glides into crisis. It follows that the present study has not discovered any evidence to support the suggestion that certain 'radical' Chinese human rights lawyers 'advocate violence'.[7]

Taxonomies that do not use the criterion of advocacy of violence but focus on the types of case lawyers take on, and their strategies and attitudes, do correspond to some real differences among rights lawyers. They are to some extent supported, as Cullen and Fu note, by the way the government and other groups in society talk about them. It is an important sociological insight that a particular social

---

6 In an electronic communication, a rights lawyer in December 2013 described hunger striking as an *ultima ratio*, and listed sit-ins, shouting slogans, performance art, sending postcards, banners/slogans, T-shirts displaying slogans, lectures in public places, 'strolls' (a name for peaceful demonstrations avoiding this term), phone calls and online expressions of resistance as alternatives. On file with author.

7 A view attributed to Peerenboom in Chapter 1. Randall Peerenboom, 'Searching for political liberalism in all the wrong places: the legal profession in China as the leading edge of political reform?', *La Trobe Law School Legal Studies Research* Paper No. 2008/7, at http://ssrn.com/abstract=1265080 or http://dx.doi.org/10.2139/ssrn.1265080.

perception, or a judgement made by the majority of people in a particular society at a given time, is in itself a social fact. It must be noted, however, that rights lawyers themselves have divergent and differentiated views about appropriate linguistic usage and about the implications of distinguishing among different kinds of (rights) lawyer. As observed in a preceding chapter, some lawyers also criticised the habit of differentiating between rights lawyers and other lawyers.[8] A differentiated view is represented e.g. by this comment by Tang Jitian in a tweet of 2 July 2013, which acknowledges the possibility of different degrees of *understanding*:

> If a lawyer does not interact with petitioners, they will have a hard time understanding the degree to which this society is sick; if they do not handle 'Falun Gong' practitioners' cases, their understanding of the human rights disaster will likely be deficient.[9]

More generally, the conception of what is radical is open to discussion, and there are divergent views. In many discussions, it is determined by the idea of system change; and while e.g. in western contexts this can gesture at some version of anarchism or dictatorship, which could not be further (it seems) from what Chinese rights lawyers advocate, the term 'radical' can also be used to describe a lawyer who takes on cases seriously challenging the State and is motivated by left-leaning political ideas that do not, however, amount to any sort of orthodox–Marxist rejection of law or rights; on the contrary. Michael Mansfield's self-description as a 'radical lawyer', for example, draws attention to the fact that he has made unconventional choices and taken non-conservative stances in his career as a lawyer defending rights.[10]

Lastly, the radical-moderate distinction underlines the system's inherent contradictions and lack of integrity, because even the most 'radical' positions supported by 'radical' rights defenders can be shown to have some basis in the system's stated principles. If being radical means to desire thorough system change or work toward change, rights lawyers of any description constitute only a small part of those who could be called 'radical' on such a conception of radicalness. Under the current system, even the text of the PRC Constitution is in some of its passages quite radical: for example, Article 33 states since 2004 that the State 'respects and safeguards human rights'.[11]

---

8 Some lawyers approached accepted the description as *weiquan* or human rights lawyers; and some insisted that they themselves were not rights (*weiquan*) lawyers, thus acknowledging the distinction.
9 Tweet accessed 28 August 2013, at https://twitter.com/tjitian/status/351868160917512192, accessed 4 January 2014.
10 Michael Mansfield, *Memoirs of a Radical Lawyer*, Bloomsbury Publishing, London: 2010; Decca Aitkenhead, 'Michael Mansfield QC interview: "What's wrong with rights?"', *Guardian*, 1 November 2013, at http://www.theguardian.com/law/2013/nov/01/michael-mansfield-qc-interview, accessed 5 January 2014.
11 PRC Constitution Article 33 as amended in March 2004.

Given that rights lawyers share many arguments and aspirations with mainstream scholars and other legal professionals, it is clear that current ascriptions of radicalness are largely dependent on the determinations of the Party–State as to who or what is 'sensitive', and this is why this ascription remains especially problematic in the context of China's repressive system. As was seen in previous chapters, the criterion of political sensitivity is one determined entirely by the authorities of the Party–State – as Teng Biao puts it, by the average level of who is currently in prison[12] – and in individual cases the Party–State may grade rights lawyers not just according to the question of how sensitive the cases they have handled were, but also according to whom they interact with, what they say to foreigners, and whether or not they are willing to accept Party–State instructions. Labelling rights lawyers radical merely because they engage in what is considered politically sensitive work, or are considered some sort of 'class A1 stability maintenance target' by the authorities, might therefore inadvertently support the repressive categorisations of the security apparatus, and psychologically support the marginalisation of rights defenders the system aims at.

Conversely, the fact that the moderate derives from the radical that, in turn, is determined by the repressive State itself makes an idea of moderation used to indicate one end of a spectrum of Chinese rights advocacy also problematic. Of course, this does not mean that the vocabulary of moderation – in Chinese, the most frequently used term is *wenhe*,[13] 'mild', 'gentle' or 'peaceful' – is wrong as such or necessarily fails to describe rights lawyers. But, rights lawyers' moderation in this sense of the term does not render them any less threatening to the repressive Chinese State, which is certain to continue labelling them as dangerous subversives; and this should be well understood.

If we take our labels from the system that represses them we may only too easily accept facile criticism of these lawyers, e.g. for being too provocative or going too far in their advocacy ('taking on sensitive cases', etc.). Relative moderation does not protect – as one rights lawyer quoted in Chapter 7 put it, just because someone shouts its own slogans doesn't mean the government will let them off; and:

> According to their way of thinking, they always need someone to be at the top of the list of enemies of the State. It is a different person at different times but there has to be always somebody.[14]

These conclusions also require us to revisit categorisations of rights lawyers according to criteria of heroism and suffering, mentioned in Chapter 1. Foreign governments, INGOs, the media, etc. tend to identify causes by drawing attention to well-known rights defenders who may even gain something of a celebrity status. The account here does not support the conclusion that concern for the individuals

---

12 Cited in Chapter 6.
13 In Chinese characters, 温和.
14 Conversation with rights lawyer, January 2010.

who have such status is merely sensationalist or obsessed with individual stories, or that it distorts a larger picture of steady human rights ameliorations. Rather, understanding human rights lawyers' stories is indispensable to understanding the darker sides of the legal and political system they try to expose to public view, mechanisms and practices extending far beyond the lives of the individuals who expose them and advocate against them. Also, while some of their worst experiences are unique, this does not turn them into exceptions from a rule. On the contrary, it has been seen that control systems for the legal profession as a whole make use of similar techniques, including surveillance, 'management' and intimidation, and that rights lawyers' advocacy and resistance address systemic human rights violations.

But it must be acknowledged that supportive external entities engaged in human rights advocacy are themselves subject to requirements and expectations affecting how they portray and present rights defender cases; and that the 'value' of a particular individual in transnational advocacy terms can fall or rise depending on how active they are and how badly they are treated by the Party–State. While internally, so far as they operate in China through offices or individuals working with them, such entities therefore have reasons to prefer 'moderation', their external profile and fund raising is assisted by active support for those who rank highly on the resistance scale. Indirectly, the Party–State's 'stability preservation' categorisations therefore also victimise transnational civil society and put it at risk of inversely replicating techniques of marginalisation, denying those pressed into categories or heroic images individuality and personality. The grading implicit in such discourse may be hard to avoid, because it originates from repression, but it carries a potentially harmful message, all the easier to internalise by those whose sense of self-worth, liberty and wellbeing has already come under sustained attack.[15]

Implications for legal reform and agency in change

Many legislative reforms have been introduced in the reform and opening era; and there is evidence to suggest that some of the reforms, for example concerning criminal procedure, State compensation and compensation for expropriations and housing demolitions, have had beneficial effects or may produce such effects in future. The experience of human rights lawyers prompts several cautionary assessments, however.

First, successes with various legislative reform agendas whose underlying goals and principles are liberal – an expanded protection of human rights such

---

15 Having experienced so many attacks on their dignity and self-respect some appeared further reduced to seeking affirmation of their own importance from what stability preservation target ranking they had been given or from how many people were on the team entrusted with their surveillance, as could also be observed in some conversations. A further fundamentally inhumane implication of such endurance rankings was that its targets would see themselves in a dehumanising enemy relationship with those who inflicted it, and pushed into becoming what another interlocutor called 'revolutionary machines'.

as the revised 2012 CPL invokes, for example – have been concurrent with the increasing public denunciation and persecution of rights advocacy and rights defence lawyers. Several chapters of this book have given examples for how *weiquan* became a denunciated concept, how rights lawyers were categorised as troublemakers and how the very ideas on which human rights defence rests were renounced and vilified especially under the new leadership in 2013. Since around 2004, if not earlier, the legal profession has been subjected to more stringent controls, rather than being gradually released from such control and interference, as discussed in Chapter 5. At the level of Party–State intentions, therefore, there is a certain degree of dualism and inconsistency. Even the new sets of rules adopted, for instance in criminal procedure, reflect a dualism that, in the context of the operations of the security apparatus especially, amounts to the principles of a 'dual state'. A better understanding of these changes justifies scepticism about incrementalist rule of law development narratives such as are preferred by some institutions and scholars.

Second, just as rights advocates, so, too, have the authorities been able to use the techniques of legal 'as if' – albeit in a different way, by pointing to State legislation and institutions as evidence of its commitment to liberal reform goals. They can insist that trials are public when, in fact, they are not, to use an example from Chapter 4, a pretence centrally relying on the existence of public rules requiring public trials, for example. The Party–State, too, can, just as liberal scholars and rights defenders, act as if the State were separate from the Party or as if the Party had no role as a political decision maker in some situations. For the authorities, this has been an advantage of the legal reform discourse cultivated at domestic and international levels, a discourse also embracing the assumption that an amelioration of public rules by itself means progress, and encouraging the strict separation between the rules and their implementation. Any concern expressed about flaws and failures to obey rules can be dismissed as unduly obsessing about individual lapses, and 'ungenerously' disregarding the progress that consists in changing the rules.

Third, top-down reform hopes are challenged by evidence that the repression of key protagonists of rule of law reform, such as human rights lawyers, is not merely incidental (or 'sensational') but, rather, systemic. While this study has not been able to further the understanding of the systemic abuses rights lawyers try to address significantly, it may have helped to further our understanding of their own systematic abuse by the Party–State, as well as of the operation of the legal system and its relationship with 'the system', its political principles and its techniques to constrain individuals. To the extent that the authorities of the security apparatus, for example, are bent on ensuring that a legislative change of the rules must not translate into the inconvenience of greater limitations of their power, the systematic intimidation and suppression of advocates pivotal in helping others use those rules is an ideal way of undermining the State-driven legal reform process. Their suppression, if successful, can ensure the continued survival of 'the system' as it was described in Chapter 3. In this context it should be remembered that even though only about one in 1,000 Chinese lawyers may be willing to identify themselves as a human rights lawyer, and even though not all human rights lawyers have suffered to equal degrees, their intimidation and suppression is complemented in subtle ways by pervasive repression of the legal profession as a whole.

The further implication of these insights must be to be sceptical of the conception of reform that the system has cultivated, as a top-down, controlled and incremental process of corrective improvement (*gaige*) affecting areas and aspects of the system the leadership wants to change. Moving to a vocabulary of 'change' rather than reform may be helpful in explaining this shift.

A shift from 'reform' to 'change' may, fourth, help to reopen the question of who the main agents of change are. This is important because many efforts, on the part of transnational society and foreign governments, as well as from the perspective of domestic academia and public interest law communities, have focused on reform conceived as something in which the Party–State must needs have paramount agency, because it has authority (or power) to determine the rules of the legal system and decide on their implementation, which, in turn, relies on various, largely subordinate entities 'inside the system'. The focus on legislative State rules, in particular, as if changing their wording were the end goal of a particular reform project, justifies support to the Party–State for whatever limited and concessionary reforms it is willing to introduce or discuss introducing. It can also serve as justification for *not* including in discussions those deemed to be 'outside the system' because it is assumed (often enough in anticipatory self-censorship) that such persons would not be tolerated, or because, quite accurately, they are thought to have no personal influence with those who make the rules. This creates a widely acknowledged bias for funded projects with measurable 'outcomes' or 'outputs' (as application forms phrase it), and against projects that could result in retaliation against participants. As a further consequence external entities promoting reform almost invariably frame their recommendations and often their ways of measuring success in terms of criteria over which the Party–State has control, and which it is willing to change. All of these modalities of developmental support for the construction of the rule of law in China – for what Woodman has called a 'shift to engagement' (indicating engagement of system-internal agencies),[16] and what Bell would characterise as 'collaboration'[17] – make sense only if the basic assumption is that the Party–State and the officials and other representatives of the system are the principal agents of change. They also support and reinforce this assumption.

---

16 Sophia Woodman, 'Driving without a map: implementing legal projects in China aimed at improving human rights', in *Ethics in Action*, Daniel A. Bell and Jean-Marc Coicaud (eds.), Cambridge University Press, Cambridge: 2006, at http://ebooks.cambridge.org/chapter.jsf? bid=CBO9780511511233&cid=CBO9780511511233A017, accessed 30 December 2013. 'The Chinese government initiated the shift toward engagement, arguing strongly that any shortcomings in its rights record were due to the country's level of development, as well as historical and cultural factors, and thus the best approach would be one that would assist the country in its efforts to develop.'

17 Daniel Bell, *Beyond Liberal Democracy: Political Thinking for an East Asian Context*, Princeton University Press, Princeton: 2006, at http://www3.nccu.edu.tw/~kangchan/readings/CPP/Bell_DA(2006book).pdf, at p. 103.

On the basis of the above we should recognised the value of 'as if' techniques as human rights lawyers use them to 'regain agency in change, without ignoring such techniques' possible abuses by the authorities. For rights lawyers and other advocates considered to be largely outside the system, 'as if' techniques are a means of achieving agency in the political and legal changes to which they aspire. For one thing, human rights lawyers' use of 'as if' techniques as described here is not merely 'pretending' or hypothetically postulating; rather, it is categorically demanding. A rights defence lawyer in court, for example, uses rights arguments 'as if' they could be expected to determine the judicial decision of the case, because rights considerations do limit justifiable uses of power. The rights-based arguments used in this way have a critical function; they define the system's flaws, even when they do not result in an acceptable outcome for that particular case. For another, rights lawyers show through their verbal advocacy and other acts of resistance that they do not consider the laws and rights they invoke as merely granted or limited at will by whosoever has the authority to create law.

Understanding law as an argumentative social practice individuals engage in as morally independent agents, rather than understanding it as a set of commands or authoritative rules sourced purely in coercive power, would not only help to recognise the agency of certain actors 'outside the system', such as human rights lawyers. It sometimes also better reflects how officials of the system try to act responsibly, not by following rules or commands but by resisting or subverting them. Chapter 4 recorded, for example, that judges would in certain instances comment that 'there is nothing I can do – you know that' – admitting with apparent unease or even guilt that the orders they received from their leadership and executed fell short of what should have been done. In another example recorded in Chapter 4, a judge furtively encouraged rights lawyers to bring external pressure to bear on the judiciary by organising a protest, in order to obtain a better decision. Lawyers, in turn, did make suggestions to improve the limitations of written law in service to imperfectly realised legal ideals, including appeals for constitutional amendments,[18] a recasting of the Constitution as in Charter 08 (which many lawyers signed),[19] appeals to ratify international human rights documents, and the introduction of a constitutional court.[20] Their advocacy and

---

18 In May 2006, Gao Zhisheng and Yuan Hongbing published a joint proposal for amending the Constitution, proposing to abolish Party leadership and guidance by the principles of Marxism–Leninism, Mao Zedong thought, and the three represents. See Gao Zhisheng and Yuan Hongbing, '修改宪法维护基本人权宣言 [Call for amending the Constitution to protect basic rights]', *Boxun*, 19 May 2006, at http://blog.boxun.com/hero/200906/xwziwj/20_1.shtml, accessed 30 December 2013.

19 Li Xiaorong and Zhang Zuhua (李晓荣、张祖桦), '零八宪章 [Charter 08]', Kaifang Press, Hong Kong: 2009, translated by Perry Link, Charter 08', *New York Review of Books*, 15 January 2009, at http://www.nybooks.com/articles/archives/2009/jan/15/chinas-charter-08/, accessed 4 January 2014.

20 Such an appeal using banners unfurled in public places was initiated by Sun Desheng and Yuan Fengchu, who were later criminally detained. Cp. Zheng Jue and Xiong Fei (郑珏、熊菲), '孙德胜、袁奉初发起的公民权利进军 [Citizen rights promoted Sun Desheng, Yuan Fengchu

myriad ways in which individual officials and other actors engage with the legal system are the often non-measurable outcomes that help promote change, without taking the form of legislative reform.

Implications for human rights advocacy

Human rights is an institutionalised international practice with offices and officials, organisations, staff, and treaties and other written instruments representing the promises made by sovereign states with regard to their human rights obligations; but human rights is also a particular view of political morality based in arguments, not social conventions. Given the domestic system's intransigence to international norms and mechanisms, the advocacy China's human rights lawyers engage in is largely an example of the latter. As it is not individuals defending human rights who are radical but, rather, the changes required by the idea they defend in the hostile political–legal environment portrayed here, it is all the more important to consider the radical implications of the very idea of human rights and of rights advocacy in repressive systems. While such systems' participation in human rights as an institutionalized practice can be criticized for conferring unmerited international respectability onto these systems, support for rights advocacy by these systems' own internal, vocal and un-coopted critics can help defuse this particular criticism.

First, when rights lawyers invoke a justifying connection between human rights principles and the acts of advocacy and resistance they engage in, they to varying extents reject the legitimacy and authority of the State whose sovereignty, as a matter of public international law, the institutionalised actors in international human rights law practices must respect. As they continue to advocate and call for better rights protection, lawyers also constantly explore and develop this justifying connection; they discuss it especially whenever a particular collective action of protest is to be taken.

Second, as noted in Chapter 1, some have described human rights thought as a new secular faith;[21] and this assessment is in some respects borne out by observations made in this book. Rights lawyers might be regarded as members of a group constituted by this global secular religion, individuals who seek membership of this community of faith. Not only can the belief that human rights are important certainly be a strongly felt conviction among people who meet for discussions or 'rights defence' activities such as lending support to a person attending a court trial. They are also more likely to trust each other just because they have shared convictions. In some cases, rights lawyers also share a religious faith.

---

further advancing]', *CHRD*, 13 April 2013, at http://2newcenturynet.blogspot.hk/2013/04/blog-post_13.html, accessed 30 December 2013.

21 Martti Koskenniemi, 'What should international lawyers lean from Karl Marx', in Susan Marks (ed.), *International Law on the Left: Re-Examining Marxist Legacies*, Cambridge University Press, Cambridge: 2011, pp. 30–52.

But the account here has also shown that rights lawyers' advocacy transcends religious faith, not just because they belong to a variety of different or no faith groups, from groups affiliated with major world religions to small communities of locally specific religions; or because they take on the cases of faith-based communities that are not their own. While the loose groups and associations rights lawyers have formed among themselves and with others also have similarity in some of their symbolism with communities of faith, they crucially exempt personal, religious conviction from scrutiny for 'access' to the group. In the case of the New Citizen Movement, for example, the degree of commitment, including emotional commitment, required of members resembles more that in a political party than in a group of faith. More important, lawyers belonging to different groups (lawyers with and without religious faith) have emphasised the importance of separating between one's religious beliefs and what they have called a 'human rights viewpoint' including the belief in religious freedom. They recognise that having faith cannot be a substitute for argument;[22] and their continuous engagement with colleagues outside their communities of faith illustrates their desire to persuade and make sense across the boundaries of their faith, which as such may not demand or allow for a perfectly rational foundation.

The significance of this finding is that it weakens the facile relativism that can motivate characterisations of human rights as 'mere' faith, or as institutionalised conventions, rules and principles drawn up and agreed on by sovereign states; the view clearly favoured by repressive governments. Rejecting conventionalist accounts of rights that focus on the established institutions administering human rights may result in a more independent and deeper account of the personal and governmental responsibilities that human rights engender. Once human rights is understood to be neither 'mere' faith nor mere (state) convention, as the examples discussed in this account suggest, it is also clear that certain views of law and rights as mere power relations cannot make sense of rights advocacy in China. As noted in Chapter 1, scholars who hold these views have argued that human rights are late expressions of imperialism, that 'global neo-capitalism and human-rights-for-export are part of the same project',[23] and that their promotion 'by western states and humanitarians' can 'blunt political resistance',[24] apparently

---

22 This is an argument in the Kantian tradition. 'Acknowledging the role of felt, irresistible conviction in our experience of value just recognizes the fact that we have such convictions, that they can survive responsible reflection, and that we then have no reason at all, short of further evidence or argument, to doubt their truth.' Dworkin, 'Law without religion', *New York Review of Books*, February 2013.

23 Costas Douzinas, 'Seven theses on human rights: (7) cosmopolitanism, equality & resistance', 13 June 2013, at http://criticallegalthinking.com/2013/06/13/even-theses-on-human-rights-7-cosmopolitanism-equality-resistance/. Douzinas' criticism was perhaps directed more against what might be described as a human rights establishment of transnational bodies, organisations and places of teaching than against domestic rights defenders, and to that extent is useful in addressing the potentially 'palliative' effects of some ideas and practices current in this human rights establishment.

24 '[The] promotion [of human rights] by western states and humanitarians turns them into a palliative: it is useful for a limited protection of individuals but it can blunt political resistance. Human rights can re-claim their redemptive role in the hands and imagination of those who return

turning rights advocates into victims of unnamed 'preachers of moralism, suffering humanity, and humanitarian philanthropy'. This would summarily suggest that Chinese human rights defenders had been duped and were victims of the workings of a cultural imperialism they had failed to comprehend and resist. At the very least, this argument would result in an odd and implausible misplacement of the source of oppression that lawyers and other people are facing in systems like the Chinese one.[25]

The fact that rights lawyers' advocacy presents a fundamental political challenge to the system is merely a further implication of the weak status of law in China. For some time, rule of law progress seemed to depend on incremental development (with western help, and promoted, albeit cautiously, by the Party–State authorities). The experience of Chinese human rights lawyers suggests that their turn to political rights advocacy, seeking more radical changes than the authorities are likely to grant, has been inevitable.

Bibliography

Constitution

PRC Constitution [中华人民共和国宪法], passed on 4 December 1982, promulgated and effective as of 4 December 1982, last revised on 14 March 2004.

Books and articles

Aitkenhead, Decca, 'Michael Mansfield QC interview: "What's wrong with rights?"', *Guardian*, 1 November 2013, at http://www.theguardian.com/law/2013/nov/01/michael-mansfield-qc-interview, accessed 5 January 2014.

Bell, Daniel, *Beyond Liberal Democracy: Political Thinking for an East Asian Context*, Princeton University Press, Princeton: 2006, at http://www3.nccu.edu.tw/~kangchan/readings/CPP/Bell_DA(2006book).pdf.

Douzinas, Costas, 'Seven theses on human rights: (7) cosmopolitanism, equality & resistance' 13 June 2013, at http://criticallegalthinking.com/2013/06/13/seven-theses-on-human-rights-7-cosmopolitanism-equality-resistance/.

Douzinas, Costas, 'Seven theses on human rights: (3) neoliberal capitalism & voluntary imperialism', 23 May 2013, at http://criticallegalthinking.com/2013/05/23/seven-theses-on-human-rights-3-neoliberal-capitalism-voluntary-imperialism/.

Dworkin, Ronald, 'Law without religion', *New York Review of Books*, February 2013.

Fraenkel, Ernst, *The Dual State. A Contribution to the Theory of Dictatorship*, translated by E.A. Shils, Oxford University Press, New York: 1941.

them to the tradition of resistance and struggle against the advice of the preachers of moralism, suffering humanity, and humanitarian philanthropy.' Costas Douzinas, 'Seven theses on human rights: (3) neoliberal capitalism & voluntary imperialism', 23 May 2013, at http://criticallegalthinking.com/2013/05/23/seven-theses-on-human-rights-3-neoliberal-capitalism-voluntary-imperialism/.

25 Coming as it does on the heels of an observation on 'imperial arrogance and cosmopolitan naivety', moreover, one cannot but fail to notice its own patronising tone.

Gao Zhisheng and Yuan Hongbing (高智晟, 袁鸿冰), '修改宪法维护基本人权宣言 [Call for amending the Constitution to protect basic rights]', *Boxun* (博讯), 19 May 2006, at http://blog.boxun.com/hero/200906/xwziwj/20_1.shtml, accessed 30 December 2013.

Koskenniemi, Martti, 'What should international lawyers learn from Karl Marx?', in Susan Marks (ed.), *International Law on the Left: Re-examining Marxist Legacies*, Cambridge University Press, Cambridge and New York: 2011, pp. 30–52.

Li Xiaorong and Zhang Zuhua (李晓荣, 张祖桦), '零八宪章 [Charter 08]', Kaifang Press, Hong Kong: 2009, translated by Perry Link, Charter 08', *New York Review of Books*, 15 January 2009, at http://www.nybooks.com/articles/archives/2009/jan/15/chinas-charter-08/, accessed 4 January 2014.

Mansfield, Michael, *Memoirs of a Radical Lawyer*, Bloomsbury Publishing, London: 2010.

Peerenboom, Randall, 'Searching for political liberalism in all the wrong places: the legal profession in China as the leading edge of political reform?', *La Trobe Law School Legal Studies Research* Paper No. 2008/7, at http://ssrn.com/abstract=1265080 or http://dx.doi.org/10.2139/ssrn.1265080.

People's Daily, '中国真正的挑战是未来 5–10 年 [China's real challenges lie in the 5 to 10 years ahead]', 1 July 2012, at http://ccnews.people.com.cn/n/2012/0731/c141677-18636091.html, accessed 30 December 2013; translation by Harold Scott' at http://chinadigitaltimes.net/2012/08/peoples-daily-chinas-real-challenge-is-the-next-5-10-years/, accessed 30 December 2013.

Woodman, Sophia, 'Driving without a map: implementing legal projects in China aimed at improving human rights', in Daniel A. Bell and Jean-Marc Coicaud (eds.), *Ethics in Action*, Cambridge University Press, Cambridge: 2006, at http://ebooks.cambridge.org/chapter.jsf?bid=CBO9780511511233&cid=CBO9780511511233A017, accessed 30 December 2013.

Zheng, Jue and Xiong, Fei (郑珏, 熊菲), '孙德胜、袁奉初发起的公民权利进军 [Citizen rights promoted Sun Desheng, Yuan Fengchu further advancing]', *CHRD*, 13 April 2013, at http://2newcenturynet.blogspot.hk/2013/04/blog-post_13.html, accessed 30 December 2013.

Websites, blog and microblog entries

Tweet accessed 28 August 2013, at https://twitter.com/tjitian/status/351868160917512192, accessed 4 January 2014.

Index

610 Offices 64, 76, 195, 241

academics 60–3, 64, 77, 138, 204, 281
access to justice 58, 85–93; courtroom advocacy *see separate entry*
access to lawyers 79, 80, 89–90, 107, 108–9, 242
acquittals 89, 126, 132
administrative litigation 39, 87–8, 90, 107; preventing trials by not filing cases 115–18; Re-education Through Labour (RTL) 116–18, 124–6, 127; reconciliation 120
Ahl, B. 60
Ai, Weiwei 艾未未 67
Ai, Xiaoming 艾晓明 67, 206
AIDS/HIV 72, 123
Aitkenhead, D. 277
All China Lawyers' Association (ACLA) 64, 115, 147–8, 151, 152–3, 154, 162, 181; American Bar Association (ABA) 179–80; assessment of law firms and lawyers 155; Charter 151; Constitutional Law Committee 165; English-language and Chinese-language websites 180
Alston, P. 4
alternative spaces for rights advocacy 136–40
American Bar Association (ABA) 179–80
Angle, S.C. 3, 26, 31, 41
Anhui Law Firm 安汇律师事务所 175
anonymisation 14–15, 241
Ansfield, J. 150
anti-corruption campaign 87, 262, 264
Anti-rightist Movement 21, 33, 36–7, 38
appointment of lawyers: obstruction and interference with 108–9
Arendt, H. 74, 256, 266
arts 136; *Herzog's Days* 137–8, 139; performance art 139
assaults/beatings 14, 70, 110, 193, 197–200, 204–5; *see also* torture

assessment systems, licensing and registration 147, 148, 154–60
association: advocacy and resistance through 248–55; freedom of 59, 60, 76–7, 79, 233–4, 237

Bai, Mei 白梅 175, 207
Bajoria, J. 58
Balme, S. 104
Bandurski, D. 75, 263
Bao, Judge 28
Bayefsky, A.F. 60
Beihai Lawyers' case 北海律师案 105, 197, 204–5, 239, 250, 251
Beijing Lawyers' Association (BLA) 149, 154, 169, 170–2
Beiyang government 31
Béja, J.-P. 64, 249
Belkin, I. 83, 130
Bell, D. 281
Bennet, I. 75
Benney, J. 8
Bentham, J. 4, 84
Berlin, I. 178
Biddulph, S. 81
blogs 68, 119, 204, 216
Bo, Xilai 薄熙来 166, 209
Bodde, D. 22, 27, 28
Boehler, P. 241, 242
Branigan, T. 71, 132
Bristow, M. 71, 242
Buckley, C. 150
Buddhism 76
burden of proof 87
bureaucratic control of legal profession; 'daily supervision and management' and enforcement of 'ethics' and 'discipline' 160–5; educational and committee activities 165–9; invasive and pervasive dimensions of

176–8; licensing, registration and assessment systems 154–60; limitations of 181–2; problems with modernisation and institutional liberalisation narratives 178–81; signs of control 146–7; 'two conjoined' and the Party 147–54; X law firm 170–5

Cai, Dingjian 蔡定剑 60–1
Cai, Zhuohua 蔡卓华 250
'cancer villages' 70
Cang, Hai 沧海 90
Cao, Guoxing 曹国星 262
Cao, Tianxiang 曹天祥 120
capitalism 32; neo- 4, 284–5
career development, cases and encounters significant for lawyer's further 66–7
Carter, L. 190
case-focused teams 250–53, 267
categorisations of lawyers 6–10, 275–8
censorship 62, 66, 74, 75–6, 77, 119; online 251; self- 79, 281
Chan, J. 23
Chan, Kin-man 陈建民 76
Chan, Melissa 123
Chang, Jian 常健 4, 63
Chang, Kai 常凯 71
Charter 08 37, 222, 282
Chen, Albert 陈弘毅 62
Chen, Geng 陈赓 33
Chen Guangcheng 陈光诚 8–9, 108, 110, 201–2, 207
Chen, Hongwei 陈虹伟 107
Chen, Jiangang 陈建刚 243
Chen, Kegui 陈克贵 108, 245
Chen, Tong 陈同 32
Chen, Weidong 陈卫东 206
Chen, Yanhui 谌彦辉 205
Chen, Yonggui 陈永贵 51
Chen, Yongmiao 陈永苗 64, 256
Chen, Youxi 陈有西 83, 251
Cheng, Bin 程斌 260
Cheng, Hai 程海 158
Cheng, Yuanjing 程远景 120
Cheung, Yiu-Leung 张耀良 166
children: 'One Child Policy' 8, 69, 70
Chin, Josh 265
Choukroune, L. 26
Chung, Dan 71
Citizen's Pledge 259–60
citizenship: New Citizen Movement 258–62, 263–6, 267, 274, 284; political conception of 255–8
civic meals 258, 261–2, 264, 265, 266
civil disobedience 235, 260

civil litigation 87, 90, 104, 107, 115, 161
civil representatives (*gongmin daili* 公民代理) 135, 176, 182
civil society 255, 257–8, 265, 274; organisations 76–7, 248–9; transnational 254, 279; *see also* non-governmental organisations
Civil War 32
Clarke, D.C. 43, 44, 71, 82, 88, 170, 210
class-based justice 34
Cohen, J.A. 43, 44, 45, 108, 119, 150, 170
Cohen, R. 2
colleagues 193–4, 200; attribution of collective responsibility 194–6
collective memories created through advocacy 122
collective responsibility 194–6
compensation 133; criminal reconciliation 120–1; employment discrimination 123; expropriation 69, 70, 71, 124, 126, 163–4, 279; *see also* damages
conciliation 107
confessions 83, 84, 85, 109, 112, 129, 130, 166, 203, 204–5, 207
Confucius/Confucianism 20, 22, 23, 26, 27, 28, 29, 30
Constitution 234, 260, 276, 277, 282; 1982 40–1, 47, 59, 257; 2004 amendment 50, 59; courts adjudicate cases independently (Art. 126) 60, 126; direct application by judiciary 48–9, 88, 124; expropriations and demolitions (Art. 13) 69; freedom of religion (Art. 36) 59, 60, 77–8; freedom of speech (Art. 35) 59, 60, 77; personal liberty and bodily integrity (Art. 37) 60, 79–82, 85; rights lawyers' perspective on 'the system' 64–5; rights and the Party 61–3; rule of law (Art. 5) 59, 62, 164
constitutionalism 48–9, 263
constraints on research and the use of sources 10–15
control *see* bureaucratic control of legal profession
Convention against Torture 60
conversion (*zhuanhua* 转化) 211, 215, 218
Cooper, E. 10
corruption 46, 70, 80, 86, 88, 89, 91, 93, 128, 135, 250; anti-corruption campaign 87, 262, 264
courtroom advocacy 104–5, 140; advocacy between 'speaking truth' and negotiation 127–30; advocacy inside tolerated zones 122–3; advocacy outside tolerated zones 124–7; constraints arising from public legal rules 106–7; dispersal of rights advocacy

into wider community 133–40; genuine 130–3; 'harmonising' judicial process 118–21; limited achievements in 121–33; 'managing' the trial 111–13; obstruction and intimidation before criminal trials 108–10; preventing trials by not filing cases 115–18; public nature of trials, reducing 113–15; rules and practices limiting 105–21

criminal investigation detention 14, 79–80, 83–4, 207

criminal justice 42–3, 45, 104, 115, 118, 161, 162, 275, 279–80; advocacy between 'speaking truth' and negotiation 127–30; advocacy outside tolerated zones 126–7; beyond reasonable doubt 88; case-focused teams 250–3, 267; constraints arising from public legal rules 106–7; conviction rates 126; Criminal Procedure Law (CPL) 60, 79–80, 88–90, 107, 111, 112, 120, 191n13, 206n80, 225–6, 238, 279–80; crowds outside court building 137–9; genuine courtroom advocacy 130–3; lawyers charged with criminal offences 202–11, 242; Luzhou trial (2009) 112–13, 114, 135–6, 158–9, 237; 'managing' the trial 111–13; obstruction and intimidation before trial 108–10; petitions 91; popular sentiment 119; public nature of trials, reducing 113–15; reconciliation 120–1; self-incrimination 89, 107; social media 136, 238–9, 275; solidarity: 'surrounding or watching' or *weiguan* 围观 137–9, 140

criminal law 79; charges against lawyers 108, 202; civil society organisations and assemblies 77; courtroom advocacy 107; 'crimes' not contained in 243–4; evidence 107, 203–6; free speech 74–6, 77; religion 74, 75, 76, 77–8; social media 76; torture 74, 83

criminals, petty 81

Cui, Weiping 崔卫平 138

Cui, Weiyuan 82

Cullen, R. 6–7, 276

Cultural Revolution 21, 33–5, 37–8, 39, 48, 50, 215, 224

damages 39; *see also* compensation

Daoism 76

De Lisle, J. 51

De Mente, B.L. 34

death penalty 46, 66n41, 67, 109, 119, 121, 129–33, 139, 166, 204, 224; China Against Death Penalty 234, 253

defamation, crime of 74–5, 137

democracy movement 46, 48

Democracy Wall Movement (1978–1979) 41–2

Deng Xi 邓隙 21–3, 24, 26–7

Deng, Xiaoping 邓小平 39–41, 47, 246

Deng, Yanhua 邓燕华 195

Deng, Yujiao 邓玉娇 245

Deng, Zhongxia 邓中夏 33

detention 14, 49, 64, 205, 233, 238, 263, 265, 266; access to lawyers 79, 80, 89–90, 107, 108–9, 242; administrative 81, 90, 241; court hearings in places of pretrial 115; criminal investigation 14, 79–80, 83–4, 207; extrajudicial systems 70, 80–2, 85, 90, 116–18, 124–7, 225, 233, 259; illegal detention in black jails 70, 81, 82, 225, 259; judicial 81, 113, 241, 242; lawyer's licence booklet 156; lawyers and soft 196–7; legal education centres 81, 85; legal study classes 81, 85; obstruction and intimidation before criminal trials 109–10; of Party members (*shuanggui*) 82, 209; psychiatric institutions 82, 109, 139, 218–19; reducing public nature of trials 114

Di (Dee), Judge 28

Ding, Jiaxi 丁家喜 242, 265

disability rights 122, 139

disappearances, enforced 12–13, 14, 80, 90, 198, 201, 205, 210–11, 224; definition 212; torture and 211–21, 240–1

disbarment 139, 148, 156, 158–9, 160, 166, 176, 182

discrimination 72–3, 123; employment 72–3, 90, 116, 118, 122–3; gender-based 66, 123

distributive injustice 73

Dou'E / Dou'E yuan 窦娥冤 29

Dong, Yunhu 董云虎 4, 63

Douzinas, C. 4, 284

drug rehabilitation 81

Du, Bin 杜斌 29

Du, Jin 杜金 28

'dual state' logic Party–State terror 224–6

Duan, Jianguo 段建国 89

Dworkin, R. 1, 2, 235, 284

economic growth/development 46, 73, 178–9

education 68, 73, 264; household registration system 69–70; legal 35, 39, 48, 60–1; right to 49, 259

electronic surveillance 13–14, 146–7, 191, 192–3

employment 67–8, 71–2; discrimination 72–3, 90, 116, 118, 122–3 enforced disappearances 12–13, 14, 80, 90, 198, 201, 205, 210–11, 224; definition 212; torture and 211–21, 240–1

environmental pollution 69, 70, 73

ethnicity 123, 224; ethnic and religious persecution 76, 78

evictions/expropriations 68–9, 70–1, 72, 73, 79, 90, 92, 107, 118–19, 259; advocacy outside tolerated zones 124, 126; compensation 68, 70, 71, 124, 163, 279; courtroom as street happening 133–5; 'daily supervision and management' 163–5; protests 137; protests and relational repression 195

false imprisonment 74, 82, 238, 243

Falun Gong 法轮功 7, 38–9, 64, 76, 77–8, 178, 190, 210, 266, 277; acquittals 126; case-focused teams 250; 'daily supervision and guidance' 162; detention 81, 85; judicial detention of lawyer 241; justice bureau visits to law firm 160; 'managing' the trial 112–13; non-local lawyers 110; obstruction and intimidation of lawyers before criminal trials 110

family of lawyer 108–9, 193–4, 197, 200–2, 205, 214, 219, 240; attribution of collective responsibility 194–6

Fan, Biaowen 范标文 260

Fan, Qihang 樊奇杭 129–30

Fan, Yanqiong 范燕琼 138

Fang, Zhida 方知达 33

Faure, G. 139

Feinerman, J.V. 43, 44, 88

Feng Yu-lan 冯友兰 29

film 62, 89, 113, 127, 166, 197, 206, 209, 253, 262; *Herzog's Days* 137–8, 139

financial disclosure 262, 264

forced disappearances 12–13, 14, 80, 90, 198, 201, 205, 210–11, 224; definition 212; torture and 211–21, 240–1

Fraenkel, E. 16, 110, 147, 191, 223, 275

France 258; Declaration of the Rights of Man and the Citizen (1789) 3

Fraser, C. 21, 27

freedom of assembly 59, 60, 76–7, 233

freedom of association 59, 60, 76–7, 79, 233–4, 237

freedom of expression/speech 23, 32, 45, 59, 60, 74–6, 77, 79, 233, 234, 237, 265, 266; freedom of religion and 78

freedom of religion 59, 60, 77–8, 284

freedom of thought and conscience 74, 237, 240

friends of lawyer 193–4, 200, 201–2, 216, 218, 219; attribution of collective responsibility 194–6

Fu, Guoyong 傅国涌 28

Fu, Hualing 傅华伶 6–7, 58, 81, 206, 223, 276

Fu, Yonggang 付永刚 260

Fuchs, J. 176

Fujian (Three) Netizens 福建三网民 137–8, 139–40

Fuller, L. 200

Gallagher, M. 72

Gang of Four 41, 42–4

Gao, Zhisheng 高智晟 10, 12–13, 67, 108–9, 200–1, 206, 207, 212, 215, 241, 251, 282

Garapon, A. 26

gender-based discrimination 66, 123

German Democratic Republic 176

Gewirth, A. 2

Givens, J.W. 6, 8–9

Global Law Firm 175

Godovits, F. 9

Goldman, M. 32, 256, 257

Gong, Gangmo 龚刚模 165–6

Gong, Ting 112

Gong, Xiantian 巩献田 63

Goodman, R. 4

Greece, ancient 24

grievances 66–8; centred in restrictions of liberty of the person and mind 73–85; stemming from social and economic rights violations 68–73; traditional submission of *shen yuan* 27, 29, 30, 50

Griffin, J. 2

groups focusing on causes 253–5

Gu, Kailai 谷开来 132

Gu, Yuejin 顾跃进 24–5

Guan, Hanqing 关汉卿 29

Guanyin Fa Men 观音法门 76

Gudjohnsson, G.H. 211

Guiyang trial (2012) 136, 238

Gulik, R. van 28

Guo, Fei 70

Guo, Feixiong 郭飞雄 (aka Yang Maodong 杨茂东) 108, 109, 207, 262, 263, 265

Guo, Guoting 郭国汀 77

Halliday, T. 175, 204

Hand, K. 80, 88, 237

harmony (*hexie* 和谐) 25–6, 28, 39, 119; 'harmonising' judicial process 118–21

Hart, H.L.A. 60, 223

Havel, Václav 176, 220, 235, 256

Hayek, F. 256

He, Haibo 何海波 117, 118
He, Weifang 贺卫方 24, 41, 60–1, 62, 87, 118, 204, 257
He, Yang 何杨 89, 129, 138, 166, 197, 206, 209, 262
healthcare 69–70, 73
Henochowitz, A. 190
Hepatitis B 72, 116, 118, 122–3
heroism 9–10, 278–9
Herzog's Days (*Hesuoge de rizi* 赫索格的日子) 137–8, 139
history 20–1, 255–6; Confucius/Confucianism 20, 22, 23, 26, 27, 28, 29, 30; distrust toward law 21–2; enduring significance of historical conceptions of justice 51–2; imperial era: tradition and counter-tradition 21–30; injustice (*yuan* 冤) 20, 21, 27, 29–30, 45, 47, 50, 52; legal advisor centres 33; limited legal reconstruction in the reform and opening eras 39–47; 'pointing to a deer and calling it a horse' 23–4, 27; popular literature 29; promises of liberalism and spectres of totalitarianism 30–9; rise of *weiquan* 维权 (rights defence) 47–51
HIV/AIDS 72, 123
hooliganism 45
house-arrest 13, 108, 114, 197, 200, 205, 249
household registration system 69–70, 72–3, 123; access to legal profession and 154–5
housing, right to 69, 71
Hu, Jia 胡佳 (胡嘉) 109, 202, 242
Hu, Jintao 胡锦涛 26, 40, 73
Hu, Shigen 胡石根 248
Hua, Sheng 42
Hua, Xinmin 华新民 68
Huang, Songyou 黄松有 49, 88
Huang, Yeqing 70
Huang, Zhaolin 黄兆麟 86
Hung, Melissa S. 181
hunger strikes 109, 208, 218, 276
Hutzler, C. 114, 206

Idema, W.L. 28
imperial China 20–1, 255–6; legal codes 22, 27–8, 45; Qing Dynasty 22–3, 25, 31, 32, 37–8, 39, 45, 52; tradition and counter-tradition 21–30
imperialism 4, 284–5
innocence, presumption of 45, 112
institutional liberalisation narratives and modernisation, problems with 178–81
International Covenant on Civil and Political Rights (ICCPR) 48, 60, 65, 257, 264

International Covenant on Social, Economic and Cultural Rights (ICSECR) 59–60, 72
international law 4
internet 66, 75, 77, 136–40, 206, 232, 237, 238, 239, 246; associative structures 249; blogs 68, 119, 204, 216; case-focused teams 251; censorship 251; 'flat' networks 266; groups focusing on causes 254; *guobao* 190; protesting retaliation against advocates 241, 242, 243; public opinion guidance 79; social media *see separate entry*
Islam 76

Jacobs, A. 62
Janzen, C. 176
Japan 31
Jasmine Crackdown (2011) 136, 140, 210–20, 224, 225, 251, 253
Jiang, Jue 姜珏 43, 44, 80, 107, 120, 121
Jiang, Ping 江平 60–1, 204
Jiang, Qiming 江启明 205
Jiang, Qing 江青 43
Jiang, Qisheng 江棋生 222
Jiang, Shigong 强世功 41, 63
Jiang, Tianyong 江天勇 158, 198, 201, 213, 240
Jiang, Zemin 江泽民 39
jokes and verses 66, 257
judicial review 88, 93, 107, 124
judiciary 86, 90–1, 93, 105, 134–5, 282; independence 60, 114, 126; 'managing' the trial 111–13; mediation 119; non-routine cases 126; performance evaluation 86, 116–17; petitioning offices 91; political and legal committees of the Party 64, 86, 112, 114, 126; preventing trials by not filing cases 115–18; professionalism 48; reconciliation quota 121; reducing public nature of trials 113, 114; 'Three Supremes' doctrine 86–7; weak position of 126, 128–9
justice bureaux, lawyers' associations and the Party: 'daily supervision and management' and enforcement of 'ethics' and 'discipline' 160–5; educational and committee activities 165–9; licensing, registration and assessment systems 154–60; 'two conjoined' and the Party 147–54
juveniles: extrajudicial detention 81

Kahn, J. 110, 250
Kai, Wen 凯文 105
Kang, Youwei 康有为 32, 256
Kant, I. 23
Keller, P. 40
Kellogg, T.E. 88, 122, 254

Kilgour, D. 9, 10
Kirchheimer, O. 44
Koskenniemi, M. 4, 283

labour rights 73, 122; collective labour action 71–2; employment discrimination 72–3, 90, 116, 118, 122–3; lawyers 72
Lam, Willy 153
Lampton, D.M. 62
Lan, Rongjie 兰荣杰 165, 166, 204
Lan, Zhixue 兰志学 158
land takings (expropriations) 68–9, 70–1, 72, 73, 79, 90, 92, 107, 118–19, 259; advocacy outside tolerated zones 124, 126; compensation 68, 70, 71, 124, 163, 279; courtroom as street happening 133–5; 'daily supervision and management' 163–5; protests 137; protests and relational repression 195
landlords 68, 174–5, 209
Lau, D.C. 23
Lawrence, S. 64
lawyers' associations 252–3; justice bureaux, lawyers' associations and the Party *see separate entry*
legal aid 254
legal education 35, 39, 48, 60–1
legal reform, 'constructive' rule of law discourse and agency in change 279–83
legal teams, case-focused 250–3, 267
'Letters and Visits' 50, 91, 115
Lewis, M.K. 45, 83
LGBT community 66, 122
Li, Changsheng 李昌盛 44
Li, Cheng 70
Li, Chunfu 李春富 158
Li, Dunyong 李敦勇 158
Li, Fangping 李方平 79
Li, Heping 李和平 158
Li, Jie 李杰 190
Li, Jinglin 李静林 110, 158
Li, Jinxing 李金星 205, 238
Li, Li 118
Li, Ling 93, 112, 114, 126
Li, Qian 栗茜 22, 27
Li, Tiantian 李天天 240
Li, Wangyang 李旺阳 225
Li, Wen 李文 80
Li, Xiaorong 李晓蓉 38, 282
Li, Xiongbing 黎雄兵 158, 219
Li, Xueyao 146
Li, Yujun 李郁军 87
Li, Zhuang 李庄 165–9, 177, 204, 209, 251
Liang, Lily 204

Liang, Qichao 梁启超 32, 256
Liang, Xiaojun 梁小军 260
liberalisation narratives and modernisation, problems with 178–81
liberalism, Chinese 21, 30–3, 36–9, 42, 47–8, 51–2, 256
liberty of person and mind: grievances centred in restrictions of 73–85
licensing, registration and assessment systems 147, 148, 154–60
Lieberthal, K.G. 62
Liebman, B. 6, 86
life, right to 42, 74, 79
Lifton, R.J. 220
Lin, Ping 林坪 73
Lin, Qi 林淇 33
Lin, Zhe 63
Lincoln, A. 259
litigation master (*songshi* 讼师) 20, 25, 27, 31, 32–3
Liu, Binyan 刘宾雁 42
Liu, Guiming 刘桂明 31, 33
Liu, Jie 刘杰 63
Liu, Jinbin 刘金斌 260
Liu, Lee 70
Liu, Shihui 刘士辉 198, 240
Liu, Shu-Hsien 22
Liu, Sida 刘思达 146, 148–9, 175, 204
Liu, Wei 刘巍 112–13, 114, 135–6, 139, 158, 238
Liu, Weiguo 刘卫国 80, 241, 242, 260
Liu, Xiaobo 刘晓波 39, 76, 132, 207, 210, 222, 256, 262
Liu, Xiaoyuan 刘晓原 79, 158, 240, 260
Liu, Yao 刘尧 252
Liu, Zhengqing 刘正青 206
Lo, Carlos 40
Locke, J. 2
Longanecker, M.K. 60, 74
Luo, Gan 罗干 63, 119
Luo, Xin 罗欣 87
Luzhou trial (2009) 112–13, 114, 135–6, 158–9, 238
Lüshi 律师 (lawyer) 31, 33
Lynch, E. 158, 166, 202

Ma, Xiaoquan 马小泉 32
McConville, M. 83, 104, 107, 119
Mansfield, M. 277
Mao, Lixin 毛立新 106, 203
Mao, Yushi 茅于轼 81
Mao, Zedong 毛泽东 20, 31, 33, 34, 36–7, 38, 39, 41, 42, 43, 51, 75, 86, 87, 118, 120, 190, 196, 221

marginalisation 58, 165, 176, 255, 275, 278, 279; and identification 92, 93–4, 132
Martin, M.S. 64
Marx, K. 4
Marxism 32, 34, 40, 45–6, 63
media 6, 9, 48, 108, 122, 129, 137, 204, 216, 232, 237, 251, 266, 278; micro-blogs 239; social *see separate entry*; *Southern Weekend* 263
mediation 92, 93, 107, 119–20, 121
mental disorder 109, 113, 139, 219, 276
Merry, S.E. 5, 50
Michnik, A. 64, 256
migrant workers 70, 119, 180, 259
Mill, J.S. 23, 45
Ministry of Justice 35, 39, 148, 149, 150, 151–2, 153, 167–8; assessment of law firms and lawyers 155, 156–7; *see also* justice bureaux, lawyers' associations and the Party
minors 113
Minzner, C.F. 29, 91, 92, 118, 224
Mitchell, T. 252
Mo, Shaoping 莫少平 236
Mo Shaoping Law Firm 175
Mo, Zhixu 莫之许 63
mobile phones 13, 14, 146–7, 191, 198
modernisation and institutional liberalisation narratives, problems with 178–81
Mooney, P. 206
Morris, C. 22, 27, 28
Moyn, S. 4
Muehlhahn, K. 28
Mueller, H. 67
Mueller, K. 74
Münzel, F. 92

National People's Congress (NPC) 60, 105, 124, 233
National Security Committee 189–90
negotiation: advocacy between 'speaking truth' and 127–30
neocapitalism 4, 284–5
Nesossi, E. 93
New Citizen Movement 258–62, 263–6, 267, 274, 284; clampdown 265–6
'New Mass Line' 86, 87
Ng, Teddy 225
Ng, Tze-wei 203, 213, 215, 240
Ni, Yulan 倪玉兰 127, 132, 206, 209
Niyaz, Hairat 108
non-governmental organisations (NGOs) 6, 123, 129, 139, 174, 180, 182, 208, 253, 278; labour rights advocacy 72; legal aid from

foreign 254; restrictions 76–7; transnational 2, 3; *see also* civil society
Nowak, M. 3

oath of loyalty 152, 176, 234–5
O'Brien, K. 195
obscenity 75
O'Connor, A. 32, 35
Olesen, A. 9
'One Child Policy' 8, 69, 70
Open Constitution Initiative (Gongmeng) 233–4, 237, 248–9, 258–9
open letters (*xianshu*) 21, 27, 109, 250
open 'suggestion' letter 49
Opium Wars 31
Osnos, E. 234

Pan, Xuanming 潘玄明 135
Parry, J. 82
Peerenboom, R. 7–8, 40, 178, 276
Peng, Jian 彭剑 158
People's Congresses 60, 86
performance art 139
Perlez, J. 190
petitioning 106, 115, 118–19, 124, 125, 126, 132, 134–5, 137, 250, 259, 277; criminal offences and petitioners 207; detention 81, 82, 85; *guobao* 190; history of 28, 29, 30, 45, 47, 49, 50; offices 91–3
Pils, E. 5, 30, 48, 68, 69, 70, 71, 75, 80, 82, 88, 92, 107, 109, 115, 124, 135, 175, 236, 250, 258
pledges, statement of (*baozhengshu*) 216–17, 218
police 13, 34, 35, 39, 89, 128, 137, 189, 190, 201, 209, 221, 250; defamation of 137; detention 14, 126, 156, 205, 212–13, 233; evidence in criminal trials 107, 111, 167, 203–6; extrajudicial detention 81; *guobao* 国保 154, 190–200, 206, 221, 241, 246, 266; obstruction and intimidation before criminal trials 110; offices of law firms 146, 175; reporting 'crimes' of 243–4; social media 240–1; torture 83–4, 127, 129–30, 167, 213; trial in police detention centre 114–15
political resistance 2–3; *see also* resistance and wider legal and political advocacy
political trials 42–4
pollution 69, 70, 73
Posner, R. 63
post-totalitarian system 47, 73–4, 75, 76, 77, 85–6, 224, 248, 266–7, 276
postmodernism 4
prison 14

prisoners of conscience 65
Propaganda or Publicity Department 75, 189
property developers 68, 69
property rights 39, 50, 60, 63
prostitution 81
protesting retaliation against advocates 241–4
psychiatric institutions 82, 109, 139, 218–19
Pu Songling 蒲松龄 29
public nature of trials, reducing 113–15
Public Security Bureau (gong'an 公安) 85, 125,
    130, 241
public services 69–70, 72–3

Qi Yuling 齐玉苓 (2001) 48–9, 88
Qian, Yanfeng 68
Qin, Yongmin 秦永民 248
Qing Dynasty 22–3, 25, 31, 32, 37–8, 39, 45, 52
Qiu, Shi 秋石 153
Qiu, Zhihong 邱志红 25, 27
Qu Yuan 屈原 27

Ran, Yanfei 203
Rawls, J. 3, 235, 256
Re-education Through Labour (RTL) sentence
    14, 80–1, 90, 116–18, 124–7, 223, 233
reconciliation 120–1
reform, 'constructive' rule of law discourse and
    agency in change 279–83
Reform and Opening (*gaige kaifang* 改革开放)
    39–47, 52, 60, 179, 279
registration, licensing and assessment systems
    147, 148, 154–60
religion: attitudes of lawyers to faith and 78,
    284; case-focused teams 250; criminal law
    74, 75, 76, 77–8; freedom of 59, 60, 77–8,
    284; *see also* Falun Gong
Ren, Baige 任白戈 33
repentance, statements of (*huiguoshu* 悔过书) 75,
    85, 215, 216–18, 220
Republic of China 31–2, 37, 39, 256
research and use of sources, constraints on
    10–15
residential surveillance 80, 90, 205
resistance and wider legal and political advocacy
    2–3, 232, 237, 283, 285; association 248–55;
    case advocacy from and beyond courtroom
    237–41; inclusive transformation goal
    266–7; logic of resistance to Party–State
    control 233–7; New Citizen Movement
    258–62, 263–6, 267, 274, 284; political
    conception of citizenship 255–8; principles
    and strategies of political action 244–8;
    protesting retaliation against advocates
    241–4; violence 245–7, 260, 276

rights' place in the system 58–9; encountering
    common grievances 66–85; institutions to
    address injustices 85–93; marginalisation
    and identification 92, 93–4, 132; overview
    58–65; Party and rights 61–3; restrictions of
    liberty of person and mind 73–85; rights
    lawyers' perspective on 'the system' 64–5;
    scholarly debates 59–61; social and
    economic rights violations 68–73
Rosenzweig, J.D. 26, 45, 75, 80, 88, 90, 107,
    120, 121
'ruling the country in accordance with law'
    (*yi fa zhi guo*) 39–40, 41

Sapio, F. 79, 80, 83, 92, 107, 189, 209
Scarry, E. 211
scepticism 4, 10
Schauer, F. 235
Schmitt, C. 63
security apparatus 68, 146, 150, 160, 176, 182,
    189–91, 255, 261–2; attribution of collective
    responsibility 194–6; combined effect of the
    measures 200–2; direct violence 193,
    197–200; 'dual state' logic Party–State terror
    224–6; enforced disappearance and torture
    211–21; individuated interaction 191–4;
    limited uses of the formal criminal process
    202–11; 'persuasive' and 'caring'
    Party–State terror 221–4; social media
    240; soft detention and similar measures
    196–7
Selden, M. 34, 118
self-censorship 79, 281
self-enforcement 220, 221–3, 236–7
self-worth, advocates' sense of 121, 176, 255,
    279
Seppänen, A.S. 61, 62, 63
Shama, S. 258
Shell, J. 256
Shen, Nianzu 沈念祖 105
Shengzhi Law Firm 175
Shi, Liang 史良 33
Shi, Qing 石青 (pen name of 李金星)
    238–9
Shirky, C. 261
Shu, Sheng 舒升 153
signature campaigns 241, 243, 249
Simon, Karla 77, 259
Skype 11, 12, 192
Smith, R.K.M. 3
social management (*shehui guanli* 社会管理) 119,
    150, 189
social media 75, 76, 137; associative structures
    249, 253; courtroom as happening on 136,

238, 275; groups focusing on causes 254;
legal teams 251, 252, 253; protesting
retaliation against advocates 240, 241;
security apparatus 240; Twitter 194, 219,
240–1, 244n67; Weibo 微博 136, 241,
244n67; *Weixin* 微信 1n1, 240, 249
social movements 7, 52, 267
social stability 25–6, 45, 67, 72, 86, 92, 119,
181; duty of lawyers to maintain 151, 163;
lawyers charged with criminal offences 206;
see also harmony; stability preservation
socialist legality 32
Socrates 24, 27
solidarity 232, 247, 284; 'surrounding and
watching' or *weiguan* 围观 137–9, 140, 225,
237, 241, 242, 276
Song, Ze 265
Songshi 讼师 (litigation master, lawyer in imperial
China) 20, 25, 27, 31, 32–3
Southern Street Movement 263, 265
sovereignty 283
Soviet Union 32, 33, 246
Spence, J. 41, 46
Spires, A. 181
stability preservation (*weiwen* 维稳) 67, 75–6, 92,
119, 140, 150, 189–92, 206, 275, 279;
offices 75, 189–90; targets 191–2, 197
State Council Information Office 75
State security cases 80, 90, 161
statement of pledges (*baozhengshu* 保证书)
216–17, 218
statements of repentance (*huiguoshu* 悔过书) 75,
85, 215, 216–18, 220
Steiner, H.J. 4
street protests 92, 136–40; Southern Street
Movement 263, 265
street and social media happening, courtroom as
133–6
subversion 74, 206, 223, 234; inciting 74, 77,
108, 136, 202, 206–7, 209–10, 214, 218,
222, 223, 234
suicides, protest 70, 71
Sun, Desheng 孙德胜 282
Sun, Di 孙狄 241
Sun, Yat-Sen (aka Sun Zhongshan 孙中山) 256,
259, 260, 262
Sun, Zhigang 孙志刚 49, 62, 233, 237
Sun, Zhongshan 孙中山 (aka Sun Yat-sen) 256,
259, 260, 262
Supreme People's Court 115, 120; *Qi Yuling*
齐玉苓 (2001) 48–9, 88
'surrounding and watching' or *weiguan*
围观 137–9, 140, 225, 237, 241, 242,
276

surveillance 13–14, 146–7, 191–3, 220, 279;
family 201; residential 80, 90, 205
Svensson, M. 75
Sweden 3

Tang, Jitian 唐吉田 112–13, 135–6, 139, 158–9,
238, 241, 242, 277
Tang, Yiming 70
Tasioulas, J. 2
taxation 234
taxonomies of lawyers 6–10, 275–9
Taylor, J. 9
teams, case-focused legal 250–3, 267
Teng, Biao 滕彪 11–12, 40, 47, 49–50, 74, 76,
77, 78, 80, 81, 82, 107, 108, 139, 158–9,
201, 206, 222, 223, 226, 233, 234, 242, 247,
251, 252, 253, 259, 261, 267, 278
terminology 5
terrorism 80
Theobald, U. 22, 27
Thompson, T. 189
'thought work/reform' 79, 82, 84–5, 174, 196,
211, 215, 218, 220, 226
Three Gorges Dam 68
'Three Supremes' doctrine: judges 86–7;
lawyers 153
Tian, Xi 田溪 198
Tibetan community 76, 78, 108, 250, 259
Tierny, B. 5
Tong, Lihua 佟丽华 71, 153, 154
torture 2, 14, 66, 67, 68, 109, 127, 243, 253,
275; confessions 83–4, 130–2, 166–7,
204–5; Convention against Torture 60;
criminal law 74, 83; investigation procedure
in death penalty cases 130–2; lawyers
prosecuted after alleging torture of their
clients 204; lawyers on range of 83–4;
lawyers and rights defenders subject to
207–9, 210, 211–21, 240–1; 'managing' the
trial: allegations of 111, 112, 238; open
protest against in court 129; 'thought
reform' 79, 82, 84–5
totalitarian and post-totalitarian systems 47,
73–4, 75, 76, 77, 85–6, 224, 248, 266–7,
276
Transition Institute 234
treason 194
Trevaskes, S. 119
Twitter 194, 219, 240–1, 244n67

Uighur community 78–9, 108
UN Human Rights Council 63
UN Special Rapporteurs 3
unions 71–2

United States 3, 256
Universal Declaration of Human Rights (UDHR) 3, 257
Universal Periodic Review (UPR) 3
universal values (*pushi jiazhi* 普世价值) 26, 31, 63, 258
universities 35
Upham, F. 104
utilitarianism 45–6, 63, 71, 85

verses and jokes 66, 257
video cameras in court 114
violence 264; assaults/beatings 14, 70, 110, 193, 197–200, 204–5; resistance 245–8, 260, 276; social status 193; torture *see separate entry*

Wang, Bo 王博 250
Wang, Chuxiang 王楚襄 (aka Wang Cheng 王成) 260, 265
Wang, Gong 王工 129
Wang, Gongquan 王功权 265
Wang, Lihong 王荔蕻 114, 139–40, 206, 242
Wang, Lijun 王立军 166
Wang, Quanzhang 王全璋 113, 241, 242–3, 249
Wang, Tiancheng 王天成 63
Wang, Xing 王星 82
Wang, Yajun 王亚军 158
Wang, Yonghang 王永航 207
Wang, Zhenmin 王振民 40
'Warning and Education' campaign 2010–11 165–9, 177
Webster, T. 72, 122
Wee, Sui-lee 68
Wei, Jingsheng 魏京生 41
Wei, Liangyue 韦良月 158
Wei, Wenhao 韦文浩 205
Weibo 微博 (generic name for micro-blogs) 136, 241, 244n67
weiquan 维权 (rights defence) movement 5, 11–12, 52; human rights lawyers as a contentious issue 6–10; rise of 47–51
Weixin 微信 (Wechat) 1n1, 240, 249
welfare 2, 21, 26, 45, 46, 69, 70, 72, 73
Wen, Chaoli 文朝利 34
Wen, Haibo 温海波 158
White Book on Human Rights (1991) 48
Wiggins, D. 257
Wolf, Frank 10
Woodman, S. 180, 281
Wu, Fengshi 吴锋时 76
Wu, Huaying 吴华英 138, 242
Wu, Kaisheng 吴开生 33
Wu, Lilan 吴立岚 33

Wu, Si 吴思 51, 61, 223
Wu, Tiaohe 吴调和 59
Wu, Zhenqi 吴镇琦 260

Xi, Jinping 习近平 63, 87, 120, 153, 189
Xi Wang 希望 (pen name) 70
Xia, Yong 夏勇 60–1
Xia, Yu 夏雨 175
Xiao, Han 萧翰 61
Xiao, Hong 晓虹 35, 36, 43
Xiao, Qiang 190
Xiao, Shu 笑蜀 236, 261, 262, 265, 267
Xiao, Yang 肖扬 48, 88
Xie, Yanyi 谢燕益 158
Xin Yu 心语 (pen name) 175
Xiong, Fei 熊菲 282
Xu, Chongde 徐崇德 41
Xu, Jianbo 徐建波 87
Xu, Zhiyong 许志永 8, 80, 108, 207, 233, 242, 255, 257, 258, 259, 260, 261, 263, 264, 265
Xunzi 荀子 31

Yan, Wangli 燕旺利 260
Yan, Xiaoling 严晓玲 137
Yang, Deshan 杨德山 39
Yang, Guobin 杨国斌 77
Yang, Huimin (Yang Huiwen 杨慧文) 158
Yang, Jia 杨佳 92, 108, 109, 245, 250
Yang, Jinzhu 杨金柱 251
Yang, Ming 杨明 69, 264
Yang, Zaixin 杨在新 158, 197, 204, 205, 251
Yang, Zhengsen 杨政森 87
Yao, Jiaxin 药家鑫 119
Ye, Qing 叶青 24–5
Yi, Xing 易兴 74
Yirenping (Beijing) 益仁平 72, 139
Yitong 亿通 Law Firm 175
You, Jingyou 遊精佑 137–8
Yu, Jianrong 于建嵘 47, 75, 91, 118
Yu, Verna 109
Yu, Xingzhong 于兴中 48
Yuan, Chengjia 袁诚家 238
Yuan, Fengchu 袁奉初 282
Yuan, Hongbing 袁红冰 282
yuan 冤 (injustice) 20, 21, 27, 29–30, 45, 47, 50, 52
Yuan, Qi 袁起 34
Yuan, Shikai 袁世凯 31

Zeng, Jinyan 曾金燕 202, 220–1
Zhai, Keith 109
Zhang, Boshu 张博树 64
Zhang, Feng 张峰 153

Zhang, Jun 张军 105–6, 130, 132
Zhang, Kai 张凯 158, 197–8
Zhang, Lihui 张立辉 158
Zhang, Qianfan 张千帆 41, 60–1, 62
Zhang, Qing 张倩 251
Zhang, Sizhi 张思之 35–6, 43, 44
Zhang, Xianming 张先明 89
Zhang, Xiong 75
Zhang, Xueran 133, 136 239, 251
Zhang, Xuezhong 张学忠 61, 62
Zhang, Zuhua 张祖桦 38, 222, 282
Zhao, Changqing 赵常青 265
Zhao, Chunfang 赵春芳 154
Zhao, Lianhai 赵连海 108

Zhao, Ling 赵凌 91
Zhao, Yanhong 赵艳红 204
Zheng, Jianwei 郑建伟 90
Zheng, Jue 郑珏 282
Zhou, Benshun 周本顺 189
Zhou, Bin 周斌 165, 167
Zhou, Ruiping 周瑞平 72
Zhou, Yongkang 周永康 150–1, 153, 154,
    173–5, 189
Zhu, Mingyong 朱明勇 129–30, 166
Zhu, Suli 朱苏力 63
Zhuang, Jinghui 139
Zimbardo, P. 9
Zou, Guoliang 邹国良 34